T0323430

All That Glittered

All That Glittered

*Britain's Most Precious Metal
from Adam Smith to the Gold Rush*

TIMOTHY ALBORN

OXFORD
UNIVERSITY PRESS

OXFORD
UNIVERSITY PRESS

Oxford University Press is a department of the University of Oxford. It furthers the University's objective of excellence in research, scholarship, and education by publishing worldwide. Oxford is a registered trade mark of Oxford University Press in the UK and certain other countries.

Published in the United States of America by Oxford University Press 198 Madison Avenue, New York, NY 10016, United States of America.

Library of Congress Cataloging-in-Publication Data
Names: Alborn, Timothy L., 1964– author.
Title: All that glittered : Britain's most precious metal from Adam Smith to the Gold Rush / Timothy Alborn.
Description: New York, NY : Oxford University Press, [2019] |
Includes bibliographical references and index. |
Description based on print version record and CIP data provided by publisher; resource not viewed. Identifiers: LCCN 2019005620 (print) |
LCCN 2019008847 (ebook) | ISBN 9780190603526 (updf) |
ISBN 9780190603533 (epub) | ISBN 9780190603519 (hardcover : alk. paper)
Subjects: LCSH: Gold—Great Britain—History. |
Gold standard—Great Britain—History. | Finance—Great Britain—History.
Classification: LCC HG295.G7 (ebook) | LCC HG295.G7 A43 2019 (print) |
DDC 332.4/0420941—dc23
LC record available at https://lccn.loc.gov/2019005620

1 3 5 7 9 8 6 4 2

Printed by Integrated Books International, United States of America

CONTENTS

ACKNOWLEDGMENTS

Although I have been working in earnest on this book since 2009, its genesis dates back to graduate school in the late 1980s, when I first confronted the strangeness of the gold standard. I thank my dissertation advisers, Barbara Rosenkrantz and Peter Buck, for encouraging me to "think outside the box" about gold and other matters back then; and Peter has generously continued to read in manuscript almost everything I write, including *All That Glittered*. Over the nearly thirty years since my Ph.D. I have developed my ideas about gold whenever I have taught British history, first at Harvard and, since 1998, at Lehman College and the City University of New York (CUNY) Graduate Center: thanks go to the many students who probably did not anticipate learning so much about that metal when they signed up for my classes.

My colleagues at Lehman and the Graduate Center have provided a friendly and intellectually stimulating environment for thinking, talking, and writing about history. At Lehman, Evelyn Ackerman, Cindy Lobel, José Luis Renique, Robyn Spencer, Chuck Wooldridge, and Amanda Wunder all provided sounding boards for ideas that made it into the book, as have Laird Bergad, Sarah Covington, Josh Freeman, Jim Oakes, Helena Rosenblatt, David Troyansky, and Randy Trumbach at the Graduate Center (special thanks to Amanda and Sarah for reading draft chapters). Laura Guerrero at Lehman and Marilyn Weber at the Graduate Center have also been amazing resources. Between 2009 and 2012, when I began working on this book while serving as Dean of Arts and Humanities at Lehman, my colleagues and staff in Shuster Hall understood that my love of research enhanced rather than impeded my administrative duties.

All That Glittered is the result of an enormous amount of work, not all of it mine. CUNY has blessed me with an abundance of funds for research assistance, and I have been lucky to be able to employ a talented group of Ph.D. students over the years. Sam Bussan, Igor Draskovich, Jiwon Han, Andrew Kotick, Esther Mansdorf, Sophie Muller, Matt Sherman, Mark Soriano, Jaja Tantirungkij, and Ky Woltering have all left their mark on this book through their tireless downloading and organization of PDF files, compilation of databases, scanning of books, checking of quotes, and tracking down of illustrations. My doctoral students Dory Agazarian, Alex Baltovski, Phelim Dolan, Jarrett Moran, and Luke Reynolds (as well as Sophie, Jaja, and Jiwon) have also read chapter drafts and generally put up with my penchant for talking incessantly about my research.

The staff of the National Archives in London, as well as Justin Cavernelis-Frost at the Rothschild Archive, Eve Watson at the RSA Archives, Alex Ritchie and Richard Wiltshire at the London Metropolitan Archives, and Joe Hewson and Margherita Orlando at the Bank of England Archives, all provided important assistance with my research. *All That Glittered* has also gained immensely from the interlibrary loan heroes at Lehman (Gene Laper) and the CUNY Graduate Center (Silvia Cho and her staff). Finally, it would have not been possible to write this book without access to electronic collections of primary sources. I'm especially grateful to Ray Abruzzi, Scott Dawson, and Theresa DeBenedictis at Gale and to Janet Munch and Stefanie Havelka at Lehman, who have provided access to many of these; and to the dozens of anonymous librarians around the world who scanned and coded the thousands of digital resources I consulted.

I have also gained from the community of literary critics and historians in the New York area, who have provided fertile soil for writing and thinking about *All That Glittered*. My Victorianist writing group—Tanya Agathocleous, Carolyn Berman, Deborah Lutz, Caroline Reitz, Talia Schaffer, and Marion Thain—provided lasting friendship and constructive feedback on several chapters and related articles over many tasty meals. For most of the time while I was working on this book I also had the privilege of discussing new books in British history over wine and cheese with Chris Brown, Evan Haefeli, Guy Ortolano, Susan Pederson, George Robb, Deborah Valenze, Kathleen Wilson, Rebecca Woods, and Alex Zevin. In and beyond New York, I have also been given opportunities to discuss my work at various workshops and seminars. For these I thank Joe Childers (The Global Nineteenth Century, Riverside), Catherine Delyfer (Gold in/and Art, Toulouse), David Lerer (European History and Politics, Columbia), Patrick Scott (Victorian Disruptions, Columbia, SC), David Weiman (Economic History Seminar, Columbia), and Carl Wennerlind (Mercantilism through the Ages and The Social, Legal, and Political Life of Money, both at Columbia). I also express appreciation to the Schoff Fund at the University Seminars at Columbia University for their help in publication. Material in this work was presented to the University Seminar: Modern British History.

In addition to these interactions, Brian Cooper, Alex Dick, Adrienne Munich, Maura O'Connor, and Carl Wennerlind have taken the time to comment on specific chapters. Many other friends and colleagues have inspired me with their conversations: these include Jenny Anderson, David Blaazer, Stephanie Burt,

Deborah Cohen, Martin Daunton, Will Deringer, Chris Desan, Jonathan Eacott, Doucet Fischer, Paul Gillingham, David Goodman, Jeannette Graulau, Anne Humpherys, Joe Kelly, Dane Kennedy, John Kleeberg, Seth Koven, Ayla Lepine, Paula Loscocco, Sharon Murphy, Paul Naish, Tillman Nechtman, Prasannan Parthasarathi, Richard Price, Erika Rappaport, Phil Stern, and Rebecca Spang.

Portions of this book have previously appeared in the *Journal of the History of Ideas* and the *Journal of Victorian Culture*; I wish to thank Martin Burke and Alastair Owen, and the anonymous referees of both journals, for their valuable feedback on those articles. Martin Hewitt, who asked me to write an entry on money in *The Victorian World*, enabled me to try on for size several ideas that made it into the book. Art Resource, British History Online, the British Museum, Columbia University Libraries, the Morgan Library and Museum, the Museum of Applied Arts and Sciences (Sydney), the Museum of the History of Science (Oxford), the National Portrait Gallery, the New York Public Library (General Research Division), the Royal Collection Trust, the Tate Gallery, and the Victoria and Albert Museum all provided valuable assistance in obtaining permission for and providing images used in this book. Last but not least, Susan Ferber has been very helpful at Oxford University Press at shepherding the book from proposal to proofs, as have been the referees of the proposal and book manuscript.

A silver lining throughout the arduous process of balancing *All That Glittered* with a full plate of teaching and administrative duties has been the unwavering support of my wife, Alix Cooper, and the constant companionship of our cat Hermione. Alix's persisting love and trust has meant the world to me in sustaining belief in myself and in this project.

All That Glittered

Introduction

Gold between Tradition and Modernity

From the early eighteenth century into the 1830s, Great Britain was the only major country in the world to adopt gold as the sole basis of its currency, in the process absorbing much of the world's supply of that metal into its pockets, cupboards, and coffers.[1] During the same period, Britons "forged a nation" by distilling a heady brew of Protestantism, commerce, and military might, while preserving important features of its older social hierarchy.[2] *All That Glittered* argues for a close connection between these occurrences, by linking justifications for gold's role in British society—starting in the 1750s and running through the mid-nineteenth century gold rushes in California and Australia—to contemporary descriptions of that metal's varied values at home and abroad. Most of these accounts attributed British commercial and military success to a credit economy pinned on gold, stigmatized southern European and subaltern peoples for their nonmonetary uses of gold, or tried to marginalize people at home for similar forms of alleged misconduct. This book tells a primarily cultural origin story about the gold standard's emergence after 1850 as an international monetary system, while providing a new window on British exceptionalism during the previous century.

The conjunction of gold with British national identity emerged as a result of shifts in global trade and new monetary policies. In the course of its expanding commerce with Asia during the seventeenth century, the East India Company drained Britain of much of its silver coin; trade with France in the early eighteenth century replaced that silver with gold. As Master of the Mint, Isaac Newton adjusted to these developments by fixing the official value of the gold guinea at twenty-one shillings, which had the effect of driving out even more silver and establishing gold as the reigning currency.[3] Trade within Britain had reached the point where larger transactions could be settled with guineas, and the majority of the population who needed smaller sums made do with token coins, copper pence, and whatever silver shillings remained in circulation.[4] Through the 1750s, when gold production boomed in Brazil, Britain's favorable trade balance with Portugal enabled a sufficient influx of gold to sustain what had become a de facto gold standard.

For a gold standard to work, de facto or otherwise, it is necessary for credit to allow a little gold to go a long way. A gold (or silver) standard works when banks promise depositors to exchange the paper money they issue as loans for metallic currency on demand. Trust that they will do so enables these banks to circulate far more notes than the gold they hold in reserve. Britain was even more advanced in this regard than the Netherlands, from which it learned many of its financial tricks. Following its establishment in 1694, the Bank of England soon evolved into a lender of last resort: its gold backed not only its own paper, but the notes issued by dozens of private banks as well, including a cluster of large and stable joint-stock banks in Scotland.[5] In addition to the gold held by the Bank, an equal quantity circulated as coin, while even more adorned Britons' bodies and houses; the result, according to one pamphlet from 1760, was that "Gold, which during half an Age had never changed its abode," now "shifted with such wonderous Quickness . . . that the Eye follows it in vain."[6]

Besides being in the forefront of commercial credit, Britain also led the way during the eighteenth century in creating and sustaining an intellectual justification for a credit economy based on gold. This was part of a more general theory of social progress, which posited that human societies advanced from hunting and gathering, through tending livestock, then farming, then finally a fully commercial economy with all the advantages bestowed by the division of labor. Although French *philosophes* produced similar theories after 1750, it was the British version (first developed by Lord Kames, then perfected in the 1760s by Adam Smith) that found special application to the problem of money. As historian Craig Muldrew has argued, such stories about social development enabled Britons to make sense of money and credit as forms of "cultural currency" that transcended the intrinsic worth of gold and silver, while extending the division of labor to commercial exchange: precious metals "existed as the ultimate means of payment within credit networks," but only "in specified areas and transactions."[7]

This was the monetary and intellectual context for Adam Smith's *Wealth of Nations* (1776), which provided much of the language by which Britain refashioned itself as an economic power. According to Smith, people initially valued gold for its beautiful appearance; its scarcity soon conferred status on those who were able to sacrifice means of subsistence to obtain it. Once these properties had endowed gold with sufficient value, the state took advantage of its additional qualities—ductility and fusibility—to press it and guarantee its weight with an official stamp. This final validation of gold's cultural currency rescued would-be merchants from the inefficiencies of barter, paving the way for commercial farming and industry—and also for international trade, where gold (as well as silver) served the additional function of balancing foreign payments. Having safely lodged gold in the Bank of England, Smith devoted the rest of his discussion of money to the complex machinations of credit. Secure in the assumption that gold would never be in short supply in Britain (thanks mainly to its advanced credit economy), he took an agnostic stance regarding its persistent ornamental uses.[8]

Subsequent Britons echoed Smith's account of gold's place in the evolution of money, but increasingly condemned ornamental gold. The political context for their new aversion to adornment was the drain of bullion occasioned by an enduring war against France (1793–1815), which led many to conclude that gold needed to be reserved for its most "civilized" function of all—as a foundation, in the form of coin and bullion, of Britain's proliferating supply of bank notes and bills of exchange. As a result, the "beauty" phase of Smith's speculative history of gold came to connote cultural inferiority, reinforced by British travel accounts of Southern European, Asian, and African men and women wearing the metal as jewelry and Italian, Russian, and Mexican cathedrals adorned with gilded saints. Meanwhile, novels, plays, and local histories quarantined gold in Britain's recent past, where aristocratic dandies had sported chains, canes, buckles, and lace that pointed to that metal's transitional role as a signifier of status.

Smith's conjectural history of gold and its later modifications hewed closely to Max Weber's twin categories of "market situation" (class) and "style of life" (status), which molded the changing contours of British politics and culture during the decades on either side of 1800. By definition, what was precious could not be possessed equally: in this sense gold set Britain apart from the rest of the world, but also set some Britons apart from others. How it did this was always complicated. As money, gold persisted throughout much of the eighteenth century as a stand-in for "market situation." Even after 1820, when gold coins mainly circulated among shopkeepers and better-off laborers, the notes and bills held by their social superiors owed their value to the vast gold supplies at the Bank of England. By the 1780s, decorative gold had passed from being a nearly exclusive marker of an aristocratic "style of life" to being relegated to the ranks of the nouveau riche, and new laws and technologies made gold or difficult-to-detect imitations accessible to nearly all social ranks after 1820. These changing functions of gold roughly reflected the arc of the British aristocracy, which established a fortuitous hegemony of both economic and social power between 1780 and 1830 before embarking on a decades-long decline.[9]

Gold's dual role in this history of class and status provides a strikingly useful map for exploring Britain's ascendance during the century after 1750. Specifically, its peculiar status as both a marker of value and a valuable commodity closely mirrored a social structure that balanced dynamic economic and social forces against traditional hierarchies. The dominant British discourse on gold, which privileged its use as currency over decoration, aligns with an interpretation of that century as radically modern, whereby Britain took a comfortable if short-lived lead in the race among nations for wealth and power. According to this account, Britain's subordination of ornament to currency accompanied a Promethean accumulation of property, ample expenditure on a "fiscal military state," and imperial expansion. This side of gold also aligns with a similarly modernizing story, pioneered by Weber, of the rise of the Protestant ethic as a cultural precondition for capitalism. By this logic, in transporting gold from cathedrals into banks and coin purses, iconoclasm indirectly fueled the demise of traditional society and the rise of a new capitalist spirit.[10]

Against a forward-looking story that identifies gold as a modernizing motor, the nagging prevalence of decorative gold in Britain and its empire supports a contrary narrative that emphasizes continuity rather than a radical break. In this story, the rise of a modern credit economy shared space with a widespread "invention of tradition" that bolstered national identity with imagined relics from the past; an empire that depended as much on ornamental splendor as on economic and racial subordination; and an impulse to draw from the past in order to create a habitable present in the face of rising levels of population and class division. The point, in most such accounts, is less to wish away all modernizing tendencies than to present these as existing in an unstable equilibrium with conservativism.[11] Gold played its part in all these backward glances, including the royal family's gilded accessories, soldiers' uniforms, and lord mayors' coaches; efforts to out-glitter native princes whose territories fell under British subjugation; and ambivalence about the absence of adornment in British churches.

Besides offering new insight into the rise of the British nation, a reassessment of gold during the decades before 1850 complicates existing scholarship on the metal's changing global role. This has almost exclusively focused on its monetary function; and even in that domain most of the attention has focused on the century after 1850, when other nations followed Britain's lead in joining an international gold standard. In this domain, scholars who present the rise of the international system as the natural and beneficial consequence of new gold discoveries have contended with those who argue that it was both highly artificial and dangerously destabilizing.[12] Recent scholarship has added a great deal to what we know about the cultural and institutional processes before 1850 that conferred legitimacy on money, credit, and the gold standard within Britain.[13] Even so, little attention has yet been paid to the enormous amount of cultural work—only partially successful—that redirected attitudes away from the many other values gold possessed as a commodity. Much also remains to be learned about the material story of gold's multiple roles as bullion, coin, and ornament during this time, both in Britain and the wider world.

The scope of this task is illuminated by the fact that only around half of all gold in Britain before 1850, and a much smaller share on foreign shores, circulated as coin or sat in bank vaults; the rest adorned churches, watches, plate, medals, canes, jewelry, and clothing.[14] By emphasizing these other roles of gold, this book tells the commodity side of the story that lay behind the rise of the gold standard and enables a fresh perspective on its monetary side as well.[15] In the process, it also counters a myth, dating back to Adam Smith, that capitalism works most efficiently when it transcends national boundaries—a myth that obscures the fact that nation-states have always acted as "an indispensable instrument . . . of global capital" and have also left distinctive and indelible cultural imprints on economic development within their borders.[16] Historians who focus on the gold standard as a transnational, and mainly stabilizing, mechanism tend to downplay the tumultuous politics it often engendered in its member states.[17] In Britain as well, during the decades when it was building a foundation for that mechanism, gold in both its monetary and ornamental forms was as likely to be destabilizing as disciplinary. Above all, attitudes about gold always drew from an emerging and self-consciously British national culture, which attached to gold its substantial ambiguities and internal contradictions.

One of the most important of these internal contradictions concerned the meanings that Scottish, Irish, and English people within the British Isles ascribed to gold.[18] These were the most pronounced in the case of money: most people in Scotland and Ireland embraced Smith's maxim that a well-developed credit system rendered gold needful but rarely relevant, while many in England insisted on a substantial stock of circulating gold coin as well as bank notes.[19] Scots also harbored a contrary sense of the influence of gold in foreign relations, owing to a history of England's use of that metal to influence Scottish affairs; while Irish Catholics loudly countered the standard British Protestant line on gold's proper place in religious worship. In general, though, these were exceptions to a rule that gold united more often than it divided, especially within the same social class and whenever Britons of all stripes contrasted their use of the metal with those practiced elsewhere in the world.

The first two chapters of *All That Glittered* describe British attempts to contrast their own acquisition and use of gold with those pursued abroad. The first chapter, "Domestication," recounts the eighteenth-century production and transit of gold from the Americas to Britain and traces efforts to contrast British industry and humanity with Iberian sloth, cruelty, and impolicy as a boastful justification for why so much Latin American gold ended up in the Bank of England. Chapter 2, "Value," explores the ambivalence that ensued when Britons puzzled over what made gold valuable once it had appeared on their shores. It considers the political debate over Britain's legal currency standard in the 1810s, when it was still an open question whether gold, silver, or state-backed paper money would serve this purpose. It then turns to figurative references to gold, which alternated between godliness, genius, and purity and condemnations of adornment and avarice.

Chapters 3 through 5 focus on gold's shifting function as a foundation of Britain's political economy, relating to war expenditure, foreign trade, and coinage. "War" explores the political debates and paranoid imaginings that surrounded Britain's bullion transfers to its allies and troops between 1756 and 1815. "Trade" describes gold's important role in Britain's balance of payments between 1815 and 1850 and in accompanying debates over the merits or otherwise of free trade. "Coinages" covers the respective circulation of guineas and sovereigns before and after 1820, emphasizing the irony that these gold coins recurrently needed to be weighed by their users despite bearing stamps that attested to their legal weight and fineness. An important supporting actor in the first two of these chapters is credit, which extended the reach of bullion and coin but also tended to exacerbate conflicts among landlords, financiers, manufacturers, and laborers.

Chapters 6 through 9 interrogate British claims that they uniquely subordinated gold's nonmonetary uses to its more "civilized" use as a basis of credit and commerce. "Distinction" describes efforts by upper-crust Britons to insist that gold should mainly be used as money, while they simultaneously carved out numerous exceptions that threatened to overwhelm this rule. "Display" discusses gold's appearance in British ethnographies of people who broadcast their foreignness with ornamental gold, while "Devotion" examines British critiques of excessive adornment in non-Protestant churches and temples. These chapters all emphasize the large patches of ambivalence that blurred the alleged binary between British and non-British uses of gold. Chapter 9, "Graven Images," discerns a parallel ambivalence about ancient gold coins and modern gold medals, which conjured nonmonetary (and, consequently, controversial) value by enabling Britons to discover their forebears, broadcast their erudition, or locate themselves in posterity.

All That Glittered concludes by returning to the theme of gold production, first in chapter 10, on British interests in gold mining between 1820 and 1848, and then in the conclusion, on the California and Australia gold rushes between 1848 and the mid-1850s. "Before the Gold Rush" recounts British efforts to find new sources of gold in Brazil, Russia, Africa, and Asia in order to enable the smooth functioning of their restored gold standard after 1820. In all these cases, their growing dependence on gold to maintain economic and political stability led them to blur previously bright lines between the sordid production of foreign gold and its beneficial use in Britain. These lines further faded with the gold rushes, which transformed the global money market and newly identified the extraction of gold with the British Empire. They also restored British economic thought back to Adam Smith's original lack of concern about ornamental gold, which emerged after 1850 as a safety valve against inflation.

Although these chapters are thematic, they all adhere to a chronology that can be roughly divided into three periods—the decades before, during, and after the Napoleonic Wars—that each betrayed distinctive monetary, ornamental, and political tendencies. The 1750s through the 1790s marked the swan song of the guinea, a coin that conjured aristocratic excess ("gold tables" where dandies dwindled their fortunes) and income inequality (the average laborer needed to work two weeks to earn a guinea in 1774).[20] As ornament, gold during these decades signaled the end of an era, when doctors began to trade in their gold-headed canes for stethoscopes and country gentlemen started to shed the gold lace from their waistcoats and hats. Politically, Britain began to make military use of the gold it received from Brazil, first in support of its allies during the Seven Years' War and then by paying mercenaries in an effort to quell the American Revolution.

It was this latter function of gold that precipitated the death of the guinea, the onset of which occurred with the suspension of cash payments by the Bank of England in 1797. This policy, which the British government deemed necessary to enable it to wage war against Napoleon, accompanied a substantial increase in prices by the war's end in 1815. Inflation helped landlords (especially the substantial proportion of debt-ridden ones), who passed a corn law in 1815 to retain the high food prices and accompanying high rents they had enjoyed during the war; and gave them ample capacity to spend their bank notes on ornamental gold, which enjoyed a surge in popularity even while military demands drained the country of its guineas. It ceaselessly bothered creditors, who feared the resultant diminishing returns on their loans. The French, for their part, diverted much gold from church treasuries into their war chest, which effected an ironic culmination of many Britons' anti-Catholic fantasies.

Soon after 1815 Britain returned to the gold standard and marked the occasion with a new coin, the sovereign, worth a shilling less than the guinea. The return to gold drove down prices for everyone except grain producers, ensnaring gold in a heated debate over the relative merits of self-sufficiency versus global interdependence. It also prompted prosperity, although this was uneven and volatile, and accompanied an unprecedented diffusion of sovereigns as well as ornamental gold. Aristocrats, meanwhile, found new corners where they could display gold in ways that reinforced social hierarchy, while newly influential aesthetes started to erode a centuries-old resistance to devotional gold in British churches. Most of these changes reflected a political structure that included more middle-class and Catholic voices. A revived British Empire, finally, afforded new opportunities to identify gold with cultural difference, which informed

free-trade debates along with commentary on Asian and African adornment—
as well as prompting wishful thinking about new gold mines.

Throughout the centuries after 1492, whether gold was used as ornament or
as money, it inspired envy and greed—and the fact that gold ornaments could
be converted so easily into money rendered them especially prone to pillage.
Britons often claimed that they peacefully acquired gold through commerce instead of violently plundering it, in contrast to Spain during the Conquest and
France during the decades after 1789. Yet try as they might to insist on this, violence was seldom far from the surface in British encounters with the metal.
Elizabethan privateers gave Spaniards a run for their money in the business of
plunder, while colonial conquests in South Asia appropriated much gold as well
as land. The simplicity that British Protestants celebrated in their cathedrals
rested on the awkward foundation of Tudor looting. Britain's efforts to find new
sources of gold after 1820 brought them into direct contact with serfdom in
Russia, slavery in Brazil, and social chaos in California and Australia. Finally, a
corollary of gold's ascendance in Britain after 1750 was the mounting frequency
of its appearance in criminal courts. Although the particulars changed over time,
one constant theme throughout this period was a rearguard effort to contain
such violence by diverting attention to financial institutions such as the Bank of
England, which strove to solidify gold's disciplinary potential in the face of ex-
ceptionally bad behavior.

As nineteenth-century geologists often observed, gold was both well concealed
and "widely scattered throughout the mineral kingdom." Gold was literally eve-
rywhere, although not always in amounts that made prospecting for it worth-
while. Indeed, for the entire period covered in this book, gold miners settled
for panning streams, using steam technology for crushing rocks, and applying
mercury to separate gold from its ore; it was not until the late-nineteenth century that new chemical processes enabled an explosion in world gold production.[21] These features all apply to the challenge of researching a comprehensive
cultural and monetary history of gold. References to its manifold forms are eve-
rywhere, from gothic romances to currency pamphlets—as well as sermons,
hymnals, travelogues, histories, conduct manuals, encyclopedias, poems, plays,
newspapers and periodicals of all varieties, Parliamentary speeches and committee reports, and criminal trials.[22]

Until the recent past, finding such references—except in the minority of cases
where gold appears in the title or subject heading—would rarely have repaid the
time and effort it took to call up volume after volume and sift through each for
the pages where gold makes its brief appearance. The arrival of searchable electronic databases has transformed access to these dusty corners—although not
without introducing a danger of losing track of the wider context or neglecting

the databases' built-in limitations.[23] This book uses these resources extensively in order to expand its range of available primary sources. Even in instances of quantitative analysis, the findings are suggestive (appealing to proportions, not absolute numbers) rather than definitive; hence a common criticism of these databases, which concerns their sins of omission, applies with less force.[24] Regarding the extent and composition of these primary sources, this table indicates the electronic resources used:

Google Books	8764
Making of the Modern World (Gale)	5790
British Periodicals (ProQuest)	4229
Eighteenth Century Collections Online (Gale)	4225
Gale News Vault and 19th Century Periodicals	3161
Other	1674

Other: Hansard 1803–2005 (Millbank Systems), House of Commons Parliamentary Papers (ProQuest), Old Bailey Online, and English Verse Drama (Chadwick Healey). Number of discrete sources = 27,843. By *discrete sources* I include multiple references to different themes from the same publication; the total number of books and articles consulted was roughly half this number.

A word cloud provides a glimpse into the number of hits, organized thematically. Most of these fit snugly in one or two chapters, while *plunder* appears in all but two.

A few clues regarding the genesis and evolution of *All That Glittered* can be gleaned from this word cloud. First, the prominence of personal adornment: goldsmiths and gilding (more hits than any other category by 4000) led to the allotment of equal time to this use of gold, a hunch that Smith's evocative and influential story about value reinforced. Second, the hundreds of references to gold as an instrument of war justified a stand-alone chapter on that topic; the same reasoning applied to coinage, buried treasure, and gold medals. Third, although references to gold as a basis of credit were rife, less time was devoted to this topic, since other scholars have ably discussed much of this material already. Finally, as with any project, many references either did not conveniently fit this story, would have led the book to balloon in size, or both, including alchemy, medicine, misers, and gold's many appearances in the Bible.[25]

A final word about the search process used in researching this book is in order: namely, regarding the presence or absence of gold's leading supporting actor, silver. With a few exceptions, *silver* was not one of the search terms used in finding the sources that went into *All That Glittered*—despite that fact that,

Figure I.1 Word cloud representing the frequency of references to gold found in the primary-source electronic databases consulted, organized by theme (total number, excluding "miscellaneous," = 27,214): personal adornment (4893), mining (3094), goldsmiths and gilding (2092), credit (1909), coinage (1599), medals (1458), trade (1119), churches (1086), avarice (1075), plunder (953), war (928), treasure (713), alchemy (710), Bible (708), misers (654), crucible (550), Spain (302), idols (297), chemistry (285), temples (253), medicine (178), Ophir (171), Midas (168), metallurgy (159), assaying (128), electricity (78), slavery (74), marriage (69), gambling (52).

By *discrete sources* I include multiple references to different themes from the same publication; the total number of books and articles consulted was roughly half this number.

as Shakespeare immortally implied, silver is one among many substances that glitters along with gold. The challenge of referring to silver in what is tantamount to a biography of gold parallels that of determining how much time to spend on a spouse or sibling in a biography of a human being. This was different, depending on the uses of gold discussed in the pages that follow. As money, Britain's preference for gold over silver is central to the story, with the result that the relationship between the two metals frequently appeared in contemporary debates. As adornment, and as money in regions that were not on the gold standard, the difference between the two metals was more often a matter of degree and relative scarcity than of economic policy. In these cases, gold and silver often featured together in descriptions of display, devotion, and plunder. A more general book about ornamental British metals and gems would have been more inclusive but less capable of making the connections among money, ornament, and national identity that are the primary focus here.[26]

The wide variety of contexts in which Britons remarked on gold testifies to that metal's protean qualities: it was, and remains today, subject to an enormous range of meanings, depending both on the form into which people molded it and the sort of people who possessed it. The same quarter-ounce of gold that originally bore the stamp of a Roman emperor might be retrieved from a ditch and turned into a guinea, a medal, an earring, an epaulette, or a communion plate; and the earring might signify very different things if worn by an English belle, an Italian peasant girl, a statue of the Virgin Mary, a Spanish pirate, or a Brahmin merchant. Even in its more contained role as money, gold was always both a commodity, subject to export as a means of balancing trade, and a precise signifier of value, as indicated by whichever national symbol it temporarily bore. It is the object of this book to follow gold's lurching, wide ambit of meanings around Britain and the world, which tended to cluster around an evolving national identity that took pride in being simultaneously traditional and modern.

1

Domestication

In his chapter on rent from *The Wealth of Nations*, Adam Smith settled into a long digression on the increased supply of precious metals produced by the conquistadors' "sacred thirst of gold." He cited one estimate that nearly 50,000 pounds of gold and over 4000 tons of silver (worth £2.3 million and £3.4 million, respectively, at the time) had entered Spain and Portugal from the Americas each year between 1748 and 1753. In addition, much gold remained in Latin America, where it was consumed by Iberian settlers, smuggled to neighboring colonies, or reburied. Later he returned to the influx of gold and silver into Europe, only to discount its allegedly positive economic impact. Although the new gold and silver made plate and jewelry cheaper, he countered, it also made money less convenient, by devaluing it and hence making it more cumbersome. Furthermore, it had transformed Spain and Portugal from makers into takers. The New World's real benefit, he concluded, lay in "opening a new and inexhaustible market to all the commodities of Europe," which had occasioned "new divisions of labour and improvements of art."[1]

Smith's perspective on precious metals was far from unique among his contemporaries, who nearly always started with gold in discussing the New World but just as often ended with the manufacture and trade of other commodities. Their discussion of gold often emphasized the plunder and enslavement of Native Americans and Africans in the course of its extraction, as well as the avarice and indolence it occasioned once it had reached Seville, Cadiz, or Lisbon. It was only during the final phase of the cycle, when northern European merchants arrived on the scene, that the truly beneficial aspects of the Conquest appeared, in the shape of the textiles and other manufactured goods that entered Iberia and Latin America in exchange for gold and silver. Taken together, the discovery of precious metals occasioned a new political and moral economy in Europe, over which Britons gradually came to pride themselves as masters.

Those precious metals included much more silver than gold. After focusing exclusively on acquiring the latter metal between 1492 and 1530, Spain turned most of its attention to Mexican and Peruvian silver mines for the next three centuries; gold only re-emerged as a major Latin American export with its dis-covery in Brazil after 1690.[2] Although Britons were equal-opportunity importers, they privileged gold in their political and moral affairs. Politically, Britain created a monetary system in the early eighteenth century that retained much of its gold while trans-shipping most of its silver to India and China; the effect, and argu-ably the intent, was to establish gold as an unshakeable basis for the country's rapidly expanding credit economy, at the significant cost of a perennial shortage of silver coin.[3] Morally, focusing on gold enabled sharper contrasts of Iberian greed and indolence with British industry—despite the fact that much more silver than gold cycled through Spain.[4] Silver, which Spaniards extracted using the latest European mining methods, existed on the same spectrum as British coal and tin, whereas gold conjured political violence. Even the Portuguese in Brazil could be tarred with the brush of slavery—but more awkwardly, given Britain's reliance on slaves to grow colonial commodities and its active role in the slave trade.[5]

Although such moral economies surrounding gold persisted well into the nineteenth century, they mainly described a world that was vanishing by 1780. The last major influx of Brazilian gold arrived in Lisbon in the 1770s and gold from Spanish America dwindled to a trickle after 1820. Global produc-tion of gold declined during the Napoleonic Wars, and when it resumed after 1820 either the context (newly independent Latin American states) or loca-tion (Russia) introduced new political and moral economies. After surveying early-modern gold extraction and export from the New World, this chapter discusses the contrasts Britons developed between their own and Iberia's encounters with gold, as well as their relief at never being subjected to the temptation of possessing gold-bearing colonies during the three centuries after the Conquest.

Early-Modern Gold Extraction

Discussing the European encounter with the Americas in the sixteenth century, the Scottish historian Adam Ferguson described in 1767 how "the inhabitants of one half of the world were let loose on the other, and parties from every quarter, wading in blood, and at the expence of every crime, and of every danger, traversed the earth in search of gold."[6] If Ferguson's interpretation of the Conquest was typical for its emphasis on violent crime, he stood out for including the rest of Europe along with Spain and Portugal in that verdict. More recent historians have largely confirmed his conclusion that the hope of finding precious metals in the Americas motivated Europeans of all nationalities; their efforts to extract gold revealed a wide variety of methods and human consequences. Concerning gold, as opposed to silver, such attempts to strike it rich were much more likely to fail than to succeed.

Although British writers after 1750 focused almost exclusively on the Americas in their discussion of post-Conquest gold production, nearly as much gold actually came from Africa through the sixteenth century, and a steady stream continued to flow until 1710.[7] The Portuguese dominated this trade through the 1550s, when English and Dutch merchants began to provide stiff competition. It was no accident that the guinea, which was originally stamped with "the jaunty image of a colonial elephant" to broadcast its African origins, began its long reign as England's primary gold coin in 1662.[8] In the New World, finding gold was Columbus's highest priority upon landing in Hispaniola, and his Arawak guides fed his desire by directing him to nuggets in its streams. In thirty years, Spaniards exhausted gold supplies in Hispaniola, Cuba, and Puerto Rico, while decimating the population through overwork and exposure to Old World disease. From the Caribbean they turned their sights on the mainland. The large majority of this gold consisted in treasure looted by Hérnan Cortés in Mexico and Francisco Pizarro in Peru. When Cortés sent his first haul to Charles V, Europeans briefly witnessed the splendor of Aztec decorative art before the Spanish king melted it down to fund his army. In Peru, Pizarro melted down his booty on site—a vast and diverse accumulation of gold artifacts from cultures that had been absorbed into the Incan Empire—for shipment to Spain, after liberally rewarding his soldiers.[9]

Spanish American gold outputs continued to increase each decade through 1620, by which point New Granada (present-day Colombia) had emerged as the leading producer. During the following century gold yields declined in all Spain's colonies, owing to a ban on indigenous miners and an accompanying reliance on higher-priced African slaves; it would not reach early-seventeenth century levels until the 1740s, by which point Brazil was producing more than 80% of Latin America's gold and 57% of the world's supply. After 1740, New Granada continued to yield more gold than any other Spanish colony, much of it smuggled to Britain in exchange for slaves. It made rich landlords richer and also benefited merchants in Bogotá and Medellin who supplied remote miners with overpriced goods, leaving the gold-producing areas mired in poverty.[10] Although Peru and Mexico continued to produce gold throughout this period, both colonies turned to silver as the mainstay of their colonial economies starting in the 1540s; between 1600 and 1660 their silver exports exceeded gold in value by a factor of nearly fifty.[11]

Throughout the eighteenth century, many of the same patterns that had first appeared in New Granada recurred in Brazil, accompanied by more explosive movements of population. What literary critic David Haberly has called "the first great gold rush of modern history" started in 1693, after a group of

Paulistas (Portuguese settlers who lived in semi-legal autonomy on the Brazilian border) discovered gold in riverbeds beyond the steep Mantiqueira Mountains. Eventually Portugal assumed something resembling control over the territory that would become known as Minas Gerais, although its isolation and wayward demography rendered this a difficult proposition at best.[12] For contemporaries, the most striking feature of the Brazilian gold rush was the extraordinary movement of people that it spurred. Gold was the main attraction for 400,000 Portuguese emigrants during the eighteenth century; hundreds of thousands of African slaves followed in their wake, first from neighboring sugar plantations and then directly from Africa. The number of slaves in Minas Gerais passed 100,000 by 1738, but they died sooner than their counterparts in the sugar fields due to poor diet and long days drenched in rivers.[13]

As in Colombia, the real local gainers from Brazilian gold were merchants, especially in Sao Paulo and Rio de Janeiro, who supplied the mines with food and slaves and exported the metal.[14] The other chief beneficiary of the gold rush was the Portuguese state, which collected 20% of all the gold its inspectors could track down; although smuggling was rife, both in the Brazilian interior and on the coast, proceeds from this *quinto* annually added as much as 1600 kg in gold to Portugal's national budget, worth around £200,000.[15] After 1770, however, gold yields, as well as their accompanying *quintos,* declined precipitously, from an annual average of 15,760 kg in the early 1750s to under 5000 kg a year after 1785. Brazil's percentage of world production (which itself diminished by nearly 30% between 1760 and 1800) fell during that time from over 60% to 30%.[16] Britain could never have established a sustainable gold standard without this gold, much of which remained in circulation, melted and reminted several times over, well into the nineteenth century.

The historian Pierre Vilar once remarked that "real gold and non-existent gold were equally important in the Discovery, the Conquest, and the Colonisation of the Americas." This was true in the time of Columbus and Cortés and equally true with regard to the moral economies that swirled around gold in succeeding centuries; it also helps explain the prevalence of gold relative to silver in accounts of the Conquest, since much more gold than silver did not exist. Spaniards experienced misses as well as hits, including Hernando de Soto's failure to find gold in Florida or Louisiana and Cabeza de Vaca's quixotic quest for the "Seven Cities of Gold" along the Colorado River. German investors sent expeditions into Venezuela and Colombia as early as 1528, with few survivors and much disappointment.[17] Most famously, explorers spent centuries seeking El Dorado, the fabled "inland country which abounded with gold." The Spaniards Francisco de Orellana and Lope de Aguirre died searching for it in the Amazon basin between 1541 and 1561. In Britain, Walter Ralegh set his sights on Guiana as El Dorado's likely home in 1595; undeterred by an inconclusive first expedition, he convinced James I to free him from prison in 1617 and his friends to finance a second, equally fruitless, voyage.[18]

Much to their subsequent relief, Britons loomed large on the list of explorers whose search for New World gold ended in failure. Martin Frobisher sidetracked his search for the Northwest Passage in 1577 when he mistook iron pyrite near Baffin Island for gold; after an assay in London incorrectly confirmed his hunch, a heavily financed follow-up mission proved to be an exercise in throwing good money after bad.[19] Prior to his El Dorado expeditions, Ralegh bankrolled the colonization of Roanoke Island in 1585, reserving a fifth of its hoped-for gold for himself; two decades later, John Smith successfully argued that the absence of gold in Virginia did not disqualify it as a source of wealth for England.[20] These efforts to find gold that proved not to be there yielded tangible colonial consequences. Frobisher's voyages set in motion Britain's North American fur trade, which ultimately prompted its annexation of Canada in 1763. Smith's turn from gold to tobacco in Virginia catalyzed Britain's plantation complex, which led to expansion in India and Africa as well as North America.[21] Less positively, from a British imperial perspective, Ralegh's second Guiana voyage prompted violent Spanish reprisals, which in turn led to the explorer's swift execution upon his return to London.[22]

At least three useful conclusions emerge from European encounters with New World gold. First, the vast majority of tangible gold extracted from the Americas lay in territory controlled by Spain or Portugal, whereas nearly all early modern British treasure existed, as literary critic William West has observed, "only in stories, as evidence, signs, or promises of the gold that is over there and in the future."[23] This contrast also applied to the diverging monetary systems of Britain and Iberia. Less than a century after Ralegh's final search for El Dorado, Britain would embark on a brave new world in which the Bank of England's promises to pay in gold supported a vast superstructure of credit—in a manner not unlike the business model British adventurers had routinely employed during the Age of Discovery. Indeed, two years after he founded the Bank of England, the Scottish company promoter William Paterson raised capital and colonists on the promise of "Great Mines of Gold" in Central America—a disastrous project that yielded no dividends and more than a thousand deaths from yellow fever.[24]

A second observation concerns the tendency of American gold to animate contrasts among European nations. Britain hardly monopolized this discourse: Spaniards interpreted their gold and silver discoveries as a sign that God had destined them to vanquish Islamic and Protestant infidels, while the Dutch identified Native American resistance to "Spanish perfidy" with their own contemporary struggles against the Catholic Hapsburgs. The only common denominator was a justification of conquest, in which the extraction of gold was never far from the surface. As historian John Smolenski has concluded, "condemnations of other European nations became stories they told themselves about themselves, authorizing continued American colonization."[25]

A final point concerns Portugal. Although later Britons considered themselves lucky to have avoided the curse of possessing gold-bearing lands, they were even more fortunate that it was Brazil and not Spanish America that contributed close to a million kilograms to the world's gold supply in the eighteenth century. The value of gold and silver has always been defined by its purchasing power—and Spain's use of its precious metals before 1800 differed markedly from Portugal's. Spain channeled a substantial share of its silver into its army (which was Europe's largest in the 1630s) and into imperial governance, both in the Americas and Asia. Adding £125 million worth of gold to that mix might very well have impeded Britain's ascendance as a world power after 1700. Portugal, meanwhile—largely due to its subordination to Spain between 1580 and 1640—entered the eighteenth century economically and militarily dependent on Britain.[26] Hence when it did strike it rich in the goldfields of Brazil, much of that windfall passed directly to London to balance a growing trade deficit, and did much to assist, rather than blunt, Britain's growing status on the world stage.

British Gold Imports in the Eighteenth Century

Looking back on his twenty-five years' experience as a British merchant based in Lisbon, John Koster recalled how he had been "in the habit of purchasing large quantities of gold bar and dust, and export[ing] it to England in his Majesty's packets and ships of war." This was "brought from the Brazils clandestinely," he reported, "but it was done without much apparent risk, nor was there any great secrecy observed in the purchase of it at Lisbon: it seems as if it had been known to, but winked at by, the government." For four years before he moved from London to Lisbon, he had "received considerable quantities of gold bar, gold dust, and coin" from there, which he purchased once it had been registered at the Bank of England's bullion office. By the 1790s, Koster concluded, the trade in Brazilian gold "began sensibly to diminish" and "was reduced to a mere trifle" by 1800.[27]

Koster's first-hand account accurately described the process by which Britain's bankers and goldsmiths acquired the majority of their gold for most of the eighteenth century, with imports peaking between 1730 and 1770. The combination of extensive Brazilian yields and Britain's massive trade surplus with Portugal was enough to establish Lisbon as gold's primary port of call on the way to London. The trade surplus dated back into the seventeenth century, when it had been balanced by Brazilian sugar; four treaties, enacted between

1642 and 1703, lubricated Anglo-Portuguese trade throughout this period, as did the easy credit and cheap textiles British merchants were able to offer. When gold imports began to dry up after 1780 they were replaced by Brazilian cotton, which by the 1790s arrived in quantities sufficient to give Portugal a trade surplus for the first time in over a century.[28]

Although Portuguese law prohibited foreign ships from carrying gold once it had arrived in Lisbon, between half and three-fourths of the gold between 1720 and 1780 that was registered at the Lisbon mint was illegally re-exported to London.[29] Portugal only sporadically enforced its export ban, partly to ensure the British navy's protection of its own merchant marine, but mainly because there was no other way to balance imports of British woolen textiles, grain, and cod that produced annual trade deficits from £500,000 to £1 million between 1705 and 1765.[30] Once it arrived in England, some of this gold remained in circulation in the form of Portuguese *moidras*, coins worth twenty-seven shillings. The rest was either converted into guineas or trans-shipped to Europe, in roughly equal proportions. Between 1750 and 1769, for instance, Lisbon took in a yearly average of 8750 kg of gold and the Mint at Tower Hill annually coined 5157 kg into guineas, worth £643,887. Over the longer period from 1716 to 1780, Britain sent a yearly average of £600,000 in gold bullion and coin out of the country, peaking at £1.25 million from 1726 to 1735.[31]

As Koster noted, the two most common methods of transporting gold to England were Post Office packet boats, which called at Lisbon at least once a month, and Navy men-of-war, which often added Lisbon to their itineraries solely to enable their captains to pocket the commission for taking on gold. Both types of ships were better armed than regular merchant vessels, offering protection against pirates, and also uniquely enjoyed diplomatic immunity from search and seizure by Lisbon customs officers. After being unloaded, the gold either entered the local economy in Falmouth (where packet boats landed), Plymouth, and Chatham (where men-of-war docked), or it moved on to London in heavily armed carriages. The Post Office charged between 0.25 and 0.5 percent for its leg of the journey, the Navy charged 1 percent, and the overland journey set bullion traders back an additional 0.375 percent.[32]

Koster, a Liverpool-bred merchant who maintained close ties with that city throughout his long residence in Lisbon, was typical of Britons who exported Portuguese gold.[33] Lucy Sutherland's case study of William Braund (1695–1774) sheds light on how such merchants moved into and out of this trade. Braund began his career importing woolen textiles into Lisbon, against bills of exchange drawn on exports of wine from Porto back to England. He made the transition to gold following the Lisbon earthquake of 1755, which disrupted his textile business, and the outbreak of the Seven Years' War, which heightened Britain's demand for bullion. The profits that attracted him to the trade arose from two sources: a higher price of gold in Britain owing to wartime demand (from the standard rate of 77s 10.5d per ounce in 1757 up to 81s 2d in 1761) and a favorable exchange rate in Lisbon owing to its earthquake-damaged economy. He mainly paid for his gold with bills drawn on export merchants in towns such as Norwich, Exeter, and Leeds, or on London bankers. A ship owner on the side, Braund bought a share in a packet boat, a useful hedge against shipping commissions.[34]

Significantly, not all Braund's gold crossed the English Channel. He sent around 8% of it to George Clifford, an English banker who worked out of Amsterdam, against bills on goods shipped to Lisbon from Hamburg, France, and Genoa. Other merchants specialized in trans-shipping Portuguese gold from London to the rest of Europe, much of which ended up being coined into ducats by the Bank of Amsterdam. In 1776, for instance, when £735,328 worth of gold left the country, £542,188 of it went to Holland.[35] Jewish merchant bankers, who played a major role in importing gold to Britain during the first decade of the eighteenth century and again after 1810, played an even larger role in trans-shipment owing to their close ties with the Amsterdam foreign exchange market.[36] In a sample of London gold exports from 1776, George Goldsmid— an Ashkenazi immigrant from Amsterdam—registered £53,500 out of £150,250 by value.[37] Re-exports, which comprised roughly half of the gold that entered Britain, stabilized international credit following financial crises, subsidized allies in times of war, and balanced trade deficits—in particular with Russia and the Baltic states, which provided much-needed timber.[38]

Although subsequent historians have confirmed Adam Smith's comment that "almost all our gold . . . comes from Portugal," Britons did acquire the metal from numerous other ports during the eighteenth century.[39] The South Sea Company traded slaves and other commodities for bullion (mainly silver, but also much gold) from Spanish treaty ports in Jamaica, Florida, and Louisiana throughout most of this period; British privateers and pirates acquired more by raiding Spanish galleons; merchants illegally exchanged gold for British and French imports in Lima, Buenos Aires, and Colombia and exchanged textiles for smuggled gold dust on the Brazilian coast. In Bahia, for instance, local merchants paid up to 40% less than they might have for Indian textiles by illicitly exchanging gold to East Indiamen crews sailing under multiple flags.[40]

Pizarro and Alonzo, Iberia and Britain

In 1783 the English writer Thomas Day published *Sandford and Merton*, a "work intended for the use of children" that was loosely modeled on Rousseau's *Émile*. One of its many anti-aristocratic fables concerned Francisco Pizarro and his brother Alonzo. In the story, Alonzo urges his brother not to give up their Spanish farm for the New World, but he agrees to accompany Pizarro when he refuses to heed his advice. Landing in Peru, Alonzo stays on the coast, tending the sheep and "four stout oxen" he had brought with him from Spain, while Pizarro sets off with an army in search of gold. They find much gold but little food and eventually return to the coast, their numbers depleted. Alonzo, meanwhile, had "laid up a considerable quantity of provisions" including salted fish, potatoes, and mutton. When the half-starved Pizarro asks for food, Alonzo requires payment in gold and soon receives the entire treasure trove in exchange for the food he had stored up. Just before they return to Spain, Alonzo returns the gold to his brother with this moral: "you have now learned, that, without . . . foresight and industry, all the gold you have brought with you would not have prevented you from perishing miserably. You are now I hope wiser; and therefore take back your riches."[41]

The fact that Pizarro never had a brother named Alonzo—let alone a relation so conveniently industrious—did not prevent Day from inventing one to prove the point that gold without industry was worse than useless. Primers and self-help manuals would reprint this apocryphal story throughout the nineteenth century, and other British retellings of the Conquest taught similar lessons.[42] In these narratives British industry was the pole star, around which orbited a wide array of Iberian crimes and misdemeanors: including a bloody brew of avarice and cruelty, a slow descent into indolence, and a Midas-like lack of foresight.[43] These associations, along with British interest in the history of New World gold, varied over time. An emphasis on avarice peaked during Elizabethan times, then rose and ebbed with the shifting tides of humanitarianism two centuries later. Indolence and lack of foresight, meanwhile, first appeared in British accounts of the Conquest early in the eighteenth century, then resurfaced during and after the Napoleonic Wars. Gold's role in this range of behaviors was similarly unstable. In many instances it exerted an attractive force that only the stoutest Alonzos of the world could resist; in other verdicts, gold merely exposed Iberian flaws that had been there all along.

The earliest British assumption concerning New World gold was that it had infected Iberians with a severe case of avarice, which in turn resulted in unrestrained violence against native Americans. This trope dated back to the "Black Legend" first articulated by the Spanish Dominican Bartolomé de las Casas, who skewered the "cruel and greedy and vicious" conquistadors whose desire "to acquire gold, and to swell themselves with riches" had led to the "devastation of the Indies." In Britain, the Black Legend flourished into the seventeenth century as a response to the perceived threats of Spanish war and papism. Following the defeat of the Armada in 1588, it implied military as well as moral superiority, and it surged after 1640 as a means of tarring Charles I with a Spanish brush.[44] Condemnations of conquistadors' bad behavior resurfaced briefly, and for similar reasons, during Spain's enemy status at the tail end of the Seven Years' War. One diatribe from *The Court Magazine* in 1763 declaimed that Spaniards had "murdered 6 or 700,000 of the poor natives; and . . . those who remained alive . . . were tortured in the most barbarous manner, in order to make them discover their treasure, or made slaves to work in the mines for life."[45]

After 1780, humanitarian sympathy toward the victims of Spanish plunder revived such associations, most prominently in Richard Brinsley Sheridan's elaborate theatric adaptation of August von Kotzebue's *Pizarro* (1799), which spectacularly exposed how "the abhorred lust for gold" had prompted the explorer to forsake "the honour of Castilians, and . . . the duties of humanity." Inspiring equal shares of praise and controversy, Sheridan's play provided an analogy between the Spanish Conquest and the recent French Terror.[46] A second important context for reviving the Black Legend was the abolition movement, which extended William Cowper's famous reference to planters as "slaves of gold" to conquistadors. James Montgomery celebrated the end of the slave trade in 1807 by recalling "rapacious Spain" as a "rabid race, fanatically bold / And steel'd to cruelty by lust of gold."[47]

Figure 1.1 "Pizarro returning from the Gold Mines in Peru" (1799). Richard Brinsley Sheridan, a target of anti-Jacobin bile, is pictured capitalizing on his depiction of Pizarro, who complains: "I must hurry home or I shall be waylaid by the Jacobin Banditti! My heart sinks and my sack seems lighter every step I go . . ." British Museum 1868,0808.12542.

Beginning in the early eighteenth century, indolence edged out avarice as the leading alleged effect of New World gold. Bernard Mandeville urged in his *Fable of the Bees* (1714) that the discovery of gold and silver had turned Spain "from a rich, acute, diligent and laborious, [to] a slow, idle, proud and beggarly People"; and a generation later Adam Anderson agreed that "from the flowing in so fast of the Gold and Silver of America," Spain "grew lazy with their Riches, and careless of the Labour required in Manufactures."[48] Others argued that gold merely heightened Iberians' true colors. In "casting the parts . . . of the several European nations who act upon the stage of America," Edmund Burke contrasted the "proud, lazy, and magnificent" Spaniards and "naturally indigent" Portuguese with the "thoughtful and cool" English, who had little gold but possessed "a large tract of a fine continent; a noble field for the exercise of agriculture, and sufficient to furnish their trade."[49]

The corollary of correlating Iberian gold with indolence was to stress its transience: Mandeville's Spaniards sat "with their Arms across, and wait every Year with impatience and anxiety, the arrival of their Revenues from Abroad, to pay others for what they have spent already." Such verdicts persisted throughout the eighteenth century: "in search of gold and of precious metals," wrote Adam Ferguson in 1767, Iberians neglected "the domestic sources of wealth, and [became] dependent on their neighbours for the necessaries of life."[50] For just as long, Britons were quite content to tolerate the goose that sent them so many golden eggs. Writing from Seville in 1759, Christopher Hervey observed that the gold that entered Iberia "must go to other kingdoms to buy what the indolence of the inhabitants denies them in their native country"—and hastened to add: "We ought, however, by no means to attempt to open their eyes. Their blindness is of too much service to England, not to wish them to continue in it."[51]

Such complacency eroded after Spain and Portugal failed to fend off Napoleon, resulting in a vast expenditure of British gold and lives in the Peninsular Wars. The prevailing explanation for Iberia's occupation by France concerned its "want of energy," which, lamented one writer, "even the possession of unearned gold can scarcely account for." Soldiers were quick to apply to their allies the view of Iberia that had long circulated in treatises and travelogues, while Britons back home held out hope that "principles of honour and independence" had sufficiently survived among the masses to counter gold's corrosive effects on elites.[52] Notwithstanding such glimmers of optimism, and despite the ultimate defeat of Napoleon, many assumed gold's long shadow would darken the Iberian landscape for generations after Waterloo. In 1838, Harriet Martineau blamed "the prevalent faults of the saucy beggars and beggarly grandees of Spain" on gold; a mercenary who assisted in a failed effort to overthrow those grandees likewise concluded that Spain's persistent "backwardness" had been "in a great degree the effect of the American gold which poisoned her energies."[53]

A final interpretation of New World encounters with gold faulted Iberians for poor political economy. Here, the timeless example of King Midas was especially apropos: the Scottish historian William Stevenson argued that when Spain "substituted the artificial stimulus of her American mines in the place of the natural and nutritive food of real industry," it had inherited Midas's near-fatal "power of converting every thing that is touched into gold"; another writer compared Iberian gold to "food taken into a stomach that has lost the powers of digestion, passing through without affording nutriment or strength."[54] Such references spoke to a deep-seated economic critique. As an article on "the nature and use of metallic money" in *Chambers's Edinburgh Journal* observed in 1841, Spaniards suffered from the "preposterous feeling that they were possessed, not of the means of making riches, but of riches itself; and dearly did they pay the penalty": while "the highest grandees could not command so much of the produce of ordinary commercial industry as a glass window, every wretched dwelling glittered with mountains of plate."[55]

The question of whether the curse of New World gold could be reversed hinged on whether gold, or Iberians, had been responsible for their actions. For those who argued that Spanish and Portuguese elites were essentially greedy and lazy, especially following the expulsion of Moors and Jews in the 1490s, there was little hope that they could recover national greatness even after gold no longer appeared on their shores.[56] Others were more hopeful. An article on Brazil in 1809 predicted that the imminent independence of Iberian colonies, by leaving "the mother countries . . . to their own natural wealth," would make each of them "a greater nation than ever she has been." Fifteen years later, a traveler in Spain urged that it would be "compelled, by the recognition of the independence of the South American states, to look for wealth at home," and would then "find within their own territory mines infinitely more productive than those of Mexico or Peru."[57]

Such diagnoses hinted at an alternative to national character (whether indolent or industrious) as an explanation for contrasting outcomes: political economy. Looking back on Iberian decline, most historians today point to absolutist policy decisions. A succession of Spanish monarchs diverted much of their incoming gold and silver to a military build-up and colonial acquisition, which incurred high maintenance costs that were ultimately unsustainable after 1700. What contemporaries called improvidence was hence really the result of a state-mandated diversion of savings.[58] Conversely, the British state, in order to appease tax-paying Members of Parliament, engaged in robust military spending after 1700 without abstracting gold from its economy, by putting it to work as the basis of an expanding system of public credit. In the process, the evolving gold standard encouraged saving and reinvestment over consumption by rewarding such activities with reliably high interest rates.[59] What economist Michael Pettis has called "the inanity of moralizing" did not, however, disappear from popular accounts of saving and spending on the global stage. The myth of Iberian indolence, which British advocates of the gold standard worked so hard to establish, has reappeared at present in contrasts between "the thrifty habits of Germans and . . . the spendthrift ways of Spaniards" within the European Union—whereas these countries' contrasting fortunes arguably have much more to do with fiscal policy than with national character.[60]

Providential Disappointment

In "An Anachronism; or, Missing One's Coach," published in the *Dublin University Magazine* in 1838, the narrator happens upon the Venerable Bede while hiking along Hadrian's Wall. After he updates Bede regarding the discovery of the Americas, the monk asks for more details. The northern continent, the narrator replies, was "a rugged waste of dark forests, bluff mountains, [and] trackless swamps . . . yet fertile enough in patches," while South America was "fat, prolific, inexhaustible: its bowels teeming with gold, silver, diamonds." When Bede assumes that "no doubt it is England that has snatched the realm of gold," he soon learns his mistake: "Nay, it is England that has snatched the rugged prize, leaving her neighbours to impoverish and enslave themselves with mountains of wealth."[61] With this story, the parable of Alonzo and Pizarro found geographic precision. When Britons evaluated their colonial past, they were repeatedly relieved that their colonial adventurers—including Frobisher on Baffin Island and Ralegh in Virginia and Guiana—did not chance upon any gold mines. The lesson was clearly stated in David Macpherson's *Annals of Commerce*: the English had been "providentially disappointed in their hopes of finding very productive mines of gold and silver, the nurses of national lethargy and ostentatious poverty."[62]

More than two centuries after Frobisher's northern expeditions, British historians persisted in emphasizing the gold he failed to discover. James Mill opened his *History of British India* with a reference to his "supposed treasure, which proved to be only a glittering sand," pairing this with his incorrect assumption that the mouth of Hudson's Bay would lead him to India's "golden shore"; and the natural philosopher John Leslie concluded his survey of polar exploration by smirking at the "absolute failure" of Frobisher's alleged gold mine. Hugh Murray in the *Edinburgh Cabinet Library* supposed that the London goldsmiths who had deemed Frobisher's ore to be "of the most precious of metals" had been either "ignorant, or . . . misled by the enthusiasm of the moment," and concluded that their "false decision threw all England into a ferment of joy."[63]

Close at Frobisher's heels came Ralegh's plan to colonize Virginia. For Adam Anderson, the early Virginia settlers had been "so eager to discover Gold and Silver Mines (now never like to be found there), whilst they neglected to prepare their Provisions in due Season," that "most of them were either destroyed by the Natives, or perished for Want." In this narrative, John Smith entered the picture as a late-arriving Alonzo, who rescued the settlers from their worst devices in the nick of time. He "relieved their wants by the resources he had created," wrote one historian, who included in his appendix a sermon in which Smith assured the settlers that "the pleasures of fishing" would "afford as good gold as the mines of Guiana."[64] The real gold mine in Virginia, of course, was not fish but tobacco, a point that was not lost on subsequent writers. Robert Southey's ode to snuff contrasted the "miserable realms" of Peru, which "furnish gold for knaves and gems for fools," with the "common comforts" produced by Virginian tobacco and concluded, "far above Pizarro's name / Write Raleigh in thy records of renown!"[65]

If tobacco absolved Ralegh of his misplaced desire to find gold in Virginia, British historians were more consistently critical regarding his subsequent search for El Dorado. Throughout the century after 1750, all British historians agreed that his expeditions were "delusive and pompous"; the only debate concerned whether Ralegh was, in David Hume's words, "a man capable of the most extravagant credulity or most impudent imposture." Scottish lawyer Macvey Napier claimed that Ralegh's "congenial spirit" had prompted him to believe in El Dorado. More common, especially as fraudulent investment came to the fore in the 1830s and 1840s, was the verdict that Ralegh was "a master in the art of puffing" who risked his friends' fortunes on a superficial inspection of the region and the "casual assertion" of untrustworthy locals. Southey split the difference: Ralegh tried "to cheat the nation into an enterprize which was undoubtedly of considerable national importance."[66]

As with many descriptions of Iberian conquistadors, most of these histories relieved their protagonists of at least some responsibility by referring to gold's irresistible sway. The lure of gold had bred an "epidemy of avarice" that equally infected English and Iberian adventurers; a "dangerous contagion" spread from the "rapacious Spaniards" to the Roanoke colony.[67] Where human agency did creep back in, it was either in the form of a bad actor who had infected his fellow men with gold-lust, or a vaguely-defined zeitgeist that present-day Britons had put well behind them. The first strategy was on display in a history of William Paterson's Darien expedition, in which that "extraordinary projector" perverted "the ordinarily cool and calculating Scots almost out of their senses" through his "visions of gold, and of nothing but gold." Ralegh's apologists often took the second tack, appealing to an "atmosphere of belief in golden legends" or to "the circumstances of the age."[68]

Against this tide, only a handful of accounts of the Age of Discovery were bold enough to pose the counterfactual of British explorers discovering gold and not following Spain's example. One such outlier was the Anglo-Irish historian George Croly, who insisted that had England annexed Peru and Mexico, "she would have converted their treasures into new canals and high-roads, new harbours, [and] new encouragements to agriculture."[69] Other historians stopped short of such sweeping assertions but did identify exceptions to the rule that the British were merely lucky not to find gold. The Puritans, for instance, were sufficiently "held in fellowship by a strong conformity amongst themselves" to avoid wasting time on "a search after the precious metals"; and Napier framed his discussion of Ralegh by identifying numerous sixteenth-century "English projectors" who had valued "the ordinary objects of industry and commerce" over the "blind passion for gold, that inflamed the Spanish adventurers."[70]

Whether they credited luck or fortitude, nearly all Britons reached the same conclusion regarding the lack of close encounters with gold in their colonial past. The fact that Spain had enslaved "the Natives for gold-finders" while at least some English settlers "gave gold for acres, and obtained the land by fair and honourable purchase," claimed the Anglo-American actor George Jones, "has made the essential difference, even to this day, in the stability of the Governments of the two European races, Spanish and Anglo-Saxon."[71] This sort of distinction was necessary to preserve space for gold as a positive good and not inevitably corrupting. Economist Josiah Tucker indicated this in 1774 when he argued that although gold and silver, when "spent in Idleness, will prove to be Destruction, . . . Gold and Silver acquired by general Industry, and used with Sobriety, and according to good Morals, will promote still greater Industry."[72]

When Britons agreed with Tucker's implication that they acquired and used gold "according to good morals," they overlooked the many forms of violence and illegality that accompanied such takings. Nearly all the gold imported into Britain depended on slavery for its production and smuggling or plunder for its transport. Although slavery in Brazil sometimes invited condemnation during the eighteenth century, as when the explorer James Cook lamented that its gold was produced "at an expence of life that must strike every man . . . with horror," most writers pardoned the gold standard's reliance on smuggling as a necessary evil occasioned by misguided Portuguese policy.[73] On the plunder side of the account, military necessity usually provided ample justification for violent seizures of gold from Spanish galleons, as was the case in 1762 when covered wagons conveyed booty from the *Hermione* to the Tower of London "with great parade"; and historians of such privateers as Francis Drake similarly focused on Spanish provocation or "activity of spirit" rather than avarice.[74]

Such efforts to keep gold's unsavory origins in the shadows paralleled the way Britons thought—or more often, failed to think—about the many other commodities they imported from exotic climes, including tea, coffee, and mahogany.[75] In all these cases, a process of domestication converted a barbaric substance into a signifier of civilization. For gold, that cultural alchemy included the honest industry embodied in the textiles, grain, and fish that departed Britain in exchange for the smuggled metal; the trust and political stability enabling the credit that hovered atop the Bank of England's bullion reserves; and a carefully choreographed social hierarchy that privileged some forms of wearing gold over others. Although varying widely, such efforts converged in proclaiming Britain to be a nation of Alonzos, who could be trusted to utilize gold less harmfully and more productively than their counterparts in the rest of the world. This work of domestication, however, did not end when gold entered the country. Throughout the century after 1750, Britons tirelessly debated the boundaries between gold's productive, unproductive, and corrosive uses, all the while pondering what exactly rendered it so valuable.

2

Value

In one of many scenes from *Robinson Crusoe* that inspired imitation, Daniel Defoe's iconic castaway finds a chest containing gold coins. Despite scoffing that he has "no manner of Business" for such "nasty sorry useless Stuff," Crusoe keeps his "drug" on the off chance that he will be rescued—as he does with a later discovery of gold doubloons and bars. In the end, the main function of gold in the plot is to teach the lesson that on this isolated island, "all the good Things of this World, are no farther good to us, than they are for our Use." Regarding his stock of gold, Crusoe "would have given it all for Sixpennyworth of *Turnip* and *Carrot* Seed out of *England*" since he "had not the least Advantage by it, or Benefit from it." Although he does ultimately bring it back to England, its value pales in significance next to the £5000 he had earned from a Brazilian sugar plantation during his absence.[1]

Many of Crusoe's fictional successors shared his initial reaction to the gold that they conveniently discovered on their desert islands. The hero of Joachim Campe's *Robinson the Younger* (1781) encounters a large lump of gold, which he calls "a contemptible thing" next to "a handfull of iron-nails"; he later recovers a cask of gold dust from a shipwreck, which "he could make no manner of use of" but keeps in case he can one day return it to the ship's captain. A French and an English castaway in Henri Lemaire's *French Gil Blas*, which appeared in English a decade later, discover "a block of virgin gold" but conclude: "in our present situation ... [this] fascinating metal had no more worth in our eyes."[2] And Sir Edward Seaward, whose apocryphal Caribbean shipwreck was recounted by Jane Porter in 1831, frets over his discovery of a large box of gold doubloons, which instills a "subtle poison" in his mind that he bravely counteracts by tending to his livestock, building huts, and educating a family of escaped slaves.[3]

As well as re-enacting Defoe's allegory regarding gold's lack of use-value, latter-day Crusoes found diverse ways to spend it on returning to Europe, all of which exceed Defoe's aside in clarifying the choice between depravity and virtue. Campe's hero locates the gold dust's rightful owner in Cadiz, where it enables the bankrupt captain to repay his debts; he also brings back the large lump but loses it at sea, leaving him to "pass the rest of his days in the same uninterrupted labo-riousness and sobriety, just as he had been used to live in his island." Lemaire's protagonists sell their wedge of gold for £40,000 upon returning to Europe and use the proceeds to marry their respective sweethearts: the Englishman's new wealth melts the cold heart of his future father-in-law, a "very rich merchant." Most prosaically, Seaward converts most of his gold into "three per cent South Sea transferable stock" and settles down with his wife on a comfortable annuity.[4]

In all these endings, gold regains its value through the active intervention of institutions, including bankruptcy court, the marriage market, and the stock exchange. Historians of the gold standard have likewise accounted for its emer-gence by emphasizing institutions rather than gold per se. Most such accounts focus on the quarter century after 1797, when a war against France drove nearly all the gold coin out of Britain. In response, Parliament relieved the Bank of England of responsibility for redeeming its notes for gold; the inflation that ensued (close to 60% over the course of the war) initiated an all-consuming debate over whether wartime scarcities or the Bank's irresponsible lending had caused it. A Whig-engineered Bullion Report, issued by Parliament in 1810, ultimately prevailed in this debate, setting the stage for the deflationary res-toration of cash payments under a newly formalized gold standard in 1821.[5] Historians have taken a keen interest in the ideological and class divisions re-vealed by this "bullionist controversy" and its aftermath,[6] while economists have hailed it as yielding "contributions of crucial and lasting importance to monetary theory."[7]

The century before 1797 appears in most accounts as a time when Britain ac-quired its "de facto" gold standard in a fit of absence of mind. The most common version holds that Isaac Newton errantly set the value of gold relative to silver too high to keep the latter metal in circulation, leaving gold as the only option.[8] More recently, this interpretation has been revised to restore agency to the Bank of England, Parliament, and the common law. Far from being accidental, polit-ical scientist Samuel Knafo has argued, the eighteenth-century gold standard continued a "long tradition of sound money in England" and specifically marked an effort by the state, in conjunction with the Bank, to impose discipline on the "new financial practices associated with banknote-issuing" that had emerged after 1700.[9] This focus on shared governance between the state and the Bank also informs most accounts of the decades after 1820, which play out as a period in which the Bank gradually adjusted to its new role as a lender of last resort. Gold's role in this institutional arrangement has long been a matter of debate. Many advocates of the gold standard at the time defended its role in preventing central banking in the modern sense, by hampering the Bank's ability to affect money supply. Others have argued that the Bank in the nineteenth century was indeed a central-banking pioneer, despite being limited by its gold reserves, since it could and did impact credit instruments other than bank notes (especially bonds and domestic bills) by adjusting prime lending rates.[10]

These mainly institutional histories of the gold standard's origins and early emergence provide important insights into the financial sources of Britain's rising global power after 1800, but they neglect the cultural underpinnings—more evocative of Crusoe's time on the island than of his return to Europe—that offered crucial support to gold's monetary function in Britain. Especially after Parliament formalized the gold standard in 1821, economists reinforced its legitimacy by building on Adam Smith's account of value in *The Wealth of Nations*, which offered an influential itinerary of its journey from Crusoe's allegorical island to its secure homeland. They also sharpened Defoe's distinction between gold's minimal use-value and its exchange-value; and, under newfound conditions of scarcity, focused attention on the diversion of gold away from ornamental purposes, which Smith had identified as a transitional phase on the way to the gold standard.

In laying out this multipronged elaboration of gold's value, political economy shared space with numerous other discourses—evident in novels, poems, essays, and sermons—which used gold as a metaphor for Christian virtue, artistic genius, and class; or which emphasized gold's poisonous potential, building on a long history of the metal as an object of monstrous desire. Gold as a positive signifier has received little attention; and although more is known about gold and avarice for the centuries leading up to 1800, it remained a focus of scorn well into the nineteenth century, through such personifications as misers, fortune-hunters, and gamblers.[11] These references to gold propped up its monetary role: either by cloaking it in godly glory or by diverting attention, through a focus on its power to tempt and corrupt specific classes of individuals, from the less visible (but often for that reason more powerful) realm of financial institutions.

Just-So Stories

In *The Wealth of Nations*, Adam Smith introduced a set of categories for discussing the value of precious metals that closely reflected emerging British sensibilities regarding gold and silver. The original "merit" of the precious metals, he argued, was "their beauty, which renders them peculiarly fit for the ornaments of dress and furniture." Status soon joined beauty in conferring value on gold and silver owing to their relative scarcity, which enabled wealthy people to exhibit "those decisive marks of opulence which nobody can possess but themselves." Smith next moved to commerce: once value had thereby been conferred, it was a logical step to circulate gold and silver as coin.[12] He reserved most of his discussion to this third stage, when statesmen measured commercial success by the accumulation of bullion; he countered that a country's bullion supply would always be ample as long as it maximized industrial and agricultural production and as long as credit made a little coin go a long way.

Smith's story about the evolution of precious metals from ornaments to coin and credit had deep roots. John Locke's famous chapter on property in his *Second Treatise of Government* (1690) identified them as "things that fancy or agreement hath put value on" in order to "take in exchange for the truly useful, but perishable supports of life." David Hume similarly suggested in his *Treatise of Human Nature* that they had "become the common measures of exchange" as the result of "a general sense of common interest"—citing the emergence of language as a comparable development. Such exercises drew heavily on New World encounters, as when Smith cited the "poor inhabitants of Cuba and St. Domingo" who "used to wear little bits of gold as ornaments in their hair . . . when they were first discovered by the Spaniards."[13]

Within forty years of the publication of *The Wealth of Nations,* its account of what Locke called "the invention of money" would become canonical, and it still resonates in the present day—despite ample evidence that it fails to describe the actual emergence of money in most cultures.[14] One common denominator in all nineteenth-century variants on Smith's just-so story was the assumption that (in the words of the Dundee banker David Milne) gold and silver currency evolved out of "the march of society from its primitive state of rudeness to civilization." Smith had provided a long list of commodities that had once passed for money, including cattle in ancient Greece, salt in Abyssinia, cowrie shells in India, dried cod in Newfoundland, and tobacco in Virginia. Relying on updated ethnographies, later writers reproduced and annotated this list. Economist Thomas Smith, for instance, cited Mungo Park on iron bars in Africa and James Cook on axes in the South Seas as further examples of "rude ideas of value."[15]

Economists of all stripes supported the case, originally made in *Robinson Crusoe,* that gold was effectively useless when it did not function as money. A gloss on *The Wealth of Nations* in 1811 asserted that gold "does not supply any of the wants of first necessity, but is merely an object of convenience and luxury"; later writers referred to its "comparative uselessness towards the ordinary purposes of life" and urged that it had "little intrinsic value applicable to human use."[16] Socialists joined capitalism's most strident apologists in endorsing Crusoe's aversion to gold. John Gray cited his preference of tools over gold to proclaim that "a rational system of exchange" would only be possible under socialism, while Jane Marcet referred to Crusoe in her *Conversations on Political Economy* to teach the lesson that gold comprised "but a very small portion" of wealth.[17]

The reason for this consensus was that gold's allegedly minimal use-value rested on a close variant of the just-so story that identified gold as a more civilized form of money, which called attention to Britain's place at the vanguard of the industrial revolution—and tabled the question of whether gold should remain as its primary currency.[18] Coal and iron appeared far more often than not on the long list of commodities that Britons routinely deemed to be more valuable than gold; others included ceramics, flax, potatoes, fish, and fertilizer.[19] Coal was "vastly more precious" than gold, concluded J. R. McCulloch, since its "hoarded power" was "applicable to almost any purpose which human labour directed by ingenuity can accomplish." Iron, claimed Scottish moralist Thomas Dick, was "intrinsically more valuable than gold" owing to "its agency in carrying forward improvements in art and science" and "in the civilization of barbarous tribes."[20]

Privileging coal and iron over gold, as well as the "numerous useful utensils" they assisted in producing, also dovetailed with the story Britons liked to tell about their good fortune in receiving gold through trade as opposed to conquest. Its coal mines, as well as "the locks, screws, knives, scissors and guns which are made at Birmingham," wrote the author of *Stories of England and Her Forty Counties*, were "treasures which people of other lands are glad enough to exchange for their gold." The mineralogist John Mawe celebrated British coal as having rendered "all the Gold mines of Peru . . . subservient to our manufactories."[21] Access to coal and iron ore was only half the story; the rest relied on Britain's superior division of labor. Unlike gold, which was "found in [its] perfect state, in the clefts of rocks," iron's "gross and stubborn ore" required "two laborious processes, before it becomes fit for use." Coal, meanwhile, assisted "every thing which labour and ingenuity can produce," rendering Britain "mistress of the industry and commerce of the earth."[22]

In the contentious decades after 1800, gold's relative uselessness marked the limits of consensus regarding how to conclude money's progress from "primitive" makeshifts through the precious metals. The victors in this debate, who succeeded in establishing gold as the sole legal basis for British currency, spent fifty years before and after 1821 developing arguments to justify their position. A minority also placed precious metals in the final stage of money's evolution but plumped for silver rather than gold as the most suitable endpoint. And a persistent set of critics—including socialists as well as Birmingham merchants and Scottish bankers—countered that gold was merely transitional on the way to a truly civilized outcome in which paper money and credit circulated on the basis of a binding social contract.[23]

Adam Smith muddied the waters in this debate by commending the efficiency of credit but worrying that it was a good deal more dangerous than metallic currency. Although he admitted that credit (whether in the form of bank notes or bills of exchange) "increase[d] very considerably the annual produce of . . . land and labour," he concluded that "the solid ground of gold and silver" provided a necessary check on "the unskillfulness of the conductors of this paper money." He also bred confusion by suggesting that people had settled on gold more by convention than because of its intrinsic value—while at the same time citing a list of "irresistible" qualities possessed by gold and silver (but not paper), including durability, divisibility, and fusibility.[24] Smith was not alone in his ambivalence. As historian Deborah Valenze has argued, the "thrust of commercial life" in Britain after 1700 embarked on a steady "drift away from intrinsic value" without ever wholly abandoning it; and Christine Desan has observed that credit's status in the eighteenth century as a "revenue-raising machinery" secured its "institutionalized equivalence" with gold coin but failed fully to supplant a "commodity money" regime.[25]

Smith spent little time distinguishing between the role of gold and silver in the evolution of money. Charles Jenkinson, the first Earl of Liverpool, was the first to develop a sustained argument for picking gold over silver as the basis for Britain's currency—and with his son in place as Prime Minster from 1812 to 1827, it was this argument, expressed in *A Treatise on the Coins of the Realm* (1805) that carried the day when Britain made the gold standard official. Jenkinson mainly appealed to the gradual adoption over the eighteenth century of gold as "the principal measure of property . . . in the opinion and practice of the people." By "the people" he meant those who made "considerable payment[s]"; he acknowledged that gold was "not well adapted for the retail trade, in which sort of traffic the greatest number of the subjects of every country are principally concerned."[26]

The second Lord Liverpool revived these arguments in 1816, commencing a five-year journey that ended with the resumption of convertibility under the new auspices of a gold standard combined with a token silver coinage. Leaning heavily on his father's treatise, he claimed that "the progress of this country in agriculture, commerce, manufactures, and riches, had made gold, in fact, the measure of value." Opponents countered that silver was "more conducive to the purposes of convenience"; griped that people in the previous century had used gold only because there had been no silver to be found; and defended silver as "the metal of those countries with which this country traded." As this last point made clear, a central theme in this debate concerned whether Britain would emerge from the Napoleonic War perched above the rest of Europe or fully integrated into its monetary system. When a silver proponent asked "why we should have a purer standard than the rest of the world," economist David Ricardo answered: "In a question of finance, if we could get a better system than our neighbours, we were surely justified in adopting it." Although prominent financiers Alexander Baring and Hudson Gurney backed silver, Ricardo's side prevailed in Parliament by a vote of 141 to 27.[27]

Silver advocates occasionally resurfaced after 1821, but more persistent opposition to gold came from defenders of inconvertible paper, for whom gold and silver were way-stations en route to a more enlightened financial system.[28] London merchant Edward Solly traced the progress from "leather and other materials" to "promissory and bank notes" to argue that connecting links in this series formed "merely an extraneous quality" in measuring value; Thomas Smith urged that precious metals were transitional between the "rude stages of society" and the present, when "bills of exchange, paper money, and banking, superseded completely the necessity of hoarding them up, or employing them at all." This stance achieved especially vocal support in Scotland, where, dating back to the 1760s, a stable network of joint-stock banks had established paper money as what was locally regarded as an endpoint of civilization. Sir Walter Scott and a cast of dozens loudly celebrated "the Scottishness of the paper pound," with little reference to the gold it represented.[29] Most Scots, however, upheld Adam Smith's original argument that the promise to pay in gold was necessary for a stable credit economy; this was not the case with the "Birmingham school" led by Thomas Attwood, who strenuously defended a return to inconvertible paper money.[30]

Paper-money advocates' claim that gold was merely an arbitrary, and hence transitory, measure pushed bullionists to insist on its intrinsic value. As early as 1808, James Mill had responded to Thomas Smith that "the value of *the metal* in the guinea," not an "abstract idea," gave the coin its purchasing power; a decade later, Robert Peel defended the resumption of cash payments on the grounds that "the only standard was a definite quantity of gold bullion." This stance grew increasingly rigid following the gold standard's restoration. Economist J. R. McCulloch claimed in 1824 that "[i]t was not the arbitrary choice of society, but their real fitness for a *medium* of exchange, which introduced the use of the precious metals," and another bullionist added in 1843 that "money, properly speaking, consists only of a certain quantity of precious metal," while a bank note merely "brings to mind the quantity of money which the issuer promises to pay."[31]

David Ricardo came closer than any other British economist or politician to bridging the gap that divided paper and gold advocates, but he ultimately failed to bring them together. A stockbroker by trade, he fully appreciated the value of credit; to preserve its benefits while still accomplishing the gold standard's disciplinary check, he proposed a law that would require banks to redeem their notes with sixty-ounce bars (worth £233 each), as opposed to quarter-ounce coins. Although his "ingot scheme" received powerful backing from friends in Parliament and was actually used during the transition to full convertibility between 1817 and 1821, his hoped-for "euthanasia of metal currency" never came to pass. It fell prey to widespread fears that the continued circulation of £1 and £2 bank notes would promote the persistence of forgery, which had risen dramatically during the war. The vocal presence of William Cobbett, whose suspicion of credit knew few bounds, also hindered what he called Ricardo's "perpetual paper-project."[32]

Ricardo offered a more sophisticated, but also more problematic, defense of gold as an invariable standard of value than Adam Smith had ever attempted. Whereas Smith had starkly contrasted gold's "continually varying" with labor's "never varying" value, Ricardo assumed, as a matter of convenience rather than dogma, that the value of gold was also invariable: claiming that it struck a "just mean" between "the varying quantities of labour required for production." This assumption, he concluded, was necessary to avoid "embarrassing myself on every occasion with the consideration of the possible alteration in the value of the medium in which price and value are estimated."[33] McCulloch embraced this approach in his 1828 edition of *The Wealth of Nations* but stripped away its epistemological modesty—and with it, Smith's accompanying claim that gold's value was a matter of social convention. He claimed that gold was "not more valuable than iron, or lead, or tin, because of its greater brilliancy, durability, or ductility, but simply because an infinitely greater outlay of capital and labour" was expended in producing it.[34]

While Ricardo was inserting gold into his labor theory of value, socialists pounced on Smith's sharper contrast between labor and gold.[35] Starting from the premise that gold owed "all its estimation to conventional usages" or was "a mere artificial contrivance," they proposed radically new conventions for measuring value that would extend the circuit of paper money well beyond Scotland or local banking networks. In Robert Owen's scheme, for instance, "notes representing labour would be given for every article when finished, according to the amount of labour that may be contained in it"; the result would be that "[a]ll bargaining, or desire to take advantage of each other, would at once cease."[36] The closer such schemes came to describing actual exchanges instead of generalized exploitation, however, the more they foundered in devilish details regarding measurement, mechanization, and competition. Even some socialists doubted that labor notes could ever replace hard cash. Shepherd Smith, calling Owen's proposals "not a whit less mystical or less ridiculous than the Koran of Mohamet," defended gold as "the emblem of incorruption, by its superior virtues in resisting external influence."[37]

Most economists who supported gold's place as the basis of British currency faced a threat that was more insidious than their ragtag array of paper and silver antagonists: this was the fact that people continued to display gold long after they started using it as a basis for their currency—and that the number of such people was increasing. In terms of Smith's just-so story, many Britons remained stuck in the allegedly savage stage of valuing gold for its beauty at the same time that many others had moved on to use it as money; in fact, most of these were the same people. Hence while economists took some comfort in assuming that "golden ornaments are most common in those countries possessed of the least manufacturing industry" and that aristocratic demand had declined in Britain, they could not fully ignore the fact that overall domestic consumption of ornamental gold was increasing.[38]

Adam Smith had expressed little concern in *The Wealth of Nations* about ornamental uses of gold impeding its ability to serve as money, since he assumed "a continual importation" of the precious metals would always counteract "the continual waste of them in gilding and plating [and] in lace and embroidery."[39] The Napoleonic Wars eroded such hubris by shunting gold to Britain's allies and by shutting down Latin American production. Bullion dealer John Koster worried in 1811 that gold-watch production "far, very far, exceeds the quantity of late years produced by all the mines in the world"; after 1821, as bullion drains periodically slowed the economy, economists amplified their impatience with "consumption on pleasures or luxuries." John Stuart Mill included gold lace on his list of "unproductive" commodities, which failed to give "any support to life or strength, but what would equally be given by things much less costly."[40]

To try and settle this question, the Board of Trade official William Jacob produced a two-volume inventory in 1831 of exactly how much gold was used for non-monetary purposes. Surveying refiners and "a junta of jewellers," he concluded that ornaments annually absorbed £1.64 million worth of gold in Britain—used, in descending order, for jewelry, toys, watches, buttons, lace, ceramics, and plate—and the rest of Europe added around £2 million more to that total (in comparison, the Royal Mint annually coined £2.33 million in gold between 1823 and 1835). Much of this, he worried, was "absolutely consumed," especially when used for plate and "the smaller personal ornaments."[41] Although McCulloch cited much lower estimates for non-monetary consumption and held out hope for improved recycling and mining methods, others were less optimistic.[42]

What Jacob called the "increased introduction of gold ornaments" into Britain during the decades after 1800 left its mark on the goldsmith trade, as well as such ancillary trades as beaters, twisters, and refiners. These thrived despite a decline in aristocratic lace and plate, although not without adapting to major changes in consumption patterns and foreign competition. For centuries, goldsmiths had stood out among the London trades as "men of considerable consequence," with an ancient guild occupying an "extensive and handsome pile" in the heart of the City of London and a leading role in that square mile's enduring history of pageantry.[43] With wider demand, they migrated beyond their medieval confines in the City, first to the West End and then into such provincial centers as Birmingham and Liverpool.[44] The proportion of London goldsmiths working in the City fell from more than half before 1800 to a fifth by the 1840s, while West End goldsmiths increased; the proportion of lower-brow "working goldsmiths" in Clerkenwell grew even more rapidly.[45]

Goldsmiths catered to their newly diverse customers by lobbying Parliament to allow more flexibility in mixing their gold with copper. All ornamental gold in the eighteenth century had to be certified by the Goldsmiths' Company as twenty-two carats, allegedly to check against fraud and "inconveniences in regard to coins"; manufacturers complained that this gave a competitive edge to goldsmiths on the continent, where lower standards enabled the production of watches and jewelry that were cheaper, "more durable, more polished, and more elegant."[46] A new law in 1798 reduced the standard to eighteen carats for some items, yielding a savings of fourteen shillings per ounce, and later laws allowed standards as low as ten carats for "such articles as by reason of their smallness, form, or rich chasing, could not be assayed."[47]

This new flexibility, however, bred confusion regarding the value of ornamental gold, which cost British goldsmiths in reputation what they gained in savings. Too many jewelers, worried the assayer John Watherston, failed to pass on all these savings to their customers, instead "affixing to most of the articles they sell the title of FINE GOLD! and, by this shameless effrontery . . . obtaining an unfair equivalent for a metal of very low value." France, in contrast, stepped up its enforcement of standards used in ornamental gold after 1815, an irony that might have ashamed Britons who took pride in the superior standard of their currency. As a travel writer observed in 1823: "If I purchase a gold chain in Paris, I inquire the price of the gold apart from the manufacture, and the vender is bound to give me a true answer. Thus I know what I am paying for the intrinsic material."[48] A proliferation of gold substitutes further tilted this scale against Britain: critics warned of a "mosaic-gold age" marked by an "abuse of cheap decoration."[49]

Not until the rise of the Arts and Crafts movement, which began to gain traction in the 1840s, did ornamental gold go from being derided by economists and suspected by consumers to being valued in its own right—or rather, subjected to a new value system altogether.[50] That movement's pioneer, John Ruskin, who maintained that "gold was meant to be seldom seen, and to be admired as a precious thing," made an exception for gilding—as long as it was used only "to express magnificence, or sacredness, and not in lavish vanity, or in sign painting." Or, as Thomas Banfield urged, beauty—by which he meant "the expression [and] the fitness of an object"—should constitute a new "standard of value, both for rich and poor," rather than "the materials of which it is made." While this would not "prevent the rich man from indulging in utensils of gold," he concluded, at least it would improve "the taste of such costly articles" as well as render "humbler material to be more beautifully worked."[51]

Metaphors

Britons embraced gold's value most fully in the realm of metaphors, which they used to order their moral world into hierarchies of godliness, genius, and social class, or to condemn the worst excesses of avarice. In this capacity, as a character in a play from the 1770s proclaimed, gold acted as "a dead Letter; where all Free-Agencies may subscribe or under-write their Names for Happiness or Misery."[52] Although the metal in its tangible form did exhibit many superior qualities over other metals and did tempt people to hoard, cheat, and steal, such instances represented part of an expansive whole: gold offered only a rough approximation of divinity or genius and acted as a relatively benign gateway to depthless avarice. In both cases the actual metal faded into the background, to be replaced by an ideal type that denoted virtue or depravity in its purest and most potent form. This active "social life" of gold, and the important cultural work it performed, put additional pressure on economists' mounting insistence that gold was "nothing but a commodity bought and sold for its value": a claim that was always true up to a point but could never be sustained indefinitely.[53]

Natural philosophers gloried in counting the ways that gold qualified as "the most perfect and indestructible of metals." As *The Young Ladies' Instructor* taught in 1799, gold was "not only the most valuable, but the purest of all compound bodies; it is proved to be the heaviest by being 19 and a half times more weighty than water; and is more ductile or malleable than any other metal." Chemistry affirmed gold's virginal purity: it was "incapable of oxydation from atmospheric air or oxygen gas, at any temperature . . . which a furnace can yield." To celebrate gold's ductility, science textbooks went to great lengths to illustrate the great lengths to which it could be stretched: a "piece of wire gilt with eight grains" of the metal could be "drawn out to a length of 13,000 feet."[54] The discovery of platinum unsettled this centuries-old enthronement of gold to an extent—by some accounts its greater specific gravity rendered it "perhaps, the most perfect of all the metals"—but its relative scarcity and failure to match many of gold's other qualities mainly made it a mineralogical footnote.[55]

Moving from mineral to metaphor, gold appeared in its most protean form in religious discourse, which cribbed from hundreds of Biblical allusions.[56] Among many other comparisons, clerics likened the Anglican liturgy to "a beautiful robe richly embroidered with gold"; called the scriptures "true, bright, precious, pure unmixed gold . . . which can never be diminished in its weight, or reduced in its value"; and referred to God's promises as "the Christian's bank note," redeemable in divine gold.[57] The just-so story that culminated in gold as a standard of value wound through many such references. Presbyterian preacher David Crichton, for instance, contrasted the "ignorant savage" who "prefers the . . . showy trifle, to the wedge of gold" with "the intelligent European [who] knows well that the value of the latter is incomparably superior"; by analogy, the "unbelieving . . . see no beauty in Christ," whereas "those whose minds have been enlightened by the Spirit of God appreciate his worth."[58]

Gold was also a prominent proxy in the humanities, standing in for genius—the true value of which required either sufficient taste or labor to be discerned. Just as the "permanent and transmissible value" of gold was "inherent in [its] weight and quality," went one such line of reasoning, Lord Byron's "true genius" exhibited a "nameless grace." Turning from discrimination to work, Thomas Carlyle urged readers to imitate those who had "laboured in refining" Immanuel Kant's "ponderous unmanageable dross," since it "may bear in it the everlasting gold of Truth!"[59] As literary critic Alexander Dick has argued for the Romantic poets, such literary appeals to gold reinforced, and received crucial support from, the economic logic of the gold standard—and also, in Carlyle's case, the labor theory of value. In developing these and other mutually supporting standards, he concludes, Britons found ways to "believe in their validity while knowing they are arbitrary."[60]

Finally, gold was a supple signifier of class, inviting all gradations of society to monopolize it in its purest or most solid form. In a comedy from 1796, an alderman whose son was about to be named a Lord exultantly referred to the peerage as "a column of pure gold, that will not adulterate." In his *Inventory of Lancashire*, Cyrus Redding opposed middle-class Liverpool's "weighty gold of simple warm manners" to "the hollowness of overwrought refinement" on display in London. And a lecturer to "the working classes of Edinburgh" contrasted "the guinea stamp of rank" with "the pure unalloyed gold of virtue" that offered a more "genuine badge of worth and talent." Those who sought to harmonize class divisions, on the other hand, discovered a single seam of gold running throughout society. Since gold was of "the same sterling quality in its bed of rough ore, as when it glitters on the breast of beauty or of royalty," urged novelist Gerald Griffin, "the rich, the elegant, and the highborn" might yet be convinced to "honour with their sympathy the pictures of humble sorrow and affection."[61]

One common feature in all these metaphors was their reinforcement of the tendency to value monetary over ornamental gold. Critics of the present time as "a showy superficial age" were most apt to insist on that binary, as when Cornelius Webbe contrasted Shakespeare's "heavy-weighing, valuable ore" with the "leaves of beaten-out gold" produced by present-day poets; or when George Henry Lewes lambasted the "prospectus-brilliancy" of Benjamin Disraeli's fiction, which required readers not to inquire too deeply "whether it be gilt or gold."[62] Against this grain, a Ruskin-sympathizing *Edinburgh Review* article on the "prodigious mass" of recently published books presented figurative gilding as the solution, not the problem: the task for genius in these circumstances, it argued, was to "give preciousness to the gold and silver by the beauty of the cup or vase into which they are moulded, and to make them as valuable for their form as for their matter."[63]

Even at its purest, gold often fell short as a suitable signifier of superior virtues. The Bible, which frequently placed gold and divinity on an equal footing, gave God the upper hand even more often—most popularly in the Psalmist's promise that God's approval was "more to be desired . . . than gold, yea, than much fine gold."[64] Britons applied variants of this theme to friendship ("more difficult to be acquired than gold") and a good wife (whose "price is above gold"), among many other virtuous qualities or people. Such references recalled Crusoe's lesson concerning gold's low value in the absence of monetary exchange—here adapted as synecdoche for grace or virtue—and in that sense appeared to confirm its arbitrary and accidental value. Citing Psalm 19, an *Evangelical Magazine* writer contrasted the Bible, which was "in itself, infinitely precious," with gold, the value of which was "merely accidental, arising from the authority and common consent of men."[65]

In *The Grampians Desolate* (1804), one of numerous British jeremiads on the deleterious effects of New World gold, the Perthshire poet Alexander Campbell interrupted a stanza describing "blood-stain'd Cortez" and Pizarro's "sanguinary crew" to divert scorn onto "the statesman sage" who insists: "Gold calls forth luxury—our wants increase; / Divided labour yields the arts of peace." Although he singled out Bernard Mandeville in a note as the statesman in question, his critique equally applied to Adam Smith's perspective on gold. In either case, he spoke for many in countering that metal's alleged economic value with a strong dose of moral outrage: "Would to heaven! ethics and political economy were not at such variance as at present they seem to be!"[66] Campbell's aside was, ultimately, exactly that: a footnote to parallel discourses that nearly never converged. During the same century that dozens of sermons, poems, and novels before and after *The Grampians Desolate* industriously amplified its outrage, economists and politicians worked just as hard, and just as effectively, to establish gold as the basis of the world's most powerful financial system.

Britons most often addressed the inconvenient truth of gold's morally corrosive effects by claiming that foreigners were more prone to its dangers than they were. As a historian of "the origin and progress of the passions" argued in 1825, "we must look back to antiquity, or to the present condition of foreign nations, if we would know the boundless thirst for gold": he cited as evidence "the iniquities of the Spaniards in Mexico," the Roman siege of Jerusalem, and "Turkish despotism in modern Greece."[67] At the end of the day, however, a horde of British thieves, misers, gamblers, speculators, and seducers threatened to undermine such wishful exceptionalism. As was the case with their responses to the violence that accompanied gold's transit from the Americas, Britons developed several overlapping strategies—which they willed into effectiveness—for containing the significance of so many apparent repudiations of gold's allegedly beneficent influence on their economy.

Among three dozen British essays, poems, and soliloquies that took "the power of gold" as their theme between 1780 and 1850, fourteen connected it to corruption and treachery ("for this the statesman sells / His friends or country to enrich himself"; "for gold base man betrays his friend") and eleven with war ("The soldier sheds, for gold, a brother's blood"). A third of the sample called it omnipotent, referring to its "all-conq'ring pow'r" and the "temporary deification" its possession enabled, or presented it as giving people power over others.[68] Only two grudgingly emphasized gold's capacity to do good as well as evil: "it hath a blessed power / In charity's fair hand," concluded one poem in 1834, after eight stanzas tallying its evils. This imbalance stood in contrast with contemporary British attitudes about money, which equally emphasized its redemptive and sinful side.[69]

The most tangible sense in which gold tempted bad behavior concerned the wide array of thefts involving that metal. Of 681 cases of felonious robbery that annually appeared before the Old Bailey between 1780 and 1800, seventy included at least one item made of gold, and the annual average of trials involving gold grew to 126 between 1822 and 1835. During both periods the majority of these involved guineas or sovereigns, but also included dozens of rings and watches, as well as snuffboxes, buckles, necklaces, and pins.[70] Newspaper reports often emphasized gold's tangible power to inspire crime: a miller's only defense for stealing a bowlful of gold coins was that "the window of the bullion-shop in question presented great temptation to the unfortunate, for . . . large quantities of money are constantly exhibited to public view." After a "daring and deep-laid scheme" in 1839 by a cluster of Jewish goldsmiths to steal £4640 worth of gold dust and convert it into bars, gold played a starring role in the ensuing press coverage. When the man in charge of keeping the ingots safe for the trial dropped them on the street, two hundred onlookers nearly bowled him over, shouting: "There goes the gold dust."[71]

The great gold dust robbery of 1839 was London's crime of the century—at least until John Thompson's "extraordinary robbery of £7000 worth of gold dust" in 1848.[72] One reason it attracted so much attention was that its cast of characters, and their behavior, snugly confirmed anti-Semitic stereotypes, which often connected gold's attractive power to the Biblical story of Israelites bowing down to a golden calf. J. F. Murray linked Nathan Rothschild's "all-absorbing thirst of gold" to working-class residents of London's Jewish Quarter, whom he deemed guilty of "worshipping the golden calf with the tenfold idolatry of their fathers," and Douglas Jerrold described "the Order of the Golden Calf" as "a lean-faced, low-browed, thick-jowled, swag-bellied brotherhood."[73] But British references to golden calves, and to "mammon-worship" more generally, spread far beyond crude anti-Semitism: they ranged from William Blake's nightmarish *Moses Indignant at the Golden Calf* to *The Golden Calf: or, Prodigality and Speculation in the Nineteenth Century*, a novel loosely based on the rise and fall of the railway speculator George Hudson.[74]

Anti-Semitism was just one of many ways in which Britons attempted to marginalize gold-induced avarice. An even more pervasive personification was the miser, at least in part because he embodied the uselessness of non-circulating gold. Shakespeare's Shylock and Ben Jonson's Volpone established lasting

Figure 2.1 William Blake, "Moses Indignant at the Golden Calf" (c. 1799–1800). Tate Britain 104134.

caricatures against which subsequent misers could be measured, while Daniel Defoe proposed a rationale for why their behavior—which "lock[ed] up the Tools of the Industrious" and hence harmed society—was worse even than that of thieves, who preyed only on individuals.[75] When subsequent Britons discussed misers, moral condemnation was the order of the day, taking a cue from the Biblical commandment against covetousness. The miser was a "hoary mass of meanness . . . gloating with sordid and unsocial joy over his treasured heaps of useless gold"; his only saving grace was that he would one day die. Poets in particular reveled in the truism that death forcibly separated misers from their gold. Eliza Cook's "Song of the Spirit of Gold," for instance, warned: "forget not, hoary-headed slave, / That *thou*, not *gold*, must fill a grave."[76]

A more sympathetic psychology of miserliness emerged by the 1820s, most elaborately explored by the Scottish philosopher Thomas Brown. He diagnosed the miser as forming, from a young age, an obsession with the value of gold, until the guinea "appears to him not a mere piece of gold. . . but the power of obtaining almost innumerable things"; hence "the very conception of the loss of it is. . . like the loss, not of one of those things only, but of every thing which it might have procured." His solution was to train children to spend their pennies in such a way as to "make the very remembrance of the little transfer pleasing." Others took heart in the transposition of wealth from gold to credit, which meant it was no longer necessary to wait for misers to die for their savings to be reproductive. As the economist Richard Whately observed in 1835, "a man who saves, hardly ever, in these days at least, hoards up gold and silver in a box; but lends it out on good security, that he may receive interest on it"—freeing it up to be "borrowed by farmers, or manufacturers, or merchants."[77]

It was revealing that the most celebrated British misers only apparently resembled the "miser of olden times who . . . locked up his beloved gold in iron-bound chests."[78] Leading this group were Daniel Dancer (1716–1794), who exhibited "the most remarkable instances of the misery which is ever attendant upon the mind cursed with the insanity of saving"; his friend Jemmy Taylor, a stockbroker who died in 1793 worth £200,000 and "lay upon nothing but rags and straw upon the bare floor"; and John Elwes (1714–1789), an MP who gambled away his father's fortune before turning to a career of "meanness." Gold appeared sparingly in biographies of these men, and usually in the abstract sense of mammon-worship—although Dancer did leave behind "large bowls filled with guineas." All three kept most of their wealth in reproductive investments— as did their closest nineteenth-century equivalent, Jemmy Wood, who died in 1836 worth nearly £2 million, mainly laid out in stocks and freehold estates.[79]

Gold appeared more prominently in the obituaries of more obscure misers, which emerged with increasing regularity in British newspapers over the course of the nineteenth century. Such reports followed a strict formula, in which neighbors' recollections of apparent poverty gave way to the surprising discovery of secreted treasure. Typical finds included 527 half-sovereigns in a London street sweeper's fireplace or £189 in sovereigns and shillings beneath a Colchester pauper's floorboards.[80] If the recurrence of such notices kept gold-hoarding misers simmering in public awareness, plays and novels brought them to full boil. Theaters regularly revived Henry Fielding's adaptation of Moliere's *The Miser* (1733), in which actors measured their mettle through their rendering of its gaunt protagonist Lovegold.[81] George Eliot's *Silas Marner* (1861) hinged on the moral transformation of its miserly title character, and Charles Dickens cycled through a succession of misers in his novels—including, most famously, Ebenezer Scrooge, whose "love of gold preponderated over his love for a virtuous and amiable woman."[82]

As Eliot and Dickens were well aware, a common denominator among unreformed misers was their willingness to privilege wealth over romantic and filial love. This pattern also prevailed in another character type associated with gold's corrosive power: the person who cynically married for money. Although the term *gold-digger* did not enter the English language in this sense until the 1920s, gold figured prominently in most descriptions of the pattern, which peaked during a hyperactive Hanoverian marriage market fueled by a shortage of eligible aristocratic men.[83] Especially in novels, these arrangements exposed turpitude on the part of scheming future brides and their parents, as when one character advises another to subordinate "love, being made up of light evanescent things," to gold, which was "substantive; palpable; solid; immutable." In real life, marriages for money as often worked in the reverse direction. The *Times* reported in 1792 that "Gold, that can give *charms* to *wrinkles* and *gracefulness* to a *pair of crutches*, last week purchased a lusty husband of thirty, for a *tender* maiden lady, of sixty-nine in Wiltshire."[84]

A final association with avarice related to gamblers, who allowed their "love of play" to shade into a "lust of gold." More even than descriptions of thefts, gold nearly always figured in accounts of gambling as an irresistible lure: "the gold which glitters on the table of the gamester" tempted people, especially from lower social orders, to try and regain their wealth in a single night, despite "the best affections of the heart."[85] Britons did their best to contain the corrosive effects of casinos or "gold hells" by rendering them "for the most part difficult to get at"—in contrast to continental casinos with their "open doors and glaring lamps." More generally, they downplayed gambling as a British vice by pointing to its more extravagant excesses elsewhere.[86] The closely related sin of financial speculation was harder to conceal or write off as foreign, since it uniquely extended "from the peer to the peasant" in Britain. Although gold seldom actually exchanged hands in such transactions, it almost always appeared in their condemnation—as when novelist Robert Bell wrote that this "gold-breeding experience" made people "fierce and insatiable in the pursuit of more."[87]

With heroic commitment to what literary critic Christopher Herbert has called "the principle of closing [their] eyes systematically to unwelcome realities," Britons generally managed to focus obsessively on gold's many immoral attributes without ever abandoning its central place as a bedrock of economic growth and fiscal probity. Their trick, in most cases, was to distinguish sharply between personal moral failings concerning gold and the solidity of financial institutions, which cleansed it of its taint once it entered their vaults and mints. Just as Sir Edward Seaward neutralized the "subtle poison" of gold by converting it into interest-bearing stock, most Britons defended the gold standard in one breath while, in the next, alluding to the metal to cast aspersions on misers, gamblers, and speculators. One important consequence of this ability to live with gold's contradictory character was that most of them stopped well short of making connections between human depravity (as measured in its many abuses) and institutional culpability.[88]

Gold, as opposed to its various paper representatives that financial institutions sent into circulation, played a crucial role in such diversionary habits. Condemnations of misers, fortune hunters, and speculators repeatedly cited their desire for gold, even though bank notes, title deeds, annuities and stock certificates prompted such people's bad behavior far more often. While guineas did change hands at gamblers' "gold tables," bank notes and letters of credit accounted for the lion's share of transactions there as well. A "love of filthy gold" or "the Gold-ocracy" stood as sweeping bywords for avarice wherever that deadly sin reared its ugly head in British society, from child labor to slavery, regardless of the metal's physical absence in most such settings. Paeans to "the power of gold" almost always referred to objects of greed or ambition that seldom actually involved the tangible metal.[89] Hence at the same time that physical gold served as a basis for British credit, metaphorical gold served as a shield for its abuses.

The same logic worked at the other end of the moral spectrum, where gold symbolized indescribable perfection. A revealing example, in this regard, was the Biblical claim that heaven was paved with gold, which hovered perilously close to a sacrilegious embrace of greed. Heaven, insisted the evangelical divine Joseph Milner, "was conveyed under the images of gold and precious stones, not with a view to feed the avarice of Christians, but to enliven their ideas of spiritual glory by such sensible images, as are most adapted to strike the imagination in our present state."[90] Gold appeared in this anguished argument as a necessary evil, to be contemplated just long enough to inspire piety but cast aside the moment before it inspired greed. The same could be said for the many other instances in which gold stood for superlative genius or humanity—and, by extension, the superstructure of credit that rested on the gold standard's foundation.

When gold moved from its status as a metaphor (whether for depravity or virtue) to its material embodiment as bullion or coin, it seldom attracted nearly as much notice, let alone anguish. As bullion, gold almost always rested out of sight in bank vaults. It only garnered attention in that form when it was used to secure Britain's borders, through the war subsidies that enabled Wellington and Nelson to defeat Napoleon, and to feed the country, through grain payments that periodically threatened public credit. As coin, gold was equally discreet. It was not a coincidence that gold coins featured prominently in the popular British genre of "it-narratives," in which objects told tales about social life. From their inconspicuous locations in purses, pockets, and vaults, they occupied prime positions to see without being seen.[91] Gold glittered more brightly, and was subject to more criticism, in the form of ornament—which increasingly appeared in contrast to its less conspicuous monetary forms as a signifier of inferior status, as measured on Adam Smith's timeline tracking humanity's progress toward civilization.

The many layers of meaning that gold took on during its emergence as Britain's most precious metal—as a portmanteau of metaphors and as a road map of civilization—make it all the more striking that most economists and politicians insisted that gold was just *gold*: nothing more or less. When Robert Peel defended the gold standard in 1844, he argued that British money consisted in "a certain quantity of the precious metals, definite in point of weight and fineness," and strenuously denied that it was "something set up in the imagination, to be regulated by public opinion"—despite the fact that Smith's whole point about gold as money had been that it arose out of a social contract among members of a sufficiently civilized community.[92] Arguably, it was gold's multiple meanings, only some of them savory, that required such sleight of hand. Much as Robinson Crusoe kept his gold hidden in the chest where he had found it, and much as the Bank of England buried its bullion in vaults to create confidence in its promises to pay, Peel concealed gold's wider variety of meanings to shore up public faith in its singular use as a regulator of credit.

3

War

An article on "The Gold of England," published in the *Illustrated London News* in 1845, complained of a "belief of the omnipresence of our gold, and its universal influence . . . among our neighbours." Spaniards, Frenchmen, and Americans, it claimed, had united in viewing the British state as "a locomotive money-bag," a perception that had peaked during the French Revolution but had never fully abated. At that time, the "gold of Pitt" had allegedly "urged forward the armies that threatened the frontiers," subsidized treasonous plots, "created famine, and . . . bore the blame that ought to have been thrown on the blunders of those on whom in that wild time, the business of governing devolved." The column countered that the true significance of English gold lay in its status as capital, not in its occasional political uses: "Capital has no opinion, no preferences, no aversions; it seeks only employment at a profit, and demands only security." Around the world, it concluded, English gold offered a convenient scapegoat for any country that "will not take the trouble to examine sufficiently to detect the true causes from which arise their perplexities."[1]

The notion that English (or British) gold was a "bugbear of the Continent," and accompanying denials that this was the case, roughly coincided with the two centuries that followed Britain's adoption of a de facto gold standard after 1700. The practice of waging wars by subsidizing or bribing allies had a longer history, but until then this history had relatively little to do with Britain. Between 1689 and 1815 it fought a series of wars against France with greater financial resources than most European counterparts but with a much smaller standing army. The result was that it devoted a significant share of its military budget to subsidizing allies and paying foreign soldiers, including £25 million, or roughly a quarter of the army's total budget, in three major wars waged between 1702 and 1763. These sums, which historian John Brewer cited to account for how Britain achieved "military glory without . . . European militarism," escalated (along with overall military expenses) during the Napoleonic Wars, when it paid more than £60 million to a shifting set of allies.[2]

Subsidizing allies or paying mercenaries, however, was seldom the same thing as lavishing gold on them: in most cases payments could be managed by discounting bills of exchange against Britain's substantial trade surplus. This had been Adam Smith's point in *The Wealth of Nations* when he scolded those who connected such payments with a drain of bullion from Britain. Foreign wars, he argued, were "maintained, not with gold and silver, but with consumable goods," and he cited the large supply of bullion in Britain throughout the Seven Years' War as proof of this.[3] It was not until the far longer and more expensive campaign against Napoleon that Britain's subsidy policy contributed to a severe bullion shortage—and even in that case, at least as much gold left the country to purchase goods, on the frequent occasions when food scarcities and a commercial blockade produced temporary trade deficits, or to supply Britain's own troops abroad.

As with so much else concerning British gold, subsidies and "influence" often stood as a proxy for a more complicated reality, involving diplomatic pressure, dynastic politics, public credit, and especially international trade. Right up through 1800, the tangible metal had relatively little to do with claims regarding gold's capacity to sway the balance of power: more often than not these built on mythologies, dating back to ancient Greece, in which gold stood for corruption or treason, for the dependence of poor countries on handouts from wealthier neighbors, and for otherwise inexplicable developments in foreign relations. For much of the eighteenth century, Britons primarily remarked on gold's sordid uses in the ancient past or by their European rivals; only after 1750 did they start criticizing such abuses by their own rulers. After 1789, constant French allusions to "Pitt's gold" prompted most British observers to discount the same associations between gold and foreign policy that they had long taken for granted as truisms of history.

Between 1800 and 1815, when British gold in circulation and in banks fell from more than £40 million to around £3 million, subsidies continued to occupy an exaggerated position in rhetoric surrounding this drain, although they clearly did play a more important role in foreign policy than had previously been the case.[4] Complicating the story were the roles of trade and credit in funding Britain's military campaign against Napoleon, and much of the gold that changed hands was shuffled from one corner of the continent to another. The major debate over the drain of gold, instigated by the Bullion Committee in 1810, pitted those who claimed trade as the culprit and those who blamed an over-issue of Bank of England notes. The result in either case was the same: twenty years of living without guineas permanently altered Britons' perception of that precious metal.

Stipendiarian Rapacity, 1739–1789

In his *History of Scotland* (1797), John Pinkerton paused to consider a "singular and treasonable treaty" that the Earl of Douglas had brokered with Henry V in 1420 after defeating the English king in Northumberland. He concluded that "the weakness of the Scottish government" must have "concurred with the English gold to instigate this irregular conduct." He also referred to the corrupting influence of gold to account for a later Scottish treaty in 1474 with England, which "found gold more powerful than steel, in fixing the fidelity of her northern neighbour"; and cited a "lively writer" (Voltaire), who had "observed that a poor state, which is adjacent to a wealthy, must . . . expect to be ruled by the money of her neighbour." Pinkerton found further solace in an ancient example: "when we behold Sparta in the pay of Persia, overturning the liberties of Greece, during the Peloponnesian War, we need not sigh at the comparison of ancient and modern virtue."[5]

In nearly all discussions of the influence of gold on foreign affairs, its rhetorical force far exceeded its physical presence. That this was the case should not come as a surprise, considering the comparably inflated role gold played in condemnations of avarice or splendor; in this sense it served as an evocative byword for unseen (and possibly nefarious) diplomatic transactions involving credit, financial services, or goods in kind. The original sin in most such narratives was Persia's strategy, following its defeat in the Greco-Persian wars (499–449 BCE), to sow discord by scattering gold among Greek city-states; Philip of Macedon, the story continued, finished what Persia had started. Britons absorbed this lesson from continental historians, then translated these narratives into lessons that resonated with their contemporary concerns.[6] They were especially keen to recall Philip's corruption of Greek politicians, often dwelling on his ability to counter Demosthenes' powers of oratory with "that powerful persuasion—gold, a sort of argument which always operates most effectually among a corrupted people." This widespread focus on gold's role in undermining Greek democracy derived from and informed a rising assault on "Old Corruption" in Britain.[7]

Subsequent European history reinforced Britons' sense that gold exerted an unsavory influence on foreign affairs. France and Spain topped the list of countries that employed this strategy, with England often on the receiving end. Whig historian William Belsham attributed England's support of France in the Franco-Dutch war (1672–1678) to the distribution of "great sums of French gold" and others associated French gold with that country's incursions on British soil, from the Norman conquest down to the Jacobite uprising in 1745. Recounting the failed efforts of Harold Godwinson and Edgar Atheling to drive William I out of England, George Lyttelton concluded that both were "defeated, not by the steel, but the gold of William, who corrupted the leaders." Seven centuries later, wrote Hugh Arnot in his *History of Edinburgh*, "the French gold which was sent over for the use of the Pretender, occasioned a considerable influx of wealth into the country."[8]

Next to France, Spain appeared most often in British descriptions of gold's sordid role in foreign policy, with the dynastic marriage of Philip II and Bloody Mary looming especially large. In John Brown's history of the Anglican Church, it was "Philip's Spanish gold" that "reconciled almost all the Papists to Mary's marriage with him" and gave her "the more opportunity to persecute the Protestants." The claim that Tudor and Stuart monarchs received French or Spanish gold fit snugly into the resolutely Whiggish narrative that dominated eighteenth-century historiography, with the clear lesson being that such shameful events could not resurface in the wake of the Glorious Revolution. The only occasions in which English monarchs appeared as payers (as opposed to receivers) of gold in histories of pre-modern Europe concerned their efforts to grab power in Scotland.[9]

When Britons moved from historical reflections to contemporary politics, they translated their skeptical take on foreign military aid into the language of mercantilism, worrying about so much gold leaving the country. These concerns began to appear in the 1740s during the War of the Austrian Succession and erupted during the Seven Years' War, when British subsidies rose to more than £10 million.[10] The drumbeat started before the war had begun: a pamphlet asked if "any of our Neighbours, that are now gaping to receive English Gold" would "generously send back a few Shillings in Pity and Compassion to us, after we have spent and *subsidied* away the last Farthing?" Five years into the war, Whig MP William Pulteney worried that Germans would invest their "immense sums of gold and silver" in manufactures, which would "soon restore their trade to its former balance" while British commerce lagged behind.[11]

By the time of the American Revolution, Britons and American loyalists focused more intently on the French use of gold to corrupt their colonies, while generally defending their own payment of £1.3 million for 11,000 Hessian mercenaries (comprising more than a third of Britain's force). George III's biographer referred to "the German mercenaries purchased by British gold" as a distasteful but necessary "counterpoise to . . . the military aid lent to the revolted colonists by France."[12] Few British observers paused to consider the possible negative impact of such payments on Hessen-Kassel (in terms of both depopulation and political turmoil), whereas many assumed that French gold had irreversibly corrupted Americans at the birth of their new nation. Writing from England in 1784, the recently arrived loyalist J. F. D. Smyth asked how, with "their rulers corrupted by French gold . . . and [the] affected amity of that artful, perfidious, gaudy people," Americans could possibly succeed in "ever again becoming free?"[13]

Even at the height of Britain's eighteenth-century war subsidies, relatively little gold actually departed the country. Adam Smith was largely correct that a substantial trade surplus enabled the Treasury to spend millions on its allies during the Seven Years' War without producing a shortage of coin at home. Although that war did occasion temporary shortfalls, reflected in a premium of a shilling per ounce of gold, the Mint also coined more guineas during its duration (an average of £688,000 per year) than in any previous decade.[14] The same was true for the American Revolution. British bullion traders trans-shipped more than £600,000 in gold to Holland between 1776 and 1780, much of it on Hesse's account, and an additional £96,127 directly to North America, but the market price of gold did not exceed the Mint price until 1783, and even then only by a few pence per ounce.[15]

Whether eighteenth-century diplomatic gold was tangible, a unit of account, or a rumored bribe, it usually flowed from richer to poorer states. Contemporaries were quick to connect this pattern to David Hume's claim in his *Political Discourses* that poor countries inevitably narrowed the gap separating them from their richer neighbors.[16] Most often they presented rulers of poor states as cravenly auctioning their allegiance, and those of their implicitly barbaric subjects, to the highest bidder. William Seward compared Pitt the Elder to "a wise keeper of wild beasts," who waited until mercenaries' services had been rendered before sating their "stipendiarian rapacity. . . . with gold itself, their best-beloved and most congenial metal." Critics of British subsidies also complained that poor German states conspired to drain their richer ally dry by calling in dynastic favors. One pamphlet in 1744 called Hanover's poverty "a poor Incentive to Envy, unless we were pretty sure of an Intention to remove [it] by the Weight of English Gold."[17]

The "Gold of Pitt," 1789–1800

When the British navy captured Port-au-Prince in 1794, at the outset of its six-year occupation of Haiti, the *Times* predicted that France would react to the loss with "a continuation of their native attachment to falsehood" and claim that "it was Pitt's Gold, and not British valour that subdued this important place." Six weeks later, when the navy captured a French convoy off the coast of New England, the same paper imagined that the Committee of Public Safety "most probably will say it was Pitt's *gold* that did that business; for, from all that he has already said on the subject, a Frenchman cannot be conquered in any other manner."[18] The *Times* was by no means alone in reprinting French reports alleging the sinister influence of British gold, then scoffing at the notion. Although this response remained constant in Britain, the context for French claims shifted over the course of the Revolution and subsequent war—from internecine rivalries during the Terror, in which factions accused each other of selling their patriotism to the highest bidder, to Napoleon's eastward expansion, in which the alleged corruption of European rulers supported his efforts to placate occupied territories.

During the chaotic years between 1793 and 1796, after Britain officially declared war on France under the premiership of Pitt the Younger, the French state blamed a wide range of military setbacks and political dissent on "Pitt's gold." As historian Norman Hampson has observed, "British gold served as an explanation of what was otherwise incomprehensible"—which, he adds, unduly flattered "both the skill and the resources of the British government." A revolutionary ideology that claimed full acceptance among its citizenry and perfect accord within its vanguard had few other explanations at its disposal. Hence a Committee of Public Welfare report blamed disturbances in Toulon on "the gold of Pitt," which "finds its way into the National Offices and Dock-yards," and a Revolutionary Tribunal charged that "liberticidal plots were concerted at very sumptuous entertainments, paid for by the gold of Pitt."[19] Especially during the Terror, such claims derived from a pre-existing suspicion of financiers, who of all scapegoats most plausibly had access to British gold; and from an endemic inability to resolve internal disputes, which made corruption charges and a swift execution of justice a convenient alternative.[20]

In at least one sense, Britons had themselves to blame for this constant refrain during the 1790s. From the start, revolutionary politicians claimed their new constitution would improve on that of England, where, in the words of one speaker at the National Assembly, "Ministers govern by means of gold"—and they found plenty of evidence of this in the many screeds against Old Corruption across the Channel. In his *Letter to a Patriot Senator* (1783), for instance, William Jones warned that "the gold of *Indian* princes . . . may easily have the same influence in our great national council, as that of *Philip* had in the assembly at *Athens*," while a defender of Charles Fox in 1784 described elections as times "when venal freemen sell their votes for gold, / And in return themselves are bought and sold."[21] Exposed as they were to a litany of such assertions, it made perfect sense for the French to assume that Pitt would simply adapt his well-oiled gold-dispensing machinery to his foreign policy.

On the frequent occasions when French allegations resurfaced across the Channel, Britons typically refused to condone any possible connection between their gold and the Terror. They often translated accusations of corruption, which revolutionary leaders made in order to claim a moral high ground against op-posing factions, into an indictment of the entire French nation. William Cobbett urged that when the French ascribed "all the horrors [their] principles have produced" to "the gold distributed among the revolutionists by the English Minister," they implied that "sanguinary avarice" was either "the *natural dispo-sition* of . . . *Frenchmen*" or "a *change* in that natural disposition, *produced by the revolution*." Another critic rejected "that silly cant which has long prevailed of attributing to English gold . . . the hideous crimes of the French"—but added that if it were true, they "must be the most profligate wretches upon earth, and as unfit to take the lead in the reformation of mankind, as a prostitute at a baptism."[22]

Pitt's gold remained in the news after 1797, when France traded internal strife for outward expansion, but its rationale shifted from explaining away tur-moil to reinforcing political legitimacy. Instead of traitors to the Revolution, the new alleged recipients of British gold included Austria's "superstitious and arbi-trary government," which had been "corrupted by the gold of the English," and "those of the senate of Berne who have been purchased by the gold of England." Napoleon also used British gold as an excuse for plundering or levying taxes in occupied territories, as when he informed Greece in 1798: "As a proper measure of precaution, I have removed all PITT's gold from the country."[23] In contrast to similar allegations about the Terror, these claims—which were broadly consistent with British policy in previous wars—met with more sympathy, at least among Pitt's opponents. The Whig MP George Tierney warned, in voting against an Austrian subsidy in 1800, that "the gold of England had found its way into every cabinet of Europe, and was the cause of prolonging all the miseries of war!"[24]

Whether used to incite treason or resist occupation, the tangible impact of British gold during the decade after the French Revolution has long been an open question. As a historian of the Terror has observed, "undercover espio-nage leaves few written sources, either for people at the time, or for subsequent investigators." Another historian, considering the French claim that "4 million *livres* of . . . British gold" abetted counter-revolutionaries in Lyon, found "no firm proof" of this and documented ample royalist funds from local contributions.[25] Once Britain started forging alliances after 1795, clearer indications appeared of "the gold of Pitt" leaving the country in large amounts, but even here there was a major gap between contemporary rhetoric and the actual movement of gold. A £4.6 million loan to Austria in 1796 included £3.4 million in Treasury bills, £200,000 in foreign gold coin and bars, and £1 million in Spanish silver dollars. Still, to paraphrase the opposition MP John Sinclair, a guinea saved would have been a guinea earned: "if the Government had not exported coin to the Emperor, they must have exported that which was equivalent."[26]

Foreign Princes and Foreign Trade, 1800–1815

In his influential *Letter on the Military Policy of . . . the British Empire* (1810), military engineer Charles Pasley cautioned against allowing "any foreign nation to imagine, for a moment, that we cannot defend ourselves without subsidizing them." That notion, he concluded, had "spread to our prejudice all over the globe: so that there is scarcely a nation, from the Persians and Affgans . . . to the extremities of Barbary and Scandinavia, that is not grasping at our gold; whilst they have not the smallest intention or wish of serving us." Although such depictions of Britain's subsidy policy as "a base and unwarlike, but, at the same time, prodigal and ruinous system" persisted throughout the Napoleonic Wars, they never achieved much traction, as evidenced by a six-fold increase in subsidies compared to the Seven Years' War. From another angle they were also inaccurate, since despite such a major increase in absolute terms, subsidies actually declined significantly as a proportion of overall military expenditure, from 21% between 1739 and 1763 to 8% between 1793 and 1815.[27]

In one sense, defenders of British subsidies had an easier task than had been the case in earlier wars. For one thing, the main recipients between 1793 and 1815 were Prussia, Russia, and the Hapsburg Empire: "poor countries" in Germany, Scandinavia, and Italy accounted for only a quarter of the £65 million in subsidies and loans.[28] As one critic of Pasley put it: "The sums that we have lately expended have been in subsidies of a totally different character from those heretofore granted . . . to petty states, who had no sort of interest in the contest for which they were taken into our pay."[29] In another sense, advocates of subsidies could usually—though not always—echo Adam Smith's point that even when Britain's allies received its cash this was usually the result of exporting goods as opposed to precious metals. Still, the matter of subsidies simmered throughout the war, since it offered the easiest target in accounting for the undeniable fact that gold all but vanished from British shores by the war's end.

Most critics of British subsidies during the Napoleonic Wars argued that they were not cost-effective. Anticipating Pasley, Henry Brougham urged in 1806 that "pressing our gold upon all the world, and running from door to door, to beg it might be accepted" had resulted in "a loss of character and influence." Others pointed to allies who pocketed British subsidies shortly before concluding a separate peace with France or who used subsidies to pursue territorial expansion. The opposition MP Thomas Jones complained in 1800: "PRUSSIA took our gold, and soon laid down her arms, and basely deserted us," while Austria had "consented to be subsidized by BRITISH GOLD" in order to "promote her ambitious views, and add to her extension of territory!"[30]

A related critique suggested that some British subsidies enriched France at least as much as its allies. Whig MP Banastre Tarleton worried that much of the gold that provided food to British and Iberian soldiers during the Peninsular War had been passed along to France: "Our money . . . is, I am afraid, conveyed into Bonaparte's treasure . . . The supply, of Cadiz, of Lisbon, and all the military operations of Britain, and her allies, is principally carried on by means of English gold and French corn." In other cases the flow of gold was more direct: a *Times* correspondent observed in 1810 that "much of our gold coin has lately been drawn into France by vessels coming with grain . . . which have refused to take colonial produce or British manufactures in return." In light of such reports, one agricultural reformer suggested that Britain would be wiser to support its farmers as opposed to its allies, since owing to perennial food shortages "we are obliged to furnish our common enemy with solid gold for the pay of his armies."[31]

As the war against France edged into its second decade, defenders of Britain's identity as a trading nation continued to echo Smith's argument that exports, not gold, mainly paid for its military effort. In 1814 Wellington's biographer quoted Napoleon's barb that "the alliances of Great Britain were mere commercial speculations, and that her merchants knew how to bring back into her coffers, the gold which she paid to Princes for the blood of their subjects"; and added that this "was a charge which, divested of its false premises and sophistry, was highly complimentary to the genius and industry of the British nation." The most strenuous articulation of this claim appeared in the Bullion Report of 1810, authored by a Whig-dominated Parliamentary Committee. It insisted that "in the sound and natural state of the British currency . . . no increased demand for Gold from other parts of the world" could possibly lead to an irreversible loss of that metal.[32]

The nearly total drain of gold between 1800 and 1815 created a serious problem for this assumption. By 1810, few doubted that such a drain was well under way: that year the market price of gold, which had hovered around 5% above the mint price up to that point, shot up by another 5%, and guineas fetched as much as nine shillings more than their face value by end of the war. The authors of the Bullion Report addressed this dilemma by blaming an overissue of paper money by the Bank of England, which had been "guilty of great practical errors" following the suspension of cash payments in 1797. They actually agreed with the many witnesses who blamed the drain of gold on "an unusual demand for it upon the Continent . . . for the use of the French Armies"—but argued that "the reduction of paper," which was "the chief, if not the sole corrective" for attracting bullion back into the country, was virtually impossible without a working gold standard.[33]

In contrast to the gap between what was said and what historians know about "Pitt's gold" before 1800, it is possible to reconstruct a reasonably accurate picture of when, where, and why nearly £40 million worth of gold departed Britain between 1800 and 1815. The picture that emerges suggests that bills of exchange drawn against British exports funded much of the war, but only up to a point. They accomplished this in two ways: by attracting gold and silver from Iberian colonies, which could be trans-shipped to allies (and sometimes enemies) in Europe; and by exporting British-produced goods into Europe, which were purchased with bills countersigned by allies. The same mechanisms worked for the much larger task of paying British soldiers and sailors, except in this case army commissaries raised supplies (including a daily pound of meat and biscuit per soldier) in local markets in exchange for bills, drawn on London, that could later be cashed in for British goods. Commissaries who managed to trade their bills for gold or silver coin could line their own pockets with the premium local farmers gave for being paid in cash instead of paper.[34]

The Austrian loan of 1796, comprising entirely bills and foreign bullion, set the pattern for this usually successful, though often precarious, war finance effort up to 1808.[35] Diverting so many foreign bills to the war meant fewer were left to pay for imports, which manifested itself in an exchange rate that constantly worked against British consumers throughout the war; defenders of the Bank of England identified this, as opposed to too many Bank notes, as the primary cause of inflation in Britain.[36] The only way to rectify this was to pay soldiers with bullion instead of bills, which is exactly what Pitt did (for the first time) in 1800. Although booming exports and a lull in war expenditure allowed exchange rates to recover over the next five years, this did not last once Napoleon's "continental system" started to clog British trade channels after 1806. Adding to the challenge was the huge increase in military spending that accompanied the British army's presence in Iberia after 1807, with the result that the vast majority of payments in 1808 (£2.59 million out of £2.78 million) came in the form of specie, including much silver but also a renewed drain of gold.[37]

Based both on the spike in the market price of gold after 1808 and on archival evidence, it seems likely that much of the gold used to pay British and allied troops between 1808 and 1812 came from London. The Bank's bullion office, for instance, received £174,000 in Spanish gold coins in 1808 and had sent all but £1458 across the Channel by 1810; a stock of £1.4 million in Portuguese gold, most of which it had received in 1804, dwindled to £10,782 between 1808 and 1812.[38] Many enterprising Britons responded to gold's rising price after 1809 by illegally exporting guineas (more than £2 million through Dunkirk alone in 1811, by one estimate). Nathan Rothschild, who had arrived in England in 1799 to expand his father's textile business, discovered his calling as a smuggler. By

1811 he was shipping "hundreds of thousands of English guineas," as well as gold bars, foreign coins, and snuff boxes, to his brother James in Paris.[39] Occupying a legal gray area was the £1.6 million worth of gold that London bullion brokers exported between 1809 and 1815 (up from £83,860 over the previous decade), which they swore to be "foreign" but much of which was suspected to be melted-down guineas.[40]

The erosion of the continental system between 1810 and 1813, together with Britain's aggressive efforts to sell in its allies' Latin American markets, breathed new life into its ability to cover costs with foreign bills of exchange—including £5.4 million of £6.2 million in subsidies in 1810 and £8.3 million of £11 million in total costs in 1811. But, as had occurred in 1800, an overreliance on bills drove up the exchange rate, which made imports painfully expensive.[41] The result was a new demand for gold, with almost none left in Britain. A windfall from India came to the rescue in 1813, enabling the Mint to coin £516,218 worth of "military" guineas and half-guineas—so called because they bore stamps of European emperors, which made them easier to spend once they arrived in Iberia.[42] Rothschild, now working for the Treasury, picked things up from there, using his family connections to buy continental coins where gold was cheapest and sell them where it was dearest (and using his now-dominant position in the European bullion market to affect those prices). This masterful feat of arbitrage built the foundation for his family's banking dynasty—and quite possibly won the war for Great Britain.[43]

Living without Guineas: France and Britain, 1789–1821

An Englishman, a French soldier, and a Parisian jeweler met in her shop in 1814. The Englishman informed the soldier, who looked askance at his "superlatively dirty and ragged" Bank of England notes, that these comprised "almost our only circulating medium, by virtue of which we had withstood all the power of Bonaparte, and finally hurled him from his throne." The jeweler, by way of accepting the payment, chimed in: "All depends upon confidence. You cannot eat gold any more than paper, and if the public faithfully agree that this paper shall represent so much provision, it is all well." Twenty years earlier, a British major wrote to a London friend about an offer from an "old *militaire*" aboard his Channel ship to "serve me, by giving me, in exchange for English guineas, twenty-four livres in paper." The French officer "brought the *assignats* in his hand to tempt me," concluded the major, "but I begged leave . . . to decline this courteous proposal. Surely gold and *assignats* cannot be deemed by all Frenchmen of equal value!"[44]

What economists Michael Bordo and Eugene White have termed this "tale of two currencies" (Bank of England notes, which circulated without being backed by gold between 1797 and 1821, and assignats, which lasted only eight years prior to 1797 in France) closely paralleled gold's role during wartime. By managing to do without guineas, Britons marshaled the military power needed to defeat Napoleon—and did so without having to sacrifice their taste for ornamental gold. By failing to live without gold coins, France first saw its revolutionary dreams dashed, then finally ran out of the hard cash it needed to succeed in a war on two fronts. Yet for the Britons who prevailed during this tumultuous time, living without guineas occasioned a seismic shift in their ideas about what constituted value. In 1789 they had viewed France's departure from a metallic standard as nothing short of an act of violence, while privileging their own paper money on the grounds that it could always be converted into gold. Twenty years later, many came close to embracing the notion that value could be conferred by public faith alone. Throughout this period, however, the fund holders who propped up that credit only did so on the assumption that the Bank of England's promise to pay in gold had been deferred, not broken, in 1797.[45] And when Britain finally restored the gold standard in 1821, its political leaders did so with a faith in that metal's disciplinary powers that bordered on religious fervor.

Britons formed their first opinions about inconvertible paper currency when they toured the United States, where inflation-inducing currencies controversially circulated throughout the 1780s, including loan office certificates issued by Congress and fiat money printed by several states.[46] A visitor to the Allegheny Mountains discovered "how choice we ought to be of our gold" when he saw its price rise with every westward mile, prompting him to contrast its value with that of democracy: "notwithstanding their great veneration for Independency," Americans "depreciated their Congress money" when measured against guineas.[47] Travelers to France in the early 1790s delivered similarly sardonic reports. A "plain neat old man with white locks" in a British pub informed one writer that "amongst other blessings of their Revolution, all the gold and silver of the country is vanished, and in order to supply its place they have paper money, called Assignats, which is looked upon to be of such precarious value, that nobody will sell you any thing for it without charging double price."[48]

Assignats, the French paper money that earned so much British scorn, first appeared in 1790 to fill a void left by a sudden drain of gold and silver in the wake of the Revolution. The original plan was for them to be backed by seized church property, but war expenditures soon created an overwhelming demand for money that produced hyperinflation by 1795, followed by a brief sequel under a new currency in 1796–1797. As historian Rebecca Spang has argued, assignats embodied the universalizing ambitions of the Revolution: more like coins than like any European paper money at the time, they bore national icons—initially a bust of Louis XVI, later a wide range of revolutionary symbols—and imagined "a currency space far more homogenous . . . than the one in which they lived."[49] British bank notes, in contrast, communicated personal trust between creditors and debtors, as opposed to faith in an abstract national ideal. All Bank of England paper was payable to its chief cashier; Abraham Newland, who held that post between 1782 and 1808, became eponymous with the notes he signed. The only iconography adorning them, mainly as a guard against forgery, was a medallion in the corner featuring Britannia holding a spear and olive branch. By the 1790s dozens of British banks issued similar notes, with their own idiosyncratic and insistently local pictorial symbols.[50]

Britons assailed assignats as a deviation from money's purpose—which, urged the Scottish diplomat Maurice Morgann, was to provide "a *natural measure of commercial value.*" He added that when France ran out of gold and silver, the only "perfect measure" of this value, its only remedy lay in "violence, injustice, and force": "they manufactured rags into paper . . . and ordained that each piece of this paper should pass for its nominal value, *by the guillotine.*" The stockjobber Ralph Broome likewise called assignats "a complete robbery upon all those who were obliged to give their goods for this ideal and uncertain money," whereas Bank of England notes, which were "not issued by government," gave holders "the option . . . of accepting paper, or rejecting payment in any thing but gold."[51]

Just as France was lurching back to a bimetallic standard in 1797, poor harvests and an averted invasion of Wales threatened to drain the Bank of England of its gold reserves. Parliament responded by relieving the Bank of its obligation to redeem its notes in gold; an impromptu "declaration movement" ensued across the country, in which local elites pledged to accept those notes, as well as those issued by regional banks, for the duration of the crisis. Together with new forms of taxation, such appeals enabled the mobilization of what a contemporary called "the patriotism of English merchants," which would, over the next ten years, undergird a remarkably stable financial system. The suspension of payments enabled the Treasury to carry a large current account without impeding the Bank's ability to lend in the private sector: a benefit that prompted Parliament to wait until well after the war ended to resume payments in gold. Although France, for its part, managed to limp into the 1810s by commandeering precious metals from occupied territories, its ruined public credit ultimately tilted the scale of wartime finance in Britain's favor.[52]

The Bank of England's status as a private joint-stock company had much to do with the credit of its notes, as did the fact that regional banks had established trust among their respective customers. The fact that the Bank had been redeeming its notes with gold for more than a century also carried substantial weight. The author of *Scarcity of Specie No Ground for Alarm* assured his readers in 1797 that "the CREDIT of the Bank . . . has come forth from the Mint stamped

with a PROPERTY—splendid, intrinsic, and immense." Five years on, novelist
Elizabeth Hamilton wrote that since she valued currency "in exact proportion
to the degree of credit in which I hold the bank that utters it," she considered
"French *assignats*—mere waste paper" and "real *Abraham Newlands*, the same as
sterling gold." The fact that the suspension of payments accompanied unprecedented prosperity added to such optimism. Agricultural reformer Arthur Young
praised its role in converting gold "from a useless metal . . . into beef, and mutton,
butter, cheese, and corn."[53]

Although Newland's signature and its regional counterparts may have struck
some in England as equivalent to gold, others yearned for the absent image of
their king, which they presented as subject to banishment. One critic of paper
money lamented in 1811 that "*country bank notes . . . swarm* in every place," while
"the precious likenesses of our beloved sovereign, are thus easily and cruelly
taken from us, and transported."[54] Opposition MPs routinely associated the
Bank's activities after 1797 with French finance during the Revolution, calling
its notes "downright assignats"; and the caricaturist James Gillray translated this
alarm into an image of Pitt as Midas, round-bellied with guineas, vomiting and
defecating bank notes in all directions.[55] William Cobbett fanned the flames of
such suspicions with voluminous bombast—most famously in *Paper Against
Gold*, which cited the renewed drain of gold after 1808 as evidence that equating
patriotism with public credit was a losing proposition.[56]

Defenders of Pitt and his successors did their best to sever any alleged identity
between Bank of England notes and assignats and, above all, offered assurance
that gold would eventually return to Britain to act in its former capacity as currency. William Playfair tackled the first point in a footnote to his 1805 edition of
The Wealth of Nations: "The assignats," he argued, "were paid away for expences;
the notes of the bank of England are lent on security, to be repaid at a short and
certain date." In 1821, with the benefit of hindsight, another writer imagined Pitt
asking the nation in 1797 to accept "a circulating medium, which passing upon
mutual confidence among yourselves in free exchange, shall have the same effect
in completing all your mercantile transactions and exchanges, as if conducted
in the valuable metals"; and predicting that the gold used "to support our own
troops, and to make good engagements to our allies," would eventually "form the
fund, which will enable you again to return to a metallic currency."[57]

A second distinction between France and Britain during their respective periods off a metallic standard concerned the fate of ornamental gold.
Throughout the decade after 1789, the French state relentlessly exchanged
assignats for "gold trinkets, jewels, rings, and . . . plate," initially from churches
and noble families and then, after 1795, from occupied territories.[58] Britons, in
contrast, actually increased their consumption of ornamental gold after 1797.
Purchases of gold plate, for instance, rose by 50% during 1798 and 1799 and

Figure 3.1 James Gillray, "Midas Transmuting All into ~~Gold~~ Paper" (1797). "The great Midas having dedicated himself to Bacchus, obtained from that Deity the Power of changing all he Touched." Midas straddles the domed roof of the Bank of England, wearing a lock and chain around his neck with the words "Power of securing Public Credit." British Museum 1851,0901.852.

by another 20% during the decade after that, while the army lavishly draped its officers with decorative gold.[59] A different proxy, reported thefts at the Old Bailey, tells a similar story. Between 1797 and 1821, an annual average of 104 gold rings, watches, and other ornaments was reported stolen in London's main criminal court, compared to 88.6 during the previous decade; the figure for guineas, in contrast, fell from 414 to 153 per year.[60]

As a matter of policy, there was almost no support in Britain for the French model of confiscating or even limiting the production of such ornaments in order to yield more gold for the war effort. When Pitt imposed a ten-shilling tax on gold watches in 1797, he did so to raise revenue and not to discourage consumption—and in any case the tax was so unpopular that he was forced to rescind it a year later.[61] The Bullion Report barely mentioned ornamental gold, and the handful of commentators who favored restricting its manufacture erred on the side of caution. One recommended the "prohibition of manufactured *Plate*, unless the workmanship exceeded the value of the Metal"; another urged that "the noble and wealthy possessors of useless and superfluous treasures, should present them as a voluntary offering to government." The reviewer who called such proposals "hackneyed expedients" was typical. Besides doubting that enough ornamental gold existed for them to have much effect, the economists who worried most about gold's disappearance opposed the "vexatious interference with the ordinary business of life" they would have entailed.[62]

Finally, Britain diverged from France in its valuation of the different precious metals after the war ended. In 1803 France had returned to its pre-war bimetallic standard, which kept both gold and silver in reserve as legal means of discharging debts. It retained this system after 1815, although a scarcity of gold meant silver mainly circulated in that country until the 1850s.[63] In contrast, Britain declared gold to be the only metal that counted as legal tender in 1819, relegating silver to a token coinage. In one sense, this new law merely confirmed gold's long-time de facto status as the primary form of bullion and coin held by British banks. But its new legal validation, combined with the rhetoric that surrounded its enactment, elevated the metal's value (in cultural as well as monetary terms) to unprecedented heights. Politicians professed an "ethical bullionism," urging a return to gold as Britain's sacred duty.[64]

The urgency with which British bullionists pressed their case had everything to do with the need to reassure the creditors who had enabled them to win the war—and to quiet the growing chorus of paper-money advocates who had learned all too well how to live without guineas. As economist Edward Copleston lamented, calling for a swift restoration in 1819: "The rich have been made poor—the creditor has been paid off with less than he lent—the helpless annuitant has sunk amidst the general rise."[65] Declaring gold to be legal tender was only part of the solution for bringing prices down and ensuring a fair repayment of the national debt. It was also necessary to attract sufficient gold back into the country, while still enabling the economy to keep producing goods and services. To do this, the government pursued the same method it had used to raise gold for war payments, exchanging foreign bills through Rothschild and other brokers for gold from the continent. The result, which netted nearly £16 million in gold between 1820 and 1822, replicated the effects of a decade earlier: it turned the exchange rate against Britain and dried up its domestic money supply. Although the new gold did add to that supply, more than half of it remained in the Bank and the rest replaced less than 60 percent of the paper money that had been withdrawn from circulation. While achieving its deflationary object—agricultural prices fell by 5 percent per year until 1825—the return to gold also coincided with persistent economic stagnation, with the result that sympathy for annuitants declined along with prices.[66]

After Waterloo

For decades after Waterloo, Britons continued to debate gold's role in their most recent war. Celebrations of their country's subsidy policy prevailed, ranging from William Stourton's simple declaration that "our riches . . . set the world at liberty" to Lord Liverpool's recollection that "British gold, Buonaparte's old and unconquerable foe," had gathered "the whole of the allied forces . . . to the French frontier."[67] Against such praise linking British credit, trade, and gold with military success, the only dissenting voices came from the radical fringe. Henry Hunt's biographer, for instance, bemoaned "the profusion of English gold" that had propped up "legitimacy . . . amongst the crowned despots of Europe" and had left behind "[a]n immense debt, which, vampire-like, gnaws our very vitals."[68] To the extent that celebrations of British subsidies won the day, they also set the tone for subsequent interpretations of gold's role in other countries' foreign policy. They presented themselves as uniquely able to combine military subsidies with the preservation of political freedom, while the rest of Europe was doomed after 1815 to revert to the millennia-old pattern of oppression and corruption. France continued to figure in this sequel, especially in connection with Iberian politics. The *Times* approvingly quoted a Portuguese politician who worried in 1822 that "the corrupting gold of France" was being "scattered in handfuls" to influence the country's constitutional convention; a year later Lord Erskine warned British supporters of "the brave people of Spain" that "French gold" was endangering their autonomy.[69]

Above all, Britons viewed Russian foreign aid as fully restoring the older rich-country/poor-country dynamic, with Greece, Poland, Denmark, and Bulgaria emerging as plausibly receptive poor countries after 1815. When Polish resistance to Russian rule eroded in 1831, British observers blamed "traitors, seduced by Russian gold"; dynastic intrigues in Denmark prompted concerns that "Russian gold . . . will give Russia a natural and preponderating influence in that monarchy, which holds the keys of the Baltic."[70] This pattern would intensify during the 1840s, when Russia became the world's leading producer of gold and allegedly wielded its strengthened sinews across central Europe.[71] Britons generally settled for alleging Russian treachery—although in the case of Greece they tried to counter its influence by subscribing to £472,000 in loans, at least some of which was paid in guineas. Skeptics predicted that much of this gold would be hoarded, converted into "spurious coins," or "used by the women as ornaments to their hair."[72]

More pervasive than these occasional aspersions were condemnations of gold's role in domestic politics, which had provided so much fodder for France in the 1780s. Such charges revived in full force after the passage of the Reform Act in 1832 and a sharpening of party divisions. Newspapers bristled with reports of "the seductions of Whig gold" in Nottingham, "the lavish expenditure of Treasury gold" in St. Albans, and "twaddle about gold from the Carlton club" in Glasgow.[73] Although much of this gold existed only in the realm of rumor, at least some was of the tangible variety: guineas were suitable denominations for this sort of bribery, which was rife in the days before the secret ballot. Douglas Jerrold poked fun at such realities in his *History of St. Giles and St. James*, in which the parliamentary agent Tangle tries to turn the electoral tide in "the independent borough of Liquorish" with the help of a chest of guineas, "all sparkling and burning from the Mint."[74]

For the most part, however, public perceptions of the movement of gold into, out of and within Britain during the three decades after Waterloo focused much less on political intrigue and much more on international trade. The *Illustrated London News* was correct to claim that the metal's true significance during this period lay in its role as capital, not as a tool of foreign relations. Yet this role did not remove it from the realm of politics. The return to the gold standard in 1821, which favored creditors by ensuring repayment of the national debt in full-value money, followed close on the heels of a new Corn Law, which protected farmers and landlords by imposing tight restrictions on grain imports. These two policies would conjoin gold and corn as key elements in the debate over free trade that simmered, and occasionally boiled over, until the Corn Law's repeal in 1846.

4

Trade

In his *Letter to the Duke of Buckingham, on the Corn Laws* (1839), a "Practical Farmer" worried that under a system of free trade in agriculture, "the moneyed capitalists, and the Emperor of Russia, would then have it all their own way." Russia, he warned, would "build Government warehouses to a great extent, and insist upon all the corn being there placed," charging fees for storage as well as transport whenever Britain required imports. The farmer next addressed the central claim of free-traders that abolishing taxes on corn imports would encourage trading partners to buy manufactured goods in exchange: "Gold would be required for the purchase of the corn: and it is absurd to expect [that] Russia would take your manufactures for corn. They would say, 'Bring gold; or go back, and let your population starve.'" Any Russian landowner who was tempted to trade their grain for textiles or hardware, he predicted, would receive, at the hands of the Russian "Autocrat," a *"journey, gratis, to Siberia:* and his property would be *confiscated.*"[1]

This type of argument, which repeatedly appeared in the enormous archive of speeches in favor of the Corn Laws between 1815 and 1846, highlighted the important role played by gold in framing that debate. Protectionists reasoned from periodic drains of gold between 1815 and 1846 to predict disastrous consequences for the country under free trade, owing to the need to pay for additional grain supplies with bullion. Their liberal opponents mainly attributed price variations and deflation to the operation of the Corn Laws, which (they argued) prevented the emergence of "regular" foreign markets that would be prepared to accept British goods in exchange for grain in times of dearth. They also diverted attention from trade to monetary policy, blaming the Bank of England and joint stock banks for failing to curtail loans in time to prevent drains from getting out of hand; and to "overtrading" merchants (both in Britain and the United States) whose demand for those loans exceeded the nation's money supply. At bottom, this debate pitted a state-centered theory of trade, which placed a central emphasis on the role of national rivalries in determining specie flows, against a more idealized international model that minimized gold's role in settling foreign accounts.[2]

Nobody denied at the time that drains of bullion were a recurrent problem between 1815 and 1846: gold supplies in the Bank of England swung between low ebbs of £4.6 million in 1826 and 1839–1841 to highs exceeding £10 million in 1821–1824 and 1838; this accompanied swings in prices, although the overall tendency was deflationary. In all cases, most contemporaries recognized that tight money supplies produced consequences that ranged from inconvenient to devastating, since the Bank of England's efforts to attract gold back into the country via higher interest rates inevitably affected economic activity. Most, but not all, of the gold that drained from the Bank was used to pay for foreign grain: poor harvests preceded drains in 1824 and 1839, but bullion also left the Bank to pay for Latin American loans and mining equipment in 1825, American cotton in 1838, and (by way of bank runs) political unrest in 1832.[3]

Although all the elements connecting gold with trade were in place prior to 1776, Adam Smith's critique of mercantilism in *The Wealth of Nations* set the terms for their intersection over the following decades. Smith did his best to wish away gold as a significant factor in Britain's foreign trade, envisioning a world in which trading partners relied almost wholly on bills of exchange to settle accounts and economized on the domestic use of gold through the extensive circulation of paper money. The near-complete drain of gold from Britain during the Napoleonic War, much of which left the country to pay for grain imports, led to a revival of economic arguments that linked self-sufficiency with gold supplies— which culminated in the Corn Law of 1815. Although economists appealed to Smith to paint this perspective as a mercantilist shibboleth, persistent debates over that law, together with recurrent drains of gold, ensured the survival of such thinking right up to the influx of gold from California and Australia after 1848.

Mercantilist Shibboleths

One of Adam Smith's most enduring sections in *The Wealth of Nations* was his spirited demolition of "the Mercantile School," which allegedly assumed that "to heap up gold and silver in any country" was "the readiest way to enrich it." One reason his denunciation endured was that it enabled future generations of liberals to describe their opponents as holding "exploded" beliefs, and thereby pre-emptively drain their arguments of apparent relevance. This was William Nassau Senior's tactic in 1827 when he walked his readers through Smith's arguments on the way to accusing nineteenth-century protectionists of "opposing the theory of a barbarous age to the theory and experience of an enlightened one."[4] Identifying protectionism with Smith's account of mercantilism turned it into a shibboleth, which diverted attention from several subsequent conditions that made it harder to defend Smith's original grounds for opposing mercantilist thinking: these included the rise of protectionism in the United States and Europe, the exponential growth of Britain's national debt and accompanying tax burden, and the three decades of deflation that followed the resumption of cash payments in 1821.

Without admitting it in so many words, Smith's attack on mercantilism paralleled David Hume's earlier critique, in his 1752 essay "Of the Balance of Trade." There, Hume had recalled the "universal pannic" that Joshua Gee had produced by his prediction in *Trade and Navigation of Great-Britain Considered* (1729) that, in Hume's words, Britain's trade deficit "was against them for so considerable a sum as must leave them without a single shilling in five or six years." He countered this with the wry reassurance that "luckily, twenty years have since elaps'd, along with an expensive foreign war; and yet . . . money is still more plentiful amongst us than in any former period." He also responded with a reassuring (if sketchy) theory, which subsequent economists would call the price-specie flow mechanism. The fall in prices occasioned by a drain in bullion, he argued, would immediately "bring back the money which we had lost, and raise us to the level of all the neighbouring nations." After arriving at that point, he concluded, "we immediately lose the advantage of the cheapness of labour and commodities; and the farther flowing in of money is stopped by our fulness and repletion."[5]

Smith's discussion of the "Mercantile School" reinforced Hume's efforts to downplay concerns about trade deficits and bullion drains. Instead of Gee, he reached further back, singling out Thomas Mun's *England's Treasure in Foreign Trade* (written in the 1630s), which had mistakenly conflated bullion with "any other useful commodities" that could be exported. Gold's only meaningful function was in the form of "utensils"; hence stockpiling it was "as absurd as it would be to attempt to increase the good cheer of private families, by obliging them to keep an unnecessary number of kitchen utensils." As "the money of the great mercantile republick," he concluded, gold could be relied on to flow efficiently among nations to balance accounts. Although he admitted that a direct trade was more profitable to Britain than a "round-about one" (whereby British goods purchased Brazilian gold via Lisbon, then exchanged that for a different commodity), he insisted, following Hume, that both sides still gained from the latter transaction.[6]

From his perspective in 1776, Smith found it relatively easy to dispense with two of the issues that would revive mercantilist arguments in the nineteenth century: a drain of bullion owing to foreign wars, and the impact of a trade deficit on the domestic supply of money. He implicitly applied Hume's price-specie flow analysis to drains occasioned by foreign wars and assumed that a "well regulated paper money" could replace a diminished supply of coin "not only without any inconveniency, but with very great advantages."[7] By taking Smith's analysis as their starting point, classical economists effectively divorced gold from trade policy—or rather, they subordinated trade policy to the sway of international gold supplies. In Joseph Schumpeter's words, they viewed gold in this context as a "moral as well as an economic ideal" that acted as a "naughty boy who blurts out unpleasant truths."[8] In the three decades after Waterloo, these unpleasant truths included a steady diet of deflation and a bulimic business cycle, which rose and fell as interest rates struggled to keep pace with trade-induced bullion flows.

Smith's early successes in turning the tide against mercantilism were impressive. William Pitt, who served as Prime Minister from 1783 through 1801, was an avowed disciple of Smith, and under his watch the passage in 1785 of the Eden Treaty provided unprecedented access for goods to flow legally between Britain and France.[9] The French Revolution and subsequent wars did more than interrupt this momentum in the spread of economic liberalism. The suspension of cash payments in 1797 refuted Smith's prediction that no foreign war could ever drain Britain of so much gold as to render such a measure necessary, Britain's debt burden rose from £262 million to £885 million between 1793 and 1815, and prices rose by 59% percent over the same period. Also, the ready supply of Brazilian gold that had persisted into the 1770s abruptly declined after 1790, and war-induced interruptions to production meant that world gold supplies would not return to their mid-eighteenth century levels until the 1830s.[10]

Robust debates over agricultural protection and the resumption of cash payments in 1819 reflected this transformed financial landscape. Two months before Waterloo, Parliament passed a Corn Law that prevented grain imports until the domestic price exceeded £4 per quarter, with the goal of keeping that price close to its inflated wartime level. Although it took three years for prices to fall to the £4 limit, after that the law effectively banned foreign grain for the next decade. In 1828 a liberal flank of the Tory government, led by William Huskisson and Robert Peel, pushed through a new law that allowed free imports when the price exceeded £3 13s and imposed a sliding scale below that price. A leading theme in these debates was the perceived need to balance self-sufficiency in grain production (a major concern during the war) with protection against famine during poor harvests; and, by returning to the gold standard, to arrest inflation and thereby pay down the national debt on terms that would be fair to Britain's creditors.[11]

The result was a delicate political balance whereby grain duties protected landowners' interests and hard money protected those of creditors, hence covering both bases of what historians Peter Cain and Anthony Hopkins have called "gentlemanly capitalism," without any specific policy in place for the benefit of industrial capital or labor.[12] As the Birmingham industrialist and radical

MP George Muntz would complain in 1840, "provision has been made for the fundholder by keeping the standard at its old position . . . and, to a great extent, the landed interests have been maintained in their position by the Corn Laws; but I do not see that any faith has been kept with the working classes."[13] Although few others at the time opposed both the Corn Laws and the gold standard (most assailed one or the other), Muntz's observation is a useful reminder that these two pillars of British economic policy between 1815 and 1846 established terms of debate in which gold supplies and foreign trade constantly crossed paths.

To resurrect Smithian ideas in the aftermath of the war, liberals diverted discussion of gold to the realm of monetary policy, where they waged a largely internecine battle over the proper function of the Bank of England; and labeled anyone who insisted on connecting gold back to trade policy as hopelessly behind the times. Toward this end, they dismissed any contemporary concerns regarding bullion drains or trade deficits as resting on grounds that had long since been "exploded" or "abandoned." In case Smith's original message was not clear enough, J. R. McCulloch prefaced his 1828 edition of *The Wealth of Nations* with a lengthy additional rebuttal of mercantilism.[14] When liberals turned from the allegedly self-evident claims of Hume and Smith to their opponents' arguments, they did qualify their verdict regarding the demise of mercantilism. An *Edinburgh Encyclopedia* article on export bounties presented mercantilism's staying power as a problem of irrefutable theory battling insufferable practice: "None but persons of obtuse intellect are, nowadays, blind to the absurdity of its principles; whilst its pernicious operation is still permitted to gratify a mercantile and manufacturing avarice, at the expense of the general community."[15]

An Orientalist Prologue

According to the East India Company official John Henry Grose, who served in Bombay in the early 1750s, India was "a bottomless pit for bullion, which can never circulate back to Europe." The Orientalist Thomas Maurice claimed that "the great treasures in gold and silver, produced by the mines of Spain, flowed [to India], to be there swallowed up in a vortex that never regurgitated the shining spoil." Such concerns dated back to the very beginning of Britain's presence in India. As early as 1611, the poet John Donne wrote of the Orient: "The West sent gold, which thou didst freely spend . . . The East sends hither her deliciousness."[16] Such concerns closely followed the logic of Gee and Mun, who provided the fodder for the assault waged by Hume and Smith on mercantilism.

When nineteenth-century British protectionists worried about the impact of free trade on gold supplies, they seldom directly appealed to these older arguments. But they did invoke assumptions that mercantilists had originally expressed and that were almost entirely absent in classical political economy: specifically, the concern that Britain's trading partners had reached a saturation point in their collective demand for British goods and that any further grain imports could only come at the expense of Britain's money supply. These concerns first appeared in eighteenth-century discussions of India, which reveal an enduring suspicion that Hume's concept of a price-specie flow mechanism did not necessarily apply where "Asiatic" customs and political rule persisted. To the extent that nineteenth-century protectionists transferred this perspective from India and China to Russia and Poland, it is possible to read the Corn Law controversy as a restaging of this earlier debate.

The drain of bullion that these writers were describing was not a figment of their imaginations. Between 1600 and 1800, a steady flow of gold and silver found its way from Latin America to India and points east: bullion exports were worth around £200,000 in 1600, rising to £750,000 in 1700 and £1.3 million by 1800. Spain and Portugal typically paid off their trade deficits with England, France, and the Netherlands out of the bullion they received from Latin America, and what the latter countries did not keep at home they sent on to East Asia (as well as the Baltic States and the Middle East).[17] Bullion included silver as well as gold, and especially in the seventeenth century (prior to new gold discoveries in Brazil), the British shipped much more silver than gold to India and points east. A severe shortage of silver coin in London in 1620 was the proximate cause of the famous mercantilist debates that Smith would refer to in *The Wealth of Nations*.[18]

To diagnose this digestion of bullion, Britons identified four related cultural and political conditions, all of which conveniently set India apart as distinct from Northern European habits and policies. First came religious superstition. Michael Symes, who accompanied an embassy to Burma in 1795, observed that "although highly valued, [gold] is not used for coin in the country, [but] . . . expended in gilding their temples." Second came a vain proclivity to adorn their bodies with gold.[19] Third, often linked to the first two, was a political system based on tyranny and plunder. As travel writer Maria Graham noted in 1813: "Where the people were daily exposed to the ravages of barbarous armies, it was natural to endeavour to keep their little wealth in that form in which it could with most ease be conveyed out of the reach of plunderers." Finally, "the peculiar benignity of the climate in which they lived" emerged as a reason that Indians "had no relish for the productions of any other country," leaving bullion as the only desirable item in trade.[20] In all these cases, the focus was on cultural difference as an explanation of a perceived economic problem, accounts of which served the similar function of marking South Asians apart from Europeans.

Such diagnoses of Asia's absorption of bullion started to recede (though they never wholly disappeared) after 1760, when the East India Company began to rely on tax revenues instead of bullion imports to purchase goods. From a share of four-fifths of its exports to India, bullion declined to one-eighth in the 1760s. This reversal made free-trade advocates optimistic that nineteenth-century drains would always be less severe than had been the case when Asia had absorbed western bullion. McCulloch, for instance, defended unilateral free trade with France in 1819 on the grounds that the flow of bullion was less sticky among European trading partners because the value of gold and silver in neighboring countries was "always extremely near a par." In Asia, in contrast, transport costs and an asymmetry in the value of the precious metals made an indirect trade less efficient.[21]

At a more basic level, the reversal of specie flows from east to west freed up bullion for other uses, not the least of which included waging war against the American colonies and France after 1776 and maintaining the gold standard despite recurrent drains of bullion to Europe and America after 1820. McCulloch cited this as one of several reasons to be hopeful that the deflation that had dogged Britain in the 1820s would soon be a thing of the past.[22] Liberal commentators also cited this reversal as predictive of the ability of an industrial nation to break into new markets. The fact that India (and later China, after the Opium Wars) only began to accept manufactured goods instead of bullion from Britain following military defeat may be the reason almost no liberals appealed to those countries by name when they predicted that Europeans would warm to the idea of trade with Britain.[23]

British protectionists, in contrast, recalled earlier "Asiatic" discourses in order to refute the claim that foreigners would to take British goods, instead of bullion, in exchange for their grain. By inviting comparisons to decidedly un-English peasants and Oriental-style despotism, they painted Britain's would-be trading partners as far riskier than liberals allowed. They departed from earlier mercantilist arguments when they pondered what eastern Europeans were likely to do with the gold they absorbed. In contrast to Asiatic despots, who wasted gold on pompous display, European autocrats had far more sinister plans for it: to invest in manufacturing, thereby bringing British industry down along with agriculture. Another departure related to the impact of bullion supplies on prices. Into the early nineteenth century, defenders of trade with India celebrated its effectiveness in blunting inflation in the West; as David Macpherson claimed in his *History of the European Commerce with* India (1812), Europe had thereby been "happily preserved . . . from being overwhelmed by the inundation of the pretious metals."[24] In contrast, protectionists after 1815 feared the deflationary impact of bullion drains, against the backdrop of an increasing scarcity of gold.

Mercantilist Wine in Protectionist Bottles

Since liberal economists studiously ignored protectionist appeals to national character and foreign political machinations, debates over these issues seldom progressed much farther than a dire prediction on one side, followed by an assertion on the other that the prediction went against the laws of political economy. At bottom, the economic principle in question was Say's Law, which denied the possibility of a general glut, in that liberals claimed that the price-specie flow mechanism would always eventually regenerate demand for British goods. To the extent that either side got beyond this stalemate, the ground shifted to the argument that even a temporary deficit in the balance of payments would have a redistributive impact, since the deflation it produced would favor financiers over the "productive" classes.

Few protectionist manifestos that appeared between 1825 and 1846 lacked some variant on the doomsday scenario in which an open grain trade would lead to a "ruinous *drain upon the metallic treasures* of the country" or "drain the bullion coffers of the Bank of England to their very dregs."[25] To support this, they needed to meet head-on the liberal claim that Americans and Europeans would accept British manufactured goods (instead of gold) in exchange for their grain and, failing that, would accept bills of exchange drawn on countries that did buy British goods. They countered the first argument by proclaiming the incapacity of European peasants to acquire a taste for British exports and by pointing to the tendency of grain-exporting autocracies to protect home manufactures at the expense of British goods. They were less successful at addressing the second claim until after the commercial crisis of 1836–1838, when the failure of the US economy to absorb excess British exports provided them with hard evidence that the global market for those goods was not reliably elastic.

The terms of this debate were already well established by the late 1820s, as rumors swirled concerning Huskisson's designs on the 1815 Corn Law. An early example was Layton Cooke's claim in 1827 that "it could scarcely be expected that the serfs of Poland and Russia would require the luxuries of life essential only to those who have arrived at a high state of civilization." Answer number eighteen on a list of *Twenty Questions submitted by the General Agricultural Committee* the same year predicted that liberalizing the 1815 law would "take the gold out of the country" to pay for corn "from poor, thinly inhabited, or semi-barbarous countries, who import few manufactured goods."[26] Such claims persisted into the 1830s: the Buckinghamshire MP Grenville Pigott argued in 1832 that "they who are acquainted with the condition of the peasantry . . . in north-eastern Germany, Poland, and Russia" knew that it would "require generations to give them even a taste for the manufactures of this country," as opposed to goods "supplied by their own household."[27]

Up to this point, protectionists only provided reasons why Europeans were unlikely to take British goods in exchange for their grain. The next plank of their argument turned to what these countries would do with the bullion that Britain sent them. Here, the presiding fear (as a Carlisle farmer expressed it in 1829) was that "the gold we pay for foreign grain will act as a bounty for all kinds of rival productions."[28] Fueling this fear was the rapid emergence of industrial protection almost immediately following the Congress of Vienna: starting with the Prussian Customs Union of 1818 (which evolved into a German-wide Zollverein by 1834) and followed by a Russian tariff on over 200 imports in 1822. Returning from Siberia in 1842, a year after Peel's first effort to reduce duties on corn, the barrister Charles Cottrell worried that the tsar had accelerated this process: he "gave the lie to the principal argument of the anti-corn law agitators, by raising the duty on British goods" and requiring Britain to "pay for [its] tallow and hemp in gold."[29]

Since it took time for the economic impact of the new foreign tariffs to be felt, protectionists in the 1820s instead extrapolated from the war years, when Britain "promoted [foreigners'] capability of creating manufacturing establishments" by sending gold to her European allies to pay for grain.[30] By the late 1830s, two decades' worth of experience with these tariffs had hardened their stance. One pamphleteer in 1843 predicted that unilateral free trade would enable Europeans to "grow rich by bringing corn, pork, and beef to your shores and taking back gold; and the surplus of their wealth . . . will be lent out at full usance to the young and enterprizing manufacturers who want capital." Adding insult to injury, some predicted that once European despots had ruined British farmers and caught up with British industry, they would be in a position to lure away British artisans, delivering a death blow to industry as well.[31]

Protectionists also needed to confront the scenario in which Britain's grain providers would accept bills of exchange issued on the security of other British export markets, hence removing the need to send them gold. They met this claim by arguing that demand was not elastic in those parts of the world that presently purchased British textiles. Such assertions became easier to make after the commercial crisis of 1837, when Americans proved to have a satiable appetite for British goods. A Doncaster lecturer specifically blamed that crash on British capitalists' "desire to multiply beyond all past precedent, the productive powers of manufactures," which meant "gold was worth more" to American exporters "than our goods"; he cited these as "facts which corn law repealers should keep in mind." Protectionists also blamed the drain of gold in 1837 on the adoption of a de facto gold standard by the United States in 1834, which (in

Scottish historian Archibald Alison's words) created "a vast magnet . . . in that country, invested with the quality of attracting the precious metals from every other part of the world."[32]

A different protectionist argument, which also tapped into their fear of un-requited trade, focused on the redistributive effects of drain-induced defla-tion, whereby creditors gained at the expense of debtors—of whom landlords comprised a sizeable portion.[33] This came out most clearly in an exchange be-tween the free-trader Thomas Perronet Thompson and an anonymous *Fraser's* reviewer. When *Fraser's* linked free trade with the "continual lessening of our circulating medium," and Thompson answered with the usual appeal to the "counteracting operations" effected by the price-specie flow mechanism, *Fraser's* responded that this "would answer tolerably well if there were no national debt, no 'dead weight,' no mortgages, pensions, fixed salaries, settlements, and other immoveable payments, interwoven with every man's affairs." The writer concluded: "By their two nostrums of 'metallic currency' and 'free trade,' our economists have contrived, in little more than ten years, to reduce the prices of all kinds of commodities."[34]

Not all protectionists were as ready to abandon the gold standard as this writer (although many were), but most would have agreed that the Corn Laws performed the essential service of propping up prices in the face of that policy's deflationary tendencies—especially in light of the high taxes that Britain's debt burden imposed on landlords and farmers.[35] This was especially the case while the Corn Law briefly coexisted with the more stringent requirements of the 1844 Bank Charter Act, which pegged note issue to the Bank of England's bullion re-serves. Alison argued that this more rigid gold standard needed Corn Laws more than ever: "the *monetary system* of the country is dependent for its very existence upon the prevention of any considerable importation of foreign grain." Or as another protectionist proclaimed in 1846, the Bank Charter Act made it all the more clear that *free trade in corn and monopoly in money cannot possibly exist to-gether.*" [italics in the original].[36]

Gold and Free Trade

The most common response among advocates of free trade to protectionist fears about a drain of bullion was to focus intently on outcomes rather than processes. With more than a little impatience, they lectured protectionists that gold would and did return to England in the end, just as Hume had predicted it would; when it did, they contended, overall output always increased. When they stopped to focus on the problems caused by drains, they either blamed this on the Corn Laws, which (they claimed) prevented a "regular trade" with grain exporters; or diverted attention to monetary policy, and specifically the numerous mistakes committed by the Bank of England and joint stock banks. All these arguments followed Smith in de-emphasizing the significance of gold in the international economy. Like Smith, they demeaned gold's use-value (it possessed "scarcely any value but as instruments of exchange," as one journalist urged in 1823) and offered their assurance that it would always be there when people needed it.[37]

Free-traders most often responded to fears about bullion drains by bemoaning the inability of protectionists to understand basic economics. Many of them led with the claim that talk of gold drains was a red herring: "a perfectly irrelevant consideration, which has nothing whatever to do with free trade, but with which it has been found peculiarly convenient, by certain sophists, to encumber the matter," one pamphleteer sneered in 1839.[38] Most appealed to Hume's price-specie flow mechanism, as when Richard Badnall offered the assurance in 1830 that "a country exporting her produce, and only importing gold, cannot continue to do so without causing a glut of that commodity, which is sure by eventually finding its own level, to return through one channel or another, to that country from which it was originally exported, in exchange for other commodities." That lines sometimes blurred between economic argument and article of faith is apparent from a free-trade tract in 1838, which simply proclaimed that "the exchanges would at all times put the matter to rights."[39]

At its most utopian, this argument rested on the belief that British ingenuity could generate an infinite demand for its products. According to one free-trade advocate, Britain possessed "a kind of natural national monopoly" on intelligence and industry, whereby "the natural current of her commerce is, to manufacture for those countries who supply her with raw materials." A reviewer of John Paget's *Hungary and Transylvania* (1839) envisioned virginal markets as opposed to protectionist despots in Eastern Europe, and saw no reason why grain imports necessarily implied a drain of gold: "What, in these days of universal movement, steam and railroads, is to hinder a taste for English luxuries and English enjoyments, to spring up amongst the owners of the vast plains of Europe"? He predicted that "instead of gold going out for corn, suddenly crippling every branch of commerce, and impoverishing the entire community, English ingenuity and English manufactures stimulated, advanced, and exchanged, in return for continental grain."[40]

A more sophisticated variant on this argument was the claim that a "regular," as opposed to sporadic, demand for corn on Britain's part would sustain a constant demand for manufactures on the other side. "If there were no restrictions on the importation of foreign Corn," argued Huddersfield minister Edmund Kell in 1840, foreigners "would then pay us in Corn for our manufactures" and would require only "a small portion of gold, to act like counters, in adjusting the trifling balances." This was an especially popular argument against the sliding scale that Huskisson had introduced in 1828, which, many argued, made British demand for grain less predictable for foreign suppliers. One lecturer argued in 1843 that under the sliding scale, "we come pouring in on them with our gold like an invading army of locusts, lay our hands on every bushel of corn that all the bullion of the Bank of England can buy, sweep their markets bare, and leave famine behind." None of this would happen, he concluded, if Britain would only "let nature alone."[41]

Free-traders were so confident of such outcomes that they promised an unlimited future supply of gold plate along with plentiful sovereigns—betraying none of the impatience they elsewhere displayed toward the consumption of ornamental gold. The author of *Paradise Regained* predicted an increase in "the demands . . . for plate and ornaments" under free trade, which would not "diminish the supply of the precious metals, but increase it, by the encouragement given to the extension of mining." In the shorter term, Britons could double their supply of gold plate overnight by repealing the "prohibitory" duty on that article, which had prevented them "from obtaining valuable specimens of art of the most exquisite kind . . . from the Continent."[42] At the root of all such arguments was an invocation of the price-specie flow mechanism. Sovereigns, reminded Perronet Thompson, were "made of gold bought in Peru or elsewhere with English manufactures either directly or in some roundabout way, just as much as gold watch-cases or drinking-cups." All were "nothing but bits of gold," which would find its natural price under free trade regardless of whether it was used as money or ornament.[43]

Such arguments, which essentially wished away any possible negative economic consequences of a drain of bullion, were effective enough when liberals were preaching to the converted at Anti-Corn Law League meetings. They were less effective when they found themselves in Parliament, where they were expected to do something about the negative impact of recurring economic downturns. One option was to blame "overtrading" by merchants and bankers, a concept that at least diverted blame for commercial crises from the landlords with whom they legislated in parliament. This was the favored approach of Malthusian financial reformers such as Lord Overstone, who assumed that businessmen who recklessly speculated beyond their means were doomed to experience endless waves of bankruptcy. McCulloch similarly blamed the drain in 1837 on American merchants, who "grossly overtraded" and shut their eyes to the inevitable "scarcity of money" that their actions helped to bring about.[44]

A second, more constructive, liberal response to commercial instability was to tinker with monetary policy. One interpretation for the vast amount of ink spilled on "the currency question" between 1820 and 1846, the majority of which was produced by people who were united in their opposition to the Corn Laws, is that it diverted attention from protectionist diagnoses of financial crises.

These debates focused on the allocation of responsibility among bankers and on which instruments of credit should be regulated; they culminated in the victory of the so-called currency school, which resulted in the Bank Charter Act of 1844, which separated the Bank of England's note-issuing and deposit-collecting departments and restricted its note issue to £14 million more than its holdings of bullion. As with most other social and political ills, the free-traders who supported this law hoped to remove all discretion from errant individuals (in this instance Bank directors) and enable, in Richard Cobden's words, "the trade and commerce of the world" to regulate money supply.[45]

As is often the case in persistent controversies, both sides were partly correct. The liberal claim that gold did always return following a drain was true for the first half of the nineteenth century, and the economy did, by most accounts, achieve significant overall growth during the same period. On the other hand, that period was also marked by bouts of devastating unemployment and persistent deflation, which could at least in some cases be traced directly to drains of gold, and which came with a clear set of winners and losers. One of the secrets to liberals' success in the battle for free trade was their ability to keep attention focused on consumer prices and "monopoly" rents charged by landlords, and away from the creditor interest that gained substantially from deflation. Periodically demonizing the Bank of England and greedy speculators helped their cause, as did the reticence with which many protectionists directly attacked the fundholder interest, for fear of being associated with political radicals.

In August 1847, a year after the Anti-Corn Law League had achieved its goal of repeal, the National Anti-Gold Law League formed with the goal of replacing the gold standard with a system of "Exchequer Notes of the value of One Pound and upwards," which it argued would enable gold "to rise or fall in price as the law of supply and demand may require." Four months before, poor harvests had combined with calls on railway stock to drain the country of £5.75 million in gold and bring markets to a standstill.[46] The Anti-Gold Law League's president blamed the crash on the gold standard (amplified by Peel's recent Bank Charter Act), which "had caused the restriction of the currency when its expansion was most required." Although not directly aligned with protectionists, league members did not spare free trade from their critique: Britain's "gigantic efforts to force a foreign trade," claimed another member, had "pauperise[d] labour." This last point underscored the League's "one motive," which was "to ameliorate the condition of the working-classes, whose position was now worse than it previously had been."[47]

Into 1849, as the British economy limped back to life, Peel's opponents continued to connect his restrictive monetary policies with his repeal of the Corn Laws. Reporting home from Frankfurt in 1848, Tory journalist William Aytoun provided a grim post-mortem of protectionism: "For a year and a half, the [German] boot and shoe trade has been remarkably thriving; the London market being the most profitable in the world, and nothing but British gold exported in return." A year later, Archibald Alison registered a similar complaint: "When free trade is sending gold headlong out of the country, to buy food, Sir Robert Peel's law sends the bank-notes, public and private, back into the banker's coffers, and leaves the industry of the country without *either* of its necessary supports!" Alison argued that the combination of the Bank Charter Act and the repeal of the Corn Laws had produced the "widespread ruin which has now overtaken nearly all the interests—but most of all the *commercial* interests—in the state."[48]

Such a close association between the gold standard, free trade, and deflation led protectionists and paper-money advocates alike to stumble after 1848, when a windfall of new gold from California and Australia suddenly removed one of the legs from their stool. The Anti-Gold Law League held its last meeting in 1848, and nine years later Edward Cayley, who had been a leading protectionist during the 1840s, informed the *York Herald* that he could easily tolerate free trade as long as gold was plentiful: "Give me gold—give me cheap paper— and I don't care for protection. We have Australia—we have, thanks to a beneficent Providence, California, and that settled the question of free trade."[49] Most Britons also assumed that class divisions would subside after 1848 owing to the rising prices that the new discoveries promised. Although such hopes erred on the side of optimism—among other things, gold-induced inflation proved to be moderate and short-lived—the gold rushes did coincide with, although they did not directly cause, the fading of Chartism and the rise of free trade as a national article of faith.[50]

In contrast, class and political divisions had seldom been far from the surface on the varied occasions before 1849 in which gold assisted commerce and foreign policy, either as subsidies to Britain's allies, bullion for balancing Britain's trade, or domestically circulating coin. As subsidies, gold polarized foreign affairs from the 1740s through the Napoleonic Wars and roiled domestic politics as both a metaphor and mechanism for corruption. Between the restoration of cash payments in 1821 and Corn Law repeal in 1846, periodic drains of gold lent force to those who complained that the postwar political settlement had unduly favored landlords and financiers. And as coin, gold pushed aside silver and copper in availability for much of the eighteenth century, leading to no end of inconvenience for workers, shopkeepers and merchants alike. Reincarnated as sovereigns after 1820, gold took on a more middle-class guise and occasionally empowered Chartist agitators who demanded to be paid notes for their gold.

5

Coinages

In the *New Monthly Magazine* for 1844, Laman Blanchard imagined a "Recent Meeting of the Coinage at the Royal Mint" occasioned by the introduction of the copper half-farthing two years earlier. Arriving late, the gold coins "were by no means delighted with the occasion on which they were summoned": taking the chair, the five-pound piece "surveyed the mixed assembly" with "heavy, haughty grandeur" before formally admitting the half-farthing and other coins "according to their rank." The rest of the assembly devolved into a heated exchange sparked by the sovereign's back-handed compliment of "his noble and ancient friend the Guinea, and those other elder coins who, though practically useless," were still "gold coins in their own right"; the guinea spluttered that although sovereigns were "very useful in trading and commercial affairs," he remained the preferred coin of philanthropists and professional men. When the sovereign made things worse by complaining that such people would not accept him without "a vulgar shabby shilling clapped to his back," the penny came to the "middle class" shilling's defense, eventually prompting the sovereign to apologize to shilling and guinea alike. The meeting concluded with guinea and sovereign exchanging "the yellowest looks of confidence and friendship."[1]

This colloquy indicates one of the many ways guineas and sovereigns, in concert with coins composed of allegedly inferior metals, reflected and contributed to British class distinctions. Although this process persisted throughout the century after 1750, its tone shifted depending on political context and on the markedly varying availability of coins that circulated during different stretches of time. Three pivotal moments highlight this dynamic: the recoinage of gold guineas in 1773–1776, which ended a counterfeiting crisis; the new coinage of gold sovereigns and token silver coins in 1816–1821, following two wartime decades in which paper had all but replaced guineas; and a second recoinage of gold in 1842–1844. The first recoinage was noteworthy for its failure to address an ongoing shortage of silver—privileging those wealthy enough to circulate guineas over the much larger mass that resorted to token coins on the frequent occasions when legal-weight silver was not available. The postwar coinage solved the shortage of silver by tokenizing it; at the same time, it enshrined the gold standard in the tangible form of circulating sovereigns—which, ironically, were initially composed almost entirely of melted-down continental coins. The recoinage in 1842–1844, finally, drew attention to subtle class distinctions that had remained after 1816 despite the new availability of small change.

Across these different generations of gold coins, one constant concerned the fraught division of responsibility between the state and its subjects regarding their bullion content. In theory, the whole reason gold was superior to barter was that it bore the state's stamp, confirming a specific weight and fineness. Although the Mint assiduously assayed and weighed every batch of coins it produced, only a small segment of the population consistently attended to their weight after they entered circulation. Most people treated coins as representatives of value, not—as they were designed—small packages of bullion. In the years leading up to the 1773 recoinage, this fostered abuse at the hands of clippers and filers; during the sovereign's early years it fostered neglect, followed by confusion and panic when it became known that friction had reduced a third of them slightly below their legal weight.

The Business of Weighing

Nearly all accounts that traced commercial exchange from barter to the precious metals culminated in coinage. Since, as Adam Smith wrote, "a small difference in the quantity makes a great difference in the value" where such metals were concerned, "the business of weighing" loomed large in establishing sufficient trust for them to measure the value of other commodities—and weighing gold, the most precious of all, was "an operation of some nicety." Additionally, the "still more difficult . . . operation of assaying" was needed to guard against "the grossest frauds and impositions": specifically, mixing an inferior metal in with its gold or silver cousins. To relieve people of the need to weigh and assay every lump of metal they received in exchange for goods, the state stepped in "to affix a publick stamp upon certain quantities of such particular metals" through "those publick offices called mints." With this account of "the origin of coined money," Smith concluded his story about money's capacity to "facilitate exchanges, and thereby to encourage all sorts of industry and commerce."[2]

As with the case of value more generally, Smith's origin story of coins has survived into the present day,[3] and ethnographic embellishments started to appear in its immediate wake. The Orientalist Thomas Maurice wrote in 1800 that before the invention of coins, the merchant would "carry a certain portion of gold or silver into the market, and, having previously furnished himself with proper instruments and scales, he cut off and weighed out . . . as many pieces as were proportioned to the purchase of it"; he noted that this process, occasioning "great inconvenience and delay," was "still practiced in China." Accounts of Africa routinely included descriptions of indigenes weighing gold "in small balances" in lieu of coin, typically accompanied by fraud. And nineteenth-century commentators smugly looked back on earlier times in England, when "most people carried Gold scales in their pockets, to weigh Gold on all occasions."[4]

This origin story did not, however, end with the establishment of mints. The quantity of gold in all coins inexorably fell below its stamped value through the process of friction; and "frauds and impositions" persisted—especially, in the case of British gold, during the mid-eighteenth century, when loss by friction reached the point that clipped coins blended in with counterparts that were nearly as light. (A final source of disparity between a coin's nominal and actual weight, debasement, had ceased to be an issue, at least in Britain, by 1600.)[5] Fraud and friction both insured that the state never monopolized the business of weighing gold. For the most part, even severely underweight gold circulated freely until it reached the Bank of England or a tax collector, but during outbreaks of clipping, or when the state issued proclamations to call in light coin, the demand for weights and scales extended much farther into the community.

Before guineas made their way in the world, the Royal Mint assayed and cut them into stamped pieces weighing five pennyweights and nine grains each (0.27 troy ounces, or 8.4 grams), and comprised of twenty-two parts (or carats) gold and two parts silver-copper alloy.[6] Members of the Goldsmith's Company in London or its provincial counterparts were authorized to confirm the fineness of gold used in watches, plate, and snuff boxes, but the Mint alone determined that quality in coins.[7] To do so, its Assay Master combined a sample of alloyed gold (received either from the Bank of England or from private bullion traders) with lead in a porous pot known as a cupel, then heated it in a furnace. This had the effect of oxidizing "copper, tin, and the other cheaper metals" and leaving only precious metals behind; to remove silver or platinum, assayers reheated the mix in combination with nitric acid and mercury. From there, they added enough alloy to achieve the legal standard of fineness, passed the mix on to the weigher to be divided into lumps of legal weight, then to the moneyer to be converted into coins.[8]

The Mint's careful task of assaying and weighing gold resonated deeply in a culture that was steeped in biblical references to "gold tried in the fire" as a wide-ranging metaphor for salvation, martyrdom, and affliction.[9] Clergymen of all denominations compared their congregants to refined gold in order to admonish them, but also to assure them that God, as a divine assayer, knew exactly when to reduce the heat. Once purified and assayed, the good Christian was ready to enter into circulation—implying an additional role for God, as moneyer as well as assayer. Welsh preacher Christmas Evans compared the

ASSAY. 69

B B B B, *fig.* 59, is a perpendicular section of *fig.* 58; *a a*, end view of the rollers; *b* the ash-pit; *c* one of the ash-pit dampers; *d* the grate, over which is the plate upon which the muffle rests, and which is covered with loam nearly one inch thick; *f* the muffle in section representing the situation of the cupels; *g* the mouth-plate, and upon it are laid pieces of charcoal, which during the process are ignited, and heat the air that is allowed to pass over the cupels, as will be more fully explained in the sequel; *h* the interior of the furnace, exhibiting the fuel.

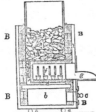

The total height of the furnace is 2 feet 6½ inches; from the bottom to the grate, 6 inches; the grate, muffle, plate, and bed of loam, with which it is covered, 3 inches; from the upper surface of the grate to the commencement of the funnel *e*, *fig.* 58, 21½ inches; the funnel *e*, 6 inches. The square of the furnace which receives the muffle and fuel is 11¾ inches by 15 inches. The external sides of the furnace are made of plates of wrought iron, and are lined with a 2-inch fire-brick.

c c c c, *fig.* 60, is a horizontal section of the furnace over the grate, showing the width of the mouth-piece, or plate of wrought iron, which is 6 inches, and the opening which receives the muffle-plate.

Fig. 61, represents the muffle or pot, which is 12 inches long, 6 inches broad inside; in the clear 6¾ : In height 4½ inside measure, and nearly 5½ in the clear.

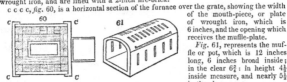

Fig. 62, the muffle-plate, which is of the same size as the bottom of the muffle.

Fig. 63, is a representation of the sliding-door of the mouth-plate, as shown at *d*, in *fig.* 58.

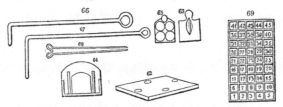

Fig. 64, a front view of the mouth-plate or piece, *d*, *fig.* 58.

Fig. 65, a representation of the mode of making, or shutting up with pieces of charcoal, the mouth of the furnace.

Fig. 66, the teaser for cleaning the grate.

Fig. 67, a larger teaser, which is introduced at the top of the furnace, for keeping a complete supply of charcoal around the muffle.

Fig. 68, the tongs used for charging the assays into the cups.

Fig. 69, represents a board of wood used as a register, and is divided into 45 equal compartments, upon which the assays are placed previously to their being introduced into the furnace. When the operation is performed, the cupels are placed in the furnace in situations corresponding to these assays on the board. By these means all confusion is avoided, and without this regularity it would be impossible to preserve the accuracy which the delicate operations of the assayer require.

Figure 5.1 "The furnace and implements used for assaying in the Royal Mint and the Goldsmiths' Hall, in the city of London." Andrew Ure, *A Dictionary of Arts, Manufactures, and Mines,* 63. General Research Division, New York Public Library.

law-abiding Christian to a coin "of pure gold; full measure, and full weight, and bearing the right and lawful stamp," and a popular pamphlet (first issued during the recoinage of 1774, then reprinted three decades later) featured a divine official who weighed people's "religious Coin" with "the Hydrostatic Balance" to prove their "Sterling Value."[10]

The task of stamping the nation's gold received added symbolic weight in the "trial of the pyx," which the British state staged in a converted chapel in the Westminster Abbey Cloisters. With every new coinage, twelve of London's most established goldsmiths joined the Master of the Mint and assorted politicians to confirm that a random sample of coins had come within a "remedy" of forty grains to the pound and within a sixth of a carat of the legal standard, "agreeable . . . to the standard trial plates kept in the Exchequer." After receiving their charge from the Lord Chancellor, the goldsmiths melted the gold in a purpose-built furnace at the Exchequer's office, occupying "nearly the whole of the day," followed by a feast at Goldsmiths' Hall.[11] Sixty-two goldsmiths served on fifteen such juries between 1817 and 1851, weighing anywhere from 349 to 15,476 gold coins against the standard weight and assaying between sixteen and 163 against the standard fineness. Well into the nineteenth century, they compared coins to lopped-off pieces of plate that had first been used in 1688, which had shrunk after multiple trials; the Goldsmith's Company produced a new test plate in 1830, with smaller replicas to be used in eight provincial towns.[12]

Estimates of loss to gold coins by friction ranged between three and four grains over the course of a century, or six to eight pence in the pound.[13] Many guineas diminished much more rapidly, however, such that some circulated in the 1760s that were as much as nine grains underweight—despite the fact that in 1733 the Treasury had called in all gold minted prior to 1660. Most people attributed the additional loss to clipping, which had spread from small change to gold after 1700. For decades, the state's only defense against this crime was the threat of the noose, operating in conjunction with an extensive network of informers and other Mint-employed "coin catchers." By the 1760s this had become a losing battle, especially in Yorkshire, where a perennial guinea shortage yielded a thriving "yellow trade" based in Halifax. Conviction rates, which had never been robust, were even lower in Halifax, where juries either supported the trade, feared retribution, or both.[14]

Shopkeepers and bankers who wanted to guard against clipped coins by weighing them faced an uphill battle until 1774, when Parliament ordered the Mint to certify all "just and true" weights and when new folding scales significantly improved ease of use and accuracy. The new models, which came with brass weights that slid along a beam in order to exhibit the extent to which a coin was deficient, were easily accessible to shopkeepers who only needed to weigh a guinea at a time.[15] Bankers and revenue officers, who might receive thousands in a single day, had more trouble identifying light coins with the machines available to them. The Bank of England, for instance, regularly faced complaints that coins paid out by one office were refused by another down the hall as underweight. This situation improved after 1842, when William Cotton, the Bank's Deputy Governor, commissioned the construction of an "automaton balance" invented by one of his tellers, which was nearly four times faster (at sixty coins per minute) and much more accurate than its manually-operated predecessor.[16]

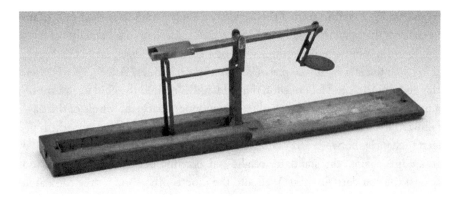

Figure 5.2 Pocket Coin Balance, constructed by A. W. Wilkinson, Ormskirk, 18th Century. Inv. 43149 © Museum of the History of Science, University of Oxford.

The other defense against light coin was to build a better guinea. As of 1774, the Mint was a century into adding milled edges to coins, which made it easier to detect fake or clipped coins. But as Lord North lamented that year, "the Art of milling. . . having got into the Hands of the Diminishers," that no longer offered much protection.[17] After 1797, when the suspension of cash payments brought the Mint's coining duties to a standstill, its officers used their free time (as Board of Trade official William Jacob stated) "in investigations and experiments to improve the fabrication of money"—and specifically to make coins "less subject to loss by abrasion." To achieve this, a Parliamentary committee called on the chemists Henry Cavendish and Charles Hatchett, who worked with an engineer to run experiments on a machine in which coins "were made to rub against each other for a considerable time." Although they confirmed that the alloy in the existing guinea was the most durable on offer, some of their ancillary recommendations did inform the design of a new mint, which opened in 1811.[18]

Restoring Guineas, 1773–1816

In his *Remarks on the Coinage of England* (1789), Nottingham hosier Walter Merrey credited the English with being "wise in the management of gold," but added: "in their management of the most useful and necessary part of money, namely their change, they are nearly as bad as the dealers in cowries." Subsequent writers confirmed Merrey's point that the recoinage that had transpired fifteen years earlier had endowed "the old English guinea" with "a preference and facility in circulation beyond that of any coin of any other realm."[19] Numerous critics also censured the government for failing to do anything about silver. The numismatist John Pinkerton complained in 1784 that "much greater wisdom would be shewn in giving us good silver" than in spending so much time and money on gold; a later writer recalled that it had been "an error of judgment that the reformation had not commenced with the silver: that of the gold only benefiting the wealthy part of his Majesty's subjects."[20]

The eighteenth-century ascendance of gold in Britain is clear enough from an overview of its coinage between 1603 and 1809. Through 1701, the Mint annually issued £160,677 worth of gold and £247,618 in silver; during the next 108 years, annual gold output ballooned to £822,726, as opposed to an anemic £8432 in silver.[21] Partly this was due to the ready availability of Brazilian gold, but mainly it was the result of Isaac Newton's readjustment of the relative mint price of gold and silver in 1717. Historians have traced this uniquely English bias against small change back to medieval times,[22] and Merrey provided numerous illustrations of the inconvenience occasioned by the perennial shortage of silver in his own day. Workmen, he noted, "lose hours every week in seeking change," while their employers were "obliged to apply to a baker, or publican weekly for a little change to pay their workmen." He also identified the aristocratic blinders that lay at the heart of Parliament's sin of omission: "If a rich man sends a guinea to change to a tradesman, efforts will be used to oblige him, hence he knows but little of what the poor suffer on this account."[23]

Considered in isolation from its inaction in the matter of small change, the state's recoinage of gold between 1773 and 1776 was much needed, relatively liberal, and well designed to put an end to what had become a full-blown clipping crisis. With no debate in Parliament, Lord North's ministry convinced George III to issue a proclamation in July 1773 calling in all guineas that had suffered weight loss "with a reasonable allowance for . . . wear"; in practice, the only coins cut by the Bank of England were those that fell below their original weight by at least six grains, or close to a shilling shy of twenty-one. By December the Mint received £3.7 million worth of guineas, around a fifth of those in circulation, which on average were nearly four shillings below their legal weight. Two more proclamations followed, in 1774 (targeting coins that were deficient by three to six grains) and 1776 (one to three grains), which called in another £11.9 million.[24]

Although it succeeded at attracting excessively light guineas to the Bank, the initial phase of the "Gold Act" was not above criticism. The most persistent related to the alleged injustice of making holders of coins pay the difference between their bullion and face value. As one correspondent complained, "the *guilty* escape unpunished after having made their market, and I, *who am innocent*, am *cruelly* and *unjustly* deprived of my property without any compensation being made me for my loss!" (North, for his part, argued that anyone holding a guinea more than a shilling short of its legal weight was either guilty of "Knavery or Neglect.") A similar complaint concerned the Bank of England's policy limiting its payment for bullion content to batches of fifty or more guineas. This forced "poor labourers and handycraftsmen," who received a lone guinea as their weekly wage, to resort to goldsmiths and refiners, who often charged an extra shilling or two for the service.[25] The law's apparent success at inhibiting fraud met with more approval. "The clippers and sweaters are already at a stand," reported the *Morning Chronicle* in early August of 1773, "and those who used to work under ground about Halifax. . . are now come up to look about them, and find more honest employment."[26]

When North resumed recoinage in May 1774, he addressed the two main complaints—the loss falling on "innocent" holders of coin and lack of access to honest bullion brokers—in one blow. In the next culling of light gold, he compensated holders "by delivering in Return others of full Weight" and appointed "proper persons for the collecting of light gold coin" (usually goldsmiths) who worked on commission in several towns. This approach did not come cheap: £72,476 for the exchangers and an additional £317,314 for the difference in weight—more than what so-called knaves had paid in 1773.[27] On top of that were suspiciously substantial Mint charges: £115,460, including "very large profits" for its Master, Lord Cadogen, and his various moneyers—prompting Edmund Burke to propose its abolition in 1780.[28]

The new guineas worked their magic almost immediately: a persistent gap between the bullion and mint prices of gold dwindled to nothing, while the Bank of England saw its shares boom in value.[29] Clipping diminished, though it did not completely disappear.[30] A larger source of light coins after 1774 would be the influx of guineas that found their way back to Britain following the American Revolution.[31] The official response to the remaining light gold was to remind people of their duty to weigh coins and to replace those that came up short. A proclamation in 1787 urged "all persons to break and deface any gold coin wanting in weight" and the Bank of England told its customers in 1799 "invariably to weigh the Gold Coin which may be offered to them in payment."[32] The Mint, for its part, coined £15.4 million from recalled guineas between 1776 and 1798, around £6 million of which it estimated had come from the United States—nearly equaling its efforts during the original recoinage of 1773–1776.[33]

To Charles Jenkinson, commenting in 1805 on the perpetual weighing and recoining that had prevailed since 1776, this was all according to plan: the continued vigilance against light guineas had kept the coinage "at nearly the state of perfection to which it was then brought." His only regret was that the state had not been more diligent in reminding the public of its duty; as a result, "the practice of weighing Coins," which had "prevailed universally" during the decade after 1774, had "been very much discontinued." Rogers Ruding, writing in 1819 and with an eye on Adam Smith's distinction between coins from lumps of gold, begged to differ. That approach, he argued, was "in direct opposition to the true principles of Coinage, and ... reduced the Money, in a great degree, to the State of Bullion after a considerable expense had been incurred in order to give it a character totally distinct."[34]

During the decade after Jenkinson published his *Treatise on the Coins of the Realm* the point became moot, since there were practically no guineas left to weigh. The Mint only issued guineas in one year between 1800 and 1815, although it did coin half-guineas and seven-shilling pieces worth an annual average of £268,814. Mainly, though, £1 and £2 notes replaced gold: the Bank of England kept around £1.5 million in circulation starting in 1798, creeping up to £9.7 million by 1814—and private bankers followed suit with notes of their own.[35] In 1802 the economist Henry Thornton claimed that guineas had "disappeared ... to a material degree," and by 1816 it was estimated that all but 500,000 had left the country.[36] Although pound notes offered ample compensation for the missing guineas in most cases (more than ample, many argued), the persistent problem of small change grew even worse during the war years. As goldsmith Benjamin Smart observed in 1811, the lack of silver had forced Britons to avail themselves of "the tolerated expedients of honest men," including tradesmen's tokens and five-shilling notes.[37]

Forging a New Coinage, 1816–1842

On October 17, 1820, Nathan Rothschild received a consignment of gold coins from the De Jonge house in Amsterdam containing 2136 Napoleons, 2022 Frederic d'ors, 240 Louis d'ors, and a few Dutch ducats, totaling 2046 ounces once he melted them down into twelve bars. He sent these, containing gold that had been coined in France, Prussia, and the Netherlands, directly to the Mint to be turned into new sovereigns and stamped with the bust of George IV.[38] Although the specific source of the coins in this case was exceptional (most of Rothschild's gold came from his brother in Paris), as was the delivery (usually he sent his gold to the Bank of England, which relayed them to the Mint), this one instance provides a unique example of what went into the millions of sovereigns that were coined in 1820 and 1821. Like modern Euros, these early sovereigns bore traces of multiple nations—although these were inside, melted and remolded into new British coins, instead of gracing a map on the front.

In contrast to the recoinage of gold in 1774, which called in light gold to be brought up to its legal weight, the Coinage Act of 1816 replaced paper with gold—and since gold coins had almost entirely vanished from Britain, this needed to be purchased from other European countries. It also introduced a new gold coin, called the sovereign, which (weighing five pennyweights and three grains, and valued at twenty shillings) succeeded the slightly heavier guinea.[39]

Another difference from the earlier coinage was a hiccup in its roll-out: after issuing a first run of more than £7 million worth of sovereigns through January 1819, the Mint abruptly shut down this operation when it became clear that the rising price of gold bullion—it increased from £3 19s 11d per ounce in 1816 to £4 2s in 1818, or 5 percent higher than the mint price—had led many to be melted down and shipped abroad.[40] Once the price fell back down it resumed operations in earnest in late 1820. In 1821 and 1822 it issued £14.8 million worth of new sovereigns, a burst that would not be matched until 1854–1855 in the wake of the Australian gold rush.[41]

Accounts from the Bank of England and Rothschild enable a partial reckoning of where this gold originated. The Bank purchased coins directly from Europe as well as ingots that bullion brokers had imported or melted down from such coins. Although it also used other brokers, Rothschild supplied 69 percent of the £3.2 million in "foreign bar gold" it received in 1816 and 52 percent of the £10.7 million it received in 1820–1821 (he sent another £600,000 directly to the Mint in 1820). During those three years, nearly 60 percent of the gold collected by Rothschild had been issued in France and flowed through his brother James's Paris agency; Spanish doubloons, ducats, and Frederic d'ors comprised most of the rest, mainly from assorted Hamburg and Amsterdam merchants.[42] The Bank drew on a wider array of foreign suppliers, resulting in a greater diversity of coins: between 1815 and 1817 this included Portuguese *moidras* (£1.5 million), Napoleons (£1.3 million), Spanish doubloons (£241,503), and Frederic d'ors (£202,701).[43] Such was the promiscuous pedigree of gold that many of these coins were themselves recycled guineas—the banker Joseph Marryat remarked in 1816 that "the amount of English guineas melted down in the mint of France" in recent years had been "immense"—and many sovereigns minted between 1817 and 1819 were in turn rapidly reincarnated as European coins, then converted back into sovereigns two years later.[44]

The decision to call the new coin a sovereign, and for it to pass at twenty shillings instead of the guinea's face value of 21s, had everything to do with the recently concluded war against France. Life without guineas had meant life with pound notes, worth twenty shillings each, as the "current medium." As a result, when Lord Liverpool and the Master of the Mint, William Wellesley Pole, tried to retain the guinea in 1816 (based mainly on traditionalism and a concern that a change would "create . . . confusion in our mercantile transactions abroad"), the reaction was uniformly hostile. One *Times* correspondent accused Liverpool of "adhering, for the mere sake of antiquity, to a barbarous and troublesome denomination," and praised the "golden pound" for its "decimal facility." Indeed, the Admiralty Secretary John Croker, who pointed out that "perpetually resorting to fractions" would still be a fact of life with sovereigns, urged that the time was ripe for "giving all the parts of our circulating medium a decimal relation to each other," following "the example set us by the French."[45]

In its very name, the sovereign offered a constant reminder of Britain's defeat of Napoleon. At the trial of the pyx in 1822 Lord Eldon directed the goldsmiths' attention to "the superscription of a gracious Monarch upon the coins submitted to your trial, and not that of a tyrant, reigning over subjects little better than slaves"; the following year he asserted that the sovereign was "taken with the greatest confidence all over the world."[46] Although his latter assurance was unwarranted—as late as 1842, a visitor to Salzburg complained that a money changer there "could comprehend neither my language nor my money"—it was also mostly irrelevant since most travelers by the 1820s had switched from using gold to using circular notes, an early version of travelers' checks.[47] In England (but not Scotland and Ireland, where sovereigns were as rare as guineas before them), early users greeted the new name with bemused acceptance, although some did wonder why the coins were not called "Georges" in the manner of Louis d'ors and Fredericks on the continent.[48]

After its false start in 1817, Parliament timed the sovereign's rollout in 1821 to coincide with the resumption of cash payments at the Bank of England. As the *Times* reported the day after resumption commenced, bankers who normally received one-pound notes from the Bank "received sovereigns only," rendering their diffusion "almost instantaneous." The same week the Bank sent gold coins "on a most extensive scale" to provincial towns and also dispatched inspectors to help bankers there "detect the forged notes that will probably on this occasion be presented." Eight years later, after Parliament passed a new law forbidding English private banks from issuing their own one-pound notes, the Bank again took steps to insure that the country would be "'irrigated' with gold" to meet the demand.[49] The large majority of the new sovereigns and half-sovereigns circulated: on average, the Bank of England held only £4.8 million of them in its vaults (as well as £3.7 million in gold bullion), around a tenth of Britain's supply. Although the Mint did also issue double sovereigns and five-pound pieces, these were "only coined in small numbers, and principally issued among collectors."[50]

If the new sovereign represented a clear contrast with the recycled guineas of the 1770s, an even more significant difference was that this time, following Jenkinson's advice, Britain started with silver: specifically, a token silver coinage that weighed 6 percent less than its face value. As economist Angela Redish has persuasively argued, this policy "accomplished the objective of concurrent circulation of high- and low-denomination coins" without reference to the relative market value of gold and silver. It did this by removing the temptation to melt down silver for export, since the price of the coins exceeded their bullion value. New technology, which among other things girded the shillings with steel collars, enabled the Mint to stamp token coins that were less prone to being counterfeited; and a well-organized state-subsidized campaign exchanged £2.6 million worth of them for the underweight and often barely legible shillings and crowns that circulated as of 1816.[51]

Although a plentiful silver coinage greatly benefited working men and women, it also sharpened class distinctions among gold, silver and copper, in a sense that paralleled the emerging division of railway travelers into first, second, and third-class carriages.[52] In sheer numbers, less-valuable coins circulated more widely: between 1826 and 1841, the Mint produced 59.5 million copper coins and 64.7 million silver, compared to 29.8 million gold.[53] An expansive vocabulary accompanied this newfound profusion: one slang dictionary listed no less than seventeen terms for sixpence (including *kick*, *cripple*, and *tizzy*) and eleven for shillings (*breaky-leg*, *stag*, and *twelver*, as well as *bob*). Sovereigns, in contrast, made do with the unassuming quintet of *canaries*, *counters*, *gold finches*, *thick-uns*, and *yellow-boys*. At the bottom of the coinage scale, some commentators wondered if the smallest denominations were even necessary. Thomas Hood acknowledged that coins such as the half-farthing might make sense in "a cheap country" such as France or Belgium—"but in England, dear England, what is there that one can purchase for such a mite?"[54]

Just as class was never a stable category in Britain, however, neither was its numismatic manifestation. With a rising standard of living and an increased reliance on paper money, sovereigns came to represent a distinctly mercantile currency. As one MP pointed out in 1842, "payments of the rich were made chiefly in bank notes, and by checks on the banker," while sovereigns resided in the pockets and cash boxes of "those engaged in petty retail business" and (evanescently) the millions of workers who received weekly wages in the form of one or two gold coins.[55] Guineas, for their part, held on as grandiose ghosts: as denominations, if not as actual coins, they continued to be used throughout the nineteenth century, most often in calculating professional fees.[56] As the *Penny Magazine* quipped in 1835: "Our old coin . . . has bodily disappeared, but still lives in the fee of the lawyer and physician, in the lists of charitable subscriptions, and on all occasions when five per cent can be slily added to the value of the sovereign, under the guise of its being more handsome and genteel than the vulgar pound." Doctors routinely charged a guinea per visit, and lawyers were even more tenacious in retaining their traditional fee.[57]

Old Bailey trials yield a snapshot of the sort of people who possessed sovereigns just prior to having them stolen. 1827 offered an especially rich harvest of thefts, with 147 tried cases (compared to an average of 107 between 1822 and 1835), of which 87 indicate the victim's occupation. Of these, only three were professional men (a solicitor, a surgeon, and an accountant); thirty pursued a wide variety of trades, including butchers, bakers, grocers, milliners, publicans, and shopkeepers (these people typically lost their gold on the shop floor, often to employees); another fifty were wage laborers (predominantly sailors and servants); and four were pensioners. Most sailors lost their gold at the pub or in the company of a prostitute, shortly after receiving it as wages. Many others lost their sovereigns from locked boxes, desks, or under mattresses—suggesting a lack of banking facilities—or from their pockets as they arrived in London seeking work.[58]

A final sense in which sovereigns at least sometimes took on a uniquely middle-class or working-class connotation concerned bank runs. Although bank runs dated back to the 1760s, Irish nationalism, the Reform Act, and Chartism provided political variants after 1830. In January 1831, Daniel O'Connell added to the momentum of his anti-Unionist movement in the wake of Catholic Emancipation by orchestrating a run on the Bank of Ireland, blanketing Dublin with notices reading "Gold for Rags."[59] On May 12, 1832, as the Reform Bill awaited approval by the House of Lords, the National Political Union urged "every man who had a 5*l.* note to turn it into gold, and hoard it till the charter of the people's liberties was won"; the ensuing run drained the Bank of England of more than £1.6 million in gold, around a third of its supply.[60] A decade later, Chartists transposed this middle-class refrain into a working-class key. An American visitor to Manchester during a Chartist general strike in 1842 noticed placards that connected the seizure of sovereignty with the seizure of sovereigns: "Run, middle-class men, trades, Odd Fellows, sick clubs, and money clubs, to the saving's-banks and all banks, for gold! gold! gold!"[61]

The "Gold Panic" of 1842

For all the apparent success of the coinage of sovereigns and token silver between 1816 and 1821, one thing the new coinage regime distinctly failed to do was to settle on who was responsible for guaranteeing that the face value of gold coins accurately represented their bullion content. Initially, the idea was to retain Lord North's original goal of rendering users as vigilant as possible through repeated reminders of the sovereign's legal weight. In 1820 the Mint tried to make the task of weighing coins easier by reducing the legal weight by a quarter grain—conceding that weighing within the previous margin was "almost impracticable in the common traffic of the public." New royal proclamations issued in February and March of 1821, prior to the resumption of cash payments, reminded the public that sovereigns under 5 pennyweight 2.5 grains "shall not pass current" and that only weights stamped by the Mint could be used to reject such coins.[62]

These were the last such proclamations to be issued for more than two decades, however—and an 1829 ruling by James Scarlett, the Attorney General, which barred "cutting . . . light sovereigns offered in payment," further worked against regularly calling in underweight coin. This ruling, which exempted "intention to defraud," was formally consistent with North's coinage regime, since it added that holders could claim "the real value of the gold" in coins that had become light through friction. In practice, though, both the Bank of England and tax collectors interpreted it to mean that light gold should be refused in payment but not withdrawn from circulation.[63] Meanwhile, the proportion of underweight gold coins steadily rose: the Bank rejected £7.4 million out of £36 million between 1837 and 1840 as below the legal weight. Although reports of clipping or sweating did occasionally appear after 1821, the Bank's tally of light sovereigns suggested wear as the likeliest cause; most predated 1823, and most were short by just a penny or two—well within the probable effects of friction.[64]

The result was that by 1842, the British money market faced a peculiar sort of crisis: around a third of its circulating coin was no longer legal tender, but not by all that much. The major sufferers were banks, which sat on large stocks of sovereigns that they could not pass along to the Bank of England; others included the many middle-class holders who tried to pay excise or custom taxes in gold or tried to deposit their coins directly with the Bank. In April the *Times* reported "much disappointment" among London bankers at the Treasury's inaction, which had resulted in "a large portion of their funds" being "unprofitably locked up"; to this end they joined the Bank of England director John Horsley Palmer in petitioning the Treasury "to authorise the Bank to clip all sovereigns presented, which power was formerly possessed in the case of guineas, and at the same time, to sanction the receipt of such light coin for account of the Mint at the standard price of 3l. 17s. 10½d. per oz."[65]

In June 1842, a royal proclamation announced that "great quantities of the gold coin of this realm deficient in weight are now in circulation, contrary to the tenor of two proclamations issued" in 1817 and 1821, and blamed this on "due attention . . . not [being] paid to the weighing of the said gold coin." As Palmer had hoped, this effectively reversed Scarlett's ruling by mandating the destruction of all light coin. Although that might have been music to London bankers' ears, it "created a considerable sensation in the city," as *The Times* reported two days after its issue. Many aspects of the ensuing controversy, which extended into 1844, closely paralleled the points of contention in 1773, with complaints about "holders . . . suddenly having their sovereigns reduced from the nominal to the bullion value" and about the Bank of England's inaccessibility to lower-class consumers.[66] Unlike the earlier recoinage, and somewhat surprisingly given the rising tide of democratic sentiment in Britain, neither Robert Peel's ministry nor the Bank made much effort to change course during a second phase in 1843.

The Bank prepared for the recoinage in 1842 in precisely the same fashion as it had in 1773, ordering tellers to exchange light sovereigns for their bullion value but only in sums exceeding fifty coins. After a volley of protests, it reduced the minimum to twenty within two weeks—but then shut down this service altogether in early July, "as the Rotunda [was] required for the payment of dividends" to its shareholders.[67] As numerous critics noted, this created a double standard whereby large businesses could count on full reimbursement for the gold in their coins, while "small tradesmen and others of the humbler classes" (many more of whom possessed gold coins in 1842) had to get what they could from "bullion dealers, pawnbrokers, and Jews." During the week after the proclamation, workers paid up to two shillings in order to change their sovereigns if they could find anyone to change them at all—although this did drop to a few pence within a month. In Parliament, Joseph Hume asked Peel why he had not "sent into every town in England . . . a public officer for the purpose of exchanging sovereigns under-weight," as North's ministry had done in 1774.[68]

Making matters worse, employers who sought to pay their workers in silver until the "gold panic" had passed quickly depleted the Bank's shilling supply, and efforts to restock were delayed by an exceptional foreign demand to fund wars in China and Afghanistan. A different shortage unfolded at the Mint, where tellers could not keep up with the demand for stamped money weights. To their credit, the Bank and the Mint amassed a larger supply of shillings ahead of the second recall, but in all other regards the same policies and accompanying complaints persisted.[69] Peel's Chancellor of the Exchequer, Henry Goulburn, responded to such complaints by fatalistically lamenting that the "lowest orders in society" always fared worse in these cases "because they were the most easily deceived by those disposed to make a profit of their ignorance." When asked why the state did not pay for the difference between the sovereigns' nominal and bullion value, Peel worried (without citing any evidence) that coiners would use this policy to create a revolving door of newly filed coins—resulting, he warned, in "a profligate loss" to the state.[70]

The one thing almost nobody complained of during the recoinage of 1842–1844 was the Royal Mint. It issued as many as 300,000 sovereigns per week (over four times the weekly average in the 1770s), and £14 million worth of sovereigns and half-sovereigns in all, at a cost (£67,861) of 60% of the Mint charge in the 1770s.[71] On the debit side, Peel's ministry emerged with little sense of how to keep from landing in the same predicament a few decades later. Goulburn's only long-term solution for friction in 1842 repeated Lord North's original plan: "clear intimations in future from time to time of the state of the law upon the subject, thereby calling the attention of the public to the necessity of weighing coins." The shortcomings of this approach became clear soon enough. By 1870 a third of all sovereigns once again circulated below their legal weight, and political inertia increased that proportion to well over half before Parliament finally approved a recoinage in 1893—this time with the margin between nominal and bullion value (£650,000) entirely paid for out of the public purse.[72]

Underlying the confusion surrounding the recoinage of gold in 1842 was a basic gap in understanding about who should be responsible for maintaining Britain's coinage at its legal weight. On one side stood Peel's ministry, which blamed the crisis on insufficient attention being paid to "weighing of the . . . gold coin." On the other stood a "Constant Reader" of *The Times*, who protested (echoing Rogers Ruding a generation earlier):

> If we are to weigh every sovereign . . . we are thrown back into a state approaching that of barter—gold and silver may take the form of ingots, and the Mint be abolished as useless. I contend that every individual is justified in considering a sovereign bearing the effigy of his Queen as of the true value both in weight and purity, and that he ought not to be a sufferer from his faith.

At least as far as the expense of the recoinage was concerned, those who argued that it fell disproportionately on working people—an "encroachment on the property of the masses," as one critic claimed—were only half right.[73] The same bankers who had lobbied for recoinage also absorbed much of its cost, which was only partly offset by the luxury of handing over their stored-up light gold directly to the Bank. In that sense, the state-funded recoinage of 1884 would symbolize the increased power of the financial classes relative to the masses, not the reverse.[74]

As much as the sovereign ensured that gold entered into increasingly wide circulation after 1820, the perennial association of the metal with poison and power retained its stamp on British coinage as well—albeit always wishfully tempered by an ounce of charity. In a "Dialogue between a Guinea and a Half-Crown," published in 1805, the "humble born" silver coin rebukes his haughty counterpart: "you are the ready instrument of seduction! . . . The gambler hails you lord"; and brags on its own behalf: "I am moderately liked by all; disliked by none." A generation later, Peregrine Oakley concluded his *Life and Opinions of a Sovereign* by recapping the coin's reflection in "the greedy gaze of the miser," "the gloating eye of the libidinous," and "the careless glance of the giddy and thoughtless," before adding, as a comforting afterthought, "the mild and gentle eye of christian charity." To illustrate England's status as "a nation of gold-worshippers," Horace Smith pointed to "the jingling of sovereigns in the breeches-pocket of some warm, portly, and purseproud reader of Clapham Common."[75]

Yet gold coins had one distinct advantage over gold in its uncoined or metaphorical manifestations: the generally revered images, and associated institutions, that graced their faces. This was especially the case with the sovereign, which replaced the guinea's African associations with a thoroughly British signification. Sovereigns did not invariably command deference, any more than their human namesakes did: the wag who joked that George III's bust was "a leetle unsound and shakey" and George IV's was "a leetle gay, [which] took the gilt off his sovereign," was proof enough of that. What they did accomplish, however, was to temper critics of capitalism by suggesting royal restraint on an otherwise wayward moral economy. In a generally critical article on "cash, corn, and coal markets," a *Chambers's Edinburgh Journal* writer cited his "very strong partiality for notes of the governor and company of the Bank of England and sovereigns of full weight and fineness" as a reason for stopping short of denouncing the "debasing love of gold."[76]

Whether gold facilitated military payment, international trade, or domestic commerce, its role in class and political tensions only occasionally rose to the forefront of public debate or subsequent historical analysis. Gold was literally on the surface in its other primary function, which was to measure status through ornamenting people's houses, clothing, wrists, necks, and fingers. How gold operated as a status symbol depended on where, when, and how much people displayed it: before 1750, it signified the usually unobtainable cachet of upper-crust fashion, typically in imitation of the latest French decorations. After that norms altered, as the *nouveau riche* caught up to their aristocratic counterparts' consuming capacity and aristocrats refigured the ostentatious display of gold as a gauche failure to stay in style.

6

Distinction

"A 'squire' is the man for matrimony": this was Innes Hoole's advice to women in *Scenes at Brighton; or, "How Much?,"* a "satirical novel" published in 1821. To snare such a man, he continued, all that was needed was to praise "the elegance of the private gentleman's dress, compared with the frippery of gold lace, gold tags, gold spurs, & c.; and while he is shingling through his fingers the gold he may have in his pocket, launch out on the wisdom of keeping it there, instead of spreading it all over the body." The point of this pointer was to divert the attention of Brighton's maidens from the local squirearchy's chief competition: British soldiers, clad in a "mine of gold lace" and other "puppet-show pieces of ordnance."[1] Hoole's contrast between the tawdry soldier and the discreet country gentleman, who kept his gold concealed in the form of circulating coin, represented a break from the recent British past. A century earlier, gold lace (along with buckles, buttons, snuff boxes, chains, and embroidery) had been the norm for gentlemen in town and country alike, and military officers had struggled to keep pace.

This transition was largely the result of the rise of a third class of people, the *nouveau riches*, who possessed wealth but had few attachments to the soil. Their presence created a crisis of recognizability, whereby hierarchical social distinctions could no longer be easily discerned on the basis of external appearance. In previous centuries, the British aristocracy had countered the prospect of being indistinguishable from similarly-clad social inferiors by passing sumptuary laws, which precisely attached the privilege of wearing gold to one's social rank. By 1800, difficulty of enforcement and new economic views rendered such laws obsolete, and aristocrats responded by replacing their gold lace and embroidery with such ineffable cultural markers as taste and sentiment, which were harder to imitate precisely because ladies and gentlemen made these up as they went along.[2] The officers in Hoole's sketch, together with servants, monarchs, and mayors, occupied an exceptional position within this new sartorial order, in which wearing gold still meaningfully signified distinction, either because the wearers belonged to an enforceable hierarchy, because their ritual status transcended shifting social norms, or both.

None of this meant that the consumption of gold for non-monetary purposes suffered any decline in the century and a half after Queen Anne. Not only did the burgeoning class of parvenus persist in converting their guineas into gilded ornaments, but military demand for gold and silver lace during the Napoleonic Wars also contributed around £500,000 annually to London's economy.[3] Squires, meanwhile, invented newly inconspicuous ways to possess gold watches and plate, while aristocratic women continued to wear gold— albeit with a new emphasis on subtlety and decorum. Finally, there was the important presence, after 1810, of the Prince Regent, the future George IV, whose very public taste for gold absorbed much of the royal purse until his death in 1830 and inspired imitation by the upper echelons of the British aristocracy.

This chapter traces the varied uses of gold in Britain between 1780 and 1850 as signifiers of social distinction, through the adornment of people's bodies, sideboards, and rituals. It opens with the central tension between the consumption of decorative gold by all who could afford it and the consternation this caused landed elites who had long relied on gold as a status symbol. It also identifies a new set of cultural markers after 1750 that were designed to denigrate the continued wearing of gold. Those who deployed these markers, including fashion critics, novelists, and aristocrats of all stripes, either relegated the metal to tasteful margins, such as the fringes of women's apparel, or contrasted properly sentimental reasons for displaying it with sus- piciously mercenary motives pursued by the new rich. The new rules regarding decorative gold were also on display in snarky descriptions of "old school" aristocrats, who had not received the message that gold lace no longer meant what they thought it did.

This chapter further discusses those people who persisted in deploying gold as a means of displaying hierarchy, including military officers, livery servants, mayors, and members of the royal family. The first two of these cases appeared in response to recent historical changes. The vast expansion of Britain's navy, standing army, and militias after 1750 spearheaded a profusion of gold lace, while servants increasingly inherited the gold that their masters newly shunned. In each case adornment could, at least up to a point, be disciplined by a strict set of rules. Monarchs and mayors, in contrast, wore their gold as embellished archaisms, which proclaimed Britain's ambivalent relationship to its glittering past. And even these exceptions invited mounting criticism from moral and po- litical reformers during the decades after Waterloo, which in at least some cases reduced their glitter.

Distinctions: Sense and Sentimentality

In Mary Meeke's novel *The Sicilian* (1798), an Italian duke entertains two English guests: his distant cousin Mrs. Studeville and her friend Mr. Chambers, a wealthy London draper. The conversation soon fixes on "an immense gold chased watch" with a matching chain, which Mrs. Studeville has given to the duke. By way of attesting to its value, his cousin assures him that the watch "had been presented to an ancestor of Sir Roger de Courcy's on the field of battle" and had passed to her as a family heirloom. Chambers interjects that the chain is worth less than the watch, adding that "the two would not fetch less than thirty or five and thirty guineas, if they were knocked to pieces, and sold for old gold." Struggling to suppress his bemusement, the duke assures Mrs. Studeville that the watch's lineage made it "infinitely more valuable" and accepts the gift with as much grace as he can muster. Chambers, for his part, grumbles that he was merely assessing its "intrinsic worth," as he "should have done old plate, or any thing else out of fashion."[4]

This three-way skirmish over the value of a gold watch captures the confusion surrounding decorative gold in Britain at the end of the eighteenth century. Chambers's straightforward assessment of the watch's monetary value awkwardly appears, in the duke's drawing room, as a source of embarrassment or mirth. In contrast, Mrs. Studeville's alternate valuation drips with sentimentality—"My father generally wore it," she affirms—which only adds to her cousin's amusement.[5] The duke sits above the fray, in possession of enough taste to accept the gift with grace—but also enough left over to pass a more severe private judgment. The three characters in this scene represent three distinct strategies for dealing with decorative gold: the parvenu with his ledger-book, the genteel woman with her sentiment, and the nobleman with his exquisite sense of taste.

Two centuries earlier, British elites had tried to clarify such conundrums through sumptuary laws, which sought to prevent non-aristocrats from wearing cloth of gold along with silk, ermine, and jewelry—both to prevent "the subversion of good and politic order" that adornment by commoners might produce and to preserve the country's bullion supply. Parliament repealed the last such law in England in 1604, with Scotland following suit in 1673, though most historians agree that enforcement was minimal even when these laws were on the books.[6] By 1800, Britons tended to follow Daniel Defoe and David Hume in condemning such laws for interfering with the honest trade of goldsmiths and for targeting "the most innocent and inoffensive" of vices.[7] Despite this consensus, a crucial underlying premise of sumptuary laws—the notion that "dress . . . could create identity"—never fully disappeared. Indeed, an advice manual in 1781 waxed nostalgic for the days when "none but persons of quality . . . were allowed to wear gold," since without such restrictions "our vanity, that whimsical thing called *fashion*, bears such an imperious sway, that it often beats poor modesty out of doors."[8]

By most accounts, the consumption of decorative gold exploded in Britain after 1760: one writer in 1829 estimated a sixfold increase in "the quantity of gold consumed in manufacture" over the previous seventy years. In his 1831 survey of precious metals, William Jacob noted that "much chemical knowledge" had recently been applied to produce alloyed gold ornaments that enabled "the more numerous class, a little below the fashionable world, to rival their superiors in fashion, and with no danger of their inferiority being detected except by the very small number who are critical judges of the metals." As Jacob's comment implied, diffusion bred confusion. One writer complained in 1794 that adornment had "become so very arbitrary, that if we were to make it the criterion of rank or fortune, we should be liable to fifty errors a day"—citing the bankrupt linen draper who "takes out a gold snuff-box, informs us of the hour from a gold watch, and is in every respect so much the man of rank and fashion, that we are ready to bow down before him."[9]

Starting in the eighteenth century, elite Britons discovered numerous ways to distinguish themselves from such deceptive characters. Taste was the most prominent, and most complicated, variant on this theme. As historian Gerald Newman has observed, their early impulse was to turn to France to find the "proper bow, compliment, wig, or waistcoat . . . invisible as a thing apart but conferring value." Letters home from the grand tour before 1750 betrayed a scrupulous regard for lessons learned on exactly where and when to wear gold. By the mid-eighteenth century, Englishmen were starting to associate good taste with plain dress, in direct contrast to allegedly effeminate French tastes for decorative gold.[10] By 1800, according to one historian, "English dress sense lacked flair and panache," preferring instead "understatement [and] unobtrusiveness."[11] Etiquette guides permitted gold watch-guards, "but not festooning over the waistcoat," and urged that "if you have a gold chain to your watch, keep it, but the less you show of it the better."[12]

Tasteful women showed more of their gold, but generally took care to do so in moderation and only around the edges.[13] The hundreds of references in British fashion magazines to gold ear-rings, chains, tassels, fringe, trimming, bracelets, bands, and cords leave little doubt as to the presence of the precious metal on upper-class women's clothing between 1780 and 1850—but most insisted on its role in enhancing "elegance" or "tasteful contrast." Popular gold accessories included simulations of the natural world, such as acorns, sprigs, flowers, and ears of corn, and more generally gold often acted to tone down the effect of more splendid gems—most universally juxtaposed on wedding and engagement rings.[14] French fashion, in this context, acted as both model and foil. Gold-laden

Parisian costumes received London fashion editors' approval only if they were "well adapted to the chaste taste, good sense, and propriety . . . characteristic of our country-women."[15]

If British tastemakers retained ambivalence about French fashion, they took off their white gloves when they turned to the nouveau riches. Snide commentary on parvenu families exploded after 1780, especially in novels, and more often than not the focus was on female characters. Such was the case with Miss Twist, a fictional heiress to a tobacco fortune, who wore "an agate essence bottle set in gold" and three gold chains to her parents' frequent balls; and Thackeray's Mrs. Bumpsher, a wholesale stationer's wife whose "gold serpents" gave her the appearance of a display table in a jeweler's shop. In another novel, a newlywed's "high-born guests . . . looked at *her,* and her surrounding gold and silver," with "a sigh of regret that such excellent things should be so grievously thrown away upon persons who did not know how to use them."[16] The most visible variety of *nouveaux riches,* the "nabobinas," flaunted their South Asian wealth. Novels bristled with such characters as Lady Mango, who glittered "with gold and jewels, like the queen of Sheba at Bartholomew-fair" after marrying off her daughter to a Bengal merchant, and Miss Bullion, who "looked and moved like an enormous ingot of gold."[17]

When British taste-enforcers turned their attention from parvenus to "old-school" aristocrats, their tone turned from contempt to pity—the timing and tenor of which makes it possible to identify precisely when different items of decorative gold faded from fashion. John Sparling's gold-laced waistcoat and cocked hat marked him as "one of the last of the old school" of Liverpool merchants in the 1790s, and the narrator of *Uncle Tweazy and his Quizzical Neighbours* (1816) remarked on the "risibility" of his older relative's "low-crowned hat . . . bound with a narrow gold lace."[18] Gold buttons followed lace on its swift divorce from gentility after 1760. In various reports from the 1780s, they accompanied "an old-fashioned pompadour coat," a "not altogether modern" claret-colored jacket, and another coat belonging to "a careful old gentleman." Buckles fared no better: a character in an epistolary novel from 1794 described an old parishioner who fastened his shoes "with small gold buckles" as "looking as if he had just awoke from a nap, commenced in the reign of good *queen Anne!*"[19]

The most striking example of fast-fading decorative gold was the gold-headed cane, which persisted into the 1780s as an accessory for assorted gentlemen and ladies "of the old school."[20] Later accounts portrayed these canes as "an antiquated emblem," carried with guileless pride by the "old-gentlemanly Plodder," the "venerable old rector," and the "lady of the mansion" whose "decay and mouldering" could not conceal "a grace, a dignity, a softened fire."[21] The gold-headed cane's outmoded character achieved professional clarity in the case of British physicians, for whom it had conferred "the visible signs of the invisible knowledge" through much of the eighteenth century.[22] By the 1790s only "a few old, grave, solid, and solemn doctors" remained who sported this professional accessory, and by the 1830s it appeared only in Punch and Judy shows, costume balls, and "the Valley of Lost Fashions" in a fantasy novel set on the moon.[23] A medical journal hammered the final nail into its coffin in 1838 when it declared that the stethoscope "would prove . . . a more certain means of obtaining public confidence as a physician, than the gold-headed cane of Sydenham, Meade, or of any other of the medical sages of former times."[24]

As many of these examples make clear, good taste enabled Britons of means to despise the wearing of gold by others without forsaking the privilege of wearing it themselves. Although most parvenus were too busy trying to learn the tastemakers' rules to notice the hypocrisy of this stance, some Protestants were quick to condemn it. Borrowing from New Testament proscriptions, Methodists banned "putting on of gold or costly apparel" and Quakers argued that such ornaments served "only to amuse the thoughtlessness, and to gratify the vanity, of fallen man."[25] Other churchmen equivocated, as when a Cheapside Anglican counseled "a medium between the affected plainness of a Quaker, and the gawdy array of a *beau* or of a *belle*." Sterner Christians greeted such allowances with scorn: a temperance reformer asked the bishops assembled at Victoria's coronation if they had "been faithful in reminding the Queen and the peeresses" of Paul's advice not to wear "*gold, or pearls, or costly array*."[26]

A less divisive strategy for removing decorative gold from the realm of crass display was to attach sentimental value to such objects. People often endowed their gold snuff-boxes, watches and family plate with personal significance, claiming sympathy or romantic love rather than money as a measure of their worth.[27] Novels often featured gold watches as symbols of devotion, as when Thackeray's character Barry Lyndon compared his "first love" to his "first gold watch (an elegant French gold repeater)": "I used to go into corners, and contemplate and gloat over my treasure; and to take it to bed with me, and lay it under my pillow of nights, and wake of mornings with the happy consciousness that it was there." Such scenes were more accessible to middle-rank families, including the staunchest evangelicals, but still could be used to put overly materialistic parvenus in their place. Hence when the Methodist minister Adam Clarke gave his wife a gold watch on their anniversary in 1799, he compared its face to hers and its gold case to her body.[28]

Students, Soldiers, and Servants

In *The Irish Tutor*, a one-act play performed at Covent Garden in 1823, a maid tells her employer Rosa that she has fallen in love with "a charming man, not like our village folks, such a fine coat, all covered with goldlace!" When the maid adds that he also wore a gold-laced hat, Rosa's cousin concludes that he was "either a parish-beadle, a two-penny post-boy, or some gentleman's servant" (the latter guess was correct).[29] Had he added military officers and Oxbridge undergraduates to this list, he would have summed up the exceptions that proved the rule of an aristocratic retreat from gold after 1780. All these cases successfully included decorative gold in hierarchies that were largely impervious to the recognizability problem that Britain's new rich posed, either by adorning aristocrats with gold in the restricted environs of the school or barracks, or by vicariously displaying status through servants. The key in either case was the uniform, which re-enacted sumptuary laws by precisely aligning gold with rank. As one historian has put it: "Where fashion confounded ranks and led to social disorder, uniforms showed hierarchy and obedience."[30] This formula worked well enough in the university and military up through the Regency period, but lost luster after 1830; British servants, meanwhile, continued to glitter with their masters' gold throughout the nineteenth century.

If money was the great leveler of social distinction in Britain after 1750, Oxford and Cambridge persisted into the 1830s as safe spaces for the nation's aristocrats to display their status for a few years before passing into adulthood. Oxford permitted only children of peers and baronets to don "silken gowns trimmed in gold lace" and to affix gold tassels to their black caps. Gold tassels also thrived at Cambridge, spawning a new species of "tuft-hunters"—defined by a cant dictionary from 1785 as "an university parasite . . . who courts the acquaintance of nobility whose caps are adorned with a gold tuft."[31] Such sumptuary survivals had the capacity to uphold a sense of social order: in a novel set in the 1790s, a banker's son praised the "gold tufts of [his] college aristocracy" as promoting "the stability of our institutions . . . and the maintenance of our unrivaled constitution." These attitudes waned after the Napoleonic War, when merit, money, and a shortage of future baronets eroded the gold tassel's sway. One critic worried in 1834 that these "threads of gold" taught noblemen "to rely upon external distinctions, which are not accorded to them afterwards in the world." By 1840 only five "tufts" were left at Oxford, leaving undergraduates to divide themselves into "sets" comprising "an enormous range of financial means and future prospects."[32]

Besides holding its own at Oxford and Cambridge, decorative gold flourished among the British officer corps, outshining even the glittering shoulders of their continental counterparts. Although English and Scottish soldiers had entered battle "gay with gold" since medieval times, their numbers and the nicety of their adornment dramatically increased after 1750.[33] One inventory of British military dress in the final third of that century included "very elaborate loops of gold embroidery" on horse guards, gold lace on life guards' collars and lapels, fur caps "with heavy gold tassels" on horse grenadier guards, gold epaulets, lace and tassels on sergeants in the dragoons, and gold lace around the pockets and on the shoulders of Coldstream Guards. A portrait gallery of British officers that William IV commissioned in the early 1830s indicated no abatement in adornment: gold tassels, bands, buttons, loops, crescents, cuffs, sashes, stripes, or sword knots sparkled from the canvas far more often than not.[34]

British regiments routinely issued general orders with painstaking rules for attire, down to the last epaulet. Gold figured prominently in most of these, signifying rank or regiment through its position and relative profusion. William IV's orders adorned all officers with gold epaulets, sashes and star loops of varying widths, then added gold wings for light infantry, braids and waist belts for life and horse guards, and girdles for light dragoons and lancers.[35] Although such rules, like earlier sumptuary laws, tended to be observed in the breach, their presence played an important role in training troops to respect their ranks.[36] As

General
The Most Noble Marquis of Anglesey G.C.B.
Colonel of the 7th Reg.t L.t Dragoons, Hussars.

Published by J Booth for the Military Costume of Europe N°8 July 20 1822.

Figure 6.1 Portrait of the Marquis of Anglesey featuring the dress costume of the 7th Regiment of Light Dragoons, Hussars. From T. Goddard and J. Booth, *The Military Costume of Europe; exhibited in a Series of Highly Finished Military Figures, in the Uniform of their Several Corps* (London: Goddard and Booth, 1822). General Research Division, New York Public Library.

a writer on the "elegances of costume" put it in 1848: "A soldier's dress is imposing, because it *is a uniform*. Because the golden epaulette on this shoulder is matched by a similar epaulette on the other; because the stripe of gold lace here is matched by another there."[37]

In addition to shoring up military discipline, gold-laced uniforms assisted in recruitment. A fictional tar recalled in 1813 that the "irresistible allurements" of a midshipman's gold loops and cocked hat had convinced him as a youth that school, compared to the navy, was "one of the stupidest places upon the face of the earth." There was also the promise that gold lace would improve officers' chances with women. The biographer of a Dublin war widow recalled how she would daily "dream of epaulettes both gold and silver" before finally meeting her future husband.[38] This recruiting potential extended well beyond Britain's officer corps. Gold epaulets, lace, and cocked hats performed a similar function for Irish rebels in 1803, volunteers throughout the Napoleonic Wars, and Kentish Chartists; and at the Admiral Nelson pub in "a large manufacturing town," a portrait of Nelson wearing a hat "with a glory of gold-lace about it" suggested to one bemused observer that "England expects every man to do his duty—at the ale-house."[39] Though a profusion of gold might have been an effective means of adding to an army's ranks (or betrothals), it came with the downside of attracting enemy fire. The British army had to tone down its bandsmen's uniforms, which originally came with gold tassels, sash, and stripes, when French snipers spotted them at alarmingly high rates.[40]

A more general military risk than vulnerability to snipers was excessive expense: the dilemma of the officer whose " 'regulation' thick" gold "lay on the wrong side [of] his waistcoat-pocket" was widespread.[41] During the belt-tightening decades after 1815, such complaints spread from soldiers to statesmen. On a nearly annual basis, Radical MP Joseph Hume regaled Parliament concerning the "gold lace and gorgeous trappings" that he saw "daily paraded about the streets, as if to mock the squalid poverty of the lower orders"—and by the late 1820s such rhetoric was starting to open cracks in Britain's military-sartorial complex. In 1828 the Adjutant-General, Herbert Taylor, announced "a reduction of useless expence in military equipments," and outside critics leapt at the chance to echo the need for reform. The *Polar Star*, for instance, urged that draping officers with "yards of lace" was a "vulgar and effeminate mode of marking a military distinction." The only vocal defense of the status quo came from lacemen, who reminded Taylor of "how many poor families would be thrown out of employ" by such a reform, which would also detract from "the beauty of the British army." These developments produced a trend toward "simplification and . . . utilitarianism" in military dress under Queen Victoria.[42]

The proliferation of gold lace among Britain's military men met its match among the liveried servants who worked for the aristocracy. The logic was the same in both cases: in contrast to masterless parvenus, servants' adornment could be regulated by their employers and thereby brandish the same hierarchy that prevailed in the officer corps. The parallels between soldiers and servants were not lost on contemporaries, who referred to the "complete armour of gold lace" worn by coachmen and to servants "drilled into new, stiff liveries, glittering with gold and embroidery."[43] As with soldiers, glitter among servants was not new—seventeenth-century footmen typically wore gold tassels and fringe—but increased in scale and appeared more prominently in contrast to its relative absence among aristocrats. Unlike military officers, who had to foot the bill for their adornment, servants wore gold that their masters provided. Female servants, in contrast, received no allotment of decorative gold, and few could afford to buy even imitation gold jewelry out of their meagre pay.[44]

Besides vicariously displaying their masters' wealth, servants recalled an earlier age when aristocratic men had directly advertised their status through external show. Washington Irving made this point in his novel *Bracebridge Hall*, set in an English manor, when he contrasted a portrait from "past times" featuring "a gallant colonel in full-bottomed wig and gold-laced hat" with the present occupant, whose page wore "a profusion of gold cord and gilt buttons about his clothes."[45] Although most British observers took this inversion in stride, foreign visitors—especially Americans—were less forgiving. After witnessing a set of smug coachmen in Piccadilly with "gold-headed batons in their white-gloved hands," a New York tourist lamented: "There must be something 'rotten in the state,' when God's creatures . . . look up to a station behind a lord's coach as a privileged place."[46] As for the servants themselves, there is some evidence that they understood that gold had radically changed its meaning as a social signifier. When social reformer Charles Cochrane complimented a Canterbury groundskeeper on "the peculiar neatness of his dress and gold braiding," the servant scoffed that it looked "rather too footmany-fied"—and asked his wife for his "plain hat, for that's more genteel."[47]

Majesty, Early and Modern

On May 12, 1842, Queen Victoria and Prince Albert hosted a fancy-dress ball at Buckingham Palace "surpassing in grandeur of costume any English fete on record." Victoria appeared in a gold crown and a cloth-of-gold mantle, "trimmed with gold lace and pearls, lined with ermine, and fastened in front with a broad gold band." A cloak "bordered by a broad gold figured lace," gold-brocade robe, gold-embroidered tunic, and "regal coronet of gold" adorned Albert. A "most magnificent display of gold plate" greeted their guests, whose gold collars, petticoats, veils, chains, robes, tunics, girdles, badges, belts, and boots added to the splendor. The ball itself was an exception for the young Victoria, who tended to make headlines in the realm of decorative gold for christenings rather than late-night extravaganzas. A closer look, however, reveals the fete to be wholly in keeping with Victoria and Albert's own interests as well as the obsessions of the British public. Most of the gold on display was explicitly feudal, reflecting a fad for historical costume drama: the couple's clothing replicated that of Edward III and his wife Philippa, and other guests attended as "a noble French lady of the 13th century," a courtier "of the time of Charlemagne," and a Crusader. The craftsmanship on display also supported Albert's patronage of British trade: the "cloth of gold, silk and velvet" used for Victoria's costume was "made at Spitalfields."[48]

Victoria and Albert's costume ball marked the latest phase in a shifting set of royal contexts for decorative gold over the previous century, starting with George III and his wife Charlotte, who tastefully presided over a restrained revival of pomp. Upon assuming the regency in 1811, George IV engaged in levels of sumptuary excess that incited revulsion if not revolution, and William IV reined in his brother's excess but still left in his wake a succession of glittering yachts and theater boxes. One constant throughout was the sense in which royal families consciously appealed to British craftsmanship as a pretext for their fondness for gold; another, especially apparent in coronations, was the close connection between majestic gold and the British past.

One reason decorative gold flourished in proximity to the crown was that social hierarchy could be more reliably choreographed in these settings. In this regard it paralleled the abundance of gold on British soldiers and servants. George III regularly included gold in his instructions for fancy-dress balls, as when he ordered male guests to don gold-laced waistcoats and knee-bands in order to give a St. George's Day fete "a very imposing and magnificent effect"; and after 1678 British monarchs selected certain officers to serve as "gold sticks," who took on the identity of the mace they carried—originally to provide bodily protection but by 1800 strictly "to add to the splendour of the Court."[49] Although few Britons recognized this parallel in their own lives, they were quick to notice it at foreign courts. Lady Blessington, witnessing an Austrian procession in Naples, observed that the identical gold-tissue robes worn by the female courtiers "conveyed the notion that they wore a livery, and were literally servants; a notion that, however repugnant to the vanity of courtiers, is seldom far from the truth."[50]

Queen Charlotte pursued a similar exercise in sumptuary engineering each January, when she invited London's nobility to celebrate her birthday. The party was a self-conscious pretext for promoting a hierarchy of splendor and also for providing employment to goldsmiths: Charlotte's actual birthday was in May, but starting in 1762 she bumped it up in order to present "a brilliant display of taste and beauty in British manufactures" and to serve as "the commencement of the London season."[51] By 1796, all six of her daughters attended every year, always wearing gold (in 1798 Augusta, Sophia and Mary wore gold spangles, tassels and fringe, while Elizabeth sprouted gold-foil oak and laurel branches)—and their female guests mostly followed suit. Although such proceedings received exaggerated publicity, they were exceptions that proved a rule of simplicity. As one observer put it in 1791, it was only at "court, and upon all grand occasions" that people "of quality and fortune" donned cloth of gold, brocades, and silks; at all other times, they "dress in plain cloth, and good linen, like a common citizen." Charlotte herself personified this rule, by appearing "elegantly plain"—and seldom with any gold—in the center of her glittering birthday cavalcades.[52]

Such decorum was brushed aside with the ascension of Charlotte's son, first as prince regent in 1811 and then as King George IV in 1820. George attended his inaugural fete as regent in a coat "so covered with gold embroidery" that "scarce a finger's breadth of the cloth ground was to be seen." As king, he inhabited what one critic described as "a glittering world of his own—a world of golden tassel, fringe, and embroidery."[53] He generated prodigious orders for gold plate with the royal goldsmiths, commissioning 4000 pieces for Carlton House in 1811 at a cost of £61,340, and laying out an additional £105,000 for gold and jewels in the 1820s. His crowning achievement was the Royal Pavilion at Brighton, which he purchased in 1800 as a summer home and augmented with a gilded dome and columns, gold-framed paintings, gold-lined sideboards, curtains and cornices, and gold-embossed doors.[54] George IV's aristocratic acquaintances reflected their king's glory with costly adornments of their own. Into the 1840s, the Duke of Wellington hosted an annual banquet for his fellow Waterloo officers, where he displayed one service of gold plate worth £300,000 (the gift of George IV), another purchased at auction from the Duke of York, and three gold candelabra.[55]

In contrast to George IV's reign, his brother William's marked a return to their parents' association of gold with family. He restored the tradition of the queen's birthday party, where (in 1832) the Duchess of Kent, among many other guests, appeared "richly embroidered . . . with gold cord and tassels; all of British manufacture"; and he appeared with Adelaide at the theatre in boxes draped with gold fringe, gold-sprigged muslin and gold-colored cords. Although William occasionally approached his brother's gaucherie—a later critic called the interior design of the newly-opened Buckingham Palace "a waste of gold, glare, and glitter, in the worst possible taste"—he also tempered the glare with sentiment, as when he gave Adelaide a solid gold bracelet with the word "gratitude" on its gold padlock, in response to her "kindness . . . during an illness."[56]

In contrast to her two uncles, Victoria's relationship to gold during the early years of her reign combined feminine taste with maternity and utilitarianism. Fifteen different London goldsmiths, embroiderers, lacemen, and jewelers attended her royal household and she often wore gold brocade in her frequent public appearances. Instead of birthday fetes, she more commonly displayed gold at christenings, which employed the same font and salver that had been used to baptize Charles II, George IV, and Victoria herself, and which occasioned prodigious displays of the growing royal family's gold plate. Victoria also managed to apply decorative gold to a new focus on British ingenuity, as when she gave an Ottoman sultan a Spitalfields-produced umbrella that came equipped with a gold handle, watch, compass, and mirror.[57] Above all, she and Albert both reflected and led a departure from the gilded excess that had marked Regency Britain. At Buckingham Palace, they retreated from "the gold and glitter of the state rooms" to relax in quarters that combined "elegance and luxury with simplicity and comfort."[58]

One common denominator in this display of royal gold between 1760 and 1850 concerned coronation regalia, nearly all of which predated the Hanoverian dynasty. Gold was the main ingredient in an orb and scepter designed in 1661, as well as a sixty-piece set of plate and "St. Edward's crown," which was refashioned with a gold cross after Oliver Cromwell had melted down the original in 1642.[59] In George III's coronation, gold played an important supporting role in presenting the young king to his subjects: a gold canopy and abundant cloth of gold supplemented his inherited regalia.[60] George IV spared no expense in his coronation, adding "gold lacings & deep gold bullion fringe" to the throne, gold straps to the scepter, and brocade and lace to the altar, kneeling cushion, and carpet.[61] Although William IV retained much of the gold in 1831 that remained from his brother's ceremony, he added almost nothing new, and Victoria displayed the same relative restraint seven years later. One reporter noted that "the state liveries were almost *gold-bare*," contrasting sharply with the "feudal magnificence" of many of her foreign guests.[62]

Although they periodically stole the spotlight, Britain's royal family did not monopolize the display of majestic regalia. Mayors—first in London, then across Britain—exercised their ceremonial authority through the display of gold on an annual basis. Like royal regalia, and often with a royal license, a mayor's gold chain (along with his collar and mace) was a hereditary symbol of office as opposed to an evanescent fashion accessory. London mayors first received the right to hold a gold mace from Edward III in 1354; their "dignity . . . was first enhanced by the addition of a gold chain" two centuries later under Henry VIII.[63] In the provinces, mayors invented their own traditions by donating decorative gold to be worn by their successors.[64] Mayoral gold also achieved exceptional status because it reflected municipal pride. This had especially been the case during the reigns of Elizabeth and James I, but it survived residually in the mayor's annual inaugural procession, in which coachmen "plastered from top to toe with gold" paraded before his state coach, "redolent of gold and glass." Finally, the dinner after the pageant gave the mayor's wife an opportunity to supplement civic pomp with feminine taste, much as Charlotte did at her birthday party. For Frances Crowder in 1829, this consisted in "a splendid dress . . . richly

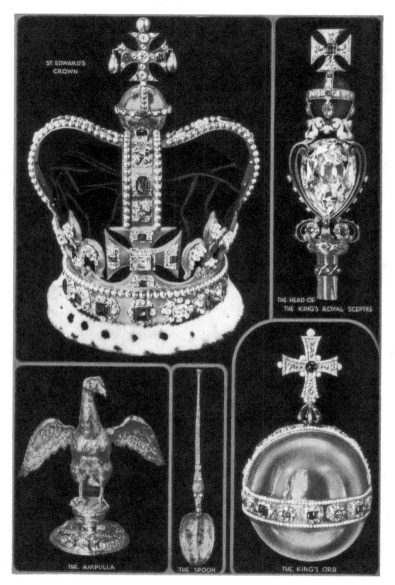

Figure 6.2 Crown Jewels of the United Kingdom. Clockwise from top left: St Edward's Crown ("a very rich Imperial Crown of gold . . . with a mound of gold on top of it, encircled with a band of the same . . . and upon the mound a cross of gold"); royal sceptre; royal orb ("a ball of gold . . . with a band of the same," with a gold pedestal); spoon and ampulla. *Illustrated London News: Coronation Record Number* (1937). Descriptions from Richard Thomson, *A Faithful Account of the Processions and Ceremonies Observed in the Coronation* (1821). Art Resource AR939911.

Figure 6.3 C. Williams, "A Wood-in Triumph, or a New Idol for the Ragamuffins"
(1809). A crowd of laborers and beggars doffing their hats or drawing the Lord Mayor's
coach, containing the fishmonger Sir Matthew Wood (Sheriff of the City of London),
on his way to deliver a resolution of support to the radical politician Francis Burdett. Art
Resource AR988296.

embroidered in gold lama, with wreaths and columns of raised gold flowers" and
"boquets of gold roses."[65]

By containing decorative gold in the past, regal display resonated with a widespread, but almost always critical, British fascination with the world they had
lost. Starting in the 1790s, detailed costume histories burst their bindings with
inventories of gold lace and embroidery.[66] These provided grist for the hundreds
of history paintings produced by Royal Academicians during this period, as
well as such historical novels as *Windsor Castle* and *The Field of Cloth of Gold*—
whose characters, "sumptuously apparelled in cloths of gold," cavorted amidst
"the most splendid mass of gold and jewels that the summer sun ever shone
upon."[67] As Britain went through a succession of coronations between 1820 and
1837, histories of past royal ceremonies—replete with exacting descriptions
of regalia—supplemented these works, as did collective biographies of past
monarchs.[68]

Most of these descriptions distanced themselves from their subjects by
associating the olden-day fondness for gold with "a puerile taste for shew and
splendour" (describing a medieval archbishop's "curious table of massy gold")
or "a prodigality of extravagance borrowed from the French" (describing the

gold-embroidered sails on Henry V's warship).[69] Front and center in most such histories were Henry VIII and Elizabeth I. Henry's gold-laden coronations (one for each queen) and "passion for magnificence" prompted condemnations of the "ruinous and useless expense" that his habits occasioned.[70] As for Elizabeth, whose splendor vied with Henry's pomp in royal biographies, John Stoughton delivered a typical verdict in his *Notices of Windsor in the Olden Times* (1844): "Much as is said about the golden days of good Queen Bess, we are fully persuaded that the golden days of good Queen Victoria are of more genuine metal, and of higher lustre."[71]

Besides reading critical accounts of their glittering past, Britons periodically viewed it in museums and manor houses. Much more than evanescent relics such as clothing and furniture, gold survived long enough to be visibly antique, ranging from the regalia and gilded armor in the Tower of London to the "gold room" at Windsor Castle, where a travel guide described "the gradations in rank and dignity of the various gold and silver plates and dishes."[72] Exhibits of gold plate also recalled olden times in the many country estates that started to open their doors to the public after 1800. Although Britain's nobility continued to add to their gold plate after 1760, most of the oldest families displayed tableware that dated back to the days of Queen Anne if not earlier. One popular destination, Warwick Castle, boasted a service of "massy and ancient gold plate . . . the finest, perhaps, to be found in England."[73]

Britons also re-enacted past displays of gold in theaters and ballrooms. The audience at London's Coburg theatre in 1830 could view the "imposing spec-tacle" of Henry VIII's tournament of the field of cloth of gold; the costume de-signer for *Ruby Red*, a melodrama set in 1712, draped all but four characters in gold lace. Historical costume balls also grew in popularity after 1800—mainly among Victoria's set, but extending at times into the industrial middle classes. A rare sighting of gold lace and embroidery in Manchester during the 1820s occurred at one such ball, in which the precious metal adorned a brewer dressed as an Arabian prince, a merchant who donned the gold fringe, tassels, medal and cross of a Knight Templar, and assorted gold-laden guests who attended in the guise of a fictional Sicilian count, the Restoration courtier Lord Rochester, and Henry V of France.[74]

Like the gold chain to which successive mayors of Hull added new links over the course of two centuries, coronations, mayor's shows, and costume balls all emphasized continuities between decorative gold in medieval and modern times.[75] While such activities count as what has come to be known as the "in-vention of tradition," they also performed the more specific task of carving out a space in which decorative gold could be appreciated for its non-economic value in upholding social distinction.[76] As such, they confirm literary critic Elaine Freedgood's argument that the "abstraction of the commodity into a

money value" was "not the only [way] of imagining the things" that crowded in
on Britons during the nineteenth century.[77] Nor did these representations ex-
haust the range of possible meanings of decorative gold. As they encountered it
in continental Europe, Asia, and Africa, they typically understood the gold that
adorned peasants, kings, and churches as barbaric, picturesque, or idolatrous.
These interpretations sharpened by contrast the significance of gold's appearance back in Britain.

7

Display

In the novel *Society in India* (1841), a party of four witnesses a military procession headed by a "Hindoo Muharajah." Throughout the ensuing encounter, past and present collide in gilded splendor: a "panoply of the dark ages rode side by side with . . . cloth of gold and silver," while "gold muslin and embroidery . . . sparkled in the bright rays of an orient sun." Towering above the company is the rajah's elephant, with tusks "bound with bands of gold and silver" and laden with "housings of bright scarlet bordered with gold." Following the procession, Lieutenant Barlow, the civil servant Mr. Morton, his stepdaughter Helen Sandys, and her suitor Captain Buxton survey the scene. Barlow "sneered at the whole affair—gaudy, bad taste, effeminate, and theatrical, were his mildest epithets"—and insists: "Good taste is always plain." Morton reminds Barlow that "gold, jewels, and shawls, are effeminate only in our eyes, because within the last half century we have confined them chiefly to the softer sex." He points to the soldier's own epaulets as a reminder that gold is not "inherently" unmanly and concludes that London's "lugubrious processions . . . might be advantageously exchanged for the brilliant confusion that has sparkled in the sun this morning." For Buxton, the pageant confirms the timelessness of eastern pomp; he suggests that "Solomon in all his glory was doubtless something very like this." For Helen Sandys, it is all about the elephant: "if I were Queen of England, I would never hide my jewelled diadem in a carriage, however gilt and carved . . . I would go in state on an elephant taller than the Muharaja's."[1]

This set piece reveals the range of responses that Britons abroad experienced upon encountering decorative gold. Their instinct was to follow Barlow in sneering at foreigners who wore gold on the grounds of bad taste, effeminacy, or illegibility. At times they extended to these cases the same critique they leveled against the *nouveau riche* at home—especially among people of color who fell short in their efforts to imitate western fashions when they wore gold. More often, especially in India, they equated getting it wrong in the matter of wearing gold with a confusion of gender roles. In such cases the problem was the opposite of inept imitation: gold ear-rings on men, gold nose-rings, bindis, or anklets on women, and the juxtaposition of gold with abject poverty removed them to a wholly foreign category that induced curiosity or, more often, disgust.

Amid the disgust, there were plenty of exceptional occasions in which Britons appreciated the appearance of gold on foreign bodies. Helen Sandys's pleasure at the sight of gilded pachyderms found multiple real-life echoes, especially among women who gloried in sighting decorative gold. Although exotic adornment was not enough on its own to merit British approval, the addition of good taste, frugality, or the adoption of a national costume usually prompted a positive response—and that response, more often than not, deployed the adjective *picturesque*, entailing a projection of British aesthetic priorities onto foreign objects. Buxton's assumption of timeless pomp and Morton's appreciation of gold's effectiveness as a governing strategy, finally, reflected what historian David Cannadine has termed ornamentalism, which marked a different sort of projection onto empire—that of "domestic social structures and social perceptions."[2] As in the case of picturesque gold, majestic gold was not sufficient on its own to confer every foreign dignitary with British approval, especially when the scene shifted from Asia to Africa, but it usually secured a warm reception, especially if Britons could identify it with their resplendent past or compare it to the exceptional glitter adorning their present-day royal family.

Whether it signified radical difference, recalled their past, or paralleled their present, gold as a means of personal ornament pervasively appeared in British accounts of travel or residence abroad—much more so, with few exceptions, than it did when Britons wrote about their fellow countrymen. Partly this was a case of wish fulfillment: they set out to India and the Near East intent on confirming gilded Oriental fantasies, and in continental Europe they went out of their way to spot picturesque glitter. To at least some extent, though, the preponderance of gold in these travel accounts was an artifact of political economy: apart from Britain, most regions in the world employed silver as their primary currency, leaving plenty of gold to be used to advertise status and enhance beauty.[3] In this sense, decorative gold in the Orient confirmed British assumptions, which they had learned from Adam Smith, about that metal's proper place relative to different stages of civilization. It also spoke to a wider diffusion of ornament among different social classes and genders—including female European peasants and well-off South Asian men, whose British counterparts seldom appeared in public wearing gold after 1780.[4]

Several assumptions and proclivities united these disparate interpretations, concerning gender and possession. Gender informed who took it on themselves to adjudicate the wearing of gold abroad: men most often delivered verdicts on gold as a signifier of governance, whereas women focused more on its role in enhancing a picturesque scene. Partly this was about access to high ranking foreign officials in the case of men and to the female wearers of gold in the case of women. Partly, though, this was also a matter of perceived expertise and interest. Men more often traveled abroad armed with expectations rooted in their reading of European historical precedent, and hence were more apt to identify gold (though not always correctly) as a governing strategy.[5] Many women, in contrast, traveled to Europe and Asia with an inclination to compare their counterparts' adornment with fashions at home.[6]

The other common feature of all British encounters with ornamental gold when they traveled abroad was that they seldom returned to Britain without taking some with them. Unlike the Oriental "other" (whether the concept or its constituent polities), which ultimately could only be partially and evanescently possessed, gold could be owned in a more tangible and permanent fashion, whether through imitation, trade, or theft. The first sense of possessing foreign gold occurred whenever British socialites donned jewelry that called attention to its exotic associations, at costume balls or as fashion statements. The second sense commonly transpired at bazaars and goldsmiths' shops from Venice to Benares, where British travelers prided themselves on being able to drive a hard bargain in acquiring gilded souvenirs. Finally, British soldiers seldom returned from a conquest of new territory without a substantial quantity of majestic gold, much of which assisted in narrowing the glitter gap between British and Asian royalty.

Barbaric Gold

In his *Dictionary of the English Language* (1756), Samuel Johnson attached two citations to the entry for *barbarick,* which he defined as "Foreign; farfetched": John Milton's allusion in *Paradise Lost* to "barbaric pearl and gold" in "the gorgeous East" and Alexander Pope's reference in "The Temple of Fame" to that structure's "eastern front . . . with diamond flaming, and Barbaric gold."[7] Johnson was hardly alone in citing such sources. Britons repeatedly resorted to this established association between barbarism and gold in making sense of the foreign display of that precious metal—especially in India and the Middle East, but also in Africa, the Americas, and even continental Europe. Mary Russell Mitford quoted Milton as an epigram for her short story "Ceylon: The Lost Pearl," and a gloating critic of Napoleon referred in 1815 to "the 'barbaric pearl and gold' of [his] evil throne, stricken into the worthlessness of which it was made."[8]

British ascriptions of barbarism to decorative gold broadly fell into two types: illegible, and often gender-bending, choices for where to place it, and a failure to do the right things with gold that had been procured through trade with Europe. The first type was apparent in Madras, where the "profusion of silver or gold rings which the natives wear on their arms, their ancles, their ears, and their toes" struck Anglican missionary Daniel Corrie as a sign of their "deep depravity, and their entire want of principle."[9] The second type of alleged barbarism was evident when Richard and John Lander encountered a chief on the Calabar River whose "only pretensions to dress consisted in a smart, gold-laced hat . . . and a handsome piece of silk tied round his loins"; by the time they ended their journey through the Niger basin, they had stripped all the gilt buttons from their jackets, which they traded to women who used them to adorn every extremity.[10]

British travelers mainly commented on the first sort of barbarism in India. They saw gold ornaments wherever they set foot on the subcontinent: from Ceylon, where women wore half-moon gold plates in their hair and gold buttons on their sleeves, to the Himalayas, where women and children alike were "weighed down under a load of silver and gold ornaments in the shape of ear-rings, nose-rings, necklaces, and bracelets." Their almost uniformly negative assessments of these people's choice of adornment had everything to do with that fact that Britain was in the process of subsuming them as colonial subjects. With the notable exception of Muslim (and very occasionally Hindu) princes, they invoked Milton's description of barbaric gold only to contrast it with the "squalid reality" of life in India, which encompassed the "coarseness of their dress, and the meanness of their habitations."[11]

Most British complaints about decorative gold in India concerned where men and women chose to place the metal on their bodies. The rings Corrie noticed were symptomatic of a more general "confusion of gender" that Britons attributed to Indian men—not because they wore gold, but because it dangled from their ears and wrists.[12] The same confusion extended to women, whose choice of where to wear gold stretched beyond the usual feminine sites in Europe (ears, wrists, necks, and the fringes of clothing) to noses, foreheads, ankles, and toes. A Benares missionary concluded that "the preposterous rings, and other appendages, which many of the females attach to their noses" were "disfigurements rather than embellishments of genuine loveliness." For most British observers, revulsion removed the possibility of the same sort of nuanced social interpretation that decorative gold invited in continental Europe; only a few took time to notice, for instance, that nose rings signified that a Hindu woman was married.[13]

Even when people in southern and central Asia wore gold in the right places, they sinned in Britons' eyes by overdoing it. The "Hindoo woman of distinction" was "always . . . overloaded with finery," according to one East India Company official; an account of Armenian women in Astrakhan dwelt on their "massive gold" robes featuring "ponderous embroidery, with large gold knobs, gold buttons, gold tassels, gold fringe, &c. &c."[14] Britons were especially quick to condemn excessive adornment of children with precious metals: one traveler worried that a boy laden with twenty gold chains "looked more like an armadillo of the picture-books than a human being." They even extended their charge of excess to Indian soldiers, who followed the British fashion of adorning their uniforms with gold but did so with insufficient sumptuary nuance. Warren Hastings's aide-de-camp complained that the gold adorning Madras native infantry officers was "too conspicuous, and totally inconsistent with their description of duty."[15]

Above all, choices in India and the Near East concerning where to hang gold struck Britons as *curious*—which, as literary critic Nigel Leask has observed, could either signify a positive desire for expanded horizons or "a negative account of the wonder aroused by distant lands."[16] Both senses of the word appeared in British accounts of the female dancers who performed for priests and princes, in Egypt as well as India.[17] At a dinner party in Calcutta in 1812, Maria Nugent found the dancers, "loaded with gold and silver trimmings," to be "really very curious and even wonderful." Other witnesses found the dancers' gold breast plates, girdles, nose rings, ankle bracelets, and eye liner alternately alluring, graceful, ghastly, or tawdry.[18] Although most Britons regarded such displays as unseemly, few could resist the chance to see them. More generally, travelers who were quick to condemn unsightly gold on South Asian subjects seldom passed up the opportunity to purchase the same adornments as souvenirs. When Fanny Parks visited Benares, famous "for its embroidery in gold, and for its tissues of gold and silver," she "purchased some to make a native dress for myself, and also some very stiff ribbon, worked in silk and gold, on which are the names of all the Hindoo deities."[19]

Beyond aesthetic judgment, especially after 1813 when the East India Company began embarking in earnest on the task of civilizing its Hindu subjects, the matter of expenditure on gold adornment became an almost constant concern. In his "estimate of the expence of a Hindu family of high rank and station," Francis Buchanan-Hamilton calculated in 1833 that gold rings, necklaces, and bindis comprised 28 percent of its assets and 10 percent of its annual expenditure. Hamilton's high-caste family, whose gold was worth roughly the same amount as its house and clothing, found many anecdotal echoes.[20] *The Friend of India*, for instance, remarked that upper-caste Hindus lavished "ornaments of silver and gold" on their children while letting them walk the streets without shoes. This sentiment echoed economist Richard Whately's verdict, concerning pound-foolish Britons, that "a mixture of finery with rags and dirt is a most disgusting sight"—but extended it to an entire nation.[21] Besides decrying these spending decisions, Britons worried that Indians imperiled women and children by draping them with precious metals. Travel accounts and fiction set in India constantly reported "nose and ear slitting" and other mutilations by thieves in the course of appropriating decorative gold.[22]

Figure 7.1 "Native Goldsmith," from John Capper, *The Three Presidencies of India . . .with
an Account of their Government, Religion, Manners, Customs, Education, &c. &c.*, 315.
"The same manual dexterity which has ever distinguished the unlettered Hindoo in the
production of fine textile fabrics, has enabled him with equal success to produce some
of the most exquisite specimens of gold and silver work." General Research Division,
New York Public Library.

What Britons found especially galling about Indian expenditure on decorative gold was that they commonly converted gold coins into jewelry in the
most literal sense: by handing them over to a goldsmith, who melted down and
refashioned them into bracelets and bangles. As a British report lamented in
1834: "Here a man is not amenable before a judicial tribunal for defacing the
king's image."[23] The muhr, which had long circulated in Madras and emerged
from East Indian Company mints after 1766, was especially popular for this purpose owing to its purity. The Company tried to deter muhr-melting in 1835 by
replacing the older coin with an alloyed version that resembled the sovereign in
fineness, but within two decades acknowledged that the primary demand for
gold coins in India continued to be as an accessory to accessories.[24] A different
strategy, which likewise met with mixed results, was to open savings banks that

would provide Indians with a "means of investing . . . money to advantage" instead of melting it down into "rude and massy armlets, bracelets, anklets, collars, and nose ornaments."[25]

While Indians were rejecting European fashion and finance, other foreigners irked Britons through improper imitation. A physician in Sierra Leone faulted residents there for "indulging their vanity in imitating the European mode of dress," resulting in a "ludicrous . . . profusion of gold and silver tinsel." In contrast to the *nouveau riche* in Britain, whose efforts to ape the aristocracy garnered anxious scorn, complacent bemusement was the more typical response abroad. Sarah Lee, who accompanied her husband on a diplomatic mission to the Gold Coast in 1816, referred to "an Ashantee fop of the highest order" who, "having rubbed himself well with grease, would sally forth, on gala days, besprinkled all over with gold dust." Harry Longueville Jones, an archaeologist and amateur fashion critic, scoffed at the "negro chief who, in a state of unclad majesty, clapped a gold-laced cocked-hat on his head, and then strutted about with an air of intense satisfaction at the result of his habilimentary effort."[26] The obsessive attention that Britons paid to such displays reflected their dual assumption that it both made perfect sense that Africans would desire to imitate British fashions and that anything approaching perfect imitation of those fashions was unthinkable.

British explorers themselves occasioned such encounters by relentlessly pedaling cheap gilded "trinkets" to indigenous people in exchange for cowrie shells or food and drink. They did so either as a basic survival strategy or as a counterfoil to the slave trade. As one Scottish merchant urged, "a scarlet coat, cocked hat, and gold-headed cane, would do wonders" in opening up "legitimate commerce in Africa."[27] The result was that British accounts of their contact with Africans often echoed their descriptions of old-fashioned gold at home, implying an encouraging transition to modernity. James Grant, a Liverpool sailor, described a Biafran chief who regularly wore "a gold-laced round hat, like those worn by gentlemen's servants," and similar attire featured in British encounters in the Congo and Sierra Leone.[28]

A more critical association of barbaric gold with *nouveau riche* excess concerned slaves in the Americas, whose adornment absurdly echoed their parvenu owner's profligate finery and tasteless indulgence. Miss Strutt, a character in a novel set in Jamaica, displayed the first vice when she took part in "slave gala days" by wearing her owner's (and her friends' owners') gold clasps, chains, bodkins, and watch. A wealthy creole widow in Lady Blessington's novel *The Governess* personified the latter vice when she provided her slave with a gold-headed cane to go along with the gold-laced hat and silver shoe buckles that she had seen "worn by a nobleman's coachman in London."[29] A British merchant noticed the same pattern in Brazil, where "the black female slaves" paraded the streets "bedecked with gold chains several times round their necks, large bracelets, ear-rings, pendants, crosses, [and] plates of gold on their foreheads."[30]

Picturesque Gold

At a London dinner party in L. E. L.'s novel *Romance and Reality* (1831), the "fascinating" Lady Mandeville reported on a scene of "exquisite coquetry" at a *fete* in a recently-visited Italian village, which featured "long gold earrings, those indispensables of their toilette—the black velvet boddice, shewing the figure to such advantage, laced with gold and coloured silks . . . all put on so neatly, and with such a fine taste for harmony of colouring." The overall effect convinced her that "national costumes [had been] invented for the express advantage of travellers."[31] A century earlier, Mary Wortley Montagu described her encounter in Adrianople with a "very becoming . . . Turkish habit" she had purchased for wearing among her aristocratic Ottoman friends, which included gold-embroidered shoes, a gold-damasked waistcoat with "deep gold fringe," a gold-fringed robe, and a gold-tasseled cap; she donned a similar outfit, adorned with gold damask, fringe, and brocade, while posing with her son in 1717. After witnessing similar costumes during her residence in Turkey, she concluded that the female inhabitants there were "the only women in the world, that lead a life of uninterrupted pleasure" in the "agreeable amusement of spending money and inventing new fashions."[32]

Taken together, these two moments capture much of what distinguished British attitudes towards decorative gold in Europe and the Near East from the parallel cases of South Asia and Africa. By finding pleasure in gold's picturesque appearance on women of inferior social rank, Lady Mandeville typified the interest taken in European adornment by her real-life counterparts, who saw little point in reporting on upper- or middle-class women whose choice of gilded décor so closely approximated their own.[33] In contrast, Montagu's articulation of what art theorist Adam Geczy has called "escape through orientalist dress" emphasized sympathy with her social equals, whose allure derived from religious and geographical difference: her reaction resonated well into the nineteenth century, as a succession of British women added variations on her discovery of the liberatory potential of the exotic.[34]

Despite such differences, these associations of gold with exoticism shared several commonalities that prevented them from appearing "barbaric" to Britons. Whether among European peasants or Turkish sultanas, wearing gold revealed connections with classical antiquity, conformity with British standards of taste, revelations of "national costume," and canny adaptations to less civilized

Figure 7.2 Jean-Baptiste Vanmour (attr.), "Lady Mary Wortley Montagu with her Son, Edward Wortley Montagu, and Attendants," ca. 1717 (detail). © National Portrait Gallery, London, 3924.

surroundings. Since they all occurred in parts of the world over which the British did not happen to rule, they were also less encumbered by a desire (so often apparent in India) to let political economy inform aesthetic judgment. Last but not least decorative gold in both contexts promised the pleasure of possession, through gift-shop purchases and re-enactment. Such glimmers of sympathy, however, were always fragile. The same southern European peasant, for instance, whose gold-fringed attire garnered appreciation, earned the scorn of British Protestants when she passed from her village square into her gold-festooned cathedral.

One source of enjoyment in viewing foreign gold adornment in both Europe and the Near East was the sense—enabled by the metal's physical durability—of connection with the ancient world.[35] Encountering "an assemblage of gold and silver tiaras and boddices" in 1836, "a Briton in Bavaria confessed: "I always derive great pleasure when I see a peasantry retaining their ancient national costumes." Travelers in Greece and Italy who were conversant with ancient inventories of jewelry were especially prone to such pleasures. One visitor to an Italian village associated the gold bells dangling from the ears of the local women with "the descriptions of Pliny" and recently-excavated relics in Pompeii; an account of Greece connected the gold chains, miters, and bracelets mentioned in Plutarch and Chrysostom with "the same kind of ornament" brandished by "modern Greek ladies."[36] Further east, the Old Testament offered recognizable antecedents to gold bridles on Turkish horses, necklaces in Nazareth, perfume boxes in Persia, and "numerous trinkets belonging to the toilet" in Egypt.[37]

If ancient precedent bred sufficient recognition for British travelers to feel at home among foreign displays of gold, another contributing factor was that, by and large, the types of ornament and their position on the body did not overly upset their preconceptions regarding proper uses of that metal. Lower-class British women did not generally wear gold drops in their ears or embroidery in their caps—but their upper-class counterparts did, which made it less surprising when British travelers encountered "peasants" thus adorned in France or Italy. Such recognition was apparent in a fictional lady's comparison of a French butter woman's "great yellow gold ear-ornaments" with the "tops and drops" that her set had once worn in Britain.[38] Since rural peasants were otherwise unlikely to be confused with urban elites, the social dyslexia inflicted by parvenus did not apply to them; nor was this an issue in the Near East, since most of the Turkish and Egyptian women who appeared in travel accounts replicated both the social class and sense of elegance of their British interlocutors.[39]

A final source of consolation concerned "national costume." The period between 1780 and 1850 was the golden age of folk costume in Europe, when increased access to the countryside by pleasure-seekers converged with elite investment of peasant garb with national symbolism. As historian Alexander Maxwell has observed, this process—initiated by J. G. von Herder in the 1790s and soon embraced throughout the continent—only took off "after international fashions displaced local costumes among other social classes" and in urban settings.[40] British travelers tapped into these romanticizing efforts but added their own picturesque fantasies to the mix.[41] They often sought out festival days, on which locals were the most likely to appear in costume—as when a visitor to Valencia spotted "peasants [who] were as picturesque as possible, in their broad-brimmed hats with gold tassels."[42]

Europe presented British travelers with an expansive array of colloquial adornment that marked off women by national type—such that, as one tourist concluded, "the female head becomes a kind of geographical index."[43] Gold often featured prominently in this display. In Calais and Lille women uniformly sported "picturesque double gold drops in the ears"; the "distinctive national costume of the pretty women of Munich" included "a cap of gold tinsel, projecting in fantastic forms"; and visitors to Friesland noted the "broad bands of gold" that women there wore around their temples.[44] Italy presented tourists with numerous microhabitats, each with its distinctive décor, including gold-beaded necklaces in Piedmont, gold chains in Venice and Padua, and "solid gold earrings, reaching to [the] shoulders" in Sorrento.[45] Although such variety may have defied the "pastoral national fantasies" of early nineteenth-century Romantics, their entertaining diversity offered ample compensation for travelers in search of diversion.[46]

The relatively recent development of national costume in Europe found its match farther east in a much longer Orientalist tradition. The *Arabian Nights Entertainments*, which first appeared in English translation in 1706, featured gold-plated castles, horses with gilded saddles and bridles, and sofas "lined with Indian Stuff of Gold," and inspired numerous gold-laden imitations.[47] On the stage as well, Britons formed Orientalist preconceptions from plays such as John Howard Payne's *Ali Pasha* (1822), the hero of which trod the boards in a gold-embroidered tunic and belt.[48] All such sources provided a distinctive blueprint for pleasurably experiencing decorative gold in the Near East. A gathering of Turkish women wearing gold-wrought girdles and embroidered sleeves struck Julia Pardoe as "a scene of the Arabian Nights in action"; and John Galt, when offered a chance to ride a vizier's horse in Greece, wryly declined: "I should have liked well enough for once in my life to have, Aladdin-like, bestrode a horse caparisoned with gold and velvet; but having no one who knew me to mortify by the sight, I thought it unnecessary."[49]

Although Mary Wortley Montagu's tradition of cross-cultural dressing did persist into the nineteenth century, most British women who visited harems treated it as a spectator sport.[50] When their hostess at a Gaza harem asked Georgiana Damer's party to "display [their] ornaments," all they could muster was a gold watch and chain.[51] Harem tourists made up for their relative lack of glitter by taking copious notes, as when Sophia Poole recounted a Cairo wedding in 1846: the bride, "supported by four slaves," wore "a yelek and trowsers of red Cashmere embroidered with gold in a florid style, equally gorgeous and elegant . . . and almost covered with embroidery of gold and jewels." Poole saw her apartment window in Cairo as "a theatre-box from which she [could] observe several 'spectacles' that 'afford various and endless entertainment'"; and it was no accident that her brother and travel-companion, Edward Lane, had translated *The Arabian Nights*, which she frequently cited by analogy.[52]

The most telling sign of the cultural value Orientalism held for British travelers in the Ottoman Empire was their willingness to excuse even the wearing of gold coins, as long as it was in the service of national costume. Wherever British travelers visited eastern Mediterranean shores, they encountered—and remarked on—women wearing gold coins on their heads, in their hair, or around their necks.[53] This custom likewise appeared in fictional accounts set in the Orient: Byron's *Don Juan* featured a Cycladic beauty whose "brow was overhung with coins of gold" and a "Bedoueen girl" in Disraeli's *Tancred* wore "gold coins . . . braided in her hair."[54] British reactions to such decorations were always at least neutral in tone and usually echoed accounts of picturesque European peasants. When archaeologist Charles Fellows described a "ladylike" woman in Antalya wearing a cap "formed of Turkish gold coins, the intrinsic value of which must have been at least £150," he concluded: "The display of wealth in [such] dresses may in description appear ridiculous, but the effect was classical."[55]

Besides appealing to picturesque or Orientalist tropes to make sense of decorative gold in Europe and the Near East, British travelers often appealed to the economic sense that wearing gold made for the women under their observation. They often noted cases in which gold jewelry had been handed down through generations, as when James Dallaway, chaplain to the British Embassy in Istanbul, conjectured that the "hereditary and unalienable" chains he spotted on Galatian women had been "first set in the time of the emperors."[56] They also identified a tendency for young women to "carry their marriage portion about with them, in the shape of gold ear-rings and crosses"; or to wear "their savings'-bank . . . around their necks, in twenty or forty piastre-pieces of modern Turkish gold."[57] Besides representing a form of saving, gold ornaments could be used as collateral for loans: visitors to Ischia and Genoa tracked the progress of their residents' gold ear-rings and caps into and out of local pawnshops as "necessary adjutants to . . . domestic economy."[58]

Sometimes Britons pointed to these putatively sensible uses of gold abroad to scold women back home who wastefully replaced their gold jewelry each year to keep up with new trends—in effect, contrasting pound-wise European peasants with penny-foolish fashion-followers.[59] More often, positive appraisals of peasants accompanied critical evaluations of the economic conditions that made their choice to wear gold appear rational—a rare instance of common ground with British views of "barbaric" gold in India. Lady Morgan attributed the "love for personal decorations of gold" in Lombardy to "the impossibility of placing money to advantage, or from a want of sufficient security" in that region. Another travel writer generalized from such examples to conclude: "Where a

Figure 7.3 "Haidée," *The Gallery of Byron Beauties; Portraits of the Principal Female Characters in Lord Byron's Poems* (1836). Engraving no. 32, after a portrait by Alfred Edward Chalon. Haidée was a character Byron described in *Don Juan*: "Her brow was overhung with coins of gold / That sparkled o'er the auburn of her hair." The editors, William and Edward Finden, commented: "No portion of this extraordinary poem is finished with so much beauty as that which relates the loves of Juan and the fair Greek girl." Columbia University Libraries.

people. . . have much wealth locked up in gold and silver ornaments, it is both a sign and a cause of a low non-progressive social condition."[60]

A different application of political economy to picturesque gold concerned commodification. Vendors of gilded jewelry in Europe and the Near East recognized this sales opportunity, and British travelers flocked to sample their wares. The gold-threaded slippers and "inviting" gold gauze in a Turkish bazaar left Julia Pardoe "with aching eyes, and a very confused impression of this great mart of luxury and expence." After viewing an exhibit of "the manufacture of the gold chains for which Venice is so famous," another tourist observed: "of course we became customers"—and recounted his purchase of several yards of chain as well as "some little models of gondolas" formed from gold.[61] Back home, upper-crust Britons displayed their picturesque gold at costume balls, where it shared space with jewelry and gold cloth that referenced the British past. Invited to a masquerade, a character in a novel from 1790 settled on "Turkish dress" as "the best adapted for an ill proportioned form"; her gold-fringed vest and wrap, "richly ornamented with gold and foil . . . conveyed a striking picture of Eastern magnificence."[62]

Gold and Governance

In December 1839, six months after the death of the Ottoman sultan Mahmud II, the *London Saturday Journal* recalled a recent occasion on which the late ruler had celebrated the "Turkish Sabbath" from the glory of his state barge. The vehicle was "not so gaudy as the state-barge of the right hon. the lord mayor of London," in the journalist's view: it was instead "more tasteful and handsome, being profusely decorated with gold leaf and gold lace, after the most approved oriental fashion." Adding to the spectacle was his charger, a "chestnut-coloured Arabian," with "saddle and horse-cloth . . . of oriental manufacture, and superbly embroidered with gold lace." All was not Oriental in this account, however: the writer was quick to add that "the bridle, bit, and stirrups were European," as befit an emperor whose primary legacy had been his introduction of western fashions into his civil and military service.[63] Across Asia, Britons grappled with the place of gold in governance, and their verdict, as in Mahmud's case, was seldom a simple matter of Orientalist condescension.

The East, literary critic Geoffrey Nash has observed, was "simultaneously the site of European origin and Europe's primitive Other by virtue of the arrested development caused by its unchanging essence."[64] This dual location was especially prominent in descriptions of Asian majesty, which Britons often compared to similar European pageants that had taken place several centuries earlier. Hence when the East India Company's Governor General met with the Sikh prince Runjit Singh in 1831, his secretary reported that its "magnificence and mutual display" called to mind "the days of 'the field of cloth of Gold.'" The same analogy surfaced in British accounts of a follow-up meeting between Singh and Lord Auckland in 1838 and an earlier peace conference that ended the third Anglo-Mysore War; and a Kandian king's gold cloth, chains and scabbard reminded a British army officer of a cross between Elizabeth and Henry VIII.[65] Biographies of early Mughal emperors presented similar tales of gilded grandeur, which echoed and usually exceeded the gold-filled royal shows that received so much attention in histories of medieval England.[66]

Such parallels with the British past spoke to a deep appreciation for Mughal, Ottoman, and Sikh statecraft, which British observers often equated with stage-craft and lamented as a lost art in Europe. An army officer reported on the "gratifying" spectacle of a royal procession in Hyderabad, which featured el-egant gold-brocade caps and "sashes of silk and gold."[67] The elephants that so captivated Helen Sandys often figured prominently in such accounts. Visiting Mysore in 1821 the East India Company cavalry officer Digby Mackworth "took an airing in the Rajah's elephant carriage," which, with its cloth-of-gold sofa and awning, was "by far the most magnificent conveyance I ever saw; the Genius of Aladdin could scarcely have done more."[68] Descriptions of royal parades in Agra, Lucknow, and Delhi likewise lingered on the elephants' gilded tusks, howdahs and caparisons.[69]

Many echoed the *London Saturday Journal* in rating these displays as supe-rior to their present-day European equivalents. After contrasting the gilt litters, umbrellas, gowns and crowns on display at the Court of Ava with the dowdy state of monarchy in Europe as of 1822, the *Monthly Magazine* thought it might soon be necessary to "send to India for an example of monarchy, as we once sent to her for science, and in later years for money and muslin."[70] The reference to Europe was not a coincidence: ever since the demise of Louis XVI in France, and in the shadow of Friedrich William of Prussia ("a decided enemy to gaudy dresses," according to an English biographer), the closest recent example conti-nental Europe had of majesty had been Napoleon—an unbecoming personifica-tion of "upstart royalty" who tried to hide his "original insignificance under the splendid scales of gold."[71]

Envy of majestic Asian gold created a quandary for would-be British rulers in that part of the world. On one hand, British dignitaries felt compelled to match the majesty in order to display authority, since, as one diplomat remarked of Sumatra, the "fondness for external show and pomp" made the precious metals "important instruments of governance" there.[72] On the other hand, the same am-bivalence that tempered British attitudes about their own glittering past altered their ornamentalist ambitions in Asia. After witnessing a Sikh pageant, army of-ficer George Francis White admitted that his regiment "of course, shewed poor in comparison" with the prince's "vaunted gold"; but he added that the British display "was of a character befitting the representatives of a nation boasting more of internal riches than of outward show."[73]

Britons who combined an interest in Asian affairs with radical politics, for whom decorative gold abetted tyranny at home as well as abroad, had no patience for such ambivalence. One of the most vocal of these critics was James Mill, who argued in his *History of British India* that there were "few indications more decisive of a poor country, and a barbarous age, than the violent desire of exhibiting the precious metals. . . as the characteristic marks and decorations of the chief magistrate."[74] Generally speaking, such verdicts had as little influence in imperial politics as they did at home; but the exceptional case of Turkey revealed the discomfort that ensued for many Britons when an "Oriental despot" actually followed western fashions. Although the middle-class *Chambers's Edinburgh Journal* praised the demise of "the ancient grotesque Turkish military equipments" as a sign that the Ottoman Empire was "rapidly acquiring . . . an estimation of the arts of civilized life," Sir Grenville Temple, a tenth-generation baronet, had his doubts. While he admired the elegance of the new "Frank uniform" introduced by Mahmud II, he could not help but wax nostalgic about the "wonderful difference that must have existed between the times of Selim I . . . at the commencement of the sixteenth century, and those of Mahmoud at the present day."[75]

Reservations about majestic gold veered closer to mainstream British opinion on the several occasions when travelers identified what they saw as clear connections between pomp and savagery. Each of the main variants of barbaric gold—far-fetched ugliness and imperfect imitation—informed verdicts on a foreign leader's incapacity to govern. The first was on display during Edward Bowdich's diplomatic mission to the Ashanti kingdom in 1817, in which courtiers wore "gilded rams' horns" and "fetishes. . . in gold and silver" and guards wore "corslets of leopard's skin covered with gold cockle shells." Back in Britain, critics pounced on this report as proof that "barbaric pomp and glitter" in Africa were "strangely blended with . . . atrocities."[76] A royal display on the other end of Africa presented a different variety of "barbaric gold." When Ranavalona, queen of the Merina territory in Madagascar, assumed power in a *coup*—which a later missionary described as "deeply stained with innocent blood"—the missionary David Jones was on hand to witness a coronation that combined the latest French fashions with idol worship. Ranavalona glistened with gold bracelets, lace, and rings, with "a row of gold filligree buttons down the back of . . . her peignoir frock." Before addressing the assembled throng, she paid homage to "the idol of the sovereign," draped in "splendid cloth of scarlet and gold."[77]

At the end of the day, the relative pecking order of world leaders in the matter of majestic display counted far less than economic and military power. The most basic reminder of this fact came on the many occasions when the British first vanquished their majestic counterparts to the east, then plundered much of the gold that had helped create such majesty. Following a short war in the mid-1820s, for instance, British troops carted off much of the splendid trappings of the Court of Ava (in modern-day Myanmar): its king's "splendid imperial state carriages" were exhibited in London within a year of the war's conclusion, "presenting one entire blaze of gold." Indeed, Britain's monarchy directly added to its own "outward show" by stripping a succession of Asian monarchs of their ornaments. In 1820, newspapers reported on the display in London of "a regal crown of pure gold, an entire suit of golden armour," and "massive gold chains of ingenious workmanship," which comprised the regalia taken from the deposed king of Kandy.[78]

The most extensive trove of plundered gold to pass from an Indian ruler to the British court followed the siege of Seringapatam, in Mysore, in 1799. Some reports at the time of the siege did condemn the soldiers' "unbridled licentiousness." Far more coverage celebrated the booty that found its way back to England—in particular, Tipu Sultan's famous throne, supported by four tigers "covered with plates of the purest gold," which drew crowds at the East India Company's baggage warehouse in 1800 before being passed along to the royal family; the throne's gilded footstool remained on display in the Company's library well into the nineteenth century.[79] Decades after the event, Tipu's treasure added to the glitter of Britain's monarchy. One of the tiger heads presided over a baptism dinner in honor of Victoria's second son, and an accompanying gold peacock worth £30,000 perched on a sideboard at Windsor for the viewing pleasure of William IV's dinner guests throughout the 1830s.[80]

Britons ultimately vindicated such displays, as well as the original plunder that made them possible, by shifting Tipu—who in fact had done much to modernize Mysore during his reign—from the category of estimable statesman to savage tyrant. Wellington's biographer wrote him off as "nothing more than a ruthless and wayward barbarian" and excused the "profusion of gold" plundered by the British as "a solid recompence for the labours they had undergone."[81] Britons also took care to domesticate this barbaric gold once it had passed onto their shores, by quarantining it in museums, trading companies and royal residences. Ten years into Victoria's reign, a treatise on poultry paused to consider "the most extraordinary Peacock in the world" that had passed from Tipu to the queen. This "specimen of Ornamental Poultry," the writer concluded, was "not unsuitable to the monarch of Great Britain." However, he assured his readers—citing Milton on "barbaric pearl and gold"—that from the queen's perspective "more pleasure is derived from the sight of its living models than from the inanimate splendours of this glittering toy."[82]

8

Devotion

In 1701 Joseph Addison took an afternoon out of his Italian grand tour to visit a small chapel, the Santa Casa de Loreto, on the Adriatic coast. In his enduring *Remarks on Italy*, he would later report that the stock of gold and silver offerings in its treasury "as much surpass'd my Expectation as other Sights have generally fallen short of it." The sheer volume of gold and jewels prompted Addison to marvel "that the *Turk* never attacks this Treasury," before helpfully suggesting that "a Christian prince" might easily pillage it using a party disguised as pilgrims. In any case, he decided, it was a shame to see "such a prodigious quantity of Riches lye dead and untouch'd in the midst of so much Poverty and Misery"; and concluded: "If these Riches were all turn'd into Current Coin, and employ'd in Commerce, they would make Italy the most flourishing Country in Europe."[1]

Subsequent British travelers to Italy in the eighteenth century provided their own inventories of Loreto's abundant gold, hatched new plunder fantasies, and joined Addison in scolding Roman Catholics for not putting the treasure to better use. After a visit in 1774, Scottish physician John Moore noted that the chapel's treasury teemed with gold lamps, angels, hearts, candlesticks, goblets, crowns, crosses, and "an infant of pure gold," donated by James II's exiled wife in thanks for the birth of her son; all were gifts of "rich bigots of all ranks," who could afford these treasures only by "oppressing their subjects." Others repeated Addison's association of treasure with rapine. After visiting in 1765, Samuel Sharp was incredulous "that some corsair . . . should not attempt to surprise and plunder this church"; in 1780 Henry Swinburne predicted: "What a pillage may, perhaps, be made here at a future day, by some now unborn Vandal!—enough to buy kingdoms."[2]

In 1796, Napoleon's forces accomplished the long-anticipated plunder of Loreto. Although much of the treasury had been moved to Rome prior to their arrival, they still made off with a million francs' worth of votive offerings.[3] For John Eustace, an Irish Catholic priest, visiting Loreto in 1806 called to mind "the fate of Delphi," the Greek temple that had been sacked by a succession of armies. Some Protestants pegged Napoleon as an agent of the apocalypse and identified "our lady of Loretto" with the whore of Babylon, whose downfall with "a golden cup in her hand" had been foretold by St. John. Millenarians reveled in Loreto's plunder, and even Eustace tempered his condemnation of Napoleon's "sacrilegious rapine" by scolding the Italians for hoarding so much devotional gold.[4] Although the restoration of Catholic kings after 1815 revived the chapel's fortunes—a cross of gold from Charles IV of Spain, a golden chalice from Pope Pius VII—postwar British visitors mainly commented on its empty cases and "trifling treasure."[5]

The range of responses that Loreto's treasures evoked, both before and after their dispersal, reappeared on the many other occasions in which Britons tried to make sense of devotional gold, whether it adorned temples in the ancient world, churches in continental Europe and Latin America, or their own houses of worship. Many of these stories about gold either started with, ended with, or were interrupted by plunder. Most condemned the use of gold in religion as wasteful, inappropriate, tawdry, and profane. All invoked a uniquely British moral economy of gold, with a strong dose of Protestant iconoclasm mixed in. Devotional gold either sat in a vault, preventing it from supporting commerce and credit, or adorned altars, adding the sin of idolatry to that of unproductive wealth. Plunder, in this context, could be justified as a necessary means of liberating gold for the greater commercial good and also as a prophylactic against future outbreaks of idolatry. This framework left room for class distinction and social stratification, which allowed for the survival of gold-fringed pulpit cloths in Anglican churches and majestic heaps of gold in royal chapels. It also reserved space for gold's affiliation with fine art, which would pave the way for more accepting attitudes in Britain by the 1840s. These varied meanings of devotional gold at home and abroad speak to the changing, and often complex, relationship between Protestantism and British national identity between 1780 and 1850.[6]

In devotion as in other occasions for ornament, gold took its place among numerous other decorations, including textiles, jewels, paintings, and less precious metals. It was almost always part of an ensemble, and not always the lead actor; as Addison remarked of Loreto, "Gold itself looks but poorly among such an incredible number of precious stones."[7] The most common, and functional, use to which it was put was in the form of cups and plates for communion and other rites. Churches that could afford it also wove gold into vestments and tapestries, and molded it into crowns (to adorn saints' skeletons as well as images of Mary and Jesus), crosses, miters, candlesticks, candelabra, altar rails and tables, and statues. Votive offerings, representing the hearts, arms, legs, or babies that were the objects of pilgrims' prayers of thanks, were sometimes made of gold as well.[8] Significantly, gold in most of these forms could be melted down and converted into money, rendering it even more prone to plunder than less portable or valuable materials—or even *more* valuable gems, which could not be monetized as readily. Gold (as well as silver) also stood out in such inventories because its devotional use necessarily withheld it from the money market.

Improper Exchanges: Idolatry and Plunder

A popular chapter in many early-nineteenth century ancient histories concerned the plunder of Herod's temple in Jerusalem by the Roman general Titus. British Protestants who retold this story followed the account of Flavius Josephus, in which Titus stood by helplessly while his army first burned and then looted the temple. The soldiers, wrote Henry Milman in his *History of the Jews*, had been captivated from a distance by the temple's "glittering front . . . covered with gold"; after setting fire to it, they "saw every thing around them radiant with gold, which shone dazzlingly in the wild light of the flames," and could not refrain from helping themselves to it, since "they supposed that incalculable treasures were laid up in the sanctuary."[9]

The association of political violence with devotional gold had a long history, which included appearances by Nero at Delphi, Cortés at Tenochtitlan, Thomas Cromwell at Canterbury, revolutionaries in France, and Napoleon's army in Europe. The justification for all these episodes, according to the Britons who recounted them, was that the plundered gold had been subjected to an improper—and unrequited—form of exchange. Misguided pilgrims deposited gold in a temple or church in expectation of a divine blessing or as thanks for a divine favor, and there it stayed, after the priests had taken a share for their upkeep. This hoarded treasure only re-entered circulation following its violent removal at the hands of bedazzled plunderers—after which (at least since Cortés) much of it fueled commercial exchange as coin, or rested in banks and multiplied exchange through credit.

The sack of Herod's temple was the final round in a cycle of theft and restoration of Judaic gold, in which Israelites were plunderers and plundered in equal measure. British readers of the Bible knew from Exodus that God's chosen people "borrowed. . . jewels of gold" from their Egyptian masters, which they ultimately donated to adorn the tabernacle. Divinely-endorsed plunder from neighboring kingdoms provided precious metals for Solomon's temple, which teemed with gold candlesticks, lamps, tables, bowls, and cups; once built, the temple's riches steadily fell prey to marauding rivals.[10] Viewed through a Protestant lens, Solomon's "richly gilded" temple had been "agreeable to that infant-state of the church, when such things were proper enough to please children"; its successive ravages, in the words of one Presbyterian cleric, attested to "the uncertainty and short duration of worldly greatness."[11]

By connecting Solomon's temple to the "gorgeous magnificence" of ancient civilizations, Britons used its adornment to make sense of the more general fate of pre-Columbian devotional gold, which always taught the same moral: it was "extremely impolitic," in Thomas Maurice's words, to make temples "the receptacle of such unbounded wealth; since it served only to spirit up every desperate invader of Asia to acts of the most nefarious plunder and sacrilege."[12] A prime example was the temple of Apollo in Delphi, which princes "loaded . . . with tripods, vases, shields, crowns, and statues, all of gold or silver"—and thereby invited plunder by Persia, Thrace, and finally Rome.[13] Other acts of devotional rapine included Rome's sack of Palmyra in 272, the Afghan sack of Gujarat in 1024, and Tamerlane's sack of Delhi in 1398, all of which attracted interest from British novelists and historians alike.[14] These and many similar pre-modern episodes involved heathen-on-heathen crimes, with the exception of the Crusades—which resulted in Muslims looting Christian gold in Jerusalem and Catholics removing Orthodox gold from Byzantium to Venice. The liberation of gold by Crusaders, concluded merchant William Jacob, did have the salutary side effect of "promoting national prosperity" through commercial intercourse between east and west.[15]

The conquest of the New World marked a turning point in the fate of plundered devotional gold: thereafter, "heathen" temples more typically ceded their treasures to Christendom. Britons often compared the "jewels of gold" adorning Aztec and Incan temples with "Israelite" counterparts, implying an analogy between Spanish and Babylonian plunder—and cited the theft of these treasures as yet another instance of Spanish greed.[16] But they also interpreted the accumulation and subsequent plunder of gold in New World temples in light of the more recent, and implicitly less culpable, British takings from South Asian temples—and folded stolen devotional gold from both corners of the world into the realm of exotic spectacle. A popular Mexican exhibit at London's Egyptian Hall in 1825, which included Aztec religious relics and "pure ores of gold," found its match in the "Hindu idols of silver and gold" that visitors to the East India House could view alongside other prizes from the siege of Seringapatam.[17]

Coinciding with the Conquest was the Reformation, which had more lasting resonance for British views on the plunder of devotional gold. Whereas Calvinists and Lutherans mainly targeted offending images, British Protestants took special aim at precious metals. In 1540, Henry VIII diverted the gold that adorned abbeys and monasteries into his own war chest and into the homes of his aristocratic allies; Edward VI finished what Henry had started in 1552, stripping parish churches of their treasure, and similar levels of dispossession soon followed in Scotland.[18] Two centuries later, British Protestants viewed Henry and his northern European counterparts with the same sort of loathing that they accorded to Cortés and Pizarro. Hence one historian diagnosed Henry as suffering from "that detestable vice, avarice," and the novel *Old London Bridge* depicted that vice in action: "The King chuckled as he thought of the treasure the two coffers from Canterbury would place at his immediate command; and when Cromwell drew forth a list of suppressed Abbeys . . . now annexed to the crown, his delight knew no bounds."[19]

If most Britons hated the Reformation's plunderers, however, they usually approved of the plunder. Poet Jane Taylor delivered a typical verdict on Luther when she lamented his theft of "gold and gems" but concluded that "according to our present light, / That barb'rous, tasteless heretic—was right."[20] Henry VIII's actions, if not his motives, similarly earned praise from many British historians. Channeling Adam Smith, they conceded that he had practiced "true political economy" by liberating the gold that the church had "abstracted from the wealth of the nation and made perpetually inconvertible and unproductive." Discussing the Reformation more generally, William Jacob's only regret was that it had not gone far enough. "The protestant religion, though it had raised its head," he concluded, had been too weak to prevent Spain from using its New World plunder to abet Catholicism's "veneration for. . . imposing and showy ritual."[21]

The final major occurrence of religious plunder took place in the 1790s, when Britain bristled with weekly descriptions of "Franco-Vandals" methodically casting devotional gold into the melting pot. Since the French Revolution threatened to sweep away Christianity along with its associated ornaments (not to mention the fact that France weaponized its plunder), more Britons responded with outrage than with *schadenfreude*. Typical was the pamphleteer who condemned "the *monsters* of rapine and impiety. . . who pay the Swedes and Danes in gold and silver, sacrilegiously plundered from the churches."[22] The only exceptions were millenarians, who rejoiced at France's fulfillment of Biblical prophecy, and radicals, who saw nothing wrong with the "splendid baubles of superstitious ceremony" being used to further the cause of the Revolution.[23]

In the restricted realm of plundering devotional gold, the tide of British opinion turned in favor of France after 1800. In part this was because Napoleon's plunder looked more like Henry's: after making peace with Rome in 1801, he promised to spare churches enough gold plate "for decent worship."[24] Also, close quarters with Catholic allies during the Peninsular War prompted British soldiers to view the plunder of cathedrals in a more positive light—a process that recurred in the 1820s, when British mercenaries and merchants witnessed the destruction of church property to pay for Latin American wars of independence.[25] Above all, the sheer efficiency with which Napoleon converted devotional gold into a war machine impressed his British foes. A visitor to Moscow in 1821 marveled when an archdeacon informed him that the French had erected a furnace in a church a decade earlier, in which they "proceeded to melt all the candlesticks and other articles of gold and silver which they could collect."[26] As with Jacob's verdict on the Reformation, many Britons thought Napoleon had been insufficiently thorough. A visitor to Toledo in 1821 lamented that its cathedral still held "innumerable urns of pure gold" after the war, and connected that "melancholy waste of property" with Spain's "deplorable condition."[27]

Such regret, however, tended to be restricted to Iberia and southern Italy, where economic distress sharpened the contrast with still-wealthy churches. The French had been sufficiently thorough at stripping their own churches of treasure that these virtually disappeared from accounts of devotional gold after 1815; and cathedrals in Germany and northern Italy, which preserved most of their gold from Napoleon's clutches, generally did so without impeding those regions' economic recovery after the war. Lingering regrets about the survival of church treasuries also increasingly conflicted with the revival of tourism after Waterloo. Although most British tourists were as critical of devotional gold after the Napoleonic Wars as they had been earlier, they also valued the chance to view it—if only because it enabled them to brag about their superior piety, artistic discernment, or both.

Encountering Catholic Gold

Recalling a stopover in Bruges in 1795 on his way to India, Scottish mercenary Donald Campbell considered its many houses of worship. "The Churches, and Church-curiosities, demand our attention," he observed: "for . . . in all rich Popish Counties, every Church is a holy toy-shop, or rather a museum, where pictures, statues, gold cups . . . and gods, of various sorts and dimensions, are hoarded up, in honour of the Supreme Being."[28] The fact that he had trouble settling on an analogy is revealing. *Holy toy-shop* spoke to the childlike fascination with gold that British Protestants routinely viewed as a Catholic fault, one that often shaded into idolatry. *Museum*, in contrast, implied craftsmanship and value, which applied to at least some of the treasuries that sprawled from Mexico to Moscow. In either case, Britons flocked to churches abroad, to gawk at their devotional showpieces or to appreciate fine art in its usual resting place. Their removal of these sites to the category of entertainment or edification marked a distinctively Protestant effort to deny gold's relevance to Christian worship.

The first impression of most Britons in Catholic churches abroad was neither entertainment nor edification but bewilderment. Naval officer Francis Collins reported in 1809 that the "brilliantly illuminated" gilded altar in a Lisbon church, "on a first entrance especially, dazzles the eyes and confuses the mind." In other travelogues, a Cadiz chapel was "adorned with a bewildering profusion of gold," the "mass of gold, silver, and jewels" in Toledo's Cathedral was "perfectly dazzling," and the cathedral in Aachen "dazzled with a profusion of gold and precious stones."[29] There was danger in the dazzle—but only for "uncultivated and rude minds." William Jacob, after visiting Seville in 1809, admitted that its cathedral's "pomp and splendour... dazzles for a moment," but insisted: "my English ideas were not to be seduced by this imposing spectacle."[30] Recoil at this possibility of becoming "half a Catholic," in the words of one visitor to a Catalonian monastery, mirrored the more general fear of "going native" that British adventurers experienced abroad. To preserve and protect their "simple and natural" piety, resting on "prayer, not pomp," they transposed Catholic gold from the category of dazzling idolatry to that of the fairy tale, the theater, or the museum.[31]

British travelers often relegated devotional gold, by process of analogy, to fairytale lands. The Oxford don T.H. White compared the Virgin Mary's cloth-of-gold robe in Antwerp's Cathedral to "those dazzling habits which we read of in the Arabian Nights or Fairy Tales"; in Rome, a young Michael Faraday remarked that St. Peter's "appears to have been erected on the plan of some fairy tale," with "Gold & silver not spread sparingly but shining & glittering in every part."[32] Such readings both tamed the sense of wonder created by gold and implied that Catholics, who basked in such brilliance on a weekly basis, were stuck in a state of perpetual childhood. They also converged with a more general British tendency to treat gold's decorative uses as paradigmatically Oriental—especially in cathedrals in Venice, Turkey, and Spain, which existed in close cultural dialogue with Islamic devotional display. Hence the "Saracenic" gilded ceiling of St. Mark's impressed Frances Trollope with its "Eastern magnificence," while the "crosses of gold enriched with precious stones" at St. Sophia Cathedral in Istanbul transported another writer to "the realms of fairy land."[33]

Closely allied with transmuting devotional gold into the stuff of fairy tales was a tendency to compare Catholic church-interiors to those of British theaters. The "damask hangings and gold lace" in a Milan church reminded a visitor in 1784 of "a tattered theatre"; in Lisbon, the "gold carving and fret-work" and "curtains of crimson velvet with deep gold embroidered borders" called to mind "a spectacle in Covent Garden."[34] While Britons grudgingly accepted an over-supply of gilding in their theaters as par for the course, they chastised Catholics for replicating that fashion in their churches.[35] They were especially annoyed by the gilded costumes of Mary, the infant Jesus, and the saints whose remains lay entombed in cathedrals, which added sartorial insult to sectarian injury. A statue of Mary with a "coronet of gold or chaplet of artificial flowers," complained one journalist, destroyed "all chaste and proper effect"; other tourists scowled at Madonnas with gold watches and bambinos with gold-tissue swaddling clothes.[36] A different sort of incongruity repelled Britons who confronted the gold-crowned skeletons of saints. These were popular sites on the cathedral circuit in Vienna, Augsburg, Cologne, and especially Milan, where St. Carlo Borromeo's "poor fleshless skeleton" was "clothed in the richest costume of silver and gold." His "noseless face" struck the Anglo-Irish clergyman Michael Seymour as "a hideous and loathsome and sickening spectacle, mocking the gorgeous and splendid trappings in which the skeleton is arrayed."[37]

Instead of relocating devotional gold to the fanciful realm of the fairy tale or the tawdry confines of the theater, a different set of British tourists turned to connoisseurship, which deflected its seductive power into the uplifting realm of edification. This had the effect of converting the church from a house of worship into a museum, which supplemented British religious superiority with aesthetic judgment. When her companions in Aachen decided to pass on its cathedral "from an idea that it would be childish to go and see relics," Anna Bray concluded that religious scruples had cost them the chance to see "such a beautiful collection of goldsmith's work as cannot be surpassed throughout the world." Earlier on her trip, in Cologne, she witnessed a medieval crucifix that was "one of the

Figure 8.1 Crucifix, gold and enamel, Cologne Cathedral Treasury. Anna Bray, who visited this treasury in 1841, observed: "Here are many relics, with the most precious and costly pieces of ancient workmanship in silver and gold, ornamented with jewels . . . The goldsmiths and the architects of the middle ages seem to be alike unrivalled in their arts" (*The Mountains and Lakes of Switzerland: with Descriptive Sketches of Other Parts of the Continent*, 3: 110). Art Resource ART499207.

Figure 8.2 Reliquary with three gothic spires, Aachen Cathedral Treasury, Palatine Chapel (1370–1390). Bray remarked: "I was so delighted with examining the subjects on these doors, that I almost forgot the costly reliquaries which were ranged on the shelves within them, and blazed forth in all the glitter of the richest Gothic work, gold and silver, radiant with gems and jewels of incalculable price" (3: 146). Art Resource ART77531.

most exquisite pieces of Gothic goldsmith's work that can be imagined" and gushed that "we have nothing that can compare with it for execution, in modern times. "[38]

By the 1840s, Bray was not alone in allowing her appreciation of the artistic merits of devotional gold to trump any qualms about its potential for idolatry. Louisa Costello expressed relief in 1846 that an altar in Milan was "still radiant with that far famed ornament, wrought by the most cunning hands that ever handled the delicate implements of the goldsmith's craft."[39] Like Bray, many of these spectators embraced cathedrals as medieval time capsules, which enabled a glimpse into a world they had lost. William Bullock, who began his career running a museum in London, marveled at an "exquisite" cathedral he visited in Mexico: "The statues, balustrades, candlesticks, candelabras, &c. of massive gold and silver, which have long disappeared in England, are here in daily use."[40] In all such cases, devotional gold lost its dangerous capacity for dazzling the viewer, since it could be coolly assessed and deemed either good or bad art—in the process requiring a capacity to discriminate that local congregants implicitly lacked. Gold without art, in this context, was worse than idolatrous: it was in bad taste. Visiting Porto in 1789, architect James Murphy noted the "profusion of gilding" in its churches and scoffed: "Gold is certainly a very effectual thing to conceal the want of art or science, or—."[41]

While such verdicts overlapped with appalled accounts of Mary draped in gold lace, the difference was that sacrilege was secondary for critics such as Murphy. This was not much of a problem for the growing number of Anglicans who were starting to redefine their theology to find room for grandeur. Moving devotional gold from the category of dangerous idol to harmless museum piece, however, remained a serious problem for more rigid anti-Catholics, who were only comfortable with such an outcome if it entailed the same sort of violent appropriation that Britons accorded to so many material objects of "heathen" worship. A Congregationalist reviewer of Bullock agreed with him that a gold altar in the Mexican cathedral that he had praised was indeed "the *ne plus ultra* of El Doradic splendour," but asked: "*Is* all this religion?" Concluding that its only suitable devotional use was for rites deemed acceptable by "Turk, Papist, or Pagan," the reviewer reached a tidy solution, which capitalized on a concurrent exhibit of Aztec temple artifacts in London: "We should exceedingly like to see it in the Egyptian Hall, Piccadilly."[42]

Gold and Social Class in British Churches

In 1840 James Abbott, an East India Company artillery officer, visited St. Paul's Cathedral with his Afghan steward, Samad Khaun, who had accompanied him on a diplomatic mission in Asia Minor. Khaun was disappointed, Abbott reported, "when he learned, that the chandeliers of St. Paul's were not of solid gold." Khaun complained: "At the theatre . . . I saw the most magnificent chandeliers of cut glass: and in the house of the Almighty, you hang dull, tawdry urns of brass." Abbott replied: "The theatre is built for the use of man, who is delighted with vain shew and splendour. The ornaments of the temple of the Most High are justice, mercy, purity of intention, and humility."[43] This response echoed

the strenuous distinction British Protestants had long made between theatrical Catholic cathedrals and their own more humble expressions of devotion.
As William Wordsworth suggested in his *Prelude*, Catholics required "a temple
rich with pomp and gold," unlike Britain's "simple worshippers" who were content with a "mere mountain chapel."[44] Most Britons resolutely consigned devotional splendor on their own shores to the middle ages, as when a historian
of St. Albans contrasted the "profusion of gold and silver ornaments" in that
cathedral's "palmy days" with its present "elegant simplicity."[45]

By the 1840s, however, Abbott's assurance to his Afghan servant was starting
to wear thin in British religious discourse. On one side the Oxford Movement,
aligned with sympathetic architects such as John Ruskin and Augustus Pugin,
loudly urged a return to medievalism. On another, resurgent English Catholics
were planting seeds for new converts and new churches. Taking a longer
view, this shift was part of a more general ebb and flow. A century after the
Reformation, for example, William Laud restored at least some of the grandeur
to English churches, until puritans violently reversed his efforts during the Civil
War.[46] After the Restoration in 1660, gold gradually made a comeback in British
churches—but in the process migrated from altar and reliquary to pulpit and
pew.[47] Notwithstanding this nuance, however, it was the Reformation that cast
the longest shadow on all subsequent discussions of devotional adornment in
Britain, by focusing attention on its absence.

Britons most commonly noticed the absence of devotional gold in local
histories and in the course of sightseeing. A history of Lincoln Cathedral took
note of St. Hugh's black marble tomb, which a seventeenth-century bishop had
installed "in lieu of that costly Gold Shrine once standing in this Place"; a visitor to Canterbury pointed out its cathedral's "figures of the apostles, &c. with
traces of the blue and gold with which it was formerly profusely ornamented."[48]
Historians supplemented these accounts with long lists of purloined gold,
drawn from "antient parchment books" and "accounts of the shrine keeper."[49]
A Hertfordshire rector lavished one such tally across several chapters of his history of St. Albans, passing from twelfth-century gold candlesticks, cups and
copes to a fourteenth-century crucifix, cloth of gold, and bibles "much inriched
with gilding and figures embossed in gold."[50] Other historians consulted Henry
VIII's account books to index the "embroidered vestments, and . . . crucifixes and
images of silver and gold" that he had stripped from England's churches.[51]

When Britons moved from providing inventories of absent gold to identifying
its meaning, their responses ranged from celebrations of post-Reformation
simplicity to nostalgic melancholy. Those on the "good riddance" side of this
fence applied to Britain's past the same anti-Catholic litany that appeared in
discussions of plundered churches on the continent. The Anglican clergyman
Edward Harington cited the votive offerings that once adorned Walsingham

Abbey, which Erasmus had described in 1511 as "shining. . . . all over with jewels, gold, and silver," as an example of the "gross deception practised on the multitudes by the designing monks." In the same vein, an article on "Popish Relics" excerpted a sixteenth-century Cambridge reliquary—including a gold-spangled coat for the infant Jesus and a gold collar for Mary—as symptomatic of the "vast sums. . . lavished upon the images of saints, &c." before "the bright dawn of the Reformation lighted upon England."[52]

Especially after 1790, with the rise of Romanticism, many Protestants tempered such critiques with melancholy over the decline of devotional splendor in Britain. In "Glastonbury Abbey: An Elegy" (1793), William Andrews recalled the abbey's destruction by "subtle Cromwell's soldiers" and asked: "Where are the Chalices of burnish'd gold, / By skilful artists elegantly wrought?"[53] An increasingly self-confident fine-arts movement reinforced these isolated laments with more sweeping critiques of the Reformation. A survey of "Early Sculpture in England" from 1833 expressed regret that Westminster Abbey, once "profusely adorned with pure gold," was "but a fragment of departed splendour, which displays itself in melancholy state"; an art critic huffed in 1843: "It is the fault of the Church that we have no religious art,—she *would* become Calvinistic."[54]

Far more typical than full-throated celebrations of gold's devotional absence or melancholic nostalgia, however, were those who regarded the Reformation as a necessary evil. One telling set of examples of this attitude concerned St. Paul's, which Daniel Defoe praised in 1724 for its "true Protestant Plainness"— but he also lamented that Londoners had foiled a plan to attach to it a dome "double Gilded with Gold" following the fire of 1666. Sixty years later, the *Times* was still castigating those "peculative ignorant citizens" who had signed off on its ugly black dome and urged that it was still not too late to see it "gilt with gold, as originally intended."[55] London historian James Malcolm expressed similar ambivalence regarding the cathedral's earlier incarnation, the altars of which had been "stripped of their precious stones, gold, silver, and cloth of gold" during the Reformation. He acknowledged that "all reverence for the Deity was lost" as a result, but consoled himself with the thought that Londoners had diverted their funds from "external religion" into "foundations of charity before unthought-of."[56]

British churches after 1780 were not all stripped altars and black domes. The gold that did survive in churches after the Reformation, however, tended to appear in a few very specific sites: on pulpits and their occupants, on parish beadles, and in royal chapels. In all these cases, the same exceptional allowance for gold as a signifier of service or majesty permitted its continued association with devotion. Beyond these spaces, the only gold in British churches adorned atavisms—or exhumed bodies, in the case of St. Cuthbert, whose gilded robe, gold crucifix and armband, and gold-wire skullcap still clung to his body when it was unearthed in 1826 at Durham Cathedral. [57] Other rare survivals, most of which were preserved as curiosities rather than aids to worship, included a gold cope in Carlisle Cathedral and an altar "highly adorned with gold" at Winchester Cathedral that the local townspeople had spared from Cromwell.[58]

More commonly, devotional gold in Britain decorated pulpits, clergymen, and their servants—but only in a minority of (mainly Anglican) churches. Of twelve instances between 1780 and 1810 in which gold was reported stolen from churches by the *Times* and in Old Bailey trials—a tiny fraction of such reports overall—nine concerned lace, fringe, or tassels "belonging to the pulpit."[59] As critics of the aristocracy, along with some clergymen, were fond of pointing out, the man behind the pulpit often sported matching gold rings, watches

Figure 8.3 Beadles. Detail from Theodore Lane, "A Parish Concern, or Prominent Reasons for Matrimony" (colored engraving). From *Pierce Egan's Anecdotes . . . of the Turf, the Chase, the Ring, and the Stage* (London: Knight and Lacey, 1827), following p. 192. In his later book *The Show Folks* (1831), Egan remarked: "The almost idiotic simplicity of the bridegroom, the *thriving* appearance of the lady, and the formidable look of the men with the gold-laced hats to witness the ceremony prove the artist to have been a man of considerable observation" (41). The Morgan Library & Museum, New York. PML 8414.

and chains.[60] Occasional complaints about "gold watch and chain divines" accompanied universal disdain for the gold-laced hats and coats traditionally worn by beadles, whose unpopular tasks included guarding poorhouse inmates and ushering upper-class congregants to their pews. A humorous sketch of "the Beadle of the Parish" in 1845 noted: "Gold-lace would degenerate directly it was worn with an humble air, and look as mean a pretension as copper-lace; and he knows that, and supports its superior worth with all the dignity he can."[61]

A final glaring exception to the rule of Protestant simplicity adorned the chapels and churches patronized by the royal family. An example was the chapel George IV commissioned to accompany his ostentatious Royal Pavilion in Brighton. Consecrated in 1822, it included a communion table with gilded rails and a large gold chalice; the *Times* remarked on its "suitable magnificence."[62] Such items copied the gold communion plate and solid gold cups on display at the Chapel Royal in St. James's and anticipated the gold altar lace and chandeliers that adorned the chapel in Buckingham Palace.[63] The intersection between devotional gold and majesty achieved its apotheosis at coronations and royal marriages, which featured "massy and costly" gold communion plate and gold-brocade altar cloths. In like manner the Princess Royal's christening in 1841 featured a temporary altar, "very richly and elegantly ornamented with broad gold lace" and bearing "a large gold salver," which glittered beneath Buckingham Palace's gilt candelabra.[64]

With the important exception of royal chapels, little of the gold in Anglican churches was either very dazzling or expensive, especially in comparison to its continental counterparts. The fringe on a pulpit cushion might cost a parish five shillings.[65] Even this much gold, however, was too much for many nonconformist critics (especially Quakers), who attacked the Church of England's "glittering apparatus of gold and power."[66] Political radicals added a class component to this religious critique, as when a Northern Political Union member hoped that "the gold and silver ornaments of our ecclesiastical establishment may . . . be spared when the people are perishing for want." The author of *David's Sling at the State Church Goliath* similarly asked how "our infidel State Christianity . . . of gold and palaces" could "ever have become attached to the name of the meek and lowly Jesus?"[67]

Against this grain, several currents converged in the 1830s to call for an extension to all British churches of the lavish adornment that had long been the exclusive preserve of royal chapels. Leading the charge was a revived Catholic clerisy, which gained momentum from political emancipation in 1829, a re-established English hierarchy in 1850, and a steady stream of Irish immigrants who provided new churches with congregants.[68] English Catholics modeled the revival of their faith on the past and present splendor of southern European cathedrals. Nicholas Wiseman, who became England's first Cardinal in 1850, defended the profusion of gold in Seville's cathedral on the grounds that "God Himself in His law would have only gold around His sanctuary."[69]

Influential architect Augustus Pugin, a Catholic convert in 1834, translated Wiseman's precepts into practice—and added some precepts of his own—in glittering designs for many new Catholic churches. Pugin, who cut his teeth in the 1820s designing gold-lined sideboards for George IV, worked closely with Wiseman to provide a cloth-of-gold altar frontal and vestments for the opening of St. Chad's Cathedral in Birmingham, and a church he designed in Wetheral featured a chancel "chastely and elegantly diapered in gold."[70] He amplified his architecture with strident medievalism, contrasting the "ancient glorious garb" of English churches before the Reformation with the "detestable" design of their modern counterparts.[71] An early example of this rising tide of English Catholicism, and of its impact on devotional gold, appeared in *The Velvet Cushion*, in which the gold-tasseled protagonist recalled its pre-Reformation glory days, surrounded by "magnificently caparisoned" fellow-cushions, then recounted its rescue from centuries of Protestant perdition by a Catholic church in London. "A good Catholic," the pillow purred, "treats even his cushion with reverence."[72]

Although Pugin's sympathies clearly lay with Catholicism, his influence extended beyond his employers. A small circle of self-proclaimed Anglican "ecclesiologists" used Pugin's ideas to co-opt a church-building campaign that had been underway since the 1820s. They provided architects with marching orders that included a generous helping of gold in everything from altar hangings to organ pipes, and looked forward to the day when British cathedrals would "glitter anew . . . with azure and gold and ruby."[73] Their architectural ardor found theological kindred spirits in the Oxford Movement, led by Edward Pusey and John Henry Newman, who strenuously defended "the externals of worship" in Anglican churches. In a sermon on "Offerings for the Sanctuary," Newman endorsed David's admonition in the Bible to prepare "for the house of my God the gold for things to be made of gold," and echoed Pugin in asking: "Is it a better thing to dress up our sinful bodies in silk and jewels, or to ornament therewith God's House and God's ritual?"[74]

The ecclesiologists' most famous fellow traveler was John Ruskin, who provided an influential justification of devotional gold in his *Seven Lamps of Architecture* (1849). The book opened with "the lamp of sacrifice," which he traced back to the Old Testament tabernacle that had required so much "overlaying with gold." Ruskin upended the prevalent Protestant view that God had commanded such ornaments in order to impress the childlike Israelites, instead arguing that His real motive was to secure from them an "enduring testimony" of their faith through the donation of "treasures of wisdom and beauty"—including "the light of gold." Like other Britons before him, Ruskin was well aware of the danger of dazzle—as was God, he urged, which is why

He included a special commandment against idolatry. But he rejected the corollary that the proper response was to keep gold at a safe distance from worship. Instead, God compelled Christians to display devotional gold as a constant reminder that they had offered up to Him their most precious metal.[75]

The revival of devotional gold in Britain did not go unchallenged. The Anglican *British Critic* accused Pugin of being motivated by "a keen relish for the beauties of the material creation," and novelist Marmion Savage captured the prevailing skepticism regarding the Oxford Movement when she mocked a fictional English monastery stocked with "gigantic and massive gold candlesticks" and draped "in the most sombre and gorgeous style of Puseyitical upholstery."[76] More generally, congregants complained that efforts in the 1830s and 1840s to revive ritualistic display had resulted in churches that were "popish" and "gaudy . . . like a theatre."[77] As for Ruskin's emphasis on sacrifice, most British Protestants were quite happy to follow the Old Testament prescription to part with their gold in order to provide "an oblation for the Lord," but much more often than not they converted that gold into unadorned pews or a missionary's travel expenses.[78]

The impact of the combined forces of the Catholics and Puseyites, however, was undeniable, in the concrete form of thousands of new Anglican and Catholic churches between 1840 and 1870, and in the lasting influence of Pugin and Ruskin on British architecture and aesthetics.[79] Their impact was also, in a way, inevitable. It had everything to do with the difficulty Britons had long had in insisting that gold should only be valued for strictly monetary functions, while at the same time tacitly accepting its important role in upholding social distinctions and deference to the crown. Wiseman identified this problem in 1845 when he faulted a tourist who had praised Napoleon's plunder of Spanish churches on the grounds that devotional gold would have otherwise remained "uselessly hoarded up, and kept from being publicly beneficial." The same reasoning, Wiseman argued, applied to "the family plate and jewels of the great, or to the regalia of the crown," which were "of no more benefit to the public than those of Loreto were." Repeating the usual justifications for aristocratic and royal gold, namely that "such thriftless accumulations are useful to society, by keeping up social distinctions . . . which are among the guarantees of a nation's honour," he concluded by asking why, exactly, religious devotion should not also be granted exceptional status in a nation that professed to be Christian.[80]

9

Graven Images

In August 1773, a month into Parliament's calling in of light guineas, an Abingdon correspondent to the *London Evening Post* reported a quirky windfall for locals who might otherwise have had difficulty finding takers for their gold. An "old Jacobite gentleman," he wrote, "buys up all the light money on purpose (as he calls it) to have a *clip at the King.*" Rejoicing at "seeing the day when the King's head might be *cut off by act of parliament,*" the Jacobite pounced on the opportunity to execute the state's command, snipping the king's nose to spite his face. He "sometime amuses himself," the writer continued, "with cutting off the nose, then cleaving up between the eyes, and then striking off the ear with his large shears." The correspondent hastened to add that he himself hated to see "our poor King's head so abused," and concluded on a philosophical note: "I have heard it said, that gold can do every thing; but this I now find to be false, for it seems gold cannot keep the King's head from being insulted."[1]

The images that adorned coins carried many meanings beyond their primary purpose of guaranteeing their full weight—which, in fact, George III's stern face had ceased to do in this instance. Besides signifying economic value, gold also provided a uniquely durable backdrop for a wide-ranging iconography, which rendered it differently valuable as a preserver of history, a spur to accomplishment, or a combination of the two. Ancient coins and newly minted medals, in this sense, had much in common with the gold lodged in the Bank of England, which by staying in one place enabled a robust circulation of paper money. The healthy circulation of antiquarian knowledge similarly relied on rescuing disinterred coins from the crucible and placing them on reserve in the museum—as did the preservation of national memory through etched images of important events and individuals, to be passed down through families or buried beneath buildings.[2]

Yet gold's value as bullion could diminish, if not destroy, its capacity to capture the past or preserve present glories—and as with so much else concerning British gold, social and economic status figured prominently in this tension. Most Britons who discovered buried coins were laborers, whose failure to appreciate their historical significance—and consequent tendency to sell them to goldsmiths, who often converted them into toys, jewelry, or coin—bothered antiquaries to no end. (A similar disparity in value judgments separated British connoisseurs of devotional gold from those who were happy to see such symbols of idolatry melted down into money.) The commission of gold medals, over which elites had more control, signified class differently, since these nearly always memorialized aristocratic accomplishments. Members of Parliament, military officers, public school and college students, and improving landlords received the lion's share of gold medals and trophies, while their lower-ranking counterparts settled for silver, bronze, or cash awards.

These social distinctions accompanied an ongoing debate over allowable senses in which gold was valuable. On one side stood "the unanswerable logic of *cui bono*," which could not comprehend "a mode of valuation so glaringly inadequate as that which the antiquary sets upon his mouldered pence."[3] This was a version of the stance that gold could never be truly valuable if it was diverted from its use as money. On the other side stood the dual forces of historical scholarship and national pride. Many interpretations of ancient gold enabled assurances of national superiority, either by staking claims for indigenous civilization or by indicating superior refinement in comparison with foreign possessors of antiquities. The thousands of gold medals issued during the century after 1750, for their part, deftly achieved a sweet spot between prideful posterity and commodity value. As Jeremy Bentham put it in *The Rationale of Reward*: "Pride proclaims aloud,—'it is not the intrinsic value of the metal which possesses attractions for me; it is the circle of glory alone with which it is surrounded.' Cupidity makes its calculation in silence, and accurately estimates the value of the material of the prize."[4]

History

"You are not to look upon a cabinet of Medals as a treasure of mony, but of knowledge," urged a participant in one of Joseph Addison's *Dialogues on the Usefulness of Ancient Medals* (1721); "nor must you fancy any charms in gold, but in the figures and inscriptions that adorn it."[5] Although this sentiment did not go unchallenged, even within Addison's dialogue, it garnered significant support over the course of the eighteenth century. Britons on the grand tour delighted in the history on display in coin cabinets from Amsterdam to Naples, and projects such as "an History of England by Coins" and "a Numismatic History of the Kings of Britain" found ready patronage.[6] William Wyon, one of Britain's leading engravers, commended coins and medals as leaving records of "battles by sea and land, processions, coronations, funeral pomps, and other ceremonies, alliances, marriages, portraits of illustrious men, and all that relates to policy or religion."[7]

Although the most concentrated collections of ancient artifacts resided on the continent, Britain offered numismatic troves under its building foundations, fields, and beaches, at least some of which found their way to museums and private cabinets. Coins minted by British kings dated back to medieval times, Roman rule left an even older cache, and Ireland boasted of Bronze Age treasures.[8] Many Britons, moreover, purchased or plundered ancient artifacts in Europe and points east, which they brought back for their compatriots' edification.[9] As the most lasting of metals, gold featured prominently in all such finds. When Michael Faraday wanted to "illustrate the durability of gold" in a chemistry lecture, he asked Britain's leading mummy expert for some "samples of very ancient date *worked by man*."[10] Besides standing the test of time, gold was also "the easiest found of metals," as one antiquary observed, owing to "its brilliancy and beauty."[11]

For antiquaries, ancient gold carried value that transcended its worth as bullion. That sort of value, however, varied in the eye of the beholder—and more often than not, the people who discovered such treasures were likely to prize them more for the gold they contained than for the history they brandished. A rough census of such people can be attained through reports of discoveries in newspaper articles and local histories that spanned the century after 1750. In descending order, the context of discovery in which at least one gold coin or other artifact was found included plowing a field (29); digging a foundation (24); digging ditches, ponds, canals, roads, sewers, railway cuttings, or wells (19); mining or quarrying (12); gardening (11); beachcombing (11); removing rubbish (8); and grave digging (5). Such accounts usually described the finders as "labourers" or "workmen," only occasionally children, and even less often property owners.[12]

Discoveries of gold coins or medals were most often solitary or limited to a small team of workers. Sometimes, however, whole communities got in on the act—as occurred in 1780, when a laborer in Lyme Regis who was filling in a sawpit found a pile of gold coins and filled his pockets instead. A watchful neighbor waited for him to leave then went to the pit, where she uncovered "a large collection of gold and silver coins, with some MSS." As a local historian recounted, "a general rush" ensued, in which "all . . . hastened to the general scramble." The neighbor sold her coins for £200, while another lucky resident "redeemed a mortgage on her house."[13] Similar scenes recurrently played out on England's shores when gales uncovered the remains of shipwrecks. Beachcombers on the Isle of Portland were "enabled to enjoy their Christmas holydays most merrily" in 1828 when a storm turned up "bars of gold and silver . . . which have been buried in the sea for many years."[14]

There was a wide gap between what finders did with the gold they encountered and what British law required them to do. Officially, they were supposed to hand it over to the coroner, whose duties included investigating "gold or silver, which appears, when found, to have been purposely hidden" in order to see if it qualified as treasure trove and hence belonged to the Crown.[15] It was newsworthy when finders actually did this, as when "a labourer trenching a field" in Lewisham who found two pots containing 420 gold coins "honestly and commendably communicated the circumstance to his employer," prompting a coroner's jury to seize them on behalf of Victoria.[16] More typical were the Westminster workmen who sold a "profusion" of Hanoverian gold coins "to promiscuous purchasers at very inconsiderable prices," or the Berwick laborers who sold a trove of Tudor coins to a jeweler "and regaled themselves with the proceeds." Sometimes the jewelers on the receiving end of such finds sold them at a profit to antiquaries or museums, but just as often they converted them into "rings and toys" or otherwise diminished their historical value.[17]

Faced with these odds against preserving the past, antiquaries uniformly condemned what one of them called "the destruction of national records in the meanest spirit of cupidity, which no wealth could restore." Cupidity, however, was not always the culprit; workmen who sold treasure to an interested antiquary stood to gain from the bargain more often than not, since a Tudor gold coin (to cite one example) could fetch more than £30.[18] The problem was at least as much legal as economic: namely, a "miserable" treasure-trove law that incentivized melting down antiquities in order to keep discoveries secret. As a result, wrote Scottish historian John Hill Burton, "[i]f a ditcher, or a set of railway navvies, find a gold torc ... no law or logic will persuade them that they ought to give it up for the public benefit."[19] Some British antiquaries sought to remedy this through "more liberal regulations"—such as those practiced in Denmark, where the state promised to pay bullion-value for discoveries that were donated to museums.[20]

Despite these obstacles, museums perseveringly accumulated gold coins and other relics by purchasing individual discoveries and either buying private collections or receiving them as donations. The British Museum built on those of Hans Sloane and Robert Cotton to amass a stock of coins and medals that one guidebook in 1850 called "superior to any existing, except perhaps that at Paris."[21] Lower-brow displays included a Kilkenny innkeeper's inventory of ancient Irish gold ornaments, which offered "a source of considerable amusement to travellers."[22] Even residence in a museum did not guarantee protection against "fearful destruction," however, as one Dublin antiquary worried in 1850: he warned that without a regular security officer, the Irish Academy's "gold antiquities" would be looted by the "London swell-mob, carried about by railroads and steamers" who visited "for the express purpose of plunder."[23]

A plunder-prone fascination with ancient gold coins and artifacts also accompanied Britons to the European continent. Although most contented themselves with viewing such relics under glass, some took a more hands-on interest in the past. In Crimea Edmund Spencer purchased "rare and beautiful specimens of gold and silver medals" from local peasants; more ambitiously, John Fiott Lee unearthed a trove of gold rings, chains, and necklaces from the Greek island of Ithaca and carted it back to his Buckinghamshire stately home.[24] The excavation of Pompeii, in particular, offered a window on ancient gold that few travelers could resist. One tourist's only regret was that "the contents of the houses could not have been allowed to remain in the state in which they were found"—but he added that "this would have been impossible" since "[t]ravellers are the greatest thieves in the world." Pompeii's treasures also inspired fictional reenactments, most famously Edward Bulwer Lytton's *Last Days of Pompeii*—which glittered with golden chains, tapestries, and bracelets, and featured a house in which "gold and jewels seemed prodigalized all around."[25]

British archaeological expeditions in the Near East yielded especially valuable stores of relics, as well as revealing rationalizations for removing them to Britain. With each successive excavation Britons replayed Addison's dialogue, baffling their local guides by insistently devaluing the bullion content of their discoveries. In Mesopotamia, Austen Layard wrote home regarding the " 'ridiculous notions' of locals that he was hunting for treasure" and breezily assured his guides they could have any gold they found, while he "cavalierly ripped through his sites on a single minded treasure hunt for the best specimens of sculpture to take back to the British Museum."[26] In most such stories, Turks, Greeks, and Arabs emerged as exaggerated versions of the dull-witted British laborers who melted down Roman and Tudor coins. Their "incurable fantasy that everything that is old must contain some of the precious metals," complained travel writer Charles Macfarlane, "has hastened and is still hastening the destruction of all ancient relics."[27]

If package tours and archaeological expeditions abroad emboldened Britons to possess antiquity's remains (with or without gold), discoveries of ancient gold closer to home provided them with a sweeping, but patchy, history of the British Isles from pre-Roman to modern times. Dates on coins recalled specific periods in the past—often times of violence when coins tended to be hoarded. Hence a pot of guineas discovered in 1830 with dates up to 1745 alluded to the Jacobite rebellion, while the stash of gold coins that Richard III hid beneath his bed in a Leicester inn shortly before dying in the Battle of Bosworth became the stuff of local legend.[28] Remnants from the Druids, such as a "fine gold *Druidical coin*, or medal" found in Essex and "much coveted by the British Museum," sparked endless fascination concerning their religious ceremonies—often inviting comparisons with Old Testament idol-worshippers or "superstitious Roman Catholics."[29]

Unearthing ancient gold in the British Isles also enabled celebrations of ethnicity, although these seldom went uncontested. Irish nationalists embraced the ornaments found in their bogs as proof that "the ancient nobility of that country possessed . . . vessels of gold and silver of excellent workmanship"; others contended that the old "lords of the soil" had received the gold in exchange for selling their vassals into slavery.[30] Across the Irish Sea, antiquaries sparred over the relative contribution of Romans and "ancient Britons" to gold coinage. Many pointed to pre-Roman gold coins minted by Cunobeline and "bearing ears of corn. . . to signify the improvements he introduced in agriculture," while others took Caesar at his word regarding the absence of "a Coinage of the more precious metals" prior to his arrival. At stake in all such debates, as Alexander Dick has observed, was "an idea of a *national* currency" defined through competing origin stories.[31]

This busy traffic in knowledge claims hinged on removing gold from its more typical functions of circulation and ornament in order to deposit it in a museum or private collection. And that, in turn, required a successful valorization of historical knowledge, starting with finders but extending to the wider public. For finders, it was mainly a matter of getting the word out, as was the case with the Dorset laborer whose master informed him that the "heathenish lingo" on a coin he had discovered rendered it "of very considerable value." The challenge of convincing a wider public was illustrated in 1827 by a novelist who recast Addison's dialogue as a conversation between a vicar and an English squire. After the vicar repeats Addison's point that an ancient coin's "erudition. . . stamps it with value," the squire insists that there is "something very inexplicable in the tastes and feelings of you patrons of antiquity."[32]

Posterity

In his "Verses Occasioned by Mr. Addison's Treatise on Medals" (1721), Alexander Pope put what literary critic Suvir Kaul has aptly termed a "manifestly imperialist" spin on his countrymen's fascination with ancient gold coins and medals, when he yearned for the day that Britain would in "living Medals see her wars enroll'd, /And vanquish'd realms supply recording Gold."[33] At the dawn of Britain's de facto gold standard, and a century before it would fully translate that metal's basis as its currency into global economic dominance, Pope pointed to a further use for gold: as a canvas on which Britons could etch a far more durable version of the "history of the present times" than that which contemporary newspapers and magazines reported.[34] Besides recording history in the making, colleges, schools, voluntary societies and sportsmen hoped that gold medals could also assist in making history, by motivating Britain's best and brightest to achieve new feats of invention, creativity, and athletic prowess.

In addition to functioning in markedly different (though overlapping) ways, gold medals and coins tended to be distinct in composition and appearance. As William Wyon explained, medals were "usually engraved in high relief," requiring "a succession of blows. . . with repeated annealings"; since they were not designed to circulate, they could forego alloy, sacrificing durability for facility in engraving. Coins, in contrast, were "usually brought up with one blow" and required enough silver or copper to alleviate the effects of friction. Although some engravers preferred working in bronze, since its cheapness enabled "more space for legends and devices," most medal commissioners opted for gold if they could afford it.[35] By any measure, gold medals proliferated after 1750, owing to an increased popularity of this method of commemorating political, military, and sporting events, and to an explosion of new schools and learned societies— which invariably came to employ gold medals as spurs to effort or invention, or as a means of honoring achievement.

At the top of the hierarchy of political gold medals sat those commemorating coronations. Although these dated back to the sixteenth century, they came into their own under George III in 1761, when 1008 were minted—including one for every Member of Parliament and 450 for the king and queen to dispense as they pleased. By the time of Victoria's coronation in 1838, that number had grown to 1409, including 106 sold by various goldsmiths for six guineas each.[36] Such medals typically provided more space than guineas or sovereigns to recount and/or allegorize the event. At 35mm in diameter, for instance, George IV's medal was 59% wider than the sovereign, offering room to depict, on the reverse, the king in Roman garb surrounded by an angel and three allegorical women.[37] Coronations yielded the most bountiful harvest of royal medals, but other occasions also prompted commemoration in gold: George III received four different gold medals to celebrate his recovery from illness in 1789 and a gilt bronze medal for being "preserved from assassination" in 1800.[38] Elderly Britons in the 1760s might have recalled a different manifestation of royal medals: until 1714, monarchs dispensed gold coins (to be worn around the neck) along with their "royal touch" as a cure for scrofula.[39]

Like coronation medals, gold medals honoring military triumphs had a long history prior to an explosive proliferation after 1760. Among many other examples, Oliver Cromwell awarded them to officers who fought at Dunbar in 1650, as did William III for naval officers during the Nine Years War; and Richard Haddock earned "a small gold medal still in the possession of the family" for his naval victory over the Dutch in 1672.[40] This trickle turned into a torrent during the Napoleonic Wars, which have aptly been described as "the real beginning of

Figure 9.1 Benedetto Pistrucci, reverse of 1821 George IV Coronation gold medal. The medal depicts the king "in a curule chair, and Roman dress, with baton in his right hand, an angel . . . behind the chair in the act of crowning," and "an altar with fire upon it" over which three helmeted women, representing England, Scotland and Ireland, swear allegiance (Thomas Allen, *The History and Antiquities of London*). Victoria and Albert Museum 1622&A-1902.

enormous public interest in the armed forces." Starting with Richard Howe's victory at Ushant in 1794, the Crown awarded 139 naval gold medals through 1815; army officers fared even better from their service in the Peninsular War, with 163 gold crosses and 584 gold medals. In addition to the substantial plunder they took home from the siege of Seringapatam, eighty-three East India Company officers received elaborate gold medals depicting a "the British Lion subduing the Tiger, the emblem of . . . Tippoo Sultan's Government."[41]

Municipal corporations did not sit idly by while the Crown dispensed appreciative gold, although they preferred gilding swords and snuffboxes over minting medals. Leading the way was London, which, as the *Times* remarked in 1787, was "as lavish of gold boxes, as if [it] had been the capital of *Eldorado*." Between 1757 and 1858 it awarded 29 gold-hilted swords and 52 gold boxes, typically coming with the freedom of the city and depicting "a particular man's good works"; fully half of the recipients were officers who served during the Napoleonic Wars.[42] Other London guilds followed suit, as did their provincial counterparts; as one critic observed, these boxes lauded "those who were interested in their country's welfare, and those who fattened on its spoils."[43] Such men included the Duke of Cumberland for suppressing the Jacobite uprising in 1745, Lord Gordon for inciting anti-Catholic riots in 1780, and multiple Lord-Lieutenants of Ireland.[44] Municipalities also often bestowed gold to radical politicians and causes, as when London gave a gold box to the Welsh MP Gwyllym Wardle for his role in removing George III's son as commander-in-chief on corruption charges; or when English towns "rained gold boxes" on William Pitt as a means of snubbing his rival, the Duke of Newcastle, in 1757.[45]

Among voluntary societies, the trend-setter in issuing gold medals was the Society of Arts, which awarded hundreds of them, as well as silver medals and cash prizes, during the century after its formation in 1754—most notably for "raising, planting, and preserving Trees proper for Timber" (a vital ingredient for a strong navy in an era of severe deforestation) and for "the culture and produce of such commodities as we must otherwise import from foreign nations."[46] The many agricultural and horticultural societies that blossomed after 1780 energetically copied its model, at times asking for advice on medal construction.

Figure 9.2 Gold box awarded in 1809 with the freedom of the City of London to Gwyllim Lloyd Wardle, M.P. for "having, unawed by Ministerial threats, exhibited serious charges against the late Commander-in Chief, which . . . induced His ROYAL HIGHNESS [Prince Frederick, Duke of York] to resign a situation of which he is unworthy" (*London's Roll of Fame*, 119). Rosalind and Arthur Gilbert Collection 454-2008, on loan to the Victoria and Albert Museum.

The Farming Society of Ireland, the Highland Society in Scotland, the Royal Agricultural Society of England, and the Smithfield cattle show, as well as many provincial societies and five different London horticultural societies, all used gold medals to motivate farmers and gardeners.[47] As scientific societies emerged in the nineteenth century, each commissioned gold medals to memorialize achievement in fields such as astronomy, geology, geography, and zoology.[48]

Gold also proliferated after 1750 as a spur to activity in colleges, schools, and sporting events. In 1751 the Duke of Newcastle endowed Cambridge with its first of what would grow to seven gold medal competitions by 1842, and starting in 1769 the Royal Academy gave gold medals to its top students in painting, sculpture, and architecture to reward "past diligence" and provide "an incentive for . . . future exertion."[49] Public schools swiftly followed suit, starting with Winchester in 1787 and spreading to Harrow and Charterhouse, among many others.[50] Organized sports also embraced gold medals and other trophies, especially on the racetrack. Between 1832 and 1839, eighty-five different horse races awarded at least 288 gold cups, shields, and candelabra, which were either endowed by an aristocratic patron or neighboring town, or paid for by subscription.[51] William IV donated "a splendid gold medal, to be competed for annually" by golfers at Saint Andrews, and athletes collected gold medals, arrows, cups, and laced hats in such sports as archery, curling, pigeon shooting, sailing, swimming, and wrestling.[52]

In all these forums, the allocation of gold medals signified social distinction in ways that paralleled the circulation of gold coins. The navy, for instance, restricted gold medals to admirals, captains, and flag officers; monarchs limited most of their gold coronation medals to Members of Parliament and foreign dignitaries, while scattering silver ones "amongst the people" in the audience.[53] Thirty years after Sir Geoffrey Copley donated funds to the Royal Society to pay for experiments, its aristocratic members decided to divert the endowment to pay for an annual gold medal—which the biographer of one of its recipients praised as a "more honourable, and a nobler object of ambition."[54] Members of the aristocracy won most if not all educational and sporting gold medals and trophies, while the snuffbox, the award of choice among municipal corporations, was a decidedly aristocratic accessory. By the same token, not everyone was convinced that gold was the best signifier of accomplishment: the Dundee clergyman Thomas Dick urged that instead of "a gold or silver medal," awards should be "of some *utility* to the person to whom it is adjudged," such as a pocket telescope for an astronomer.[55]

The Society of Arts, which catered to a mixed clientele of landed gentry, farmers, and mechanics, employed an especially precise calculus of social distinction in allocating its awards.[56] Although its original charter called for cash prizes only, it soon switched to offering gold and silver medals in most of its tree-planting categories—"with a view to exciting emulation among . . . persons of condition, with whom pecuniary premiums could have no weight"—and offering a choice of a gold medal or money in many other cases. Tellingly, one reason for the second provision was that since "such a token of honour and Regard is lasting, and may be handed down to posterity . . . many will prefer it to money, which is soon spent, and leaves no memorial behind." (The other reason was that at a cost of £5 per medal, the society stood to save a good deal of money if recipients took them up on their offer: the average cash prize between 1785 and 1800 was £25.) Just as tellingly, two-thirds of the winners during that period who were given the choice took the cash. One of these, Lincolnshire farmer Edward Presgrave, told the secretary he could not "with strict duty to an increasing family make choice of the medal."[57]

By the 1820s, the construction of gold medals had moved beyond voluntary societies to entrepreneurs, who sought subscribers to pay for gilded memorials of history in the making. One of the most industrious was the Birmingham silversmith Edward Thomason, whose masterpiece was a series of sixteen "numismatic monuments" to science and technology (including optics, phrenology, and steam engines), housed in "an elegant case" with red velvet and a magnifying glass. One reviewer praised this "metallic encyclopaedia of useful knowledge, which . . . as far as durability is concerned, are undoubtedly certain to outlive every record on paper."[58] A less successful venture was James Mudie's "grand series of national medals," which memorialized forty historical events stretching from the settlement of Bombay in 1602 to the Congress of Vienna; although he attracted 259 subscribers (at £630 for the gold medals or £42 for a silver set), the venture landed him in insolvent debtor's court within two years of issuing them.[59]

The prospect of posterity raised the stakes regarding the artistic quality of the busts and other embellishments that graced gold coins and medals. In terms of both skill and design, it took decades for Britons to achieve something approaching self-confidence in this matter. As late as 1820 they contrasted Napoleon's "handsome, commodious, and intelligible" coinage with the "barbarous workmanship" of their own.[60] The Treasury Office assigned the first sovereigns, coronation medals for George IV and Victoria, and a series of Waterloo medals to Benedetto Pistrucci, an Italian who brought to his task an "intense study of the great examples of ancient Art existing in Rome." Jean Merlen, a French immigrant, designed the reverse images for many of its coins.[61] Well into the nineteenth century, even homegrown engravers hewed so closely to "Roman customs and ceremonies" on their coins that, as Joseph Addison worried a century earlier, posterity would think its kings "paid a great devotion to Minerva [and] Apollo."[62]

By the 1840s a competing British style in gold medals and trophies finally started to emerge, and with it a newly nationalist aversion to foreign designs. As a writer on horse racing noted in 1848, "the old-fashioned, fashionless gold cups" of the previous century were giving way to "attractive triumphs of art" designed by local goldsmiths: one such "rich gold cup" could be admired "at the manufactory of Messrs. Fentem, Webster, and Danby" in Sheffield prior to a Rotherham race.[63] William Wyon's appointment in 1828 as the Mint's chief engraver provided a British foil to Pistrucci's classical—and often controversial—panache. For some, this changing of the guard was long overdue. When the Mint unveiled Pistrucci's bust of George IV on the sovereign, an anonymous critic stormed that "both head & neck *has a cropt appearance, as if it had been guillotined*," and alleged that "that tasteless Italian," with his "vulgar affectation of grandeur," deserved all the blame.[64]

Images on medals commissioned by municipalities or voluntary societies generated less controversy, but at least as much thought went into designing and presenting them. The New London Bridge occasioned two gold medals—one for the laying of its foundation stone in 1825 (featuring the Lord Mayor on the front and a stone, mallet and trowel on the back) and another when it opened in 1831 (featuring William IV on the front with the bridge and its dimensions on the back). When the mayor presented William with the latter medal and a gold cup at the opening ceremony, the king praised London's "magnificent improvements," of which the new bridge was "a most extraordinary instance."[65] Revealingly, given the encroaching commonplace that gold was only useful as currency, a proposed Society of Arts gold medal in 1756 went out of its way to devalue the metal that comprised it. Depicting "the most impressive instruments of arts and manufactures" against a backdrop of "a windmill, a paper mill, a water engine &c," it sported as its legend: "More Worth than Mines of Gold."[66]

In the case of coins, iconography may have been a topic of keen discussion but was always decidedly secondary to their primary function as a circulating medium.[67] In the most basic sense, medals also circulated, at least potentially. The *Farmer's Magazine* pointed out that although they were less "imposing" than monuments, they could be "circulated into every household, there to add fire to the fire of rising genius."[68] By design, however, the typical circuit of a gold medal was usually far shorter than that of a sovereign or guinea. Many became family heirlooms, as when Horatio Nelson left a gold box and sword to his nephew. Others decorated uniforms: four victorious captains were required to don "gold medals descriptive of the action in the Adriatic . . . on all occasions."[69] Medals and trophies also adorned stately homes; a racing enthusiast gushed that the twenty-nine gold cups lining the sideboard in Sir Thomas Stanley's Cheshire estate "presented a most brilliant, a most magnificent appearance."[70] Finally, as

Figure 9.3 Gilt bronze medal commemorating the construction of the New London Bridge, 1831. 28 mm. The inscription on the other side reads: "New London Bridge. The first stone was laid by the Rt. Hon. The Lord Mayor . . . on the 15 June 1825, and the bridge open'd by their majesties, the 1st August 1831. Cost 560,000 pounds." British Museum M.6089.

with the elaborate sets produced by Thomasson and Mudie, many gold medals were intended to travel straight to the collector's case.

An even more direct sense in which medals and coins earned a place in posterity concerned their ceremonial burial beneath buildings. In London alone between 1760 and 1844, gold coins found homes beneath the foundation stones of churches, prisons, the New Royal Exchange, the West India and London Docks, and at least five different bridges.[71] Provincial examples included the lunatic asylum and borough court in Glasgow, the Humber Dock in Hull, and Durham's "county courts, new gaol, &c."[72] Besides attempting to shape future archeologists' perceptions of nineteenth-century Britain, the presence of gold coins in their foundations embellished structures with regal dignity. Local officials clambered for coronation medals to undergird new building sites, as when J.D. Skelton asked the Mint, "on behalf of the good old loyal town of Sheffield," for two of George IV's medals to bury beneath a church. The same reasoning worked in reverse: an account of a "perfectly well bred" Holderness squire compared his education and manners to "coins of purest gold in the stony corners of our greatest buildings." [73]

In the final chapter of the meandering *Adventures of a Rupee* (1782), the titular gold coin, which had traveled from India to China, Batavia, St. Helena, and finally England, found itself "safely laid up in the storehouse of a society of antiquarians," where it endlessly conversed "with medals, busts, inscriptions, and other of my learned brethren . . . separating truth from the ashes of time." Cato, for instance, "spoke with much severity against corruption, from which he naturally passed to censure the British parliament."[74] With suitable suspension of disbelief, a similar conversation could well have been imagined among the coins in Horace Walpole's extensive collection at Strawberry Hill, before it was scattered on the auction block in 1842. In that scenario, gold coins featuring Philip of Macedon, Julius Caesar, Augustus, Nero, Hadrian, and Marcus Aurelius might have joined Edward III, Henry VI, and James I at the banquet table—while a veritable Congress of Vienna perched in the gallery, with representative gold coins from Venice, Austria, Rome, Sweden, Poland, Bavaria, Geneva, Holland, Turkey, Spain, Portugal, and France.[75]

It was no accident that an obsession with ancient gold artifacts, a proliferation of commemorative and motivational gold medals, and a newfound scrutiny of the images that adorned them, accompanied Britain's awkward embrace of greatness during the century after 1750. Just as a surfeit of gold bullion guaranteed Britain a seat at the table in the contest for commercial power, gold in these more evocative senses promised a different form of status, which overlapped with its economic might. William Bullock's Egyptian Hall, for instance, framed its numerous pre-Columbian exhibits in ways that contrasted Britain's noble preservation of treasures with the Conquistadors who obliterated Latin American history by melting it down into bullion.[76] Gold medals, meanwhile, wedded national greatness to Britain's favorite precious metal. Waterloo inspired George IV to commission a medal that would "for surpassing magnitude, become to future ages an enduring type of the great event"; and Cambridge University made "Waterloo" the topic for its Chancellor's gold medal in 1819—prompting a winning poem (penned by a veteran of the battle) that concluded: "proudly shall posterity retrace . . . That giant fight, which crushed Napoleon's power, / And saved the world."[77]

Besides assisting Britons in the task of distinguishing themselves from the rest of the world, gold also worked in the other direction—especially during the war that ended at Waterloo. Britain spent most of its stockpile of £40 million in gold coin and bars to forge a shifting series of alliances with European states, which propelled it to victory. Much of that gold ultimately returned to Britain to form its newly minted sovereigns. But more evocative reminders of the war also washed ashore. Although Nelson received numerous gold medals and boxes from his many British admirers, he received similar tokens from foreign ports of call: a gold-handled sword from the Greek island of Zante as well as gold boxes from Palermo, Sardinia, and Russia.[78] With medals as with money, gold sometimes signified international accord as well as national rivalry. In yet another register, the British search for new sources of gold after 1820 would yield occasions for co-operation and occasional sympathy with foreign cultures in such diverse regions as Brazil, Russia, and Southeast Asia.

10

Before the Gold Rush

Writing from Java in 1811 to India's Governor General, Stamford Raffles assessed Indonesia's potential contribution to the Napoleonic War effort. Javanese timber, he proposed, would "render our navy independent of the stores formerly derived from the precarious friendship of the northern powers." What was more, "the acquisition of a range of countries, apparently possessing the most valuable gold and diamond mines in the world," was a matter of serious consideration "in our present situation, in which the drain of our specie has been great in an unprecedented degree, and when for the restoration of the precious metals among us, as a circulating medium, we are likely to be left in a great measure to our own resources." Four years later, as Britain was trying to decide whether to return Indonesia to the Dutch, Raffles returned to this theme. "The great Island of Borneo," he urged, was "as rich perhaps in the precious metals as Mexico or Peru; possessing in one convenient spot a population of nearly 100,000 Chinese, who work on the gold mines of their own accord, and for their own benefit; but who would gladly submit to, and have invited British regulations."[1]

Between 1816, when Britain first officially adopted the gold standard, and 1848, when the discovery of gold in California doubled the world's supply of that metal overnight, Britons struggled with a recurrent shortage of gold, which depressed economic activity and exacerbated financial crises. Although economists expressed confidence that foreign trade, once unfettered, would supply the country with sufficient gold for a robust currency, many others followed Raffles's advice and hedged their bets by seeking what might be termed "gold sovereignty." They set their sights globally, ranging from Africa to India and Indonesia, but mainly focused on Latin America (especially Brazil) and, after 1820, Russia. In the first three locations, the search for gold accompanied Britain's expanding empire; in Latin America it was part of Britain's efforts to form financial relationships with newly independent states; and Russia, finally, posed the challenge of Britain's leading European rival becoming its leading supplier of gold.

Raffles's optimism regarding gold's accessibility and ease of extraction pervaded British descriptions of foreign gold during the first half of the nineteenth century. Many Britons assumed their moral and technological superiority would transform gold mining from a sordid tale of enslavement and plunder to a get-rich-quick scheme, perfectly suited to a rising class of armchair investors; they also assumed local miners would be more than happy to cooperate with freedom-loving Britons, following centuries under various feudal yokes. With their more direct involvement in mining came a blurring of traditional distinctions between Iberia's extraction of gold and Britain's acquisition of it through trade. That subtle shift in tone foreshadowed a more seismic change after 1850, when the British Empire—first in Australia, then in Canada and South Africa—became the world's largest producer as well as consumer of gold.

This chapter selectively surveys the wide sweep of British efforts to find gold, starting with Latin America and Russia and concluding with less successful searches in Africa, India, and Southeast Asia.[2] The presumptive power of British capital, which lured investors to stake a claim in potential gold deposits, was seldom far from the surface in any of these regions. The devil, as the different cases suggest, lay in the details, ranging from the use of slave labor in Latin America, serfs in Russia, and fiercely independent Chinese miners in Indonesia; to difficulties in getting Africans and Asians to part with their gold; to a failure to find substantial quantities of the metal in India.

Latin America

Among thousands of his countrymen in the early 1820s, Lord Byron contemplated buying "a principality of auriferous soil in Chili or Peru." South America's "vast quantities of gold," he thought, would form "powerful weapons in contending with an enemy." And long before Benjamin Disraeli entered literature and politics, he emerged as a leading defender of the many mining companies that sprouted in 1825 as part of a larger stock market boom. Disraeli echoed numerous prospectuses and promotional guides when he asked: "what mind can resist speculating on the effect, which may be produced on the metallic depositories of America, by the machinery, the science and the enterprise of Europe?"[3] According to the Colombia Mining Association, that country's "metallic treasures" had been "hitherto but very partially developed"; the General South American Mining Association promised that the continent's "inexhaustible Resources in Gold . . . and other metals" opened "a wide field for the employment of British Capital, skill, and enterprize, and afford encouraging assurances of the probable success of the present undertaking." Besides skill and enterprise, companies emphasized the power of British capital to reverse the fortunes of Latin American mining, by paying for drainage of flooded veins and for crushing ore.[4]

In sharp contrast to the eighteenth century, when Spain and Portugal excluded direct access to their colonial mines, newly independent Latin American states warmly welcomed foreign capital and technology. In 1823 Colombia's secretary of state promised investors that "the working of our gold mines . . . will be greater in time to come," and official publications issued in Venezuela and Brazil urged that foreign aid would reverse the economic decline caused by shortsighted colonial policies.[5] Of the various regions in Latin America that invited direct investment in gold mining, Brazil stood at the top of the list, owing to its dominant position as a gold exporter in the previous century and uniquely liberal accommodations. Although Colombia actually produced more gold than Brazil in the first half of the nineteenth century, the predominance there of alluvial panning over large-scale mining rendered it less reliant on British capital. Mexico and Chile did yield gold around the edges, but mainly specialized in silver and copper, respectively, after 1820.[6]

Although Britain had absorbed much of the gold produced in Brazil since the early eighteenth century, nearly all of it first passed through Lisbon before being semi-legally trans-shipped to London. Direct access to Brazilian gold was much slower in coming. When Captain James Cook visited Brazil in 1768 on his way around the world, he reported that the gold mines lay "far up the country, though we could never learn where," since they were "concealed as much as possible, and troops are continually employed in guarding the roads that lead to them." Naval chaplain Richard Walter provided a bit more intelligence on mining methods during a prior visit.[7] That remained the extent of British knowledge about the whereabouts of Brazilian gold until 1804, when Portugal's prince regent, John VI, invited the mineralogist John Mawe to inspect that colony's "extensive gold and diamond districts"—making him "the first Englishman, perhaps the first foreigner, who visited the interior of Brazil with the sanction of government."[8]

Four years later, British merchants achieved new access to Brazil when John VI moved his entourage there ahead of an imminent French invasion of Portugal. Of the dozens who flocked to Brazil, some used their new access to venture into the interior and transplanted their old trade of gold smuggling from Lisbon to Rio. One such merchant was John Luccock, a wool importer who shipped more than £10,000 a year in gold dust, bars, and coin back to London between 1809 and 1812.[9] Along with their gold, Luccock and others sent home accounts of their travels, most of which employed the same stereotypes that had long marked British histories of gold mining in South America. The Portuguese miners were "ignorant, vain, and idle," according to Luccock; another writer observed that gold had been a "fatal gift" that had diverted labor from neighboring cotton and sugar plantations. The result, concluded Mawe, was that Brazil lay "neglected . . . like that of Eden after the fall; while its infatuated possessors, like the offspring of Cain, hungering for gold, kept aloof from the rich feast which nature here spread before them."[10]

The more these visitors learned about the gold-mining regions, however, the more they realized what Brazilians had known for decades: that Brazil's "golden age" had long since faded. Most of the mining towns Mawe encountered were "fast hastening to decay," and most of the miners observed by a later British traveler eked out "a miserable and uncertain subsistence." They greeted such desolation with mixed feelings. On one hand, they expressed relief that the inhabitants had moved on to more virtuous agricultural occupations. John Barrow, who visited Brazilian sugar plantations in 1792 on his way to Indochina, praised Portugal for its overdue recognition that "the increased demand for this valuable product, in the markets of Europe," would enable them to recover from declining gold production; other visitors identified iron, cotton textiles, and a more general "advance of agriculture" as sources of economic recovery.[11] Indeed, the ghost towns they visited were exceptional enclaves in the thriving, diversified economy of Minas Gerais, only a fifth of which relied on gold and diamond exports by 1808.[12]

By the same token, Britons could not help but speculate that a substantial quantity of gold remained buried in Brazil's mountains (which were "still virgins," as one visitor noted) and that only a woeful lack of mineralogical skill had prevented Brazilians from finding it.[13] One reviewer of Mawe observed that mining labor in Brazil had been "applied in a manner far less ingenious, than in procuring coal in our own country," and Luccock attributed a failure to trace alluvial gold dust to its mountainous source to ignorance of basic geology. He blamed this on "a Priesthood, almost as ignorant as that of the darkest ages"; another writer faulted "the crooked policy of Portugal," which had "never permitted the introduction of scientific and learned persons into Brazil."[14] As for local efforts to extract ore from the mountains, Britons consistently lamented their want of proper pumps and dredges and their over-reliance on manual labor for crushing rocks.[15]

Brazil's declaration of independence from Portugal in 1822 provided an ideal test of the prediction that British ingenuity could squeeze additional gold out of its mountains. John VI's son Pedro, who sided with nationalists to become Brazil's first emperor, actively encouraged direct British investment in the new country. Two firms emerged as durable stakeholders in the reopened Brazilian mining sector: the Imperial British Mining Association (IBMA), which received concessions in 1824 to work the abandoned Gongo Soco mine; and the St. John d'el Rey company, which formed in 1830 and settled on two adjacent mines. (Less fortunate firms included the Brazilian Company and the Cachoeria Gold, Silver, and Copper Mining Company, both of which yielded more lawsuits than

Figure 10.1 "Manner of Washing for Gold in the Brazilian Mountains," in Edward Polehampton, *The Gallery of Nature and Art* (London, 1821), vol. 2, p. 312. The Morgan Library & Museum, New York. PML 142348-53. Bequest of Gordon N. Ray, 1987.

gold.)[16] Gongo Soco was more productive at the outset, while the St. John's mines yielded more gold over the long term. Together, the two companies extracted more than 25,000 kg of gold between 1825 and 1850 (a third of Brazil's total output), enough to assist in a moderate revival in the country's mining fortunes but nothing close its former yields.[17]

Promoters of the new companies raised capital on the promise that their "improved science of mining" would revive that sector by tracing the depleted alluvial sands upriver and "excavating the Mountains whence these Streams have their source." This mainly involved drilling shafts into mountain faces, then crushing and stamping the extracted ore. By the 1830s, the IBMA was applying steam power to the drilling process, and by 1840 the St. John del Rey had doubled its recovery of gold by using mercury amalgamation instead of hand-washing the stamped ore "after the Brazilian manner." On the debit side of this balance sheet, the hoped-for technology transfer from British coalfields to Brazil fell short of expectations. Gongo Soco's first mining superintendent discovered that his Newcastle recruits proved to be "quite unfit for the mode of working in use at the gold mines."[18]

A focus on mining acumen fit comfortably into the standard British narrative of providing a technical as well as financial fix to Latin American backwardness, but it left open one awkward question: if gold mining had been a "fatal gift" under the Portuguese, what was to prevent a return to those dark ages once the British had revived that sector? Robert Walsh, a physician who visited Gongo Soco in 1829, cleverly defended economic imperialism by presenting the new arrangement as a mutually beneficial division of labor. He argued that since the British companies were focusing on mountainous areas, which were mostly bereft of vegetation, their presence did not interfere with the more virtuous focus on agriculture by Brazilian farmers and planters—vocations that, in any case, were more suited to their natural abilities. Relying on "others of more capabilities" to seek gold "in the heart of the sterile rock," he claimed, would "leave uninjured the prolific soil of the country," which would enable locals to gain from "the pursuits of agriculture." This, he concluded, was "the best and wisest policy the Brazilians could adopt, in the present state of their country."[19]

The most obvious flaw in this argument lay in the fact that British mining companies fared worse than their Brazilian forebears had. A more immediate flaw concerned the one area of substantial overlap between British and Brazilian mining practices—their almost exclusive reliance on slave labor. Echoing condemnations of early modern Spanish gold mining in the sixteenth century, British visitors to Brazil had long emphasized its heavy reliance on slaves in the goldfields, which generally resulted in higher mortality than on plantations.[20] As of 1840, British companies owned around 2000 slaves; after 1845 they adapted to a new law banning expatriates from owning slaves by renting them from failed mines and plantations. From early on these firms broadcast their efforts "to ameliorate and soften" the condition of the slaves who worked for them—although this claim did not appease abolitionists in Britain, including some of their own shareholders. In any case, this paternalist defense began to fray around the edges once renting had replaced ownership, since this discouraged longer-term investment in the wellbeing of their human capital.[21]

Such arguments also became harder to sustain as companies shifted to more industrial methods, which subjected slaves to unprecedented levels of injury and toil. As an abolitionist petition noted in 1849, the St. John del Rey's introduction of a more powerful stamping machine, which was capable of breaking 50 percent more ore, was accompanied by an extra four hours' labor per day for the slaves who extracted it, and resulted in a "hideous sacrifice of human life"; in the first half of the year, it reported, forty-eight had perished from overwork.[22] Hence the same technological superiority that prompted Britons to defend gold-mining as an ideal type of economic imperialism undermined the anti-slavery posture that marked their most strident application of cultural imperialism to Brazil—which included, after 1826, cautious efforts to prevent newly imported slaves from entering the country.[23]

An even more pronounced passage from optimism to disappointment accompanied British involvement in the extraction of gold from other Latin American regions. One visitor in the mid-1820s found "very unproductive"

Colombian mines that had "never produced more than twenty or thirty pounds of gold per annum, from want of capital to work them properly"; another described "wretchedly poor women and children" loitering at deserted mines, filling vultures' quills with gold dust.[24] Far from despairing, company promoters assumed they could reverse such abject conditions with their superior "information as to what supplies will be required [and] . . . capital to procure them." Others hoped they could convince "the native indians . . . of the benefit that would result to themselves from their free labour in the mines," diminishing an expensive and unpalatable reliance on slave labor.[25]

Even more than in Brazil, most British designs to accelerate gold production in other newly independent Latin American states bore little fruit. Wholly dashed hopes greeted gold mining companies in Argentina, "a country which produced nothing but horses, beef, and thistles"; Chilé, where poor roads rendered the mines "of little or of no value"; and Haiti, where "sanguine assurances" gave way to a "considerable waste of capital" within three years.[26] Although Mexican gold production was more robust, especially in the newly opened region of Sonora, it mainly persisted as a sideline to silver, while Colombia's output of gold was, in one historian's words, "more constant . . . but also constantly disappointing."[27] The reasons for such disappointments paralleled the Brazilian case, with local variations. Companies sent steam engines to semi-arid mountains and "shiploads of Cornish and Welsh miners" who "were utter strangers" to gold mining; and, especially in Colombia, failed to appreciate that its treacherous terrain meant "the patient industry of the natives," not "European machinery and skill," was the only viable means of extracting gold from the soil.[28]

Russia

For Europeans whose hopes for a second golden age in Latin America had waned by the 1840s, Russia offered considerable solace. As German explorer Alexander Humboldt, one of many interested onlookers who diverted their attention from Latin America to Russia, proclaimed, "since the supplies of gold from the Brazils have so far diminished, those of Northern Asia . . . have attained an unexpected degree of importance." Although gold had been extracted from the Ural Mountains since the seventeenth century, Russians did not begin prospecting in earnest until the 1820s; a decade later, the Urals were producing more than 5000 kg of the metal each year, and when that supply leveled off new discoveries in Siberia provided record levels: in the five years before the California gold rush, alluvial deposits in Russia produced 130,000 kg of gold, which was 40 percent of the world's yield during that time and almost twice as much as Brazil had produced during its mid-eighteenth-century heyday.[29]

Unlike Brazilian gold, which required relatively little processing on its journey from the ground to the mint, Russian gold settled in miniscule flakes in the beds and shores of rivers, requiring more ingenuity to separate it from the sands. A new invention by the mining engineer Lev Brusnitsyn in the 1820s improved this separation process, and the many British visitors to Russia who reported home from the Hotel des Mines in Saint Petersburg witnessed similar devices— including a "most ingenious" machine for removing gold from micaceous sand, another for extracting it from clay, and a "carriage laboratory" for assaying ores in the field. The result of such inventions was a previously unsurpassed capacity to turn a profit from such thinly scattered gold. One Briton noted that the typical Siberian mine prospered despite recovering only an ounce of gold in every 3600 pounds of sand.[30]

Notwithstanding this record of Russian accomplishment, many British visitors to the Urals and Siberia went out of their way to identify past episodes of British ingenuity and boast of possibilities for remunerative investment in the region. It "would be a most profitable speculation," concluded one traveler in Siberia, "for any clever inventor of machinery to go out there, to devise some new plan for cleaning the materials from which the gold is extracted."[31] Several accounts related the story of a Birmingham mechanic named Major, who arrived in the boomtown of Ekaterinberg in the 1790s to serve as "principal engineer to the Oural mines," and proceeded to invent a new steam pump and a gold-washing machine. He soon built a bustling trade among the local peasants, "who had never in their lives seen any mechanical tools, except an axe and a saw," and acquired a small fortune by prospecting for gold in his spare time.[32]

If mechanical ingenuity appeared around the edges of British self-congratulation, its more central claim regarding Russian gold lay in geology— personified by the "King of Siluria," Roderick Murchison, who Nicholas I invited to survey the Urals in 1840. Although Murchison was not the first European geologist to investigate Russian gold, he took credit for producing the first accurate geological map of the Urals and identifying its strata, which he used to assuage Nicholas's concerns about whether "the gold alluvia were likely to last much longer." With help from the French paleontologist Edward de Verneuil, whose identification of Silurian fossils was crucial for accurate stratigraphy, and with the czar's financial backing, he reported the fruits of his survey in the lavish *Geology of Russia*, which, as Robert Stafford has observed, added "new territories to Murchison's scientific empire" while praising Russia as an imperial power worthy of British emulation, not fear.[33]

Although British visitors to Russia were not all so fulsome in their praise, the large majority delivered verdicts on Russian gold mining that betrayed less ambivalence than had been the case in discussions of Brazil. The suggestion that gold mining had been pursued at the expense of agriculture was almost wholly absent in this case, for the simple reason that Siberia and the Eastern Urals were largely bereft of arable land. Indeed, the main obstacle to mining in Siberia— that the permafrost restricted the mining season to five months in the year— applied doubly to agriculture. Further south, Britons expressed confidence that the large-scale movement of people east of the Urals would become "the firmest support of... agriculture" once "mining and washing operations shall have been reduced to a more regular system."[34]

On balance, British writers on Russian gold were also more forgiving regarding the people employed in its extraction than they were with Brazil. In the Urals, this mainly concerned the use of serfs, who, as one visitor reported in 1825, received a daily ration of "two pounds of black bread, with a suit of clothes and a sum amounting to 13s. 6d. sterling yearly" for their efforts; besides washing for gold, they chopped down trees for use in melting ice and smelting ore.[35] In Siberia, exiled prisoners (political or otherwise) performed much of the work. Murchison favorably compared this system to the British policy of transporting felons to Australia and urged that the "introduction of European manners and mining industry" had thereby "cleared and civilized" eastern Russia.[36] Criticisms of employing serfs and convicts in the mines tended to point to economic inefficiency rather than human costs. Liberating the "peasant slaves" who toiled in the Urals, argued John Cochrane, would yield far more in tax revenue than securing the "paltry profit accruing from their coercive labour." Others noted that the starvation wages paid to serfs incentivized fraud and theft.[37]

Britons grew more anxious when they turned from the extraction of Russian gold to its shipment abroad. Unlike Brazil, where the only obstacle to importing gold after 1825 was a 20 percent tax collected by the state, the transit of gold from Russia to Britain was more fraught. The Russian crown outlawed the export of its gold by private traders, although it did grant licenses in certain cases, and it often exported the gold that had been mined by the state.[38] In general, British perceptions about the incoming gold ranged from anxiety that there would be too much of it to concern that insufficient supplies crossed the Channel. The *Economist* thought it necessary to placate readers in 1844 who worried that an influx of Siberian gold would lower "that the general value of the metal," noting that most of it would be absorbed by the "rapidly increasing . . . consumption of gold for ordinary trade uses." More commonly, Britons expressed annoyance that much Russian gold either stopped only temporarily in their country or directly flowed elsewhere—for instance, £30,000 each year to India.[39]

If Portugal had enabled Britain to embark on an informal gold standard from the early eighteenth century until the suspension of payments in 1797, Russia arguably enabled it to sustain its gold standard following a financial crisis in 1847. Russian gold flowed into the country starting in 1846 and imports increased dramatically the following year in the wake of the crash, which had been occasioned by overinvestment in railways. The Bank of England replenished its gold reserves from £7.1 million in May 1847 to £12.2 million in September 1848, with half of the gold consisting in Russian coin. As one journalist remarked at the time, an "influx of Muscovian cash" arrived "just in the nick of time": "Precisely as the water butts in Threadneedle Street were getting rather empty, the Emperor turns on the cock, and pours into them a fresh supply." In exchange, Russia received a significant share of Britain's national debt, in a series of deals arranged by the St. Petersburg banker Alexander von Steiglitz.[40]

Britons balanced their grudging gratitude for the Russian gold that arrived on their shores with nervous suspicion regarding the gold that stayed in Russia. In the eyes of most Britons, Russia's windfall dramatically enhanced its capacity to engage in "systematic and subtle diplomacy," which allegedly altered the balance of power throughout the post-Waterloo world from Canada to Crimea.[41] One writer warned in 1834, in an effort to inspire British investment in Latin American mining: "the Colossus of the North is drawing yearly from her Siberian mines the sinews of war—the means of at length realizing those gigantic projects of ambition, which have been her hereditary policy since the days of the great Catherine."[42] Another worried, amid ongoing divisions within Britain's diplomatic corps regarding Russia's designs, that Nicholas diverted "his golden sands" to "agents, informers—spies if you will . . . at every court of Europe."[43]

The financial crisis of 1847 brought such anxieties to a head: although some expressed relief that Russia had enabled Britain to remain on the gold standard, many argued that such a standard was not worth it if it implied dependence on a national rival. As Francis Bennoch told the Anti-Gold Law League in 1847, "we ought not to bind ourselves to [gold] for our home trade, and place ourselves at the beck and command of Russia." The tsar, he worried, "could easily purchase 10,000,000*l*. in our funds," driving down their price and bankrupting British investors. Not everyone subscribed to this line. Free-trade advocate Richard Cobden was fond of insisting, as he did at the London Tavern in 1849, that "Russia was neither powerful, nor rich—that the tales of the produce of the gold mines of Siberia, and the investment of millions upon millions in the French, English, and American Funds, were altogether fabulous." More prevalent, however, were Cobden's many detractors, who warned that it was "not . . . altogether wise to calculate too far upon the assumed weakness of an empire like Russia."[44]

Global Gold: Africa and Asia

As Britons ventured forth across the globe after 1780, facing a potential shortage of gold and a vast map of yet-to-be colonized territories, they took solace in the Biblical account of King Solomon, who had amassed much gold from the uncharted land of Ophir. Ophir routinely appeared on early world maps in Peru, Armenia, Oman, Indonesia, Burma, the Gold Coast, or Mozambique; and in their headlong pursuit of new markets after American independence, British merchants and explorers eagerly followed suit. Africa and Asia featured prominently in such wishful thinking. In 1803, for instance, seven years into Britain's occupation of Ceylon, maritime historian James Clarke identified it as Solomon's "celebrated and mysterious country." Although most such suggestions were shot down in short order, the underlying premise—that gold might well lurk beneath colonial soil—persisted throughout the first half of the nineteenth century.[45]

British desires for African and Asian gold remained vibrant even as hopes for a revived Latin American supply revived in the 1820s and as news of Russian gold emerged in the 1830s: in the first case as insurance against potentially dashed hopes, and in the second to find a source of gold more firmly under British control. All these cases featured the same assumptions about superior British finance and technology that had fueled the Latin American mining mania of the 1820s. But they also presented numerous uncertainties, starting with the most basic question of how much gold stood to be extracted. Prospects ranged from optimistic in southeast Asia to questionable in India and Africa. Another uncertainty concerned how much gold stood to be exported to Britain. Here, West Africa spawned predictions far rosier, in the wake of the abolition of the slave trade, than actual supplies warranted; India sparked interest for similar reasons, as British merchants sought new imports in the wake of Indian deindustrialization.

Though gold production in Africa precipitously declined relative to Brazil during the eighteenth century, in absolute terms it did not fall off that much: down to 1700 kg per year from 2000 kg in the previous century. After 1720, however, much of this remained in Africa, and when Brazilian supplies leveled off after 1780 Britain joined France and the Ottoman Empire in looking to that continent for renewed imports.[46] When the French regained control over Senegal from Britain in 1783 they immediately revived prior ambitions to exploit alluvial deposits that, by their lights, indigenous Africans had lazily and ineptly let lie fallow.[47] Across the continent, the Egyptian pasha Muhammad Ali set his sights on the Sudan, where (in the words of a skeptical British Africanist) he sought "the gold mines of Quâmâmyl, recorded by early antiquity, and exaggerated by distant rumour." A commissioned German incursion in the 1820s and a follow-up expedition in 1838–9 both proved to be "expensive failures."[48]

In the same vein, Britain's leading explorers at the end of the eighteenth century paid keen attention to Africa's potential for untapped gold. Both Mungo Park and William Bruce emphasized the imperfect manner in which indigenes had gone about extracting it, and subsequent explorers and mineralogists echoed these observations.[49] An article on gold in *Bradshaw's Journal* from 1842 disparaged the "wasteful and disreputable manner" in which Africans carried out the trade in that metal. Others condemned the calabashes and baskets that yielded such small quantities of the metal during rainy seasons that, as one Africa Company officer reported, "only old women think it worth their trouble to wash for it."[50] Such inefficient methods worried Britons more than was the case in Latin America owing to their lack of direct access to the gold. As one colonial writer put it, "various mines of inestimable richness must exist in the interior of the country," but the "deadliness of the climate" would prevent their full exploitation until natives could be taught to "shake off the indolence with which they are so often reproached."[51]

Despite these reservations, a striking uptick in West African gold yields greeted the end of the Napoleonic War in 1815, aided by the abolition of the slave trade during the previous decade. The disruption of the triangle trade enabled ships to return directly to England from the Gold Coast, laden with bounties of gold and ivory that had been awaiting the end of the war; and British merchants hoped that recently secured Ashanti control over the Fanti gold regions would enable a reliably steady supply. As early as 1788, William Pitt had singled out gold dust in his request that William Wilberforce investigate which "commodities, besides slaves," could be imported from Africa in the event of abolition. After 1807 this "improveable possession" loomed large on inventories of legitimate trade, which regularly celebrated the "caravans of gold merchants" that showed up in Sierra Leone.[52] A buoyant stock market supplemented abolitionists' hopes. The Gold Coast Mining and Trading Company, which formed during the 1825 mania, promised to work "with the Native Chiefs and Princes" in order "to introduce a better method of working the Mines and Pits"—which, together with increased trade, would be "the means of . . . conducing to the civilization of its inhabitants."[53]

Against this wishful thinking, a steady stream of pessimists predicted that West African gold production would fall woefully short of filling the vacuum left by the end of the slave trade. They worried that recurrent strife between the Ashanti and neighboring nations (and also with Britain) would inhibit the trade and pointed to evidence that Africans earned more from smuggling slaves than legally exporting gold dust.[54] Pessimists also alleged endemic fraud as a sign that nothing short of direct access to gold would enable its profitable extraction— a verdict that indicated deep skepticism about the success of the abolitionists' civilizing mission.[55] The pessimists had statistics on their side. Total African gold production during the half-century before 1850 declined to an annual average of 1260 kg, down by 25 percent from eighteenth-century levels. For much of the nineteenth century, palm oil rather than gold proved to be a more reliable West African export; when gold yields finally did pick up, in the 1890s, its annual average of 3655 kg would pale in comparison to the more than 60,000 kg that South Africa, Australia, and the United States produced.[56]

Many of the same motivations that prompted a revived interest in West African gold suggested India as a potential source of the metal. Remarking on the "considerable quantities" of gold dust found in Malabar's rivers, colonial enthusiast Montgomery Martin predicted in 1836 that "when the riches of India begin to be appreciated in England, the precious metals will flow in abundance from the eastern to the western hemisphere." In case anyone missed the Latin American connection, he added in a footnote: "If the money which was expended in South American mines had been spent in India, how different would have been the results!"[57] In 1840, when Madras engineer Frederick Burr examined "the very extensive occurrence of auriferous deposits in various parts of the Indian peninsula," he found grounds for optimism in the recent Russian discoveries. Since "a large proportion of the gold of the Ural is produced from exceedingly poor auriferous sands," he noted, a "skilful mining Engineer" should be able to "yield a profit" in the similarly low-yield Indian soil.[58]

Wishful thinking about Indian gold generally consisted of counting the many low-caste peasants who eked out a living panning for the metal and adding the elixir of British capital and technology. In Lucknow, gold washers were "of the poorest class" and limited in number and remuneration by high taxes levied by the local rajah; in Mysore, members of "the Pariah or Sheroo cast" dug pits near river beds and ground the ore into dust using borrowed iron tools.[59] Britons invariably disparaged indigenous panning or mining methods, including wooden platters, trays, troughs, and trenchers, as simple, rude, or "very coarse."[60] Many of the mining operations British explorers encountered did employ mercury to separate gold from ore, but wasted the mercury along with the "ignited cowdung" they used in the amalgamation process; they also lost some gold when they subsequently separated it from silver and copper.[61]

Regarding future prospects, a divide emerged between East India Company surveyors, who bemoaned low yields in the mines they visited, and those who faulted them for possessing too little "practical science" to envision success.[62] Hopes for innovation were pinned on the capitalists who arrived in the wake of the new Company charter of 1813, which opened India to outside investment; a spokesman for the Tea Committee of Calcutta hoped that "some rich bed of gold might be discovered" in Assam along with its tea. Some offered technical fixes, such as the "graduated wire-sieve washing machine" that a Bengal major proposed for "reducing. . . manual labor," while others urged that even without new technology "the very low price of labour in this country" would render Indian gold competitive in the world market.[63] As in Africa, nearly all of this thinking remained of the wishful variety until the 1870s, when transformative changes in mining technology finally made gold profitable, at least for a decade or two, in Malabar.[64]

East of India, Britons saw more tangible evidence of gold in the decades before 1850, but also fewer opportunities to carry it back to Britain. Southeast Asia had long been a favored location of Ophir, dating back to Ptolemy's identification of present-day Malaya as "the Golden Chersonese."[65] That peninsula, together with Borneo and Sumatra, amply delivered on Ptolemy's golden promise during the first half of the nineteenth century, yielding between 3500 and 6000 kg of gold each year—around a quarter of the world's total between 1810 and 1830. [66] From a British perspective, however, such statistics could be deceiving: the consensus was that (in William Jacob's words, regarding Malaya) "little or none" of the gold "makes its appearance in the trading world, but must be used by the natives as personal ornaments." Another writer estimated that "a considerable part (perhaps one half)" of Sumatra's gold "never comes into the hands of Europeans."[67]

For some imperialists, this gap between Asian production and European consumption only made them keener to enhance the supply side of the equation. To this end, most of the familiar tropes regarding mining methods and personnel appeared in discussions of gold in Southeast Asia, dating back to the 1780s. The "petty excavations" they observed in Sumatra's gold regions "scarcely deserve[d] the appellation of mining"; the "imperfect industry" with which Malaccans hunted for gold meant that whatever they found was merely "the voluntary tribute of the earth."[68] When they turned to the thousands of Chinese immigrants who had been extracting gold from Malaya and Borneo since the mid-eighteenth century, their tone shifted. Some did credit the Chinese with "systematically, skilfully, and effectually" excavating gold from mines, as opposed to skimming the alluvial surface. Most, however, offered the mixed verdict that this "ingenious and plodding people" used the same "rude mining process" that was favored by indigenous miners, without being handicapped by their "native indolence."[69]

The presence of industrious Chinese miners in Indonesia was a double-edged sword from a British perspective. On one hand, it was a leading cause of preventing exports to Britain, since it diverted much of the gold to China. On the other hand, at least some Britons shared Stamford Raffles's hope that the Chinese could be convinced both to learn improved mining methods from them and to reward them with a share of the gold these yielded. The miners' resentment (and evasion) of taxes by local Malay princes provided an apparent basis for such optimism, but this perspective altered when the British took over from the Malays—as the adventurer James Brooke did upon declaring himself Rajah of Sarawak in 1841. Brooke viewed the tax on gold to be a "ruinous bargain," which he only temporarily agreed to observe. "When I find myself a little better in the saddle," he promised in 1845, "I shall most decidedly apply the spur, and make them pay a proper amount for their high privilege." His efforts to do so led to a rebellion in 1857—his brutal suppression of which "literally destroyed the once-flourishing gold industry of Upper Sarawak," according to one recent historian.[70]

While British involvement in foreign gold production before 1850 seldom surpassed the level of interested onlookers, their closer connections to its extraction often prompted a retreat from earlier suspicions that the metal had been a "fatal gift" in those regions—especially Latin America—where it had been discovered before 1800. After visiting South America during the heady 1820s, travel writer Maria Graham observed that the "insatiable thirst of gold" that had motivated mining in Brazil a century earlier had, after all, "led to useful and to honourable things"—including the opening up of "unknown lands" and the extirpation of "brutal customs." Although she lamented "the waste of human life in searching for gold," she argued that the recently concluded war of independence, and Europe's religious wars before these, had cost more lives.[71] References to the civilizing potential of gold mining in West Africa and India similarly edged toward upending the longstanding British identification of gold mining with moral turpitude.

Nobody in the 1840s was as convinced of gold's civilizing potential as Roderick Murchison, whose tour of Russia taught him that gold had turned "a large portion of the Siberian flank of the Ural" into "one of the most civilized tracts of the empire, whether as regards the industry and intelligence of the natives or the state of arts and manufactures." Hence it was not surprising that he readily turned his gaze from Russia to the British Empire, just as dozens of other Britons were starting to do after 1820. Famously, he appealed to geology to single out Australia as a likely source of gold, several years before its large-scale discovery there. Writing to a Polish geologist in 1844, he compared the Urals to the Blue Mountains on that continent, and two years later he urged an assembly of Cornish miners "to emigrate and dig for gold in Australia."[72]

Although Murchison's own friends admitted that he "knew nothing personally, and very little more by report, of the geological structure of Australia" at the time, and that the Sydney geologist W.B. Clarke had provided more compelling evidence for the presence of Australian gold as early as 1841, this did not prevent him from adding Australia to his geological "empire."[73] Revealing as this priority dispute was of Murchison's imperial ambition (and, by extension, that of many other British gold-seekers), just as revealing was the reason for the gap between the first credible information about gold in New South Wales and its "discovery" by Edward Hargraves, to much fanfare, in 1851. According to local legend, when Clarke initially informed the governor of New South Wales of gold in the Blue Mountains, he was urgently told to "put it away. . . or we shall all have our throats cut" in a nation still largely populated by ex-convicts. Though likely apocryphal, this popular story, which has circulated ever since, reveals the persistence of gold's allegedly negative impact on civil society in the British Empire, which always provided a strong countercurrent against its economic promise.

Conclusion

Gold Rushes

In 1850, "A Voice from the West" informed a Quaker magazine in London about "the sufferings and disappointments of the great bulk of emigrants to the golden region of California"—and hoped that "none of our friends in Great Britain or Ireland will be induced to turn their attention to that quarter, where . . . not only disease prevails to a great extent, but iniquity abounds to an almost unparallelled [*sic*] degree." Two years later, John Capper offered a more optimistic verdict in his *Emigrants' Guide to Australia*, although not without setting his bar rather low: he included as an example of the diggers' "orderly behaviour" the fact that most of them "cease from labour on the Sunday, and spend that day as they would spend it if they were in town," and that there were "few fields . . . at which a miner might not have his wife and family." He also reported on a miner "who, being drunk, had dropped the bottle which contained his gold, [and] had the bottle and its contents duly restored to him by the finder, who took some trouble to find him."[1]

This contrast reflects the grudging and gradual process whereby Britons moved from being outsiders looking in on world gold production to being major players in the production as well as consumption of gold. By the 1860s, after further discoveries in New Zealand and British Columbia, the British Empire yielded more than 40 percent of the world's gold supply, and additional finds in South Africa and the Yukon pushed that proportion past 50 percent by 1910. In this context, the burgeoning British interest in foreign gold between 1825 and 1850 served as a test run for its experience of gold in its empire. Many of the same positive thoughts Britons expressed regarding Brazilian and Russian gold would appear with more force once the scene had shifted to Australasia. Just as Murchison had lauded gold as a force of civilization within Russia, Scottish journalist R. H. Patterson praised the "golden argosies" on their way to Australia as producing a "vast and sudden spread of civilised mankind over the earth, making deserts and waste places to bloom, [and] cities to rise amid the solitude."[2]

Many Britons were quick to temper such prognoses by fretting over the moral consequences of the new gold—especially in California, but also in Australia, a continent that until recently had mainly been synonymous with convict labor.[3] Still, sheer physical distance lessened moral panic back in Britain. Although they tried to leaven Australia with upright emigrants, and did their best to contain excesses at the "diggings" through enlightened governance, they also credited the gold rushes with draining their own society of a hungry surplus population. Overall, confidence in superior Anglo-Saxon enterprise and moral fiber trumped pessimism regarding both California and Australia. The gold rushes in the 1850s offered a welcome opportunity to test the question, entertained since the Conquest: would Anglo stock be better able than Iberians to withstand an unbridled acquisition of gold without falling prey to greed and indolence?

The real concern lay less with morals than with the impact of the new discoveries on the gold standard. The gold rushes both added fuel to and shifted the terms of the debate between those who criticized that standard's deflationary impact and those who praised its capacity to discipline overtrading. Although the gold standard ultimately survived the 1860s without requiring its advocates to lose too much face, it did so only by opening its doors to other nations, which in turn subverted the traditionally exceptional meanings with which Britons had once endowed the metal. A related upending emerged regarding British views of decorative gold. Instead of scorning ornament as an unseemly and unproductive diversion of gold from its more civilized monetary function, economists now embraced it as a crucial means of absorbing an excess supply. In doing so, they took advantage of the pliable nature of Adam Smith's just-so story about the origin of money, without abandoning their condescension toward non-European habits.

Passages to England

In January 1848, John Marshall, an employee of John Sutter, famously struck gold near Sacramento. A Swiss merchant turned debt-dogged frontiersman, Sutter had arrived in California in 1839 after a frantic itinerary through New Mexico, Missouri, Oregon, Hawaii, and Alaska; he established a quasi-military presence north of San Francisco, where he traded with Russian furriers and navigated an "extremely complicated and fluid world of Indian, provincial, national, and international intrigue." California was in the process of passing under American rule following the end of the Mexican-American War: nine days after Marshall's gold strike, Mexico ceded it to the United States. The Native Americans on Sutter's land soon handed over their mineral rights to him, although the territory's new governor quickly annulled that treaty in order to claim the property on its own behalf.[4] By the end of the year, the region had yielded close to 15,000 kg of gold, which approached Russian levels; by 1853 annual US production neared 100,000 kg and would continue to exceed 75,000 kg per year through the end of the decade: a third more than the world's annual output prior to the discovery, and triple that of any time on record prior to 1840.[5]

An estimated 80,000 self-styled argonauts found their way to California in 1849 alone, joined by 300,000 more immigrants by 1860. Although most hailed from the United States, many fled the Taiping Rebellion in China or ventured east from Australia, while others flocked north from Mexico; thousands of British adventurers steamed around Cape Horn or cut through Central America to reach the mines. Most miners either ran out of money before striking it rich or spent whatever they earned. One of these was Edward Hargraves, a Brighton native who had worked as a sheep farmer in New South Wales for fifteen years before spending a disappointing year in California. As had been the case in the earlier Brazilian gold rush, the real gainers were those who charged the miners inflated prices for clothing, mining supplies, food, drink, news, and sex.[6] The new Californians, sensing they were at the epicenter of history and desperate for a modicum of law and order, applied for statehood in November 1849 (with an anti-slavery clause in their constitution)—which President Zachary Taylor approved over objections from southern congressmen.[7]

British newspapers first mentioned gold discoveries in "the northern districts of Upper California" in September 1848, announcing: "El Dorado is no longer a fabulous locality."[8] The following month Rothschild and Sons, London's leading bullion importer, learned of "considerable tracts of land with rich Gold Washings" in a letter from Benjamin Davidson, its agent in Chile; Davidson cautioned that such reports were "somewhat exaggerated by the time they reach us" but added more hopefully that "several samples of the gold have been already received here." For most of that year, his main focus had been on the price of Mexican quicksilver and "the late most disastrous events in France." It was not until November that he informed Rothschild's agent in Havana that "400 million $ worth have already been received by various parties at different places on this coast," which provided "the best possible proof of the accuracy of the statements of the gold actually existing." By the following August he had decamped to San Francisco.[9]

In January 1850, Davidson sent his first shipment of gold dust to Rothschild, with four boxes holding 2857 ounces of the metal arriving in London in April. Thereafter, the Tennessee, Oregon, New Orleans, and Carolina steamers unloaded between £5000 and £20,000 worth of gold on Rothschild's account each week. In all, Davidson sent 44,926 ounces during 1850, more than half of the firm's receipts, and worth nearly £175,000; another 21,108 ounces came from suppliers in Mazatlan and Panama. He sent more than twice that amount in 1851 (91,039 ounces, worth £354,000), but this comprised less than a third of Rothschild's total gold receipts that year. By June the firm had started receiving fresh-minted American eagles from its New York agent, August Belmont, totaling 159,404 ounces of gold; Russian gold that passed through Europe rounded out its imports in both years. By one estimate, Rothschild and Sons netted around £6000 on their bullion trade in 1851 alone, and profits increased in ensuing years; they also earned substantial profits from arbitrage operations, taking advantage of rapid fluctuations in the prices of gold and silver in London and Paris.[10]

Rothschilds sold most of their imported gold to the Bank of England, where it joined record quantities of the metal; the increased supply had attracted several newcomers to the bullion trade.[11] Starting in April 1851 the Bank began importing gold coins directly from the United States, totaling £3.33 million through the end of 1852. To smooth this process it shared the task of receiving American gold with its Liverpool branch, which accounted for half of that total. Russian imperials, which had comprised most of the Bank's direct gold imports in 1847–1849, receded in California's wake but certainly did not disappear, adding £1.95 million to the total in 1851–1852. The Bank's bullion reserves swelled by 23 percent overall, from a monthly average of £13.07 million in 1847–1849 to £16.14 million in 1850–1851.[12]

By the time Edward Hargraves arrived from California in January 1851, the governor of New South Wales had gone from discouraging mining to offering a reward to anyone who found gold in the colony. A month later, Hargraves discovered enough of the metal near Bathurst to claim the prize, which the geologist Samuel Stutchbury confirmed later that spring. The widely broadcast discovery fostered the same cycle of rapid immigration, rampant inflation, and urbanization (in both Sydney and Melbourne) that had occurred in California: over 700,000 immigrants arrived in the 1850s, including 484,000 from Britain, and 40,000 each from China and continental Europe. Of the British emigrants, 84,000 hailed from Ireland, which was still reeling from the recent potato famine.[13] Annual Australian gold production in the 1850s exceeded 75,000 kg a year, a little more than California. Together, Australia and the United States yielded nearly 80 percent of the world's gold supplies during that decade, which carried a worth of £200 million; total North American and Australian yields between 1848 and 1870, estimated at 3.1 million kg, exceeded the entire estimated world production of gold between 1700 and 1840. Australia further bolstered the Bank of England's bullion reserves, which ballooned to a quarterly average of £20.4 million in 1852.[14]

The ultimate destination for much of the gold that passed through the Bank from Russia, California, and Australia was the Royal Mint, which coined huge quantities of sovereigns after 1850—peaking in 1855, when nearly £9 million worth of gold coins rolled from its presses. The only prior year with a higher total had been 1821, with the major difference being that then nearly all the coins contained gold that had been recycled from their melted-down European counterparts, whereas nearly all the coins in 1855 added to the net supply of gold in circulation.[15] The gold rushes coincided with a decision to license the Mint's refining operation to Rothschilds, which jumped at the chance to add "Royal Mint Refinery" to their calling card; three other firms joined them as "approved refiners" by 1861.[16] A royal proclamation in 1860 relieved the Mint from coining so much Australian gold by declaring coins minted in Sydney to be legal tender in Britain. The coins, which had circulated locally since 1854, featured the same bust of Victoria on the front but showed "Australia" on the back framed by a laurel wreath, beneath the words "Sydney Mint."[17]

With the new shipments of gold came resounding and sustained popular fascination: Londoners seeking diversion could choose from multiple gold-related spectacles in the early 1850s. Harry Lee Carter's "Two Lands of Gold," a "Musical and Panoramic Entertainment," took audiences from a Liverpool dock, through a San Francisco "Gambling House in Full Work," to "Emigrants. . . on their way to the 'Diggins'" from Melbourne, and finally back to Euston Square. Saville House countered with George Payne's "Nights in the Land of Gold," a "panoramic Tour of America, California, and Australia." And John Skinner Prout in Regent Street offered "a visit to the Australian Gold Diggings for one shilling," depicting its "bustling animation . . . thronged with hard-working gold-finders."[18] Those seeking more edifying fare could examine gold nuggets and "a steam-engine quartz crusher" from California at the Great Exhibition or attend one of many available lecture series on Australian geology.[19]

The gold rushes also coincided with an infusion of illustration into British journalism. The *Illustrated London News* treated its readers to numerous visual depictions of the California goldfields, starting with an engraving of an "Encampment in the Sacramento Valley" in February 1849. Following the money, in September it presented an engraving of the "arrival of Californian gold . . . at the Bank of England," in which bullion-laden carriages trail off into the distance as an admiring crowd looks on. The newspaper devoted even more space to Australia, beginning in October 1851 with an account of the spot where Hargraves had made his first find. Along with a portrait of Hargraves next to his horse, jauntily waving his hat, the series depicted a "lump of gold . . . actual size; weight 3lb. 10oz." and a panorama of the diggings, showing "one of those busy fields of enterprise which remind us of the splendours of geographical fable, yet convey the lesson of history, that the reputed 'wonders' of one age become the matter-of-fact occurrences of another."[20]

Besides gold, Benjamin Davidson sent Rothschilds unvarnished opinions about the impact of the gold rush on California. With his first shipment he

Figure C.1 "Arrival of Californian Gold and Mexican Dollars at the Bank of England,"
Illustrated London News September 22, 1849. "The freight of precious metals was
conveyed to London by special train on the South Coast Railway . . . It was transferred
from the London-bridge terminus in fifteen vans, escorted by police, to the Bank of
England, where its receipt occupied the whole day. The amount of Californian gold thus
received was about £120,000." General Research Division, New York Public Library.

included a private letter describing "three English men who have been working
during the winter at the mines," who anticipated that they would soon "be able
to return to England & live like Gentlemen." He expressed relief that an "editor of one of the newspapers" had not "seen the gold dust in the hands of these
men, & heard their observations," since the resulting report "would have sent
out thousands of labouring men to this country." He added: "I look upon gold
digging like gambling with the exception that in the first instance a man risks his
health & in the second his property." Aware of his audience, Davidson concluded
on a more practical note, urging the formation of "a regular Banking establishment" in San Francisco: "I am convinced that an immense amount of gold dust
would fall into our hands, could we create notes payable in different places." By
the end of 1850 he had founded two banks in San Francisco.[21]

Most Britons who considered the gold rushes in California and Australia
echoed Davidson by worrying about the new gold's impact on British emigration
and on civil society at the "diggings," then moving on to assess its implications for
money and credit. The first response paralleled the common reaction to gold's
"poisonous" potential that had developed in Britain over the previous century
and a half, involving a process of quarantine in order to preserve (and, for some,

sanctify) gold's more respectable function as an enforcer of fiscal discipline. This required relatively little effort for California, which was far from home and only distantly "British"; it was more complicated for Australia, where the impulse to isolate the gold-infected colony vied with an urge to settle it with emigrants who could be trained to avert the "vice and immorality" that had accompanied gold in California.[22] In both cases, chauvinism suggested that if anyone could overcome gold's corrupting influence it would be Anglo settlers. Britons were less sure what to make of the new gold's impact on their monetary system: critics of the gold standard (including many Scots) embraced its subversion of that policy's disciplinary premise, while defenders tried to downplay the new gold's long-term effect on prices.

Poison

Commenting on "the recent discoveries of gold in Australia, and the immense numbers thereby attracted to that country," *The Rambler*—a "Catholic journal of home and foreign literature" based in London—reminded its readers in 1853 of what had become by that time a centuries-old truism: "large and successful gold-mining operates too often upon society as a poison," accelerating wealth's "natural tendency to sap moral and religious principles." Three years later, a sketch of North American geography and history in the *Preston Guardian* lingered on the California gold rush, which "spread . . . like the pestilence floating before the wind." The "freeborn sons of civilization," concluded the writer, "were not behind the bigoted and selfish children of Spain of three centuries ago in their thirst for the acquisition of the yellow dust"—the only difference being that the new breed of California miners were "more successful in their search, and were equally as indifferent about the means used."[23]

Britons identified symptoms of gold's poisonous power in California and Australia as amplified versions of those they had long catalogued at home. A poet in the *Metropolitan Magazine*, for instance, warned her readers that in California, "Ye may pine in want and hunger, or may fall in deadly strife, / While strangers grasp the treasure that ye purchased by your life!"[24] Those who moralized about California did hope that their American cousins could resist gold's most poisonous effects: here the contrast with Spain, which had played such a major role in Britain's moral economy over the preceding century, reappeared in stark geographical focus. Recalling how "the gold of Mexico and Peru" had reduced Spain "from busy and barbaric splendour to solitude," one British writer predicted that "the gold of California" would, in contrast, "spread a spirit of peaceful enterprise over all Spanish America in the place of sloth, immorality, and destructive discords." Another credited the gold rush itself, along with its likely beneficial effects, to the new Yankee presence: "The inert Mexican lazily and barely existed in California; but no sooner is the country transferred, by conquest, to the civilized American, than he scratches the ground beneath his feet, and finds flakes, and nodes, and particles of gold."[25]

Britons' propensity to contrast Spanish sloth with American enterprise helps to account for their general confidence that depravity in California would soon give way to a robust new society. One writer, for instance, referred to that territory's multiethnic population as a "world's parliament . . . presided over by the best specimen of our race, the first in freedom, in enterprise, in colonisation—the Anglo-Saxon." Such hopeful strains reflected a firm belief that Anglo settlement could not help but improve the world. George Croly predicted in 1849 that "when the mines are exhausted . . . the more valuable mine will remain, in the existence of a new nation, in the commerce of the Pacific, and in the richness of a soil unploughed since the Deluge."[26] Others viewed the gold rush as a catalyst for Anglo colonization closer to home: by emptying "the labour-markets of the Eastern States of the Union," R. H. Patterson urged, "this Californian discovery . . . ma[d]e room for the starving myriads of Ireland, who, in their turn, left an opening in the Emerald Isle for the energy and Protestantism of the Anglo-Saxons."[27]

When moralists turned from California to Australia, they focused mainly on gold's perversion of domesticity and its potential effect on emigration. Typical in the first regard was a *Household Words* article on the Melbourne marriage market: "When the bride was sober enough to walk pretty well, she would go out shopping; and no silk nor satin that cost less than a guinea a yard was good enough for the likes of her."[28] Fueling much of this alarm was the combustible combination of gold mining with convict labor. In the words of the Scottish clergyman William Tweedie, Australia's penal colonies had "poured forth their felon stream as if from the open gates of Sodom or Gomorrah, and in many cases the gold which is amassed only helps the finder to be more signally profane, more brutified and shameless."[29] Finally, the anti-Semitism that had long accompanied condemnations of gold in Britain reappeared in depictions of Australia. Charles Reade's *Gold!*, which brought "nightly full houses" to the Drury Lane Theatre, featured an unscrupulous Jewish banker in Melbourne (Isaac Levi, also known as "old sixty per cent") who separated foolish miners from their fortunes.[30]

If British depictions of gold's poisonous side in Australia tended to exaggerate its effects, however, the colony's distant location offered ample compensation; and finding solace in distance came instinctively to those who for decades had been socially and morally marginalizing thieves, misers, gamblers, and mercenary spouses at home. In this regard Australian gold was doubly consoling to some, who hoped it would drain Britain of its underclass. *The Lady's Newspaper* remarked in 1852 that "the draughting off of our surplus population" would convert "the workhouse . . . for want of able-bodied inmates, into an asylum for the aged and sick only."[31] Emigration equally enticed those who eyed their own economic rather than others' moral improvement. Emigrants' handbooks flourished, often sprinkled with maps, first-hand descriptions of the goldfields, and copious illustrations; a *Leeds* Mercury advert for the Earl of Charlemont steamer simply proclaimed "Gold! Gold! Gold!" and identified its destination, Sydney, as "the nearest port to the Gold district."[32]

Not all Britons were so ready to turn their backs on gold-seeking emigrants once they had departed. *The Rambler* accompanied its warning of gold's seductive powers with a high-minded call for "guiding from our shores a purified stream of emigration, the worthy germ of a great people"; and the Religious Tract Society aspired to provide all emigrants, "when ready to sail," with "a neat packet, consisting of . . . a variety of tracts, together with a selection of small picture books for children." On arrival in the Victoria gold district in 1854, settlers could choose among six Protestant ministers and four "Romish Priests," while three Wesleyan missionaries made the rounds to twelve chapels and supervised "seventy-two Local Preachers and other subordinate Agents."[33] As had been the case for centuries, missionaries sold salvation by appealing to a glorious afterlife; and here, at least, the recent gold rushes made their task easier. In 1853 *The Christian Emigrant's Guide to Heaven* described that destination's "abundance of fine gold . . . that dazzles ten thousand Perus, and Ophirs, and Californias, into the shades of everlasting darkness."[34]

Moving from church to state, the colonial office valiantly struggled to impose order on the Australian gold regions, learning what they could from California. Both Victoria and New South Wales allotted land through licenses, which cost 30s a month in Victoria and limited each miner to less than 150 square feet. Local commissioners and judges tried to enforce these payments, on top of preventing violence against the Chinese, attacks from bushrangers (escaped convicts who regularly raided the camps), and general rowdiness. Their heavy-handed efforts in the matter of licenses prompted an open rebellion in Ballarat, which quickly resulted in far-reaching reform: a "miner's right" for a pound a year in 1855 in lieu of the license fee and, ultimately, limited self-government by 1859.[35] Armchair observers in Britain often wishfully toned down the rough edges of this struggle. Owing to "the Englishman's respect for *law* and good governance," claimed the Anglo-Irish *Dublin University Magazine*, the Australian gold miner "naturally allows himself to be ruled and kept in order."[36]

Finally, most Britons predicted that, as in California, the newly settled colonies in Australia would provide a vanguard for spreading civilization in neighboring regions. An emigrants' guide commissioned by the Society for Promoting Christian Knowledge envisioned an Australia that would soon "undertake the task of infusing, if possible, civilization" into Polynesia and assist in developing "our East Indian possessions . . . until we shall have reached, not for conquest, but for commercial and civilizing purposes, the confines of Tibet."[37] Gold-induced settlement in Australia also conjured visions of a Greater Britain, sustaining British virtue through family ties. "As it is gold that created the western world," the *Times* noted in 1856, "it is gold that now creates another empire in the antipodes"—such that "Melbourne has, in fact, its daily paper, its illustrated paper, its comic paper"; and "its relations with the mother country are not less intimate" than those across the Atlantic. *Punch* proclaimed in 1852: "every ounce of gold discovered at Melbourne reflects its light upon an English fireside . . . the adventurers at one side of the world have their hearts beating towards their kindred at the other."[38]

Prices

Four years after California's 1848 gold rush and a year into Australia's sequel, a Sydney correspondent lamented to the *Times* that "the palmy days of gold, as the superior and most valuable metal, are waning fast away." Numerous echoes of this proposition emerged over the course of the 1850s, with varying inflections. R. H. Patterson at *Blackwood's,* no friend of the gold standard, hoped that the inflationary effects of the discoveries would extend suffrage (since an £8 rental would now be worth £10) and give "wings" to railways and steam navigation.[39] A *Punch* cartoon shifted its perspective to the "reduced goldsmith" who plaintively offered his customer "a handsome gold snuff-box . . . for a penny"; while an earlier article quipped that gold was "being picked up in such abundance at Port Philip, that we should not be astonished at finding some eccentric ticket-of-leave man sending over, in a fit of liberality, a remittance in payment of the National Debt. "[40]

More prosaically, British bankers and merchants debated the impact of the new gold on monetary policy. News of California came four years after the passage of Robert Peel's Bank Charter Act, which had linked the Bank of England's note circulation to its bullion reserves, and a year after a financial panic had crippled the British economy. Scots in particular, who had long opposed restrictions on paper money and were especially restive concerning the extension of Peel's Act to their country in 1845, greeted the gold rush with sardonic glee. One referred to it as "the currency extension act of nature," and the Secretary of the Edinburgh Chamber of Commerce expected that "these discoveries of gold would effect the improvement of the currency which Sir Robert Peel and his pupils . . . had so long resisted."[41] Annuitants, who had long been held up as unfairly benefiting from gold's deflationary tendencies, emerged as objects of thinly veiled *schadenfreude.* A *Household Words* writer urged "Mrs. Easiday" to

STARTLING EFFECT OF THE GOLD "DIGGINS."

Reduced Goldsmith (loq.). "Now then, Here you are!—a Handsome Gold Snuff-Box and a Ha'porth of Snuff for a Penny!"

Figure C.2 "Startling Effect of the Gold 'Diggins,'" *Punch* July 24, 1852. General Research Division, New York Public Library.

prepare for the day when, "having drawn your dividends, you find your house-rent, wages, fish, flesh, and fowl all raised to what you think a famine price; while your working-men tell you calmly that the sovereign has changed its value."[42]

Politicians and economists who had defended Peel's monetary policies by appealing to the "natural" scarcity of gold did their best to emphasize that inflation would be gradual and unlikely to disrupt business as usual. Citing the "vastly increased field for the employment of gold" in the wake of California and Australia, J. R. McCulloch offered the assurance that inflation would "be brought about. . . by slow degrees" and "will not occasion any injurious disturbance."[43] Roderick Murchison offered geological support for this stance, pronouncing a "General Gold Restriction Bill of Nature" whereby Australian yields would diminish once miners had scraped clean the quartz veins near the surface.[44] (One policy implication of the new gold on which most Britons could agree concerned war expenditure, which had been the focus of so much debate during the preceding century. The Crimean War abstracted £8 million in gold from the United Kingdom, but this barely made a dent in the £69 million that the Mint coined between 1844 and 1858.)[45]

In fact, the inflationary consequences of the gold rushes in Britain were relatively mild (roughly 2 percent per year through 1873) and short-lived. Part of the reason was that returns from the United States and Australia declined, from a peak of 150,000 kg per year in the 1850s to 85,000 in the 1880s.[46] More important, Britain's two leading commercial rivals adopted the gold standard: first Germany in 1871 (after leavening its coffers with reparation payments following the Franco-Prussian War), then the United States in 1879 (after seventeen years using Civil War-induced "greenbacks"). Although Britons routinely ascribed these conversions to national hubris (in Germany's case, its "traditional policy . . . to obtain glory by following every road that leads to it"), both countries had sound reasons to make the move. German industry relied on British loans, which were cheaper to repay in gold. Americans hungered for stable prices, much as the British had done after Waterloo, and a strong dollar made it easier to attract foreign capital to their growing manufacturing sector. The result, amplified by new American silver discoveries, was to drive up the value of gold relative to silver, and to drive down British prices by 3 percent a year between 1873 and 1886.[47]

Even as other nations joined Germany and the United States on the gold standard (France and Scandinavia in the 1870s, followed by Russia and Japan by 1900), the Bank of England had little trouble attracting enough gold to back its notes. And after waning in the 1880s, world gold production reached unprecedented levels after 1890, partly due to new discoveries in the Yukon and South Africa, but mainly to new technologies (including the use of cyanide to separate gold from ore and improvements in hydraulic dredging) that boosted yields in every corner of the world.[48] Indeed, British financiers in general prospered as never before between 1880 and 1914, as they shifted from home to foreign investment—since for the first time they could depend on most foreign stocks and bonds being repaid in full-value currency. Much of this investment took the form of gold mines, to an extent and with returns far exceeding Latin America in the 1820s. Although the Yukon rush paralleled Australia and California with its anarchy of emigrant diggers, South Africa (as well as a revival of mining in Australia) relied almost entirely on share capital, heavy machinery and low-paid wage labor.[49]

Deflation after 1873 was not as kind to other sectors of the British economy. Farmers suffered from heavier mortgage payments, while manufacturers watched with concern as demonetized silver swamped India and China. This wrought havoc in those countries, where imports became punishingly expensive and foreign investment vanished, but it also took its toll on British industry, which now had to contend with inexpensive Asian goods as well as "cheap and nasty" German and American products. In a failed attempt to balance the playing field, a robust bimetallist movement sprang up in Britain that "achieved little or nothing, but ... ... illustrated much"—not least "a substantial increase in the importance of the banking and service sector." Prodded by City bankers, the Colonial Office efficiently dispensed with their complaints in 1898 by placing India on a "gold-exchange" standard, which pegged the rupee to the pound and rattled South Asian markets for the second time in a quarter century by stifling incipient growth in its manufacturing sector.[50]

As historian Martin Daunton has persuasively argued, none of these inequities did much to shake the gold standard's status in Britain as an article of economic faith during the half-century after 1850. All boats rose during the prosperous (and inflationary) 1850s and 1860s, and when prices started to fall after 1870 wages remained "sticky"—leading to rising living standards, in sharp contrast to the volatile situation in the hungry forties. Many of the countries that joined Britain on the gold standard, including the United States and France, faced far more serious political and class divisions as a result of their decision to do so: there was certainly no equivalent in Britain to the "cross of gold" populism of William Jennings Bryan.[51] In contrast to those countries, economists and politicians in Britain had been building a multilayered defense of gold as a basis of its currency for decades prior to the shock of California and Australia. As one journalist put it in 1852: "Considering what it has cost this country in times past to maintain the existing standard, it is hardly likely that any *party* will ever seriously propose an alteration of it."[52]

Ornament

An article in the *New Quarterly Review* from 1853 added a new twist to the growing chorus of assurances that foreign trade and coinage could easily absorb the gold of California and Australia. After predicting (correctly) that "Germany must change her lacquered counters for gold pieces" and (incorrectly) that gold muhrs would make a comeback in India and gold crowns would supersede silver in Britain, the writer passed from the metal's monetary to its ornamental uses: the "multitudes who are raised to opulence by emigration will wear gold ornaments," while the "goldsmiths of London may. . . be prohibited from selling slightly adulterated brass for genuine gold." In sum, "the whole world, in its vast complexity, true to the traditions of six thousand years, esteems gold as the most precious of all things, and is eager to circulate, to exhibit, or to hoard it."[53]

Somewhere between the allegedly poisonous effects of the new gold in California and Australia and its much-debated impact on prices lay the fact that around half of the world's supply (at least prior to 1849) adorned people's bodies and homes instead of jingling in their pockets or resting in bank vaults. Ornament, which had long annoyed economists as diverting gold from its higher purpose as money, suddenly appeared in a new light. Although some insisted that demand for gold in that form had reached its limit, most argued that it was endlessly elastic. The result reshaped, if it did not wholly reverse, traditional cultural assumptions about those who wore their gold rather than spending or saving it. Britons after 1850 tended to view the conspicuous consumption of gold with as much condescension as ever, but newly welcomed it as providing a safety valve that would let them keep their gold standard.

Many Britons contemplated a world turned upside down by gold's sudden glut, based on the premise, as *The London Journal* proclaimed in 1851, "that gold is but an article of merchandise, and enjoys no magic exemption, any more than potatoes, from the rule that plenty is cheapness." One writer took solace in the thought that "if gold and silver can be procured as plentifully as copper, we shall be enabled to use pleasant utensils without risk of thieves." Another anticipated that "the smooth waters of the Avon" would be "spanned with a glittering pathway, suspended by bright, aerial chains of eternal strength and durability, as delicate as beautiful."[54] These whimsical forecasts added to a stock of similar predictions that had always appeared on occasions of anticipated precious-metal windfalls: the mining mania of 1825, for instance, had conjured visions of "a poor ragged labourer cooking beef sausages in a golden frying-pan."[55]

Such exaggerated accounts contained more than a grain of truth, however, all of which pointed to an acceleration of the democratization of decorative gold that had been underway since the early nineteenth century. *Fraser's Magazine* pointed out that the invention of "electro-gilding and plating" promised to absorb much gold by "substituting plated goods for those of inferior material, and by extending the use of them to classes which would never have purchased similar utensils made of pure metal." Britain's pioneer in this trade, George Elkington, died worth £365,000 in 1865 after patenting his application of galvanism to gilding in 1836. Although he made most of his money plating silver, his Birmingham window in 1849 featured "a gorgeous display of electro specimens in gold" along with "gilt *plateaus* most lightly and equally deposited." Besides being immeasurably cheaper than earlier methods, electroplating—as Harriet Martineau marveled in 1852—enabled gold to "become one substance with the material on which it is deposited, instead of being a mere covering, liable to be rubbed off by use."[56]

Ascending from the populace to the nobility, a *Satirist* article on the "Glorious Effects of California Gold" predicted in 1849 that the Queen's coach would be "Californiaised— . . . thickly plastered with fine gold." Again, comic exaggeration in the immediate wake of the gold rush gave way to more prosaic, but still tangible, outcomes. The late-Victorian landscape yielded thousands of varieties of gilded souvenirs to accompany celebrations of Victoria's long tenure as queen, including beakers, bowls, buckles, caskets, cups, glasses, and brooches on the occasion of her Diamond Jubilee.[57] British churches, meanwhile, accelerated their restoration of gold to its pre-Reformation pride of place after 1850, stitching more of the metal into their altar cloths and wall hangings. St. Paul's Cathedral, the stark design of which had long evoked mixed feelings, stuck out as epitomizing "the superstition of false simplicity" by 1872.[58]

An apparently elastic demand abroad provided further grounds for optimism that gold's ornamental uses would absorb enough of the metal to keep prices stable. To console the annuitant who "dreads a depreciation of the value of gold," a writer in *Chambers's Edinburgh Journal* predicted that "the qualities of 'beauty and utility' possessed by gold will be for a long time guarantees for its 'scarcity' whatever be its abundance." The article suggested that "India alone would absorb the results of many years' digging," which would "supply their insatiable desire for it." Its concluding observation, that Indians "habitually invest their savings in gold ornaments, which they wear on their persons," newly appeared as both a saving grace and a symptom of woeful barbarism, instead of only the latter.[59] In Australia as well, miners were quite happy to convert their gold directly into jewelry: they gave their wives and sweethearts "digger's brooches" displaying nuggets or gilded mining implements, and the Melbourne *Argus* in 1855 advertised "a ring of pure colonial gold . . . so contrived as to show, in separate compartments, small specimens from the different goldfields in its native nuggety form. "[60]

Against these hopes that decorative gold might save the day, some suggested that past efforts to condition people against adornment had been all too effective. French statesman Michel Chevalier influentially warned that "the progress of comfort and luxury does not appear calculated, so long at least as gold shall retain its present value, to offer a rapidly increasing outlet to the quantities of that metal supplied by the mines." In Britain, he concluded, "luxury . . . is less extravagant. People are becoming more economical. The wealthy even calculate more, and spend less for ostentation." R. H. Patterson (who, unlike Chevalier and his English admirers, welcomed gold's imminent downfall as a regulator of money supply), reached the same conclusion from a different premise: "if gold were no longer to be condensed wealth, but simply a metal like the others," he

Figure C.3 Digger's gold brooch with shovels, picks, winch, bucket, and pan (1850s). Museum of Applied Arts and Sciences, Sydney, A4478.

wrote, its "demand for it as an ornamental luxury" would decline—since "it is the value, not the beauty, of the yellow metal that makes it so much prized nowadays in ornaments."[61]

Looking back in 1863 on the "striking incidents of the gold-fever of the last dozen years," Patterson imagined a "wandering spirit from another planet" who witnessed "men in myriads rushing across oceans and continents to . . . waste places in the uttermost parts of the earth." Were he "to show a piece of the yellow metal to one of the natives of the country, and ask its use," Patterson continued, "the savage would tell him that it served to make rings for wearing in the nose and ears, or on other parts of the body, by way of ornament, but otherwise was of no account,—it could neither head an axe for him nor point a spear." The solution to this puzzle, he concluded, resided in "the great monetary emporium in Threadneedle Street" and "the gay crowds who go a-shopping in Regent Street"—both sites that revealed gold to be "the recognised symbol of Property, into which we can convert our wealth."[62]

Patterson's allegory captures the sense in which Adam Smith's just-so story continued to offer a plausible explanation for gold's persistent value in a world where supplies had doubled overnight—as, indeed, it still does, when mining output exceeds 2.5 million kg a year. In the decades after 1850, the status of gold as Britain's most precious metal was stirred, not shaken. The assumption that the rest of the world would catch up to Britain and start using the new gold as money largely proved to be the case in the United States and Western Europe, at least up to 1914. The fallback position, that people worldwide would absorb any excess by sating their desire for ornament, has continued to be the case up to the present, accounting for around three-fourths of the world's supply as of 1997, or roughly 100 million kg (nearly half an ounce per capita). And as historian Niall Ferguson has noted, with more than a hint of the combination of condescension and relief expressed in mid-Victorian Britain: "the cultures most addicted to gold as a decoration are currently enjoying rapid growth of both population and income."[63]

Most histories of the gold rushes, mainly by North Americans and Australians, present them as transformative watersheds—which they doubtless were, demographically as well as economically, for the continents in question and for the "international system" of gold reserves that prevailed between 1870 and 1914.[64] In Britain, they mainly reinforced and extended moral and political economies that had been developing over the previous century, though not without significant modification. Although warnings about the Iberian curse of greed and indolence did reappear in British accounts of California and Australia, they did so in gentler tones, which drew on the metal's long association with discipline and virtue in the Anglo world. The gold rushes also accelerated many economic and cultural processes that had appeared before 1850, including the spread of gold as money and ornament to more Britons, its newfound inclusion in church services, and its place in a widening embrace of empire. For all these reasons, the gold rushes marked a culmination of Britain's ambivalent embrace of gold— while at the same time newly extending that embrace around the globe.

Once this extension was underway, however, Britain's place in the world would never be the same again. Before the gold rushes, Britain had been the only country in Europe or the Americas with enough wealth to be modern and ancient at the same time. A continued supply of gold between 1750 and 1850 had burnished Britain's standing as a thoroughly modern nation of shopkeepers by supporting ample credit and cheap imports; it also fueled a war machine that insured its global commercial dominance. Yet the same supply of gold, half of which was diverted to ornamental uses, also enabled a persistence of older markers of social status. Military officers and servants continued to display gold in carefully choreographed arrangements, while the royal family handed over a significant share of its fortune to London's goldsmiths. Even parvenus, who earned scorn from aristocratic tastemakers for gauchely brandishing gold in a failed effort to imitate, in turn invited imitation from would-be parvenus. Although Britons sniffed at the use of gold as ornament in other parts of the world between 1780 and 1850, they did not give an inch in wielding it as a form of social distinction and national pride.

The windfalls of gold after 1848 altered both sides of this equation. Britain's status as the world's most modern economy met competition, especially from Germany and the United States. Although a newly international gold standard consolidated London's financial dominance for nearly a century after the gold rushes, it did so at the expense of British manufacturing might. City bankers during this period provided easy credit for the explosion of growth abroad that came to be known as the Second Industrial Revolution.[65] Ornamental gold, by which British elites had always nervously compared themselves with their continental and Asian counterparts, grew in prominence as a measure of international status. "Grand public displays of royal pageantry" became the norm on the continent, as "the *parvenu* monarchies of Germany and Italy. . . sought to rival the more venerable dynasties of Europe." Britons awkwardly adjusted, in a manner that highlighted growing tensions between their ancient and modern identities. At Edward VII's coronation in 1901, for instance, "the whole machinery of state was employed," using "electric wires" to proclaim his rule throughout the empire. Yet at his state functions, one biographer noted, he "revived all the pomp and circumstance of medieval days"—replete with gold coaches and liveries, gold-laced tabards, and "glints of gold splashed with silver."[66]

If the extension of the gold standard to Britain's economic and political rivals altered its own place in the world, the world also inherited many of the contradictions that gold had engendered in Britain prior to 1850. Foremost of these was the myth that world gold supplies, acting as a proxy for international trade, would consistently stabilize financial markets. Within Britain, gold's capacity to soothe savage markets had always been ambiguous if not illusory; Britons resorted to institutions such as the Treasury Office and Bank of England when they truly sought an assurance of stability. Once this role had been extended to the rest of the world, the fiscal responsibilities of central banks proliferated. It was precisely this irony that prompted Karl Polanyi to expose as delusory the notion of an automatically acting international gold standard. The choice, he concluded, was henceforth between a collection of state-empowered financiers who had taken on the Sisyphean task of combining economic stability with growth, and a "pure gold standard" that "would have transformed national economies into a heap of ruins."[67]

The control of national financial systems by a set of interlocked central banks, under the deceptive guise of a "natural" metallic standard, was only half the story. The other half concerned the equally Sisyphean effort by economists, politicians, and taste-makers to subordinate gold's many non-monetary uses beneath its more "civilized" function as the basis of credit. Gold's desirability as an aesthetically pleasing commodity constantly undercut its utility as a basis of credit; and even in the form of coin (whether guineas, sovereigns, or the foreign currencies that joined them after 1870) gold's materiality always annoyingly broadcast the paradox of simultaneously displaying "only the appearance of matters" (in Karl Marx's phrase) and possessing "intrinsic" value as a commodity.[68] This paradox, more than any other, accounts for both gold's durable appeal and its eternally protean capacity to embody monetary and aesthetic value, national identity, vice, virtue, and everything in between.

NOTES

Introduction

1. *Numismatic Journal* 1 (1836): 49; William Jacob, *An Historical Inquiry into the Production and Consumption of the Precious Metals* (London: John Murray, 1831), 2: 53, 274–275; W. Stanley Jevons, "On the Condition of the Metallic Currency of the United Kingdom," *Journal of the Royal Statistical Society* 21 (1868): 444; J. Laurence Laughlin, "Gold and Prices, 1890–1907," *Journal of Political Economy* 17 (1909): 260. For most of this period Portugal and Brazil also based their currency on gold; the United States adopted a *de facto* gold standard starting in 1834.

2. Linda Colley, *Britons: Forging the Nation* (New Haven: Yale University Press, 1992); Richard Price, *British Society, 1680–1880: Dynamism, Containment and Change* (Cambridge: Cambridge University Press, 1999).

3. Roy W. Jastram, *The Golden Constant: The English and American Experience 1560–2007* (Cheltenham: Edward Elgar, 2009), 10–14; Thomas J. Sargent and François R. Velde, *The Big Problem of Small Change* (Princeton: Princeton University Press, 2001), 293–298.

4. Samuel Knafo, *The Making of Modern Finance: Liberal Governance and the Gold Standard* (London: Routledge, 2013), 106–113; Peter Mathias, *The Transformation of England: Essays in the Economics and Social History of England in the Eighteenth Century* (Abingdon: Routledge, 2006), 190–208.

5. H. V. Bowen, "The Bank of England during the Long Eighteenth Century, 1694–1820," in *The Bank of England: Money, Power and Influence, 1694–1994*, ed. Richard Roberts and David Kynaston (Oxford: Clarendon Press, 1995), 1–18.

6. *To Whom It May Concern: The Manifesto of Pam the Illustrious* (Dublin: privately printed, 1760), 12.

7. Ronald L. Meek, *Social Science and the Ignoble Savage* (Cambridge: Cambridge University Press, 1976); Craig Muldrew, "'Hard Food for Midas': Cash and Its Social Value in Early Modern England," *Past and Present* 170 (2001): 81–85.

8. Adam Smith, *An Inquiry into the Nature and Causes of the Wealth of Nations* (London: Strahan and Cadell, 1776), 1: 29–33, 46–47, 216, 236–239; 2: 1–23.

9. *From Max Weber: Essays in Sociology*, ed. H. Gerth and C. Wright Mills (New York: Oxford University Press, 1946), 181, 187; Colley, *Britons*, esp. 147–320; David Cannadine, *Aspects of Aristocracy: Grandeur and Decline in Modern Britain* (London: Penguin, 1994), 9–36; David Cannadine, *The Decline and Fall of the British Aristocracy* (New York: Vintage, 1999), 8–15.

10. Colley, *Britons*, 11–100; Peter Mathias, *The First Industrial Nation: An Economic History of Britain, 1700–1914* (London: Methuen, 1969); John Brewer, *The Sinews of Power: War, Money, and the English State, 1688–1783* (Cambridge: Harvard University Press, 1990); Joyce Appleby, *The Relentless Revolution: A History of Capitalism* (New York: Norton, 2010), 17–18, 87–162.

11. Eric Hobsbawm and Terence Ranger, eds., *The Invention of Tradition* (Cambridge: Cambridge University Press, 1992); David Cannadine, *Ornamentalism: How the British Saw Their Empire* (Oxford: Oxford University Press, 2001); Penelope Ismay, *Trust Among Strangers: Friendly Societies in Modern Britain* (Cambridge: Cambridge University Press, 2018); James Vernon, *Distant Strangers: How Britain Became Modern* (Berkeley: University of California Press, 2014); Timothy Alborn, "Were the Victorians Ever Modern?" *Journal of Victorian Culture* 12 (2006): 154–160.

12. See, e.g., Luca Einaudi, *Money and Politics: European Monetary Unification and the International Gold Standard (1865–1873)* (Oxford: Oxford University Press, 2001); Marc Flandreau, *The Glitter of Gold: France, Bimetallism, and the Emergence of the International Gold Standard, 1848–1873* (Oxford: Oxford University Press, 2004); Barry J. Eichengreen, *Globalizing Capital: A History of the International Monetary System* (Princeton: Princeton University Press, 2008); Karl Polanyi, *The Great Transformation: The Political and Economic Origins of Our Time* (Boston: Beacon Press, 1957); Marcello De Cecco, *Money and Empire: The International Gold Standard, 1890–1914* (Oxford: B. Blackwell, 1974).

13. Alexander Dick, *Romanticism and the Gold Standard: Money, Literature, and Economic Debate in Britain, 1790–1830* (London: Palgrave Macmillan, 2013; Knafo, *The Making of Modern Finance*; Angela Redish, *Bimetallism: An Economic and Historical Analysis* (Cambridge: Cambridge University Press, 2000), 1–164; Deborah Valenze, *The Social Life of Money in the English Past* (Cambridge: Cambridge University Press, 2006); Mary Poovey, *Genres of the Credit Economy: Mediating Value in Eighteenth- and Nineteenth-Century Britain* (Chicago: University of Chicago Press, 2008); Christine Desan, *Making Money: Coin, Currency, and the Coming of Capitalism* (New York: Oxford University Press, 2015); Pierre Vilar, *A History of Gold and Money 1450 to 1920* (1960; London: Verso, 1976).

14. Jacob, *Historical Inquiry*, 292; National Archives, MINT 7/1. For more details see chapter 2.

15. As such, *All That Glittered* joins the growing ranks of commodity histories, ranging from popular to scholarly: see, e.g., Peter L. Bernstein, *The Power of Gold: The History of an Obsession* (New York: Wiley, 2004); Jennifer L. Anderson, *Mahogany: The Costs of Luxury in Early America* (Cambridge: Harvard University Press, 2012).

16. Ellen Meiksins Wood, *Empire of Capital* (London: Verso, 2003), 24; Frank Dobbin, *Forging Industrial Policy: The United States, Britain, and France in the Railway Age* (Cambridge: Cambridge University Press, 1996), 10–26.

17. For a corrective see Ted Wilson, *Battles for the Standard: Bimetallism and the Spread of the Gold Standard in the Nineteenth* Century (Aldershot: Ashgate, 2000).

18. Few if any significantly distinctive Welsh perspectives on gold are evident between 1750 and 1850, regarding either its ornamental or monetary uses.

19. On England and Scotland see chapters 2 and 5; on Ireland see Philip Ollerenshaw, *Banking in Nineteenth-Century Ireland: The Belfast Banks, 1825–1914* (Manchester: Manchester University Press, 1987), 22–27.

20. Desan, *Making Money*, 377. On gold tables see Jesse Molesworth, *Chance and the Eighteenth-Century Novel: Realism, Probability, Magic* (Cambridge: Cambridge University Press, 2010), 130–134.

21. George Gleig, *Supplement to the Third Edition of the Encyclopaedia Britannica* (Edinburgh: Thomson Bonar, 1801), 2: 232; Benjamin Mountford and Stephen Tuffnell, eds., *A Global History of Gold Rushes* (Berkeley: University of California Press, 2013), 207–272.

22. Although archives figure in parts of this book (involving coinage and the bullion trade), its primary focus is on the cultural meanings of gold that emerged in printed sources. The main archives used are Treasury and Mint papers housed in the National Archives, bullion account books held by Rothschild, and reports and account books held by the Bank of England.

23. Patrick Spedding, "'The New Machine': Discovering the Limits of ECCO," *Eighteenth-Century Studies* 44 (2011): 437–453; Ian Milligan, "Illusional Order: Online Databases, Optical Character Recognition, and Canadian History, 1997–2010," *Canadian Historical Review* 94 (2013): 540–569.

24. These include thefts of gold and references to "the power of gold" (chapter 2), women who wore gold coins as jewelry (chapter 7), gold objects stolen from churches (chapter 8), and contexts for buried treasure (chapter 9).

25. These topics have been addressed in published articles (referred to in chapters 2, 5, and 10) or will be in future projects.

26. Works that include gold in a more general treatment of decorative metals and gems include Shirley Bury, *Jewellery 1789–1910: The International Era* (Woodbridge: Antique Collectors' Club, 1991); Marcia R. Pointon, *Strategies for Showing: Women, Possession, and Representation in English Visual Culture, 1665–1800* (Oxford: Oxford University Press, 1997).

Chapter 1

1. Adam Smith, *An Inquiry into the Nature and Causes of the Wealth of Nations* (London: Strahan and Cadell, 1776), 1: 262–263; 2: 24–26, 96–97, 154, 215–216.

2. Peter Bakewell, "Mining in Colonial Spanish America," in *Colonial Latin America*, ed. Leslie Bethell (Cambridge: Cambridge University Press, 1984), 105–149; C. R. Boxer, *The Golden Age of Brazil, 1695–1750* (Berkeley: University of California Press, 1964), 36–60.

3. Christine Desan, *Making Money: Coin, Currency, and the Coming of Capitalism* (New York: Oxford University Press, 2015), 371–380.

4. For instance, William Robertson's *The History of America* (London: Strahan and Cadell, 1780), an influential British account of the Conquest, mentioned gold 126 times and silver only 41 times. A full-text search in Eighteenth Century Collections Online for "lust of gold" and "Spain" yielded 158 hits, compared to one for "lust of silver" and "Spain."

5. Adrian Finucane, *The Temptations of Trade: Britain, Spain, and the Struggle for Empire* (Philadelphia: University of Pennsylvania Press, 2016).

6. Adam Ferguson, *An Essay on the History of Civil Society* (Edinburgh: A. Kincaid and J. Bell, 1767), 324.

7. According to the most frequently cited estimate of sixteenth-century gold yields, Africa contributed 253,600 kg out of 714,000 kg (35.5 percent) between 1493 and 1600, compared to 279,200 kg from the Americas (39.1 percent): Robert H. Ridgway, *Summarized Data of Gold Production* (Washington: US Government Printing Office, 1930), 6.

8. Gavin Hilson, "Harvesting Mineral Riches: 1000 Years of Gold Mining in Ghana," *Resources Policy* 28 (2002): 16–19; David Eltis, "The Relative Importance of Slaves and Commodities in the Atlantic Trade of Seventeenth-Century Africa," *Journal of African History* 35 (1994): 237–249; Deborah Valenze, *The Social Life of Money in the English Past* (Cambridge: Cambridge University Press, 2006), 127.

9. Kendell W. Brown, *A History of Mining in Latin America from the Colonial Era to the Present* (Albuquerque: University of New Mexico Press, 2012), 1–5; Pierre Vilar, *A History of Gold and Money 1450 to 1920* (London: Verso, 1976), 19; John R. Fisher, *The Economic Aspects of Spanish Imperialism in America, 1492–1810* (Liverpool: Liverpool University Press, 1997), 20–28.

10. John Jay TePaske, "New World Gold Production in Hemispheric and Global Perspective 1492–1810," in *Monetary History in Global Perspective, 1500–1808*, ed. C. E. Núñez et al. (Seville: Universidad de Seville, 1998), 29–30; Anthony McFarlane, *Colombia Before Independence: Economy, Society, and Politics under Bourbon Rule* (Cambridge: Cambridge University Press, 1993), 66–82, 89–91, 111–119; William Frederick Sharp, *Slavery on the Spanish Frontier: The Colombian Chocó, 1680–1810* (Norman: University of Oklahoma Press, 1976), 46–79.

11. Vilar, *History of Gold and Money*, 194.

12. David T. Haberly, "Colonial Brazilian Literature," in *Brazilian Literature*, ed. Roberto Gonzalez Echevarria and Enrique-Pupo (Cambridge: Cambridge University Press, 1996), 63; Boxer, *Golden Age of Brazil*, 34–37.

13. Maria Luiza Marcílio, "The Population of Colonial Brazil," in *Colonial Latin America*, ed. Leslie Bethell (Cambridge: Cambridge University Press, 1984), 47–48.

14. Boxer, *Golden Age*, 37, 54–60; Marcílio, "The Population of Colonial Brazil," 60; A. J. R. Russell-Wood, *The Black Man in Slavery and Freedom in Colonial Brazil* (New York: St. Martin's Press, 1982), 122–123.

15. Junia Ferreira Furtado, "From Brazil's Central Highlands to Africa's Ports: Trans-Atlantic and Continental Connections in Goods and Slaves," *Colonial Latin American Review* 21

(2012): 143–148; Dauril Alden, "Late Colonial Brazil, 1750–1808," in *Colonial Brazil*, ed. Leslie Bethell (Cambridge: Cambridge University Press, 1987), 621.

16. Virgflio Noya Pinto, *O Ouro Brasileiro e o Comércio Anglo-portugues* (Sao Paulo: Companhia Editora Nacional, 1979), 114.

17. Vilar, *History of Gold and Money*, 107–109; Charles Hudson, *Knights of Spain, Warriors of the Sun: Hernando de Soto and the South's Ancient Chiefdoms* (Athens: University of Georgia Press, 1997), 39–61, 303–314; William K. Hartmann, *Searching for Golden Empires: Epic Cultural Collisions in Sixteenth-Century America* (Tucson: University of Arizona Press, 2014), 257–284.

18. Robert Southey, *History of Brazil, Part the First* (London: Longman, Hurst, Rees and Orme, 1810), 371; Anthony Smith, *Explorers of the Amazon* (Chicago: University of Chicago Press, 1990), 39–136.

19. James McDermott, *Martin Frobisher: Elizabethan Privateer* (New Haven: Yale University Press, 2001), 153–203.

20. Willard Wallace, *Sir Walter Raleigh* (Princeton: Princeton University Press, 1959), 31–42; Jim Egan, *Authorizing Experience: Refigurations of the Body Politic in Seventeenth-Century New England* (Princeton: Princeton University Press, 1999), 40–41.

21. Jonathan Eacott, *Selling Empire: India in the Making of Britain and America, 1600–1830* (Chapel Hill: University of North Carolina Press, 2016), 16–24.

22. Anna Beer, "Textual Politics: The Execution of Sir Walter Ralegh," *Modern Philology* 94 (1996): 19–38.

23. William N. West, "Gold on Credit: Martin Frobisher's and Walter Ralegh's Economies of Evidence," *Criticism* 39 (1997): 316.

24. Eric Richards, "Darién and the Psychology of Scottish Adventurism in the 1690s," in *Imperial Expectations and Realities: El Dorados, Utopias, and Dystopias*, ed. Andrekos Varnava (Manchester: Manchester University Press, 2015), 26–46.

25. John Smolenski, "Violence in the Atlantic World," in *The Atlantic World*, ed. D'Maris Coffman, Adrian Leonard, and William O'Reilly (London: Routledge, 2015), 247.

26. TePaske, "New World Gold Production," 30; Regina Grafe, *Distant Tyranny: Markets, Power, and Backwardness in Spain, 1650–1800* (Princeton: Princeton University Press, 2011), 5; Katherine Bjork, "The Link that Kept the Philippines Spanish: Mexican Merchant Interests and the Manila Trade, 1571–1815," *Journal of World History* 9 (1998): 25–50; S. Sideri, *Trade and Power: Informal Colonialism in Anglo-Portuguese Relations* (Rotterdam: University of Rotterdam Press, 1970).

27. John Theodore Koster, *Short Statement of the Trade in Gold Bullion* (Liverpool: Harris Brothers, 1810), 14–17.

28. H. E. S. Fisher, *The Portugal Trade: A Study of Anglo-Portuguese Commerce, 1700–1770* (London: Methuen, 1971), 20–39; L. M. E. Shaw, *the Anglo-Portuguese Alliance and English Merchants in Portugal, 1654–1810* (Aldershot: Ashgate, 1998), 33–42; Christopher Ebert, "From Gold to Manioc: Contraband Trade in Brazil during the Golden Age, 1700–1750," *Colonial Latin American Review* 20 (2011): 113–119.

29. Leonor Freire Costa et al., "Social Capital and Economic Performance: Trust and Distrust in Eighteenth-Century Gold Shipments from Brazil," *European Review of Economic History* 15 (2011): 6.

30. J. G. Lydon, "Fish and Flour for Gold: Southern Europe and the Colonial American Balance of Payments," *Business History Review* 39 (1965): 171–183; Fisher, *The Portugal Trade*, 36–43, 92–106; Pinto, *O Ouro Brasileiro*, 290–294; Sideri, *Trade and Power*, 49–52.

31. G. P. Dyer and P. P. Gaspar, "Reform, the New Technology and Tower Hill, 1700–1966," in *A New History of the Royal Mint*, ed. C. E. Challis (Cambridge: Cambridge University Press, 1992), 432; Artur Attman, *Dutch Enterprise in the World Bullion Trade, 1550–1800* (Göteborg: Vitterhets-Samhället, 1983), 47–48; John Clapham, *The Bank of England: A History* (Cambridge: Cambridge University Press, 1966), 1: 136, 233; Thomas Snelling, *A View of the Coins at This Time Current throughout Europe* (London: T. Snelling, 1766), 13.

32. Fisher, *The Portugal Trade*, 93–106.

33. S. G. Checkland, "John Koster, Anti-Bullionist," *Manchester School* 20 (1952): 174–179.

34. Lucy Sutherland, *A London Merchant 1695-1774* (Oxford: Oxford University Press, 1933), 19–36.

35. Sutherland, *London Merchant*, 19, 37–38; Attman, *Dutch Enterprise*, 57; National Archives CUST 3/76.

36. Gedalia Yogev, *Diamonds and Coral: Anglo-Dutch Jews and Eighteenth-Century Trade* (Leicester: Leicester University Press, 1978), 39–41, 50–55; Stanley Chapman, *The Rise of Merchant Banking* (London: Unwin Hyman, 1984), 2–3. On the post-1810 period, when the Rothschild family dominated the gold import trade, see chapters 3, 5, and conclusion.

37. London Metropolitan Archives COL/SJ/27/039; Abigail Green, *Moses Montefiore: Jewish Liberator, Imperial Hero* (Cambridge: Harvard University Press, 2012), 15–17.

38. David Ormrod, *The Rise of Commercial Empires: England and the Netherlands in the Age of Mercantilism, 1650-1770* (Cambridge: Cambridge University Press, 2003), 73–74; P. G. M. Dickson, *The Financial Revolution in England: A Study in the Development of Public Credit, 1688-1756* (London: Macmillan, 1967), 167–169.

39. Smith, *Wealth of Nations*, 2: 136; Sideri, *Trade and Power*, 51.

40. Richard B. Sheridan, *Sugar and Slavery: An Economic History of the British West Indies, 1623-1775* (Kingston: Caribbean Universities Press, 1974), 318; Finucane, *Temptations of Trade*; Tim Beatie, *British Privateering Voyages of the Early Eighteenth* Century (London: Boydell and Brewer, 2015); Ruth Hill, *Hierarchy, Commerce, and Fraud in Bourbon Spanish America* (Nashville: Vanderbilt University Press, 2005), 107–140; William F. Sharp, "The Profitability of Slavery in the Colombian Chocó, 1680–1810," *Hispanic American Historical Review* 55 (1975): 489–494; C. R. Boxer, "Brazilian Gold and British Traders in the First Half of the Eighteenth Century," *Hispanic American Historical Review* 49 (1969): 460–464.

41. Thomas Day, *The History of Sandford and Merton, a Work Intended for the Use of Children* (2nd ed. London: John Stockdale, 1784), 126–133. On Day's animus against the Frenchified fashions of the Hanoverian aristocracy see Gerald Newman, *The Rise of English Nationalism: A Cultural History 1740-1830* (New York: St. Martin's Press, 1997), 100–106.

42. See, e.g., *Lessons for Youth* (London: Darton and Harvey, 1795), 111–117; *The Death and Burial of Cock Robin; to which is added, Pizarro and Alonzo, or, Industry Better than Gold* (York: J. Kendrew, 1825), 17–29; John Guy, *The Class Book, for the Use of Schools and Private Families* (London: Wright, Simpkin, 1858), 151–168; "The Two Brothers," *Political Economy Reading Book*, ed. R. H. Inglis Palgrave (London: National Society's Depository, 1882), 74–79.

43. As mentioned previously, British diagnoses of the sources of Iberian avarice and indolence found plenty of space for silver as well, but focused disproportionately on gold.

44. Bartolomé de las Casas, *The Devastation of the Indies: A Brief Account* (1552; Baltimore: Johns Hopkins University Press, 1992), 31, 41; William S. Maltby, *The Black Legend in England: The Development of Anti-Spanish Sentiment, 1558-1660* (Durham: Duke University Press, 1971), 11–30, 76–88, 112–130.

45. "An Account of Cuba," *Court Magazine* (1763): 293.

46. August von Kotzebue, *Pizarro; a Tragedy, in Five Acts … adapted to the English Stage by Richard Brinsley Sheridan* (London: James Ridgway, 1799), 41; R. Cole Heinowitz, *Spanish America and British Romanticism, 1777–1826: Rewriting Conquest* (Edinburgh: Edinburgh University Press, 2010), 78–85; Heather McPherson, "Caricature, Cultural Politics, and the Stage: The Case of *Pizarro*," *Huntington Library Quarterly* 70 (2007): 607–631.

47. William Cowper, "The Negro's Complaint" (1788), in *Poems* (London: J. Johnson, 1800), 1: 333; James Montgomery, "The West Indies," in *Poems on the Abolition of the Slave Trade* (London: R. Bowyer, 1809), 6. .

48. Bernard Mandeville, *The Fable of the Bees: or, Private Vices, Publick Virtues* (London: J. Roberts, 1724), 177–178; Adam Anderson, *An Historical and Chronological Deduction of the Origin of Commerce* (London: A. Millar et al., 1764), 1: 350. As with las Casas's critique of greed, this message stood in close dialogue with Spanish self-criticism: Ruth McKay, *"Lazy, Improvident People": Myth and Reality in the Writing of Spanish History* (Ithaca: Cornell University Press, 2006), 209–234; Elvira Vilches, *New World Gold: Cultural Anxiety and Monetary Disorder in Early Modern Spain* (Chicago: University of Chicago Press, 2010), 95–144.

49. Edmund Burke, *An Account of the European Settlements in America* (London: R. and H. Dodsley, 1757), 2: 55.

50. Mandeville, *Fable of the Bees*, 177; Ferguson, *History of Civil Society*, 222.
51. Christopher Hervey, *Letters from Portugal, Spain, Italy, and Germany* (London: J. Davis, 1785), 1: 259.
52. William Playfair, *The Statistical Breviary* (London: T. Bensley, 1801), 34; J. C. Curwen, *Hints on Agricultural Subjects* (London: J. Johnson, 1809), 148–149; Gavin Daly, *The British Soldier in the Peninsular War: Encounters with Spain and Portugal, 1808–1814* (New York Palgrave Macmillan, 2013), 126–133.
53. Harriet Martineau, *How to Observe: Morals and Manners* (London: Charles Knight, 1838), 30; Charles Frederick Henningsen, *The Most Striking Events of a Twelvemonth's Campaign with Zumalacarregui, in Navarre and the Basque Provinces* (London: John Murray, 1836), 1: 2.
54. William Stevenson, *Historical Sketch of the Progress of Discovery, Navigation, and Commerce* (Edinburgh: William Blackwood, 1824), 517; Brooke Boothby, *Observations on the Appeal from the New to the Old Whigs, and on Mr. Paine's Rights of Man* (London: John Stockdale, 1792), 256.
55. "The Nature and Use of Metallic Money," *Chambers's Edinburgh Journal* 9 (1841): 148.
56. See, e.g., John Bigland, *Letters on the Modern History and Political Aspect of Europe* (London: Longman, Hurst, Rees, and Orme, 1804), 200; Elias Hiam Lindo, *The History of the Jews of Spain and Portugal* (London: Longman, Brown, Green, and Longmans, 1848), 284–294.
57. "Gold Mines of Brazil," *Literary Panorama* 5 (1809): 1166; Michael J. Quin, *A Visit to Spain* (London: Hurst, Robinson, 1823), 356. On the complex discourse navigating Britain's alliance with Spain and its tacit support for Spanish American independence see Heinowitz, *Spanish America and British Romanticism*, 132–157.
58. Henry Kamen, "The Decline of Spain: A Historical Myth?" *Past and Present* 81 (1978): 24–50; Dennis O. Flynn, "Fiscal Crisis and the Decline of Spain (Castile)," *Journal of Economic History* 42 (1982): 139–147.
59. John Brewer, *The Sinews of Power: War, Money, and the English State, 1688–1783* (Cambridge: Harvard University Press, 1990).
60. Michael Pettis, *The Great Rebalancing: Trade, Conflict, and the Perilous Road Ahead for the World Economy* (Princeton: Princeton University Press, 2013), 19–20.
61. "An Anachronism; or, Missing One's Coach," *Dublin University Magazine* 11 (1838): 709.
62. David Macpherson, *Annals of Commerce, Manufactures, Fisheries, and Navigation* (London: Nichols and Son, et al., 1805), 1: 395.
63. James Mill, *The History of British India* (London: Baldwin, Craddock, and Joy, 1817), 1: 5; John Leslie, "Polar Ice, and a Northwest Passage," *Edinburgh Review* 30 (1818): 43; John Leslie, Robert Jameson, and Hugh Murray, *Narrative of Discovery and Adventure in the Polar Seas and Regions* (Edinburgh: Oliver and Boyd, 1830), 196.
64. Anderson, *Origin of Commerce*, 1: 427; James Grahame, *The History of the Rise and Progress of the United States of North America* (London: Longman, Rees, Orme, Brown, and Green, 1827), 1: 59, 515.
65. Robert Southey, "Snuff," *The Annual Anthology* (Bristol: Biggs, 1800), 2: 115–116.
66. William Russell, *The History of Modern Europe* (London: G.G.J. and J. Robinson, 1786), 3: 222; David Hume, *The History of Great Britain under the House of Stuart* (London: A. Millar, 1759), 1: 60; Macvey Napier, "Sir Walter Raleigh," *Edinburgh Review* 71 (1840): 23; John Lingard, *A History of England* (London: J. Mawman, 1825), 6: 164; Southey, *History of Brazil*, 374.
67. "Concise Account of Brazil . . . from Its First Discovery in 1500," *La Belle Assemblée* 24 (1817): 263; S. S. Hill, *The Emigrant's Introduction to an Acquaintance with the British American Colonies* (London: Parbury, 1837), 33–34.
68. George L. Craik, *The Pictorial History of England* (London: Charles Knight, 1841), 4: 95; Coventry Patmore, "European Navigators in Early Times," *North British Review* 18 (1853): 435; Patrick Fraser Tytler, *Life of Sir Walter Raleigh* (Edinburgh: Oliver and Boyd, 1833), 146.
69. George Croly, "Portugal," *Blackwood's Edinburgh Magazine* 56 (1844): 106.
70. John Howison, *Tales of the Colonies* (London: Colburn and Bentley, 1834), 2: 433; Napier, "Sir Walter Raleigh," 10, 12.

71. George Jones, *The History of Ancient America, anterior to the Time of Columbus* (London: Longman, Brown, Green, and Longmans, 1843), 1: 190–191. For one of the many present-day echoes of this view see Gregory Jusdanis, *Political Nations* (Princeton: Princeton University Press, 2001), 149.

72. Josiah Tucker, *Four Tracts, on Political and Commercial Subjects* (Glocester: R. Raikes, 1774), 43–44; Valenze, *Social Life of Money*, 260–270.

73. James Cook, *An Account of a Voyage Round the World* (London: W. Strahan, 1773), 34. On smuggling see Maria Graham, *Journal of a Residence in Chile, during the year 1822, and a Voyage from Chile to Brazil in 1823* (London: Longman, Hurst, Rees, Orme, Brown, and Green, 1824), 51–52.

74. Thomas Mortimer, *A New History of England* (London: J. Wilson and J. Fell, 1765), 3: 771; John Barrow, *The Life, Voyages, and Exploits of Sir Francis Drake* (London: John Murray, 1844), 55–57; Anna Eliza Bray, *Traditions, Legends, Superstitions, and Sketches of Devonshire* (London: John Murray, 1838), 2: 197–198. On Drake see Christopher Hodgkins, "Stooping to Conquer: Heathen Idolatry and Protestant Humility in the Imperial Legend of Sir Francis Drake," *Studies in Philology* 94 (1997): 428–464.

75. Erika Rappaport, *A Thirst for Empire: How Tea Shaped the Modern World* (Princeton: Princeton University Press, 2017); Brian Cowan, *The Social Life of Coffee: The Emergence of the British Coffeehouse* (New Haven: Yale University Press, 2005); Jennifer L. Anderson, *Mahogany: The Costs of Luxury in Early America* (Cambridge: Harvard University Press, 2012).

Chapter 2

1. Daniel Defoe, *The Life and Strange Surprizing Adventures of Robinson Crusoe* (London: W. Taylor, 1719), 39, 66, 152–153, 228–229, 337. For Defoe on value see James Thompson, *Models of Value: Eighteenth-Century Political Economy and the Novel* (Durham: Duke University Press, 1996), 87–131; David Wallace Spielman, "The Value of Money in *Robinson Crusoe, Moll Flanders*, and *Roxana*," *Modern Language Review* 107 (2012): 65–87; Richard Braverman, "Crusoe's Legacy," *Studies in the Novel* 18 (1986): 1–26.

2. Joachim Campe, *Robinson the Younger* (Frankfort: J. J. Kesler, 1789), 203, 300, 539; Henri Lemaire, *The French Gil Blas; or, Adventures of Henry Lanson* (London: C. and G. Kearsley, 1793), 4: 102–103.

3. Jane Porter, *Sir Edward Seaward's Narrative of His Shipwreck, and Consequent Discovery of Certain Islands in the Caribbean Sea* (New York: J. and J. Harper, 1831), 1: 157–158, 164.

4. Campe, *Robinson the Younger*, 667, 671–672; Lemaire, *French Gil Blas*, 4: 242–244, 298–300; Porter, *Sir Edward Seaward's Narrative*, 2: 196.

5. Arie Arnon, *Thomas Tooke: Pioneer of Monetary Theory* (Ann Arbor: University of Michigan Press, 1991), 17.

6. See especially Boyd Hilton, *Corn, Cash, Commerce: The Economic Policies of the Tory Governments 1815–1830* (Oxford: Oxford University Press, 1977), 31–97.

7. David Laidler, "The Bullionist Controversy," in *Money*, ed. John Eatwell, Murray Milgate, and Peter Newman (New York: W. W. Norton, 1989), 60. See also Frank Whitson Fetter, *The Development of British Monetary Orthodoxy, 1797–1875* (Cambridge, MA: Harvard University Press, 1965), 1–143.

8. See, e.g., Peter L. Bernstein, *The Power of Gold: The History of an Obsession* (Chichester: John Wiley and Sons, 2005), 244; Anna J. Schwartz, foreword to Michael J. Bordo, *The Gold Standard and Related Regimes* (Cambridge: Cambridge University Press, 1999), ix.

9. Samuel Knafo, *The Making of Modern Finance: Liberal Governance and the Gold Standard* (London: Routledge, 2013), 106; see also Christine Desan, *Making Money: Coin, Currency, and the Coming of Capitalism* (New York: Oxford University Press, 2015).

10. Knafo, *Making of Modern Finance*, 127–175; Timothy Alborn, *Conceiving Companies: Joint-Stock Politics in Victorian England* (London: Routledge, 1998), 53–170; John H. Wood, *A History of Central Banking in Great Britain and the United States* (Cambridge: Cambridge University Press, 2005), 1–116.

11. See, e.g., Richard Newhauser, *The Early History of Greed: The Sin of Avarice in Early Medieval Thought and Literature* (Cambridge: Cambridge University Press, 2000); Jared Poley, *The*

Devil's Riches: A Modern History of Greed (New York: Berghahn Books, 2016); Deborah Valenze, *The Social Life of Money in the English Past* (Cambridge: Cambridge University Press, 2006), 92–94.

12. Adam Smith, *An Inquiry into the Nature and Causes of the Wealth of Nations* (London: Strahan and Cadell, 1776), 1: 216, 30.

13. John Locke, *Second Treatise of Government* (1690; Indianapolis: Hackett, 1980), 28; David Hume, *A Treatise of Human Nature* (London: John Noon, 1740), 3: 59–60; Smith, *Wealth of Nations*, 1: 219.

14. Locke, *Second Treatise*, 23; David Graeber, *Debt: The First 5,000 Years* (Brooklyn: Melville House, 2011).

15. David Milne, *On Circulating Credit: With Hints for Improving the Banking System of Britain* (Edinburgh: William Tait, 1832), 60; Smith, *Wealth of Nations*, 1: 27–28; Thomas Smith, *An Attempt to Define some of the First Principles of Political Economy* (London: J. M. Richardson, 1821), 22.

16. Daniel Boileau, *An Introduction to the Study of Political Economy* (London: Cadell and Davies, 1811), 70; Francis Corbaux, *The Doctrine of Compound Interest* (London: n.p., 1825), xv; Walter Scott, *Tales of a Grandfather* (Paris: Baudry's European Library, 1833), 2: 11.

17. John Gray, *The Social System: A Treatise on the Principle of Exchange* (Edinburgh: William Tair, 1831), 19–20; Jane Marcet, *Conversations on Political Economy* (London: Longman, Hurst, Rees, Orme, and Brown, 1816), 28, 25.

18. Conveniently, British science and technology before 1850 offered only a handful of exceptions to the rule that gold had few important useful, as opposed to ornamental or monetary, applications. The most prominent of these was the gold-leaf electrometer, invented by Abraham Bennet in 1786, followed by the use of gold in dentistry: see Tiberius Cavallo, *A Complete Treatise on Electricity, in Theory and Practice* (London: C. Dilly, 1795), 3: 94; "On the Education of Mechanical Dentists," *Mechanics' Magazine* 30 (1839): 325–326.

19. John Ferrar, *A Tour from Dublin to London in 1795* (Dublin: n.p., 1796), 35; A. M'Donald, *An Essay upon Raising and Dressing of Flax and Hemp* (Edinburgh: William Creech, 1784), 68–69; Walter Davies, *General View of the Agriculture and Domestic Economy of North Wales* (London: Richard Phillips, 1810), 206; Henry Bliss, *On Colonial Intercourse* (London: James Ridgway, 1830), 47–48; Francis Mackenzie, *Hints to Highland Tenants and Cottagers* (Inverness: Robert Carruthers, 1838), 84.

20. J. R. McCulloch, *A Dictionary, Practical, Theoretical, and Historical, of Commerce and Commercial Navigation* (London: Longman, Rees, Orme, Brown, Green and Longman, 1832), 268; Thomas Dick, *The Christian Philosopher, or, The Connection of Science and Philosophy with Religion* (New York: G. and C. Carvill, 1826), 141.

21. Dick, *Christian Philosopher*, 141; Hannah Ransome Geldart, *Stories of England and her Forty Counties* (London: Jarrold and Sons, 1849), 162–163; John Mawe, *Familiar Lessons on Mineralogy and Geology* (London: Longman, Hurst, Rees, Orme, and Brown, 1820), 43.

22. William Robertson, *The History of America* (London: Strahan and Cadell, 1780), 2: 125–126; Neil Arnott, *Elements of Physics, or Natural Philosophy, General and Medical* (London: Longman, Rees, Orme, Brown, and Green, 1829), 2: 147.

23. Alternative endpoints included diamonds and "the average market-prices of a large number of the commodities in most general and constant demand": Gerard Graulhié, *An Outline of a Plan for a New Circulating Medium* (London: James Ridgeway, 1832); George Poulett Scrope, *An Examination of the Bank Charter Question* (London: John Murray, 1833), 25–26.

24. Smith, *Wealth of Nations*, 1: 28, 388–389.

25. Valenze, *Social Life of Money*, 42–43; Desan, *Making Money*, 387–388 and *passim*.

26. Charles Jenkinson, *A Treatise on the Coins of the Realm* (Oxford: The University Press, 1805), 12–14, 138–139. Jenkinson's equally influential argument on behalf of tokenizing silver is discussed in chapter 5.

27. *Parliamentary Debates* (1st ser.) (1816), 34: 913, 1122 (speech of Lord Liverpool), 918, 1236 (Lord Lauderdale); *Parliamentary Debates* (2d ser.) (1821), 5: 145 (speech of John Irving), 147 (vote tally) and 4: 1330–1331 (speech of David Ricardo, responding to Alexander Baring); Frank Whitson Fetter, *The Economist in Parliament: 1780–1868* (Durham: Duke University Press, 1980), 92–93.

28. Later proponents of silver, who mainly repeated the arguments used in 1816–1821, included Henry Lambert, *A Letter on the Currency* (London: W.H. Dalton, 1832), 6–7, 18 and Edward Stillingfleet Cayley, *Agricultural Distress—Silver Standard* (London: Mirror of Parliament, 1835), 22–33.

29. Edward Solly, *The Present Distress, in Relation to the Theory of Money* (London: James Ridgway, 1830), 5–6; Smith, *First Principles of Political Economy*, 19, 183; Matthew Rowlandson, *Real Money and Romanticism* (Cambridge: Cambridge University Press, 2010), 53 and 33–99 *passim*. Scottish banks did manage to retain the right to issue £1 notes well into the twentieth century, whereas that practice was banned in England in 1826: S. G. Checkland, *Scottish Banking: A History, 1695–1973* (Glasgow: Collins, 1975), 435–439.

30. S. G. Checkland, "The Birmingham Economists, 1815–1850," *Economic History Review* 1 (1948): 1–18.

31. James Mill, "Smith on Money and Exchange," *Edinburgh Review* 13 (1808): 43; *Times* May 25, 1819; J. R. McCulloch, "Money," *Kaleidoscope* 4 (1824): 422; Robert William Dickinson, *Two Addresses on the Depreciation of the Currency* (London: J. Clarke, 1843), 9–10.

32. J. Bonar, "Ricardo's Ingot Scheme," *Economic Journal* 33 (1923): 296–298. On the Bank of England's unpopular role in bringing forgery cases to trial during the suspension of payments see Randall McGowen, "Managing the Gallows: The Bank of England and the Death Penalty, 1797–1821," *Law and History Review* 25 (2007): 241–282.

33. Smith, *Wealth of Nations*, 1: 38–39; David Ricardo, *On the Principles of Political Economy, and Taxation* (3rd. ed. London: John Murray, 1821), 44–45. See Alexander Dick, *Romanticism and the Gold Standard: Money, Literature, and Economic Debate in Britain 1790–1830* (Houndmills: Palgrave Macmillan, 2013), 24–25 and Maria Cristina Marcuzzo and Annalisa Rosselli. *Ricardo and the Gold Standard: The Foundations of the International Monetary Order* (London: Macmillan, 1991), 41–50.

34. Smith, *Wealth of Nations* (Edinburgh: Adam Black and William Tate, 1828), 4: 203 (note by J. R. McCulloch).

35. Noel W. Thompson, *The People's Science: The Popular Political Economy of Exploitation and Crisis 1816–34* (Cambridge: Cambridge University Press, 1984), 82–110.

36. John Francis Bray, *Labour's Wrongs and Labour's Remedy* (Leeds: David Green, 1839), 141; John Gray, *An Efficient Remedy for the Distress of Nations* (Edinburgh: Adam and Charles Black, 1842), 189; Robert Owen, *Report of the Proceedings at the Several Public Meetings, held in Dublin* (Dublin: J. Carrick and Son, 1823), 127.

37. Gregory Claeys, *Machinery, Money and the Millenium: From Moral Economy to Socialism, 1815–1860* (Princeton: Princeton University Press, 1987), 125–160; James Elishama Smith, *The Little Book; or, Momentous Crisis of 1840* (London: B. D. Cousins, 1840), 20–21.

38. *The High Price of Bread, Shown to be the Result of Commercial Prosperity* (London: John Hatchard and Son, 1827), 25–26.

39. Smith, *Wealth of Nations*, 1: 54.

40. John Theodore Koster, *Short Statement of the Trade in Gold Bullion* (Liverpool: Harris Brothers, 1811), 22–23; John Stuart Mill, *Principles of Political Economy* (London: John W. Parker, 1848), 1: 64.

41. William Jacob, *An Historical Inquiry into the Production and Consumption of the Precious Metals* (London: John Murray, 1831), 2: 282, 284, 285, 288–292, 313; 1: 154; National Archives, MINT 7/1.

42. J. R. McCulloch, "Supply and Consumption of the Precious Metals," *Edinburgh Review* 45 (1832): 52–54; *A Concise Treatise on the Wealth, Power, and Resources of Great Britain* (London: Treuttel, Würtz and Richter, 1833), 119; *Circular to Bankers* July 1, 1831.

43. Jacob, *Historical Inquiry*, 2: 284–285; James Peller Malcolm, *Londinium Redivivum, or an Ancient History and Modern Description of London* (London: John Nichols & Son, 1803), 2: 412; Edward Brayley, *A Topographical and Historical Description of London and Middlesex* (London: Sherwood, Nealy, and Jones, 1810), 2: 370; William Herbert, *The History of the Twelve Great Livery Companies of London* (London: The Library, Guildhall, 1837), 1: 208.

44. "Diets of Gold and Silver," *Household Words* 7 (1853): 20; Henry Smithers, *Liverpool, Its Commerce, Statistics, and Institutions* (Liverpool: Thomas Kaye, 1825), 188–189.

45. Ambrose Heal, *The London Goldsmiths, 1200–1800* (Cambridge: The University Press, 1935); *Post Office London Directory* (London: B. Critchett, 1846 and 1851).

46. *Parliamentary Register* n.s. 3 (1781): 136–137, 296; Denis O'Bryen, *A View of the Treaty of Commerce with France* (London: J. Debrett, 1787), 89; C. Este, *A Journey in the Year 1793... to Switzerland* (London: J. Debrett, 1795), 137.

47. James H. Watherston, *A Familiar Explanation of the Art of Assaying Gold and Silver* (London: Smith, Elder, 1847), 44–46; Shirley Bury, *Jewellery 1789–1910: The International Era* (Woodbridge: Antique Collectors' Club, 1991) 1: 266, 344–345.

48. Watherston, *Familiar Explanation*, 52–53; "The Annual Exhibition in the Louvre," *European Magazine* 84 (1823): 243.

49. "The Lovers: An Every-day Life Sketch," *Monthly Magazine* 2 (1839): 98; Harry Longueville Jones, "The Aesthetics of Dress: The Cut of a Coat and the Good of a Gown," *Blackwood's Edinburgh Magazine* 57 (1845): 612. On mosaic gold (a sulfur-tin compound) and other imitations see Bury, *Jewellery 1789-1910*, 1: 271.

50. Talia Schaffer, *Novel Craft: Victorian Domestic Handicraft and Nineteenth-Century Fiction* (New York: Oxford University Press, 2011), 50–57; Supritha Rajan, *A Tale of Two Capitalisms: Sacred Economics in Nineteenth-Century Britain* (Ann Arbor: University of Michigan Press, 2015), 59–92.

51. John Ruskin, *The Seven Lamps of Architecture* (London: Smith, Elder, 1849), 1: 45–46; Thomas Charles Banfield, "State of the Nation: Handloom-Weavers' Report," *British and Foreign Review* 13 (1842): 157.

52. *The Fortune-Hunter; Or, The Gamester Reclaim'd* (London: printed for the author, ca 1775).

53. Mill, "Smith on Money and Exchange," 49; Valenze, *Social Life of Money*.

54. T. Garnett, *Outlines of a Course of Lectures on Chemistry* (Liverpool: J. M'Creery, 1797), 137; Ann Murray, *The Sequel to Mentoria; or, The Young Ladies Instructor* (London: C. Dilly, 1799), 279; John Murray, *Elements of Chemistry* (Edinburgh: T. Maccleish, 1801), 2: 24; Simeon Shaw, *Nature Displayed in the Heavens, and on the Earth* (London: Richard Phillips, 1823), 1: 38.

55. George Gregory, *The Economy of Nature Explained and Illustrated* (London: J. Johnson, 1796), 2: 267. Although Spaniards found platinum in Colombian gold mines as early as 1700, export restrictions hindered its availability in Britain for nearly a century: Kris Lane, "Gone Platinum: Contraband and Chemistry in Eighteenth-Century Colombia," *Colonial Latin American Review* 20 (2011): 61–79.

56. Timothy Alborn, "The Greatest Metaphor Ever Mixed: Gold in the British Bible, 1750–1850," *Journal of the History of Ideas* 78 (2017): 427–447.

57. Thomas Tregenna Biddulph, *Practical Essays on the Morning and Evening Services of the Church of England* (London: Longman, Hurst, Rees, and Orme, 1810), 40; Samuel Medley, *The Spiritual Merchant Described* (London: J.W. Pasham, 1778), 10; William Huntington, *Works* (London: T. Bensley, 1811), 3: 71.

58. David Crichton, "Believers Living Stones in the Spiritual Temple," in *The Free Church Pulpit* (New York: Robert Carter, 1848), 2: 509.

59. Egerton Brydges, *Recollections of Foreign Travel, on Life, Literature, and Self-knowledge* (London: Longman, Hurst, Rees, Orme, Brown, and Green, 1825), 2: 160; Thomas Carlyle, *The Life of Friedrich Schiller* (London: Taylor and Hessey, 1825), 179.

60. Dick, *Romanticism and the Gold Standard*, 4.

61. *The Picture; or, My Own Choice* (London: Sampson Low, 1796), 7; Cyrus Redding, *An Illustrated Itinerary of the County of Lancashire* (London: How and Parsons, 1842), 128; James Simpson, *Brief Reports of Lectures delivered to the Working Classes of Edinburgh* (Edinburgh: John Johnstone, 1844), 27; Gerald Griffin, *Tales of the Munster Festivals* (London: Saunders and Otley), 120.

62. Constantine Normanby, *Matilda: A Tale of the Day* (London: Henry Colburn, 1825), 288; Cornelius Webbe, *Glances at Life in City and Suburb. Second Series* (London: Sherwood and Bowyer, 1845), 175–176; George Henry Lewes, "Benjamin Disraeli," *British Quarterly Review* 10 (1849): 127–128.

63. Henry Rogers, "The Vanity and the Glory of Literature," *Edinburgh Review* 89 (1849): 312.

64. Psalms 19:10 (King James version).

65. Samuel Carr, *Sermons, on Practical Subjects* (London: Rivington, 1795), 2: 263; Mary Alcock, *Poems* (London: C. Dilly, 1799), 166; "The Gospel a Treasure," *Evangelical Magazine* 11 (1803): 467.

66. Alexander Campbell, *The Grampians Desolate: A Poem* (Edinburgh: Vernor and Hood, 1804), 47, 209.

67. Samuel Walter Burgess, *Historical Illustrations of the Origin and Progress of the Passions, and their Influence on the Conduct of Mankind* (London: Longman, Hurst, Rees, Orme, Brown, and Green, 1825), 1: 293.

68. "On the Pursuit after Gold," *Monthly Miscellany* 2 (1774): 51; William Hetherington, *Branthwaite Hall, and Other Poems* (Carlisle: Charles Thurnam, 1837), 88; Mary Elizabeth Robinson, *The Wild Wreath* (London: Richard Phillips, 1804), 13; Gustavus Gale, "Fatal Effects of Gold," in *Miscellanies in Prose and Verse* (London: G. and J. Robinson, 1794), 55; Smith, *Gaieties and Gravities*, 2: 224.

69. "Gold," *Fraser's Magazine* 10 (1834): 266; Timothy Alborn, "Money's Worth: Morality, Class, Politics," in *The Victorian World*, ed. Martin Hewitt (London: Routledge, 2012), 210–214.

70. oldbaileyonline.org. Owing mainly to a lack of guineas in circulation between 1801 and 1821, gold-related thefts plummeted during that period to just thirty-six annually, or less than 4 percent of total thefts.

71. *Times* October 29, 1827, May 8 and 11, 1839.

72. *Morning Chronicle* March 6, 1848.

73. J. F. Murray, "Foreigners in London," *Blackwood's Edinburgh Magazine* 51 (1842): 28; Douglas Jerrold, *Cakes and Ale* (London: Bradbury and Evans, 1852), 322.

74. Richard Henry Horne, *The Golden Calf: or, Prodigality and Speculation in the Nineteenth Century* (London: T. C. Newby, 1849). On mammon-worship see Valenze, *Social Life of Money*, 92–97.

75. Craig Muldrew, "'Hard Food for Midas': Cash and Its Social Value in Early Modern England," *Past and Present* 170 (2001): 116.

76. Robert Robinson, *Seventeen Discourses on Several Texts of Scripture* (Cambridge: W.H Lunn, 1796), 448; John Philip Wilson, "Observance of the Tenth Commandment," *Imperial Magazine* 2nd ser. 2 (1832): 305; Eliza Cook, *Poems. Second Series* (London: Simpkin, Marshall, 1840), 109.

77. Thomas Brown, *Lectures on the Philosophy of the Human Mind* (Edinburgh: W. and C. Tait, 1824), 3: 447, 456; Richard Whately, *Easy Lessons on Money Matters* (London: John W. Parker, 1836), 48.

78. H.J. Mathetes, *Can Things be Better? An Address to the Working Classes* (Manchester: Grant, 1848), 21.

79. *The Strange and Unaccountable Life of the Penurious Daniel Dancer, Esq., a Miserable Miser* (London: Ann Lemoine, 1797), 6, 27, 29; Edward Topham, *The Life of the Late John Elwes* (Newcastle: M. Brown, 1790), 12–15, 29; *Northern Star* August 14, 1841.

80. *Morning Post* Oct 27, 1838; *Leicester Chronicle* May 9, 1835.

81. Henry Fielding, *The Miser* (Edinburgh: n.p., 1733); *Morning Post* September 24, 1776 (on Edward Shuter), October 14, 1818 (on William Farren); John Galt, *The Lives of the Players* (London: Henry Colburn and Richard Bentley, 1831), 2: 291–292 (on John Emory).

82. *Morning Post* Feb 6, 1844 (review of *A Christmas Carol* at the Adelphi Theatre); Jeff Nunokawa, "The Miser's Two Bodies: 'Silas Marner' and the Sexual Possibilities of the Commodity," *Victorian Studies* 36 (1993): 273–292; Logan Delano Browning, "Reading Dickens's Misers" (University of North Carolina PhD dissertation, 1999).

83. *Oxford English Dictionary* online; David Cannadine, *Aspects of Aristocracy: Grandeur and Decline in Modern Britain* (London: Penguin, 1994), 10–18; Esther Godfrey, *The January-May Marriage in Nineteenth-Century British Literature* (Basingstoke: Palgrave Macmillan, 2009), 147–156.

84. Robert Bage, *Mount Henneth: A Novel* (London: T. Lowndes, 1782), 2: 155–156; *Times* April 25, 1792; Elsie Michie, *The Vulgar Question of Money: Heiresses, Materialism, and the Novel of Manners from Jane Austen to Henry James* (Cambridge: Harvard University Press, 2011), 18–22, 40.

85. William Combe, *The Tour of Doctor Syntax, in Search of the Picturesque* (London: R. Ackermann, 1815), 147; James Bell, *Sermons* (London: A. Strahan, 1790), 36; Hugh W. Williams, *Travels in Italy, Greece and the Ionian Islands* (Edinburgh: Constable, 1820), 1: 367.

86. "France," *Companion to the Newspapers* 4 (1836): 196; John Booker, *Travellers' Money* (Stroud: Alan Sutton, 1994), 74–75; Roger Munting, *An Economic and Social History of Gambling in Britain and the USA* (Manchester: Manchester University Press, 1996), 21.

87. David Morier Evans, *The Commercial Crisis 1847–48* (London: Letts, Son and Steer, 1849), 52; Robert Bell, *The Ladder of Gold: An English Story* (London: Bentley, 1850), 1: 207.

88. Christopher Herbert, "Filthy Lucre: Victorian Ideas of Money," *Victorian Studies* 44 (2002): 185–213; Patrick Brantlinger, *Fictions of State: Culture and Credit in Britain, 1694–1994* (Ithaca: Cornell University Press, 1996), 160.

89. Hannah More, "The Sorrows of Yamba; or, The Negro Woman's Lamentation" (1796), quoted in *What Does Your Sugar Cost?* (Birmingham: Richard Peart, 1828), 9; Richard Oastler, *Eight Letters to the Duke of Wellington* (London: James Cochrane, 1835), 108.

90. Joseph Milner, *Gibbon's Account of Christianity Considered* (York: A. Ward, 1781), 122–123; see Alborn, "Greatest Metaphor," 439–444.

91. Jonathan Lamb, *The Things Things Say* (Princeton: Princeton University Press, 2011), 28–54, 129–150.

92. *House of Commons Debates*, 1844, 76: 724, 730.

Chapter 3

1. "The Gold of England," *Illustrated London News* April 5, 1845.

2. "The Gold of England"; John Brewer, *The Sinews of Power: War, Money, and the English State, 1688–1783* (Cambridge: Harvard University Press, 1990), 7, 32, 41–42, 60; Jeremy Black, *Britain as a Military Power, 1688–1815* (London: UCL Press, 1999), 269.

3. Adam Smith, *An Inquiry into the Nature and Causes of the Wealth of Nations* (London: Strahan and Cadell, 1776), 2: 16, 9–12.

4. "Account of gold coinage and the supposed amount left for circulation at the end of the year 1798," National Archives, MINT 9/31. According to this estimate, £43,896,042 was available in 1799; on estimates of the Bank of England's gold reserves in 1815 see *Report of the Committee of Secrecy on the Bank of England Charter* (London: James and Luke G. Hansard and Sons, 1832), appendix 5 (pp. 36–37) and for circulating gold see chapter 5.

5. John Pinkerton, *The History of Scotland under the House of Stuart* (London: C. Dilley, 1797), 1: 100, 283.

6. See, e.g., Ludvig Holberg, *An Introduction to Universal History* (London: A. Linde, 1755), 63; Pons-Augustus Alletz, *The History of Ancient Greece* (Edinburgh: J. Bruce, 1768), 219.

7. Andrew Dalzel, *Substance of Lectures on the Ancient Greeks* (Edinburgh: Constable, 1821), 1: 95; Philip Harling, *The Waning of Old Corruption: The Politics of Economical Reform in Britain, 1779–1846* (Oxford: Clarendon Press, 1996).

8. William Belsham, *Essays, Philosophical, Historical, and Literary* (London: C. Dilly, 1789), 307; George Lyttelton, *The History of the Life of King Henry the Second* (London: Sandby and Dodsley, 1767), 1: 36; Hugo Arnot, *The History of Edinburgh* (Edinburgh: W. Creech, 1779), 229.

9. John Brown, *A Compendious History of the Church of England* (Glasgow: John Bryce, 1784), 1: 112; James Pettit Andrews, *History of Great Britain, from the Death of Henry VIII. to the Accession of James VI* (London: Cadell and Davies, 1796), 2: 273.

10. Stephen Conway, "War and National Identity in the Mid-Eighteenth-Century British Isles," *English Historical Review* 116 (2001): 887–889; William Eldon, *England's Subsidy Policy towards the Continent during the Seven Years' War* (Philadelphia, University of Pennsylvania Press, 1938), 162–163.

11. *The Important Question concerning Invasions, a Sea-war, Raising the Militia, and Paying Subsidies for Foreign Troops* (London: R. Griffiths, 1755), 4; William Pulteney, *Reflections on the Domestic Policy, proper to be Observed on the Conclusion of a Peace* (London: A. Millar, 1761), 59–60.

12. James Brown, *Memoirs of George the Third* (Liverpool: Caxton Press, 1820), 623; Rodney Atwood, *The Hessians: Mercenaries from Hessen-Kassel in the American Revolution* (Cambridge: Cambridge University Press, 1980), 257; Charles W. Ingrao, *The Hessian Military State: Ideas, Institutions, and Reform under Frederick II, 1760–1785* (Cambridge: Cambridge University Press, 1994), 135–153. British payments included subsidies (around 2 million thaler, or £300,000) and wages for soldiers (estimated at 120 thaler per year for each soldier, or £1 million).

13. J. F. D. Smyth, *A Tour in the United States of America* (London: C. Robinson, 1784), 2: 450; Peter K. Taylor, *Indentured to Liberty, Peasant Life and the Hessian Military State, 1688–1815* (New York: Cornell University Press, 1994), 165–200.

14. Bank of England Archives, 2A109/1; G. P. Dyer and P. P. Gaspar, "Reform, the New Technology and Tower Hill, 1700–1966," in *A New History of the Royal Mint*, ed. C. E. Challis (Cambridge: Cambridge University Press, 1992), 432.

15. National Archives CUST 3/76; Bank of England Archives 2A109/1; Taylor, *Indentured to Liberty*, 22.

16. Istvan Hont, *Jealousy of Trade: International Competition and the Nation-State in Historical Perspective* (Cambridge, MA: Harvard University Press, 2005), 267–322.

17. William Seward, *Anecdotes of Some Distinguished Persons* (London: Cadell and Davies, 1795), 3: 382; *The English Nation Vindicated from the Calumnies of Foreigners* (London: M. Cooper, 1744), 25.

18. *Times* July 28 and September 4, 1794; David Patrick Geggus, *Slavery, War, and Revolution: The British Occupation of Saint Domingue, 1793–1798* (Oxford: Clarendon Press, 1982), 118–123; Urey Lisiansky, *A Voyage Round the World* (London: John Booth, 1814), xvii–xviii (editor's preface).

19. Norman Hampson, *The Perfidy of Albion: French Perceptions of England during the French Revolution* (Houndmills: Palgrave Macmillan, 1998), 144; *Times* January 11 and April 19, 1794.

20. Michael Rapport, *Nationality and Citizenship in Revolutionary France: The Treatment of Foreigners 1789-1799* (Oxford: Clarendon Press, 2000), 245–247; Marisa Linton, *Choosing Terror: Virtue, Friendship, and Authenticity in the French Revolution* (Oxford: Oxford University Press, 2013), 196–200.

21. Hampson, *The Perfidy of Albion*, 56; William Jones, *A Letter to a Patriot Senator* (London: n.p., 1783), 20; James Hartley, *History of the Westminster Election* (London: J. Debrett, 1784), 451.

22. William Cobbett, *Annals of Blood* (Cambridge: F. Hodson, 1797), 90, 92; H.R. Yorke, *A Letter to the Reformers* (Dorchester: T. Lockett, 1798), 24.

23. *A Collection of State Papers, relative to the War against France* (London: J. Debrett, 1798–1799), 6: 54; 7: 125; *Anti-Jacobin* 2 (1798), 536.

24. *Parliamentary Register* 3 (1800), 445.

25. Linton, *Choosing Terror*, 199; *Collection of State Papers*, 5: 47; W. D. Edmonds, *Jacobinism and the Revolt of Lyon, 1789–1793* (Oxford: Oxford University Press, 1999), 259–260.

26. *Third Report from the Committee of Secrecy on the Outstanding Demands on the Bank* (1797; London: HMSO, 1826), 8 and appendix, 86; *Times* March 23, 1797.

27. Charles William Pasley, *Essay on the Military Policy and Institutions of the British Empire* (London: Edmund Lloyd, 1810), 334–335; Brewer, *Sinews of Power*, 32; Maria Cristina Marcuzzo and Annalisa Rosselli, *Ricardo and the Gold Standard: The Foundation of the International Monetary Order* (New York: St. Martin's Press, 1991), 71.

28. John M. Sherwig, *Guineas and Gunpowder: British Foreign Aid in the Wars with France 1793–1815* (Cambridge: Harvard University Press, 1969), 365–368. Sherwig points out that the "economic weakness" of Prussia, Russia, and Austria as of 1793 did render Britain an unequal partner even on this more level playing field (11).

29. "Pasley on Military Policy," *British Review* 2 (1811): 207.

30. Henry Brougham, *An Inquiry into the State of the Nation* (London: Longman, Hurst, Rees, and Orme, 1806), 137–138; Thomas Jones, *Substance of the Speech . . . on his Motion for Peace* (London: J. Debrett, 1800), 20–22. For context see Sherwig, *Guineas and Gunpowder*, 5–7, 130–135, 170–174.

31. Banastre Tarleton, *Substance of a Speech intended for the Vote of Credit Bill* (London: J. Ridgway, 1810), 20; *Times* January 16, 1810; Lewen Tugwell, "On Cottages," *Letters and Papers . . . of the Bath and West of England Society* 12 (1810): 331–332.

32. Francis L. Clarke, *The Life of the . . . Earl of Wellington* (London: J. and J. Cundee, 1814), 3: 318; *Report . . . into the Cause of the High Price of Gold Bullion* (London: J. Johnson, 1810), 4–5.

33. Bank of England Archives, BE 2A109/1; *Bullion Report*, 59, 6, 38.

34. Niall Ferguson, *The House of Rothschild: Money's Prophets 1798–1848* (New York: Viking Penguin, 1998), 84–85; S. G. P. Ward, *Wellington's Headquarters: A Study of the Administrative Problems in the Peninsula 1809–1814* (Oxford: Oxford University Press, 1957), 78–80; Ian Robertson, *A Commanding Presence: Wellington in the Peninsula, 1808–1814* (Stroud: Spellmount, 2008), 319–320.

35. The drain of gold that led to the suspension of payments in 1797 is discussed in the next section.

36. Frank Whitson Fetter, *The Development of British Monetary Orthodoxy, 1797–1875* (Cambridge, MA: Harvard University Press, 1965), 43–51.

37. Sherwig, *Guineas and Gunpowder*, 78, 88–89, 133–134, 233. On the Continental System see François Crouzet, *L'Economie Britannique et le Blocus Continentale (1806–1813)* (Paris: Presses Universitaires de France, 1958), vol. 1.

38. Weekly balance books, Bank of England Archives 9A314/1.

39. "Bullion Certificates, 1696–1741," London Metropolitan Archives COL/SJ/27/038; Gavin Daly, "Napoleon and the 'City of Smugglers', 1810–1814," *Historical Journal* 50 (2007): 345; Ferguson, *House of Rothschild*, 49–52; Herbert H. Kaplan, *Nathan Mayer Rothschild and the Creation of a Dynasty. The Critical Years, 1806–1816* (Stanford: Stanford University Press, 2006), 60–61.

40. Certificates of Bullion Received, 1792–1816 (London Metropolitan Archives COL/SJ/27/041); *Bullion Report*, appendix, 18–22, 26–27, 32–38; *Multum in Parvo . . . to which is added, A Bullion Catechism* (London: J. M. Richardson, 1811), 28–29.

41. Sherwig, *Guineas and Gunpowder*, 232, 255; Crouzet, *L'Economie Britannique*, Vol. 2.

42. National Archives, MINT 7/1; Dyer and Gaspar, "Reform," 472.

43. Ferguson, *House of Rothschild*, 89–95.

44. William Shepherd, *Paris, in Eighteen Hundred and Two, and Eighteen Hundred and Fourteen* (London: Longman, Hurst, Rees, Orme, and Brown, 1814), 250–251; Walkin Tench, *Letters Written in France, to a Friend in London* (London: J. Johnson, 1796), 23–24.

45. Michael D. Bordo and Eugene N. White, "A Tale of Two Currencies: British and French Finance During the Napoleonic Wars," *Journal of Economic History* 51 (1991): 303–316.

46. Woody Holton, *Unruly Americans and the Origins of the Constitution* (New York: Hill and Wang, 2007), 57–62, 77–90.

47. Thomas Anburney, *Travels through the Interior Parts of America* (London: William Lane, 1789), 2: 35, 40.

48. "Poor Richard; or, the Way to Wealth and Content in These Troublesome Times," *Liberty and Property preserved against Republicans and Levellers* 12 (1793): 13–14.

49. Bordo and White, "Tale of Two Currencies," 309–310; Rebecca Spang, *Stuff and Money in the Time of the French Revolution* (Cambridge: Harvard University Press, 2015), 137–138; Richard Taws, *The Politics of the Provisional: Art and Ephemera in Revolutionary France* (University Park: Pennsylvania State University Press, 2013), 13–42.

50. "The Bank of England Note: A Short History," *Bank of England Quarterly Bulletin* 9 (1969): 215; Mary Poovey, *Genres of the Credit Economy: Mediating Value in Eighteenth- and Nineteenth-Century Britain* (Chicago: University of Chicago Press, 2008), 45; R.M. Fitzmaurice, *British Banks and Banking: A Pictorial History* (Truro: D. Bradford Barton, 1975), figs. 47–50, 53.

51. Maurice Morgann, *Considerations on the Present Internal and External Condition of France* (London: J. Debrett, 1794), 31–33; Ralph Broome, *Observations on Mr. Paine's Pamphlet, entitled the Decline and Fall of the English System of Finance* (London: J. Debrett, 1796), 8, 13.

52. Hiroki Shin, "Paper Money, the Nation, and the Suspension of Cash Payments in 1797," *Historical Journal* 58 (2015): 420–423, 432 (quoting the *Newcastle Advertiser*, 442); Bordo and White, "A Tale of Two Currencies," 311–312, 315.

53. Shin, "Paper Money," 417–418; Simeon Pope, *Scarcity of Specie No Ground for Alarm, or British Opulence Unimpaired* (London: W. Richardson, 1797), 7; letter to Hector Macneill, 1802, in Elizabeth Benger, *Memoirs of the Late Mrs. Elizabeth Hamilton* (London: Longman, Hurst, Rees, Orme, and Brown, 1819), 2: 198–199; Arthur Young, *An Enquiry into the Progressive Value of Money in England* (London: B. McMillan, 1812), viii.

54. "On the Scarcity of Gold and Silver Coins," *Weekly Entertainer* 51 (1811): 242.

55. *Parliamentary Register* 13 (1800), 391 (speech of Thomas Jones); Alexander Dick, *Romanticism and the Gold Standard: Money, Literature, and Economic Debate in Britain 1790–1830* (Houndmills: Palgrave Macmillan, 2013), 45–47.

56. William Cobbett, *Paper Against Gold* (London: William Cobbett, 1810–1815); Poovey, *Genres of the Credit Economy*, 181–196.

57. Smith, *Wealth of Nations* (11th ed., London: T. Cadell, 1805), 3: 507; *The Reply of the People to the Letter from the King* (London: Rivington, 1821), 14–15.

58. *Times* January 7, 1796, April 20, 1795, January 23, 1793. On churches see chapter 8.

59. William Jacob, *An Historical Inquiry into the Production and Consumption of the Precious Metals* (London: John Murray, 1831), 2: 392; *Bullion Report*, 24 (Appendix 17). These sources report ounces of plate on which duties were paid; hence inflation does not figure in these increases. On military uniforms see chapter 6.

60. oldbaileyonline.org.

61. E.P. Thompson, "Time, Work-Discipline, and Industrial Capitalism," *Past and Present* 38 (1967): 67.

62. *Consideration on the Present State of Bank Notes, Specie, and Bullion* (London: privately published, 1811); "Bullion! Or a Patriotic Proposal," *The Scourge* 5 (1813): 125–126; *Monthly Review* 57 (1812): 315; James Mill, *Elements of Political Economy* (London: Baldwin, Cradock, and Joy, 1821), 45.

63. Angela Redish, *Bimetallism: An Economic and Historical Analysis* (Cambridge: Cambridge University Press, 2000), 168–186.

64. Boyd Hilton, *Corn, Cash, Commerce: The Economic Policies of the Tory Governments, 1815–1830* (Oxford: Oxford University Press, 1977), 39–40.

65. Edward Copleston, *A Letter to the Right Hon. Robert Peel . . . on the Pernicious Effects of a Variable Standard of Value* (Oxford: John Murray, 1819), 21.

66. National Archives, MINT 9/32; *Report of the Committee of Secrecy*, Appendix 5, 13–25; Roger Lloyd-Jones and M. J. Lewis, *British Industrial Capitalism Since the Industrial Revolution* (London: Routledge, 2003), 21. Between 1817 and 1822, circulating Bank of England notes diminished from £29.5 million to £17.5 million, compared to an increase of around £7 million worth of circulating gold coins.

67. William Joseph Stourton, *Three Letters . . . on the Distresses of Agriculture in the United Kingdom* (London: J. Mawman, 1822), 127; *Memoirs of the Public Life and Administration of the . . . Earl of Liverpool* (London: Saunders and Otley, 1827), 503.

68. Robert Huish, *The History of the Private and Political Life of the Late Henry Hunt* (London: John Saunders, 1836), 1: 330–331.

69. *Times* March 25 and June 14, 1823. For context see Bear Braumoeller, *The Great Powers and the International System* (Cambridge: Cambridge University Press, 2012), 124–126; Gabriel B. Paquette, *Imperial Portugal in the Age of Atlantic Revolutions: The Luso-Brazilian World, c. 1770–1850* (Cambridge: Cambridge University Press, 2013), 235–315.

70. *Derby Mercury* September 7, 1831; *Morning Chronicle* November 21, 1843; *John Bull* January 19, 1829 (on Greece); George Thomas Keppel, *Narrative of a Journey across the Balcan* (London: Colburn and Bentley, 1831), 1: 358–359 (on Bulgaria).

71. See chapter 10.

72. David Brewer, *The Greek War of Independence: The Struggle for Freedom from Ottoman Oppression and the Birth of the Modern Greek Nation* (Woodstock: Overlook Press, 2001), 220–225; Leicester Stanhope, *Greece in 1823 and 1824* (London: Sherwood, Gilbert, and Piper, 1825), 376.

73. *Times* July 3 and June 22, 1841, January 31, 1837.

74. Douglas Jerrold, *The History of St. Giles and St. James* (New York: Burgess, Stringer & Co., 1845), 30, 110.

Chapter 4

1. *Letter to the Duke of Buckingham, on the Corn Laws* (London: Cadell, 1839), 16–17.
2. Monetary historians have devoted relatively little attention to the Corn Laws, nor have historians of trade policy referred much to bullion drains. For exceptions see Boyd Hilton, *Corn, Cash, Commerce: The Economic Policies of the Tory Governments, 1815–1830* (Oxford: Oxford University Press, 1977), 108–126, 132–134, 278–301; Anna Gambles, *Protection and Politics: Conservative Economic Discourse 1815–1852* (London: Royal Historical Society, 1999), 134–142.
3. Arie Arnon, *Thomas Tooke: Pioneer of Monetary Theory* (Ann Arbor: University of Michigan Press, 1991), 17–19; M. J. R. Healy and E. L. Jones, "Wheat Yields in England, 1815–59," *Journal of the Royal Statistical Society* 125 (1962): 578. Prices fell by roughly 40 percent between 1819 and 1850. As much as £10 million in bullion left England in 1839 to pay for corn: Peter Mathias, *The First Industrial Nation: An Economic History of Britain, 1700–1914* (London: Methuen, 1969), 230.
4. Adam Smith, *An Inquiry into the Nature and Causes of the Wealth of Nations* (London: Strahan and Cadell, 1776), 2: 2; William Nassau Senior, *An Introductory Lecture on Political Economy, delivered before the University of Oxford* (London: J. Mawman, 1827), 31.
5. David Hume, *Political Discourses* (Edinburgh: R. Fleming, 1752), 81–83.
6. Smith, *Wealth of Nations*, 2: 7–8, 15–16, 23, 78–80. See Istvan Hont, *Jealousy of Trade: International Competition and the Nation-State in Historical Perspective* (Cambridge, MA: Harvard University Press, 2005), 77–81.
7. Smith, *Wealth of Nations*, 2: 20, 9–12.
8. Joseph Schumpeter, *History of Economic Analysis* (Oxford: Oxford University Press, 1954), 732.
9. Iain McLean, *Adam Smith, Radical and Egalitarian: An Interpretation for the Twentieth Century* (Houndmills: Palgrave Macmillan, 2007), 22–24; Charles Walton, "The Fall from Eden: The Free-Trade Origins of the French Revolution," in *The French Revolution in Global Perspective*, ed. Suzanne Desan, Lynn Hunt, and William Max Nelson (Ithaca: Cornell University Press, 2013), 44–56.
10. George Richardson Porter, *The Progress of the Nation* (London: Methuen, 1912), 617; Arnon, *Thomas Tooke*, 17; John Jay TePaske, "New World Gold Production in Hemispheric and Global Perspective 1492–1810," in *Monetary History in Global Perspective, 1500–1808*, ed. C. E. Núñez et al. (Seville: Universidad de Seville, 1998), 30.
11. Hilton, *Corn, Cash, Commerce*, 3–15, 278–301. "Per quarter" refers to "quarter hundredweight," equal to around 13 kg.
12. Peter J. Cain and A. G. Hopkins, *British Imperialism: Innovation and Expansion 1688–1914* (London: Longman, 1993), 78–81.
13. *Report from the Select Committee Banks of Issue* (London: HMSO, 1840), 103.
14. John Ashton Yates, *A Letter on the Present Depression of Trade and Manufactures* (Liverpool: G. and J. Robinson et al., 1841), 16; William Waterston, *A Cyclopaedia of Commerce, Mercantile Law, Finance, and Commercial Geography* (Edinburgh: Oliver and Boyd, 1843), 43; Smith, *Wealth of Nations* (Edinburgh: Adam Black and William Tate, 1828), 1: xii–xviii.
15. "Bounty," *Edinburgh Encyclopaedia* 4 (1832): 364.
16. John Henry Grose, *A Voyage to the East-Indies, began in 1750; with Observations continued till 1764* (London: S. Hooper, 1766), 324; Thomas Maurice, *Indian Antiquities: or, Dissertations, relative to . . . Hindostan* (London: H. L. Galabin, 1800), 7: 492; John Donne, *Poetical Works* (London: G. Cawthorn, 1800), 3: 189.
17. Artur Attman, *American Bullion in the European World Trade, 1600–1800* (Göteborg: Kungl. Vetenskaps-och Vitterhets Samhallet, 1986), 5–8, 77–78. Factoring in the precious metals that were smuggled out of Latin America, the actual volume was perhaps twice as large.
18. William J. Barber, *British Economic Thought and India 1600–1858* (Oxford: Clarendon Press, 1975), 9.
19. Michael Symes, *An Account of an Embassy to the Kingdom of Ava, sent by the Governor-General of India, in the Year 1795* (London: W. Bulmer, 1800), 260. On Indian adornment see chapter 7.

20. Maria Graham, *Journal of a Residence in India* (Edinburgh: Archibald Constable, 1813), 3; "The History of India," *Asiatic Annual Register . . . for the Year 1801* (1802): 13.

21. J. R. McCulloch, "Commercial Embarrassments—Trade with France," *Edinburgh Review* 32 (1819): 59; Rama Dev Roy, "Some Aspects of the Economic Drain from India During the British Rule," *Social Scientist* 15 (1987): 40–41.

22. J. R. McCulloch, *A Dictionary, Practical, Theoretical, and Historical, of Commerce and Commercial Navigation* (London: Longman, Rees, Orme, Brown, Green and Longman, 1832), 57.

23. *Substance of a Debate . . . on East and West India Sugar* (London: J.S. Brickwood, 1823), 13 (William Huskisson); *Report of the Public Meeting at Liverpool* (London: W. Lewer, 1829), 36 (motion by John Ewart); Prasannan Parthasarathi, *The Transition to A Colonial Economy: Weavers, Merchants and Kings in South India, 1720–1800* (Cambridge: Cambridge University Press, 2001).

24. David Macpherson, *The History of the European Commerce with India* (London: Longman, Hurst, Rees, Orme, and Brown, 1812), 337.

25. Archibald Alison, *The Principles of Population, and Their Conjunction with Human Happiness* (Edinburgh: William Blackwood and Sons, 1840), 2: 443; James Charles Dalbiac, *A Few Words on the Corn Laws* (London: John Ollivier, 1841), 53.

26. Layton Cooke, *Practical Observations on the Importation of Foreign Corn, under a Graduated Scale of Duty* (London: James Ridgway, 1827), 24; *Twenty Questions submitted by the General Agricultural Committee* (London: by Order of the Committee, 1827), 10.

27. Grenville Pigott, *A Letter on the Nature of the Protection afforded by the Present Corn Laws, and on the Probable Result of a Free Trade in Corn* (London: Roake and Varty, 1832), 48.

28. *A Refutation of a Catechism on the Corn Laws, by a Cumberland Farmer* (London: James Ridgway, 1829), 22.

29. Charles Herbert Cottrell, *Recollections of Siberia, in the Years 1840 and 1841* (London: John W. Parker, 1842), 399; Toni Pierenkemper and Richard H. Tilly, *The German Economy during the Nineteenth Century* (New York: Berghahn Books, 2004), 31–37; Boris Ananich, "The Russian Economy and Banking System," in *Imperial Russia, 1689–1917*, ed. Dominic Lieven (Cambridge; Cambridge University Press, 2006), 400.

30. Thomas Gardner Bramston, *The Principle of the Corn Law Vindicated* (London: J. Hatchard and Son, 1827), 76.

31. *Reflections on the Designs and Possible Consequences of the Anti-Corn-Law League* (London: Marchant, Singer and Smith, 1843), 15; *Fallacies of the Philanthropists! A Candid Appeal to Common Sense* (London: W. H Dalton, 1841), 18–19.

32. G. Calvert Holland, *Lecture on the Corn Laws* (Doncaster: R. Hartley, 1840), 12–13; Holland, *An Exposition of Corn-Law Repealing Fallacies and Inconsistencies* (London: Longman, Orme, Brown, Green, and Longmans, 1840), 84; Archibald Alison, "The Late Commercial Crisis," *Blackwood's Edinburgh Magazine* 42 (1837): 213. See Jessica M. Lepler, *The Many Panics of 1837: People, Politics, and the Creation of a Transatlantic Financial Crisis* (Cambridge: Cambridge University Press, 2013), 1–42, 123–156, 204–218.

33. On aristocratic debt see John Habakkuk, *Marriage, Debt, and the Estates System: English Landownership 1650–1950* (Oxford: Clarendon Press, 1994), 263–269, 340–356.

34. "On National Economy," *Fraser's Magazine* 9 (1834): 359, 361. This article was a response to Thomas Perronet Thompson, "A Free-Trader's Defence of the 'Mercantile System,'" *Westminster Review* 19 (1833): 269–283.

35. See, e.g., *Alarming State of the Nation Considered; the Evil Traced to Its Source, and Remedies Pointed Out* (London: James Ridgway, 1830), 37–39; Gambles, *Protection and Politics*, chs. 4–5.

36. Archibald Alison, "Wellington," *English Review* 4 (1845): 304; "Currency and Corn," *Hood's Magazine* 5 (1846): 90.

37. *Edinburgh Annual Register* 16 (1823): 116.

38. Jelinger C. Symons, *Arts and Artisans at Home and Abroad: with Sketches of the Progress of Foreign Manufactures* (Edinburgh: William Tait, 1839), 261.

39. Richard Badnall, *Letter to the Lords and Commons, on the Present Commercial and Agricultural Condition of Great Britain* (London: Whittaker, Treacher, 1830), 129–130; *The Injury Inflicted*

upon the People by the Corn Laws and the Prosperity that would result from their Repeal (New Brentford: Charles James Murphy, 1838), 15.

40. George Browning, *The Domestic and Financial Condition of Great Britain* (London: Longman, Rees, Orme, Brown, Green, and Longman, 1834), 420–421; "Hungary and Transylvania," *London Saturday Journal* 3 (1840): 121.

41. Edmund Kell, *The Injurious Effects of the Corn Laws, on All Classes of the Community, including the Farmer and the Landowner* (London: Smallfield, 1840), 23; Philip Harwood, *Six Lectures on the Corn-Law Monopoly and Free Trade* (London: John Green, 1843), 104–105. On the impact of the sliding scale on supply and demand see Wray Vamplew, "The Protection of English Cereal Producers: The Corn Laws Reassessed," *Economic History Review* 33 (1980): 382–395.

42. James Graham, *Free Trade in Corn, the Real Interest of the Landlord and the True Policy of the State* (London: James Ridgway, 1828); *Report from the Select Committee of the House of Commons on Import Duties* (London: HMSO, 1841), 21 (Joseph Hume). The duty on imported gold plate stood at £3 16s 9d per ounce as of 1841, very close to the value of its constituent metal.

43. T. Perronet Thompson, *Letter of a Representative, to his Constituents* (London: Effingham Wilson, 1836), 26.

44. Boyd Hilton, *The Age of Atonement: The Influence of Evangelicalism on Social and Economic Thought, 1795–1865* (Oxford: Oxford University Press, 1988), 131–136; J. R. McCulloch, "Causes and Consequences of the Crisis in the American Trade," *Edinburgh Review* 66 (1837): 234.

45. Richard Cobden, testimony before the Parliamentary Committee on Banks of Issue (1840), quoted in Frank Whitson Fetter, *The Development of British Monetary Orthodoxy, 1797–1875* (Cambridge, MA: Harvard University Press, 1965), 176. On the Bank Charter Act see Ibid., 182–197.

46. Anti-Gold Law League, circular, September 29, 1847; Rudiger Dornbusch and Jacob A. Frenkel, "The Gold Standard and the Bank of England in the Crisis of 1847," in *A Retrospective on the Classical Gold Standard, 1821–1931*, ed. Michael D. Bordo and Anna J. Schwartz (Chicago: University of Chicago Press, 1984), 233–264.

47. "Anti-Gold Law League," *Daily News* September 30, 1847; Jonathan Duncan, *The Principles of the League Explained* (London: John Ollivier, 1847), 5; "Anti-Gold Law League," *Morning Chronicle* October 22, 1847; Gambles, *Protection and Politics*, 226.

48. W. E. Aytoun, "A Glimpse of Germany and Its Parliament," *Blackwood's Edinburgh Magazine* 64 (1848): 534; Archibald Alison, "The Crowning of the Column, and Crushing of the Pedestal," *Blackwood's Edinburgh Magazine* 66 (1849): 122.

49. "Currency—Standard of Value—Free Trade and Protection," *Standard* February 22, 1848; *York Herald* April 11, 1857, quoted in H. I. Dutton and J. E. King, "An Economic Exile: Edward Stillingfleet Cayley, 1802–1862," *History of Political Economy* 17 (1985): 215.

50. On prices after 1849 see this book's conclusion; on Chartism see Margot C. Finn, *After Chartism: Class and Nation in English Radical Politics, 1848–1874* (Cambridge: Cambridge University Press, 2003); on free trade see Frank Trentmann, *Free Trade Nation: Commerce, Consumption, and Civil Society in Modern Britain* (Oxford: Oxford University Press, 2009).

Chapter 5

1. Laman Blanchard, "The Recent Meeting of the Coinage at the Royal Mint," *New Monthly Magazine* 72 (1844): 469–470, 472.

2. Adam Smith, *An Inquiry into the Nature and Causes of the Wealth of Nations* (London: Strahan and Cadell, 1776), 1: 30.

3. See, e.g., Glyn Davies, *History of Money* (Cardiff: University of Wales Press, 2002), 34–65.

4. Thomas Maurice, *Indian Antiquities: or, Dissertations, relative to . . . Hindostan* (London: H.L. Galabin, 1800), 7: 470; Mungo Park, *Travels in the Interior Districts of Africa* (London: W. Bulmer, 1799), 306; Rogers Ruding, *Annals of the Coinage of Britain and Its Dependencies* (London: Lackington, Hughes, Harding, Mavor, and Jones, 1819), 3: 178.

5. Christine Desan, *Making Money: Coin, Currency, and the Coming of Capitalism* (Oxford: Oxford University Press, 2014), 232–235.

6. When French refiners figured out how to turn a profit by extracting silver from sovereigns in the 1820s, the Mint switched to copper-only alloys, despite the fact that this diminished the coin's durability: G. P. Dyer and P. P. Gaspar, "Reform, the New Technology and Tower Hill, 1700–1966," in *A New History of the Royal Mint*, ed. C. E. Challis (Cambridge: Cambridge University Press, 1992), 486.

7. On the assaying duties of the Goldsmith's Company see J. S. Forbes, *Hallmark: A History of the London Assay Office* (London: Unicorn Press, 1999), 16–31, 127–130, 210–218, 238–257.

8. Andrew Ure, *A Dictionary of Arts, Manufactures, and Mines* (London: Longman, Orme, Brown, Green, and Longmans, 1840), 61; James Cochrane, *The Modern Receipt Book* (London: A.L. Newman, 1824), 241; Ruding, *Annals of the Coinage*, 1: 78–81, 142. By the 1830s, sulfuric acid had started to replace nitric acid (more commonly known at the time as aquafortis) as the preferred solvent in removing or "parting" silver or platinum from gold: Ure, *Dictionary*, 75.

9. Revelation 3: 18 (King James version). This paragraph draws from Timothy Alborn, "The Greatest Metaphor Ever Mixed: Gold in the British Bible, 1750–1850," *Journal of the History of Ideas* 78 (2017): 432–439.

10. Christmas Evans, "On Justification," in *Sermons on Various Subjects* (Beaver, PA: W. Henry, 1837), 260; John Clark, *The Coin Act: or, Scales for Professors. Intended to Assist Them in Proving and Ascertaining the True State of their Souls, and the Sterling Value of Their Religion* (London: T. Williams, 1803), 5, 18.

11. *Annual Register* 21 (1779), 181; Charles Jenkinson, *A Treatise on the Coins of the Realm* (Oxford: University Press, 1805), 182–183; *Gentleman's Magazine* 131 (1822), 390; *Times* July 14, 1823.

12. National Archives, MINT 7/132, 1/28; Forbes, *Hallmark*, 53, 65–68, 166, 243–244.

13. *Journals of the House of Lords* 34 (1774–1776): 196; W. Stanley Jevons, "On the Condition of the Metallic Currency of the United Kingdom," *Journal of the Statistical Society of London* 31 (1868): 454–455.

14. Malcolm Gaskill, *Crime and Mentalities in Early Modern England* (Cambridge: Cambridge University Press, 2000), 123–199; John Styles, "'Our Traitorous Money Makers': The Yorkshire Coiners and the Law, 1760–83," in *An Ungovernable People: The English and Their Law in the Seventeenth and Eighteenth Centuries*, ed. John Brewer and John Styles (New Brunswick: Rutgers University Press, 1980), 172–249.

15. National Archives, T 1/510/89–90; Michael A. Crawforth, *Weighing Coins: English Folding Gold Balances of the 18th and 19th Centuries* (London: Cape Horn Trading Co., 1979), 1–3, 36–49.

16. *Times* September 12, 1839, November 25, 1841, November 24, 1843; Bank of England Archives 13A84/7/75 ("'Report of the Deputy Governor on weighing Gold Coin," March 23, 1842); "Description of the Automaton Balance for Weighing Coins," *Architect, Engineer and Surveyor* 4 (1843): 283–284.

17. Thomas J. Sargent and François R. Velde, *The Big Problem of Small Change* (Princeton: Princeton University Press, 2001), 270–274; *St. James's Chronicle* May 10, 1774.

18. William Jacob, *An Historical Inquiry into the Production and Consumption of the Precious Metals* (London: John Murray, 1831), 2: 173; Charles Hatchett, "Experiments and Observations on the Various Alloys . . . and on the Comparative Wear of Gold," *Philosophical Transactions of the Royal Society of London* 93 (1803): 125; Christa Jungnickel and Russell McCormmach, *Cavendish* (Philadelphia: American Philosophical Society, 1996), 346–348; Dyer and Gaspar, "Reform," 455–461.

19. Walter Merrey, *Remarks on the Coinage of England from the Earliest to the Present Times* (Nottingham: S. Tupman, 1789), 84; William Nugent Glascock, *Naval Sketch-book; or, the Service Afloat and Ashore* (London: Henry Colburn, 1826), 1: 70–71.

20. John Pinkerton, *An Essay on Medals* (London: James Dodlsey, 1784), 159; John Locker, *Address . . . on the Present State of the Money System of the United Kingdom* (London: Samuel Tipper, 1809), viii.

21. Ruding, *Annals of the* Coinage, 1: 239–242.

22. Desan, *Making Money*; Sargent and Velde, *The Big Problem of Small Change*; Deborah Valenze, *The Social Life of Money in the English Past* (Cambridge: Cambridge University Press, 2006), 34–43.

23. Merrey, *Remarks*, 66, 68.

24. *General Evening Post* July 17, 1773; *Annual Register. . . for the Year 1778* (4th ed. London: W. Otridge and Son, 1800), 231; *Journals of the House of Lords* 34 (1774–1776): 196 (evidence of Samuel Etheridge, May 16, 1774).

25. *Craftsman* July 24, 1773; *St. James's Chronicle* May 10, 1774; *Lloyd's Evening Post* July 21–23, 1773; *General Evening Post* July 31, 1773.

26. *Morning Chronicle* August 5, 1773. Another report two months later suggested that the clippers' loss was the smugglers' gain: their fences were able to trade goods for light gold "as quick as it is possible for the Smugglers to procure them": *London Chronicle* October 26, 1773.

27. *St. James's Chronicle* May 10, 1774; National Archives T 1/500/184 (letter to Lord North, July 19, 1774); "A Particular Account of All Charges Attending the Late Recoinage of Gold in this Kingdom," National Archives, T 1/500/74; Styles, " 'Our Traitorous Money Makers,' " 236. Commission paid to the 24 exchangers ranged from 0.3 percent to 1 percent depending on their distance from London.

28. "A Particular Account"; Dyer and Gaspar, "Reform," 441.

29. Bank of England Archives 2A 109/1; Larry Neal, *The Rise of Financial Capitalism: International Capital Markets in the Age of Reason* (Cambridge: Cambridge University Press, 1993), 127.

30. *Times* May 14, 1785, May 5, 1791, June 22, 1792, December 19, 1786; Ruding, *Annals of the Coinage*, 4: 64.

31. "Observations on the Gold Coinage" (1799), National Archives, MINT 9/7.

32. *Times* September 24, 1787 and April 8, 1799.

33. "Memorandum relating to the Wear of the Gold Coin and the Expense Attending It," National Archives, MINT 9/224.

34. Jenkinson, *Treatise on the Coins of the Realm*, 5, 216; Ruding, *Annals of the Coinage*, 4: 53.

35. *Report of the Committee of Secrecy on the Bank of England Charter* (London: James and Luke G. Hansard and Sons, 1832), appendix 5 (pp. 13–25). By one estimate, private banks kept and average of £26.8 million worth of notes (including £5 notes) in circulation between 1808 and 1821: Douglas Adie, "English Bank Deposits Before 1844," *Economic History Review* 23 (1970): 292.

36. Henry Thornton, *An Enquiry into the Nature and Effects of the Paper Credit of Great Britain* (London: J. Hatchard, 1802), 115; *Parliamentary Debates* (1st ser.) (1816), 34: 964 (speech of Alexander Baring). A survey of guineas reported stolen at Old Bailey yields the same result: on average, the court processed claims of 430 stolen guineas per year between 1781 and 1800; that number fell to 164 between 1801 and 1810, and to 86 between 1811 and 1817: oldbaileyonline.org.

37. Benjamin Smart, *A Letter. . . on the Necessity of an Immediate Attention to the State of the British Coinage* (London: J. Hatchard, 1811), 7–8. See Kevin Clancy, "The Recoinage and Exchange of 1816–17" (University of Leeds PhD dissertation, 1999), 54–57.

38. Rothschild Archives VII 2/1.

39. The name was not new: sovereigns and half-sovereigns had circulated in the sixteenth century, although not in great quantities. See C. E. Challis, *The Tudor Coinage* (Manchester: Manchester University Press, 1978), 59, 111–112, 219–221, 244, 277.

40. Bank of England Archives 2A 109/1. By one estimate, £2.5 million of the sovereigns coined since 1817 "had disappeared": *Times* April 30, 1818.

41. National Archives, MINT 9/62.

42. On Nathan Rothschild's European connections at this time see Stanley Chapman, *The Rise of Merchant Banking* (London: Unwin Hyman, 1984), 18–19.

43. Bank of England Archives C 66/1; Rothschild Archives VII 2/0-1. National origin can only be determined when the Bank or Rothschild did the melting; when they purchased gold bars this information is not available. In Rothschild's case that accounts for 45 percent of imports in 1816 and 38 percent in 1820–1821 (66 percent of bar gold came from non-French sources). The figure of 60 percent for French gold is based on the proportion of coins received from Paris (78.3 percent French) and other sources (29.1 percent) and assuming this for the bar gold received from French and non-French sources. Rothschild's bullion import records for 1817 through February 1820 are lost.

44. *Parliamentary Debates* (1st ser.) (1816), 34: 1025 (speech of Joseph Marryat).

45. *Parliamentary Debates* (1st ser.) (1816), 34:1022 (speech of Wellesley Pole), 1024 (John Wilson Croker); *Times* May 31, 1816; Clancy, "Recoinage and Exchange," 65–67.

46. *Gentleman's Magazine* 131 (1822), 390; *Times* July 14, 1823.

47. John Alton, *Eight Weeks in Germany* (Edinburgh: William Whyte, 1842), 58; John Booker, *Travellers' Money* (Stroud: Alan Sutton, 1994), 63–70, 124–131.

48. *Times* July 7 and December 1, 1817; "The 'Sovereign' Coin," *Gentleman's Magazine* 97 (1827): 504.

49. *Times* May 9, 1821, March 9, 1829. In 1825, when Parliament ended the Bank of England's power to issue £1 and £2 notes, the Bank issued a record £7.5 million in gold coins: *Report … on the Bank of England Charter*, appendix 5 (p. 72).

50. *Report … on the Bank of England Charter*, appendix 5 (pp. 13–25; annual average from 1816 to 1832); William Miller, "Estimate … of the total amount of the Gold Currency in the United Kingdom" (1858), Bank of England Archives M 5/592; Henry Noel Humpherys, *The Coins of England* (London: Longman, Brown, Green, and Longmans, 1848), 117–118.

51. Angela Redish, "The Evolution of the Gold Standard in England," *Journal of Economic History* 50 (1990), 796, 799, 802; George Selgin, "Steam, Hot Air, and Small Change: Matthew Boulton and the Reform of Britain's Coinage," *Economic History Review* 56 (2003): 478–509; Clancy, "Recoinage and Exchange," 110–147, 237.

52. On railways and social class see Simon Bradley, *The Railways: Nation, Network, and People* (London: Profile Books, 2015), 54–102.

53. National Archives, MINT 7/1. This period was chosen to exclude the gold recoinage of 1842–1844.

54. John Camden Hotten, *The Slang Dictionary: Etymological, Historical, and Anecdotal* (London: Chatto and Windus, 1874), 62–63; Thomas Hood, "The Little Browns," *New Monthly Magazine* 65 (1842): 418.

55. *Parliamentary Debates* (3d ser.) (1842), 64: 198 (speech of Charles Buller).

56. Guineas did continue to circulate as legal tender in Britain after 1821: in Old Bailey trials, they comprised 11 percent of gold coins stolen between 1821 and 1825 and 6.5 percent between 1826 and 1835 (oldbaileyonline.org).

57. "Gold," *Penny Magazine*, April 25, 1835; Anne Digby, *The Evolution of British General Practice, 1850–1948* (Oxford: Oxford University Press, 1999), 99–105; A. H. Manchester, *A Modern Legal History of England and Wales 1750–1950* (London: Butterworths, 1980), 69.

58. oldbaileyonline.org.

59. *Times* January 19 and 29, 1831; Patrick M. Geoghegan, *Liberator: The Life and Death of Daniel O'Connell 1830–1847* (London: Gill Macmillan, 2010), chapter 3.

60. *Report … on the Bank of England Charter*, 23–24 (evidence of J. Horsley Palmer) and appendix, 25; *London Interiors* (London: Joseph Mead, 1841), 72; Nancy D. LoPatin, *Political Unions, Popular Politics and the Great Reform Act of 1832* (Houndsmills: Palgrave Macmillan, 1999), 131–159.

61. John P. Durbin, *Observations in Europe, principally in France and Great Britain* (New York: Harper and Brothers, 1846), 2: 121. On Chartism and bank runs see Thomas Milton Kemnitz, "Approaches to the Chartist Movement: Feargus O'Connor and Chartist Strategy," *Albion* 5 (1973): 69.

62. National Archives, MINT 1/21 (Wellesley Pole to Privy Council, November 13, 1820; "Notice: Money Weights," March 1, 1821).

63. *Parliamentary Debates* (3d ser.) (1842), 63: 1492 (speech of John Childers); National Archives, MINT 1/27; 1/28 (James William Morrison to J. Rippon, June 15, 1830).

64. *Examiner* October 23, 1841; National Archives, MINT 9/226 (letter from W. D. Haggard, Bank of England bullion office, December 4, 1841). For reports of counterfeit gold currency see *Standard* August 24, 1829; *Manchester Times* August 17, 1833; *Preston Chronicle* April 9, 1836.

65. *Times* April 19, 1842; *Parliamentary Debates* (3d ser.) (1842), 63: 229 (speech of Robert Peel).

66. *Times* June 8 and 9, 1842.

67. *Times* June 10 and 18 and July 5, 1842.

68. *Times* June 10, 13, 15, 20 and July 20, 1842; *Parliamentary Debates* (3d ser.) (1842), 64: 233.

69. *Times* November 21 and 23, 1843; National Archives, MINT 5/110 (report of James Hill, July 20, 1842).

70. *Parliamentary Debates* (3d ser.) (1842), 64: 215, 220 (Henry Goulburn), 231 (Robert Peel).

71. Bank of England Archives C 66/2; Dyer and Gaspar, "Reform," 484.

72. *Parliamentary Debates* (3d ser.) (1842), 64: 222 (speech of Henry Goulburn); Timothy Alborn, "Coin and Country: Visions of Civilisation in the British Recoinage Debate, 1867–1894," *Journal of Victorian Culture* 3 (1998): 252–281.

73. *Times* June 8, 1842, October 5, 1843; James J. Macintyre, *The Influence of Aristocracies on the Revolutions of Nations* (London: Fisher and Son, 1843), 98.

74. Alborn, "Coin and Country," 292–293.

75. "Dialogue between a Guinea and a Half-Crown," *Walker's Hibernian Magazine* 35 (1805): 228; Peregrine Oakley, *Aureus; or, The Life and Opinions of a Sovereign* (London: George Wightman, 1824), 118; Horace Smith, *Gaieties and Gravities: A Series of Essays, Comic Tales and Fugitive Vagaries* (London: Henry Colburn, 1825), 3: 78.

76. W. Jones, "Light Sovereigns," *Penny Satirist* July 16, 1842; "Cash, Corn, and Coal Markets," *Chambers's Edinburgh Journal* 17 (1852): 42.

Chapter 6

1. Innes Hoole, *Scenes at Brighton; or, "How Much?": A Satirical Novel* (London: A.K. Newman, 1821), 1: 196–199.

2. Alan Hunt, *Governance of the Consuming Passions: A History of Sumptuary Law* (New York: St. Martin's Press, 1996), 375–376; Lynn Festa, *Sentimental Figures of Empire in Eighteenth-Century Britain and France* (Baltimore: The Johns Hopkins University Press, 2006), 67–110.

3. Patrick Colquhoun, *A Treatise on the Wealth, Power, and Resources, of the British Empire* (London: Joseph Mawman, 1814), 93.

4. Mary Meeke, *The Sicilian* (London: William Lane, 1798), 2: 154–158.

5. Ibid., 154–155.

6. Hunt, *Governance of the Consuming Passions*, 156, 302–311, 322–324, 368. The quote, from a 1533 law, is from p. 311.

7. Daniel Defoe, *The Complete English Tradesman* (London: Charles Rivington, 1727), 100; David Hume, *The History of England* (London: A. Millar, 1763), 2: 513.

8. Martha C. Howell, *Commerce Before Capitalism in Europe, 1300–1600* (Cambridge: Cambridge University Press, 2010), 243; Mary Deverell, *Miscellanies in Prose and Verse* (London: J. Rivington, 1781), 1: 144.

9. *Bankers' Circular* July 31, 1829, 11; William Jacob, *An Historical Inquiry into the Production and Consumption of the Precious Metals* (London: John Murray, 1831), 2: 286; "On the Prepossessions of a First Sight," *Universal Magazine* 94 (1794): 109.

10. Gerald Newman, *The Rise of English Nationalism: A Cultural History 1740-1830* (New York: St. Martin's Press, 1997), 37; James T. Boulton and T. O. McLoughlin, eds., *News from Abroad: Letters Written by British Travellers on the Grand Tour, 1728–71* (Liverpool: Liverpool University Press, 2013), 10; David Kuchta, *The Three-Piece Suit and Modern Masculinity: England, 1550–1850* (Berkeley, CA: University of California Press, 2002), 121–125.

11. Paul Langford, *Englishness Identified: Manners and Character 1650–1850* (Oxford: Oxford University Press, 2002), 158.

12. "Dress—Male Attire," *London Journal* 1 (1845): 184; Harry Longueville Jones, "Aesthetics of Dress: Minor Matters," *Blackwood's Edinburgh Magazine* 57 (1845): 738. On the gold watch as "a prestigious piece of male jewellery," see Amanda Vickery, *Behind Closed Doors: At Home in Georgian England* (New Haven: Yale University Press, 2009), 264.

13. On distinctions between "fashionable femininity" and "fashionable masculinity" see Sumaio Li, "Fashionable People, Fashionable Society: Fashion, Gender and Print Culture in England, 1821–1861" (University of Michigan PhD dissertation, 2008), 139–196.

14. "Fashions for September," *Le Beau Monde* 2 (1807): 159; "Fashions," *Edinburgh Annual Register* 5 (1812), 216; Adam Clarke, *Christian Theology* (London: Thomas Tegg and

Son, 1835), 303; Hannah Greig, *The Beau Monde: Fashionable Society in Georgian London* (Oxford: Oxford University Press, 2013), 48–52.

15. "Parisian Fashions," *La Belle Assemblée* 1 (1810): 145.

16. Edward Nares, *Thinks-I-To-Myself* (London: Sherwood, Neely and Jones), 1: 118; William Makepeace Thackeray, "*Our Street*" (London: Chapman and Hall, 1848), 43–44; Theodore Edward Hook, *Sayings and Doings, a Series of Sketches from Life* (London: Henry Colburn, 1824), 1: 115, 117.

17. John Moore, *Mordaunt. Sketches of Life, Characters, and Manners, in various Countries* (London: G. G. and J. Robinson, 1800), 2: 203–204, 212–213; Eugenia de Acton, *The Microcosm* (London: J. Mawman, 1801), 2: 133. On nabobinas see Tillman W. Nechtman, *Nabobs: Empire and Identity in Eighteenth Century Britain* (Cambridge: Cambridge University Press, 2010), 185–220.

18. Robert Syers, *The History of Everton* (Liverpool: G. and J. Robinson, 1830), 163; *Uncle Tweazy and his Quizzical Neighbours* (London: Simpkin and Marshall, 1816), 1: 53.

19. Henry Mackenzie, *Works* (Edinburgh: Constable., 1808), 4: 133, 5: 115 (quoting newspaper articles from 1779 and 1785); "A Whimsical Disappointment," *Edinburgh Magazine* 48 (1780): 307; Mary Elizabeth Robinson, *The Shrine of Bertha* (London: W. Lane, 1794), 1: 54.

20. Robert Macnish, *The Philosophy of Sleep* (New York: William Pearson, 1835), 48.

21. Obadiah Lapstone, "Views of Life," *Newcastle Magazine* 8 (1829): 553; Cornelius Webbe, *Glances at Life in City and Suburb* (London: Smith, Elder, 1836), 201–202; John Gamble, *Views of Society and Manners in the North of Ireland* (London: Longman, Hurst, Rees, Orme and Brown, 1819), 170; Gerald Griffin, *The Collegians* (London: Saunders and Otley, 1829), 1: 164–165.

22. "Empiricism—Medical Practice in Ireland," *National Magazine* 1 (1830): 573–574.

23. Friederich Wendeborn, *A View of England towards the Close of the Eighteenth Century* (London: G.G. J. and J. Robinson, 1791), 2: 74–75; Hermann Pückler-Muskau, *Tour in England, Ireland, and France* (Philadelphia: Carey, Lea and Blanchard, 1833), 46; *Lancaster Gazette* June 30, 1838; John Russell, *Adventures in the Moon, and Other Worlds* (London: Longman, Orme, Brown, Green and Longmans, 1841), 88–90.

24. "Diseases of the Chest," *Medical-Chirurgical Review* 32 (1838): 33.

25. 1 Peter 3:3; *The Nature, Design, and General Rules of the Methodist Societies established by the Rev. John Wesley* (London: George Whitfield, 1798), 6; Joseph Gurney, *Observations on the Distinguishing Views and Practices of the Society of Friends* (Norwich: S. Wilkin, 1824), 342.

26. George Jerment, *Early Piety, Illustrated and Recommended* (London: T. Conder, 1798), 193; Joseph Livesey, *The Moral Reformer* (London: R. Groombridge, 1838), 147 (quoting 1 Timothy 2: 9).

27. Festa, *Sentimental Figures*, 67–69.

28. William Makepeace Thackeray, "The Luck of Barry Lyndon: A Romance of the Last Century," *Fraser's Magazine* 29 (1844): 44; J.B.B. Clarke, *An Account of the Infancy, Religious and Literary Life, of Adam Clarke* (New York: B. Waugh and T. Mason, 1833), 2: 33.

29. Richard Butler Glengall, *The Irish Tutor, or, New Lights; a Comic Piece, in One Act* (London: John Lowndes, 1823), 7. Starting in 1793, mail-coach drivers and guards wore gold-braided uniforms and letter carriers wore gold hat bands: Phillis Cunnington and Catherine Lucas, *Occupational Costume in England from the Eleventh Century to 1914* (London: Adam and Charles Black, 1967), 240–243. On beadles see chapter 8.

30. Alexander Maxwell, *Patriots Against Fashion: Clothing and Nationalism in Europe's Age of Revolutions* (Houndmills: Palgrave Macmillan, 2014), 69.

31. John Eglin, *The Imaginary Autocrat: Beau Nash and the Invention of Bath* (London: Profile Books, 2005), 17; Francis Grose, *A Classical Dictionary of the Vulgar Tongue* (London: S. Hooper, 1785), entry "tuft hunter."

32. Horace Smith, *The Moneyed Man, or, The Lesson of a Life* (Philadelphia: Lea and Blanchard, 1841), 1: 17; George Cox, *Black Gowns & Red Coats, or, Oxford in 1834* (London: James Ridgway, 1834), 19; M.C. Curthoys and C. J. Day. "The Oxford of Mr. Verdant Green," in *The History of the University of Oxford: Nineteenth-Century Oxford, Part I*, ed. M. G. Brock and M. C. Curthoys (Oxford: Clarendon Press, 1997), 270–271.

33. Edward Churton, *Lays of Faith and Loyalty* (Cambridge: John Thomas Walters, 1845), 7; Adrian R. Bell et al., *The Soldier in Later Medieval England* (Oxford: Oxford University Press, 2013), 56–64.

34. W.Y. Carman, *British Military Uniforms from Contemporary Pictures* (New York: Arco, 1957), 79–83, 90–91; Jenny Spencer-Smith, *Portraits for a King: the British Military Painting of A. J.-Dubois Drahonet* (London: National Army Museum, 1990), 12–92.

35. *Regulations for the Dress of General, Staff, and Regimental Officers of the Army* (London: William Clowes and Sons, 1834), 5–154.

36. Scott Hughes Myerly, *British Military Spectacle from the Napoleonic Wars through the Crimea* (Cambridge: Harvard University Press, 1996), 69, 109.

37. "The Beautiful and Picturesque," *British Quarterly Review* 8 (1848): 507.

38. Edmond Temple, *The Life of Pill Garlick* (London: John Miller, 1813), 15; William Maginn, *The Military Sketch-book* (London: Henry Colburn, 1827), 1: 127.

39. *Times* September 7, 1803; Linda Colley, *Britons: Forging the Nation* (London: Pimlico, 2003), 288; Myerly, *British Military Spectacle*, 135; James Montgomery, *Prose, by a Poet* (London: Longman, Hurst, Rees, Orme, Brown, and Green, 1824), 1: 159, 166–167.

40. Spencer-Smith, *Portraits for a King*, 67.

41. Henrietta Jenkin, *Wedlock; or, Yesterday and To-Day* (London: Richard Bentley, 1841), 3: 75.

42. *Times* June 9, 1819, December 2 and 26, 1828; "Prices of Military Equipments," *Polar Star* 1 (1829): 405; Carman, *British Military Uniforms*, 132.

43. James Smith, "Miss Pope," *New Monthly Magazine* 19 (1827): 495; Anna Maria Hall, *Lights and Shadows of Irish Life* (London: Henry Colburn, 1838), 2: 290.

44. Cunnington and Lucas, *Occupational Costume*, 176–177; William Kitchiner, *The Traveller's Oracle* (London: Henry Colburn, 1827), 2: 27, 30. A coachman's coat with a gold-laced collar and buttonholes added around £15 to his employer's annual budget, with an extra £5 for a gold-laced hat; in both cases the gold comprised close to half of the expense. On female servants see Shirley Bury, *Jewellery 1789–1910: The International Era* (Woodbridge: Antique Collectors' Club, 1991), 1: 147–148.

45. Washington Irving, *Bracebridge Hall: or, The Humorists* (London: John Murray, 1822), 1: 60–61, 75.

46. Catharine Maria Sedgwick, *Letters from Abroad to Kindred at Home* (New York: Harper and Brothers, 1841), 1: 51.

47. Charles Cochrane, *Journal of a Tour . . . through Great Britain and Ireland* (London: Simpkin and Marshall, 1830), 1: 68. On footmen see Lucy Lethbridge, *Servants: A Downstairs History of Britain from the Nineteenth Century to the Modern Times* (New York: W.W. Norton, 2013), 44.

48. "The Queen's Fancy-dress Ball," *Court Magazine* 20 (1842): 488–498; Adrienne Munich, *Queen Victoria's Secrets* (New York: Columbia University Press, 1996), 28–35.

49. *Times* April 4, 1805; J. N. P. Watson, *Through Fifteen Reigns: A Complete History of the Household Cavalry* (London: Spellmount, 1997), 16–17; *Royal Military Chronicle* 1 (1811), 277.

50. Marguerite Blessington, *The Idler in Italy* (London: Henry Colburn, 1839), 2: 141–142.

51. *Edinburgh Weekly Magazine* 59 (1784), 140; *Times* January 19, 1809. For context and continuities dating back to 1700 see Greig, *The Beau Monde*, 100–130.

52. *Weekly Entertainer* January 29, 1798; Percival Barlow, *The General History of Europe* (London: W. and J. Stratford, 1791), 6; *Parker's General Advertiser* January 21, 1783.

53. "Character of the Prince Regent," *Reflector* 2 (1811), 11; "The King at Brighton," *Examiner* 6 January 1822.

54. Christopher Hartop, *Royal Goldsmiths: The Art of Rundell and Bridge, 1797–1843* (Cambridge: John Adamson, 2005), 15–17, 86–88; John Bruce, *The History of Brighton, with the Latest Improvements, to 1835* (Brighton: John Bruce, 1835), 27–29, 32; John Parry, *An Historical and Descriptive Account of the Coast of Sussex* (Brighton: Wright and Son, 1833), 125.

55. "Apsley House," *Mirror of Literature* 30 (1838): 159; *Morning Chronicle* June 19, 1841.

56. "Archives of the Court of St. James's," supplement, *Royal Lady's Magazine*, 3 (1832): 12; *Times* April 20, 1831; "A Little Talk About Buckingham Palace," *Sharpe's London Magazine* 3 (1847): 376; Bury, *Jewellery*, 1: 264.

57. *British Imperial Kalendar* (1844), 112–114; *Times* February 11, 1841; *Examiner* January 29, 1842.

58. "A Little Talk About Buckingham Palace," 377.

59. William Taylor, *Chapters on Coronations* (London: John W. Parker, 1838), 16–17; Claude Blair (ed.), *The Crown Jewels: The History of the Coronation Regalia in the Jewel House of the Tower of London* (London: The Stationery Office, 1998), 2: 2–4, 183, 235, and *passim*. Of 61 pieces of gold plate, all but six were added to the regalia before 1761, as well as 19 of 26 other pieces.

60. David Hughson, *London; Being an Accurate History and Description of the British Metropolis* (London: J. Stratford, 1805), 1: 47–48. On the "aesthetically performed politics" of George III's coronation see Holger Hoock, *Empires of the Imagination: Politics, War, and Arts in the British World, 1750–1850* (London: Profile Books, 2010), 23–36.

61. Christopher Hibbert, *George IV: Regent and King, 1811–1830* (London: Allen Lane, 1973), 190; Hugh Roberts, "Royal Thrones, 1760–1840," *Furniture History* 25 (1989): 67; Blair, *The Crown Jewels*, 2: 185; Robert Huish, *An Authentic History of the Coronation of His Majesty, King George the Fourth* (London: J. Robinson, 1821), 108–110.

62. Blair, *The Crown Jewels*, 2: 257; *Mirror of Literature* September 10, 1831 and July 7, 1838.

63. Hughson, *London*, 1: 78; A. T. Thomson, *Memoirs of the Court of Henry the Eighth* (London: Longman, Hurst, Rees, Orme, Brown, and Green, 1826), 2: 372.

64. See, e.g., William Hargrove, *History and Description of the Ancient City of York* (York: William Alexander, 1818), 1: 323; Thomas Allen, *A History of the County of Surrey* (London: Isaac Taylor Hinton, 1831), 2: 119; Henry Englefield, *A Walk through Southampton* (London: T. Baker, 1841), 29; *Times* April 13, 1787 and January 5, 1836.

65. Scott A. Trudell, "Occasion," in *Early Modern Theatricality*, ed. Henry S. Turner (Oxford: Oxford University Press, 2013), 236–237; "The Lord Mayor's Show," *Tait's Edinburgh Magazine* 4 (1833): 363–364; *Times* November 10, 1829.

66. Joseph Strutt, *A Complete View of the Dress and Habits of the People of England* (London: J. Edwards, 1796–1799); James Planché, *History of British Costume* (London: Charles Knight, 1834); Frederick William Fairholt, *Costume in England: A History of Dress from the Earliest Period until the Close of the Eighteenth Century* (1846; London: Chapman and Hall, 1860).

67. Alice Mackrell, *An Illustrated History of Fashion: 500 Years of Fashion Illustration* (New York: Costume & Fashion Press, 1997), 147; W. Harrison Ainsworth, *Windsor Castle: An Historical Romance* (London: Henry Colburn, 1843), 1: 57; George Payne Rainsford James, *Darnley; or, The Field of the Cloth of Gold* (London: Colburn and Bentley, 1830), 252.

68. Huish, *Authentic History*; Taylor, *Chapters on Coronations*; James Planché, *Royal Records; or a Chronicle of the Coronations of the Queens Regnant of England* (London: Chapman and Hall, 1838); Agnes Strickland, *Lives of the Queens of England* (London: Henry Colburn, 1840–1847).

69. John Aikin and William Enfield, *General Biography* (London: G. G. and J. Robinson, 1799), 1: 421; Emma Roberts, *Memoirs of the Rival Houses of York and Lancaster* (London: Harding and Lepard, 1827), 1: 253.

70. Patrick Tytler, *Life of King Henry the Eighth* (Edinburgh: Oliver and Boyd, 1837), 58; George Craik, *The Pictorial History of England* (London: Charles Knight, 1839), 2: 343.

71. John Stoughton, *Notices of Windsor in the Olden Times* (London: David Bogue, 1844), 142–143. See Michael Dobson and Nicola J. Watson, *England's Elizabeth: An Afterlife in Fame and Fantasy* (Oxford: Oxford University Press, 2002), 147–158.

72. David Henry, *An Historical Description of the Tower of London, and Its Numerous Curiosities* (London: Thomas North, 1800); Johann Georg Kohl, *England, Wales, and Scotland* (London: Chapman and Hall, 1844), 1: 174.

73. Jacob, *Historical Inquiry*, 2: 206–207; *Morning Chronicle* December 7, 1816. On Warwick Castle see Peter Mandler, *The Fall and Rise of the Stately Home* (New Haven: Yale University Press, 1997), 71–88.

74. *Times* June 22, 1830; Thomas Egerton Wilks, *The Ruby Ring; or, the Murder at Sadler's Wells!* (London: J. Duncombe, 1840); *John Bull* October 13, 1828. For similar examples of historical costume dramas see Diana De Marly, *Costume on the Stage, 1600–1940* (London: B. T. Batsford, 1982), 64–82.

75. John Tickell, *History of the Town and County of Kingston upon Hull* (Hull: Thomas Lee, 1798), 218.

76. Eric Hobsbawm and Terence Ranger, eds., *The Invention of Tradition* (Cambridge: Cambridge University Press, 1992).

77. Elaine Freedgood, *The Ideas in Things: Fugitive Meaning in the Victorian Novel* (Chicago: University of Chicago Press, 2010), 7–8.

Chapter 7

1. *Society in India; by an Indian Officer* (London: Henry Colburn, 1841), 1: 272–274, 276–279.

2. David Cannadine, *Ornamentalism: How the British Saw Their Empire* (Oxford: Oxford University Press, 2001), 10.

3. William Jacob, *An Historical Inquiry into the Production and Consumption of the Precious Metals* (London: John Murray, 1831),1: 300–306; *Cambridge Economic History of India*, vol. 1, ed. Tapan Raychaudhuri and Irfan Habib (Cambridge: Cambridge University Press, 1982), 263–268, 364–365.

4. On "non-existent . . . regional or peasant jewelry" in England, see Shirley Bury, *Jewellery 1789–1910: The International Era* (Woodbridge: Antique Collectors' Club, 1991), 1: 149.

5. See, e.g., William Dalrymple, *Return of a King: The Battle for Afghanistan, 1839–42* (New York: Alfred A. Knopf, 2013), 18 (on Lord Elphinstone).

6. Chloe Chard, *Pleasure and Guilt on the Grand Tour: Travel Writing and Imaginative Geography, 1600–1830* (Manchester: Manchester University Press, 1999); Ann Bermingham, "The Picturesque and Ready-to-Wear Femininity," in *The Politics of the Picturesque: Literature, Landscape and Aesthetics Since 1770*, ed. Stephen Copley and Peter Garside (Cambridge; Cambridge University Press, 1994), 81–119.

7. Samuel Johnson, *Dictionary of the English Language* (London: J. Knapton et al., 1756), entry *barbarick*; John Milton, *Paradise Lost* (Indianapolis: Hackett, 2005), 40; Alexander Pope, *Works* (London: J. Wenman, 1778), 1: 149.

8. Mary Russell Mitford, *Works* (Philadelphia: James Crissy, 1841), 563; *Observations on the Public and Private Life of His Royal Highness the Prince Regent* (London: J. Swan, 1815), 41.

9. Daniel Corrie, *Memoirs* (London: Seeley, Burnside and Seeley, 1847), 37 (journal entry from 1806).

10. Richard and John Lander, *Journal of an Expedition to Explore the Course and Termination of the Niger* (London: John Murray, 1832), 3: 322; 1: 235–236; 2: 43.

11. Robert Percival, *An Account of the Island of Ceylon* (London: C. and R. Baldwin, 1803), 141–142; "Himalaya Mountains, and Lake Manasawara," *Quarterly Review* 17 (1817): 413 (quoting F. V. Raper); review of W. S. W. Ruschenberger, *Narrative of a Voyage round the World, Athenaeum*, April 28, 1838.

12. Michael J. Franklin, *Romantic Representations of British India* (London: Routledge, 2006), 174.

13. Daniel Tyerman and George Bennet. *Voyages and Travels . . . from the London Missionary Society* (Boston: Crocker and Brewster, 1832), 3: 120; "Native Life in India," *Monthly Review* 127 (1832): 236. On bindis see John Hobart Caunter, *The Romance of History: India* (London: Edward Churton, 1836), 20–21. On toe rings see R. Montgomery Martin, *History of the British Colonies* (London: James Cochran, 1835), 1: 193.

14. James Forbes, *Oriental Memoirs* (London: White, Cochrane, 1813), 1: 74; Edward Daniel Clarke, *Travels in Various Countries of Europe, Asia, and Africa* (Cambridge: University Press, 1810), 1: 311.

15. Basil Hall, *Fragments of Voyages and Travels. Second and Third Series* (Philadelphia: Edward C. Mielke, 1833), 1: 256; George Fitzclarence, *Journal of a Route across India, through Egypt, to England* (London: John Murray, 1819), 109.

16. Nigel Leask, *Curiosity and the Aesthetics of Travel Writing 1770–1840* (Oxford: Oxford University Press, 2002), 4.

17. Joep Bor, "Mamia, Ammani and other *Boyadères*: Europe's Portrayal of India's Temple Dancers," in *Music and Orientalism in the British Empire, 1780s–1940s: Portrayal of the East*, ed. Martin Clayton and Bennett Zon (Aldershot: Ashgate, 2007), 39–70.

18. Maria Nugent, *A Journal . . . including a Voyage to and Residence in India* (London: T. & W. Boone, 1839), 1: 326; John Henry Grose, *A Voyage to the East-Indies* (London: S. Hooper, 1766), 141–142; Elijah Hoole, *Personal Narrative of a Mission to the South of India*

(London: Longman, Rees, Orme, Brown, and Green, 1829), 85; William Osborne, *The Court and Camp of Runjeet Sing* (London: H. Colburn, 1840), 86; Mary Eliot Carmichael, *A Year and a Day in the East, or, Wanderings over Land and Sea* (London: Longman, Brown, Green, and Longmans, 1846), 83.

19. Fanny Parks, *Wanderings of a Pilgrim, in Search of the Picturesque* (London: Pelham Richardson, 1850), 2: 62. On Parks see Leask, *Curiosity and the Aesthetics of Travel Writing*, 227–241.

20. Francis Buchanan-Hamilton, *A Geographical, Statistical, and Historical Description of the District . . . of Dinajpur* (Calcutta: Baptist Mission Press, 1833), 115–131. As Hamilton went down the social scale gold's share in annual expenses dwindled to nothing, but silver filled the gap to yield a substantial proportion of ornament across the board.

21. "On Circumstances Favorable to the Happiness of India," *Friend of India* 2 (1819): 353–354; Richard Whately, *Easy Lessons on Money Matters* (London: John W. Parker, 1836), 29.

22. Martin, *History of the British* Colonies, 1: 381; John A. Heraud, "The Indian Somnambule," *Howitt's Journal* 1 (1847): 131.

23. "The Sonah Wallah," *Saturday Magazine* 5 (1834): 171; Parks, *Wanderings*, 1: 44.

24. Report . . . *to consider of the Petition of the East India Company for Relief* (London: HMSO, 1840), 94; "The Gold Question in India," *Allen's Indian Mail* 12 (1854): 171, 206.

25. *Sketch of the Commercial Resources and Monetary and Mercantile System of British India* (London: Smith, Elder, 1837), 51–52; "Bombay," *Household Words* 5 (1852): 187.

26. Thomas Winterbottom, *An Account of the Native Africans in the Neighbourhood of Sierra Leone* (London: John Hatchard, 1803), 1: 98; Sarah Lee, *Stories of Strange Lands; and Fragments from the Notes of a Traveller* (London: Edward Moxon, 1835), 70; Harry Longueville Jones, "Aesthetics of Dress: Minor Matters," *Blackwood's Edinburgh Magazine* 57 (1845): 731. On Lee see Travis Glasson, *Mastering Christianity: Missionary Anglicanism and Slavery in the Atlantic World* (New York: Oxford University Press, 2012), 192.

27. Macgregor Laird, "Remedies for the Slave Trade," *Westminster Review* 34 (1840): 141–142.

28. Hugh Crow, *Memoirs . . . with Descriptive Sketches of the Western Coast of Africa* (London: Longman, Rees, Orme, Brown, and Green, 1830), 275; James Hingston Tuckey, *Narrative of an Expedition to Explore the River Zaire* (London: John Murray, 1818), 62; John Matthews, *A Voyage to the River Sierra-Leone* (London: B. White, 1788), 77.

29. *Marley: Or, a Planter's Life in Jamaica* (Glasgow: Richard Griffin, 1828), 292; Marguerite Blessington, *The Governess* (London: Longman, Orme, Brown, Green, and Longmans, 1839), 1: 144–145.

30. Thomas Ashe, *A Commercial View, and Geographical Sketch, of the Brasils* (London: Allen, 1812), 124. On "the impossibility of non-white sartorial imitation" among South American slaves in the nineteenth century see Rebecca Earle, "'Two Pairs of Pink Satin Shoes!!' Race, Clothing and Identity in the Americas (17th–19th Centuries)," *History Workshop Journal* 52 (2001): 184–187.

31. Letitia Elizabeth Landon, *Romance and Reality* (London: Colburn and Bentley, 1831), 2: 114, 122.

32. Mary Wortley Montagu, *Letters . . . written, during her Travels in Europe, Asia, and Africa* (London: T. Becket and P. A. de Hondt, 1763), 2: 28–30, 3: 28–29; Adam Geczy, *Fashion and Orientalism: Dress, Textiles and Culture from the 17th to the 21st Century* (London: Bloomsbury Academic, 2013), 67–68.

33. See, e.g., Jonathan Gray, *Letters Written from the Continent* (York: W. Blanchard, 1819), 108.

34. Geczy, *Fashion and Orientalism*, 67.

35. On the "familiarity of the ancient past" see Chard, *Pleasure and Guilt*, 82–83.

36. Edmund Spencer, *Sketches of Germany and the Germans* (London: Whittaker, 1836), 2: 314; George W. D. Evans, *The Classic and Connoisseur in Italy and Sicily* (London: Longman, Rees, Orme, Brown, Green, and Longman, 1835), 3: 9; John Trusler, *The Habitable World Described* (London: Literary Press, 1793), 13: 266–271.

37. Thomas Williams, *The Song of Songs . . . a New Translation* (London: C, Whittingham, 1801), 172–174; James Silk Buckingham, *Travels Among the Arab Tribes Inhabiting the Countries East of Syria and Palestine* (London: Longman, Hurst, Rees, Orme, Brown, and Green, 1825), 49–50; Samuel Burder, *Oriental Customs* (London: C. Whittingham, 1807), 143; Gardner Wilkinson, *The Manners and Customs of the Ancient Egyptians* (London: John Murray, 1837), 3: 225.

38. Peter George Patmore, *Rejected Articles* (London: Henry Colburn, 1826), 27.

39. Geczy, *Fashion and Orientalism*.

40. Alexander Maxwell, *Patriots Against Fashion: Clothing and Nationalism in Europe's Age of Revolutions* (London: Palgrave Macmillan, 2014), 154–155.

41. As many scholars have noted, English travelers engaged in similar interpretive activities closer to home, especially in the Celtic fringe, with two differences: the "national costume" they encountered seldom included ornaments made of gold, and their Romantic response as English outsiders always competed with an indigenous patriotic celebration of national costume. On Ireland see Katie Trumpener, *Bardic Nationalism: The Romantic Novel and the British Empire* (Princeton: Princeton University Press, 1997), 22–34 and on Wales see Maxwell, *Patriots Against Fashion*, 161–170.

42. Richard Phillips, *A Tour through the Principal Provinces of Spain and Portugal* (London: Richard Phillips, 1806), 35.

43. Joseph S. Forsyth, *Remarks on Antiquities, Arts, and Letters during an Excursion in Italy, in the Years 1802 and 1803* (Geneva: P. G. Ledouble, 1820), 435.

44. Marianne Baillie, *First Impressions on a Tour upon the Continent in the Summer of 1818* (London: John Murray, 1819), 352; "Foreign Costumes," *Chambers's Information for the People* (Edinburgh: William and Robert Chambers, 1842), 2: 562–563; Charles Boileau Elliott, *Letters from the North of Europe* (London: Richard Bentley, 1832), 27.

45. Anna Riggs Miller, *Letters from Italy* (Dublin: W. Watson et al., 1776), 1: 165; Selina Martin, *Narrative of a Three Years' Residence in Italy, 1819–1822* (London: John Murray, 1828), 74; James Silk Buckingham, *France, Piedmont, Italy, Lombardy, the Tyrol, and Bavaria: An Autumnal Tour* (London: Peter Jackson, 1848), 2: 422.

46. Maxwell, *Patriots Against Fashion*, 155.

47. *Arabian Nights Entertainments* (London: Andrew Bell, 1713), 2: 101, 114, 134; Charles Morell, *The Tales of the Genii* (London: J Wilkie, 1764), 5–21; *The School for Majesty: An Eastern Tale* (London: S. Colbert, 1780), 6–8; *The Palace of Enchantment* (London: W. Lane, 1788), 68–70, 134–137, 230–236. See Srinivas Aravamudan, *Enlightenment Orientalism: Resisting the Rise of the Novel* (Chicago: University of Chicago Press, 2012), 17–18, 50–58.

48. Wallace Cable Brown, "The Near East in English Drama, 1775–1825," *Journal of English and Germanic Philosophy* 46 (1947): 68–69.

49. Julia Pardoe, *The City of the Sultan, and, Domestic Manners of the Turks, in 1836* (London: Henry Colburn, 1837), 2: 369–370; John Galt, *Letters from the Levant* (London: Cadell and Davies, 1813), 82.

50. On Montagu's Victorian legacy see Dianne Sachko Macleod, "Cross-Cultural Dressing: Class, Gender and Modernist Sexual Identity," in *Orientalism Transposed: The Impact of the Colonies on British Culture*, ed. Julie F. Codell and Dianne S. Macleod (Hants: Ashgate, 1998), 63–85.

51. Georgiana Dawson Damer, *Diary of a Tour in Greece, Turkey, Egypt and the Holy Land* (London: Henry Colburn, 1841), 2: 71.

52. Sophia Lane Poole, *The Englishwoman in Egypt . . . Second Series* (London: Charles Knight, 1846), 81, 84; Elisabetta Marino, "Three British Women Travelers in Egypt: Sophia Lane Poole, Lucie Duff Gordon, and Emmeline Lott," in *The Legacy of the Grand Tour: New Essays on Travel, Literature, and Culture*, ed. Lisa Colletta (Lanham, MD: Farleigh Dickinson University Press, 2015), 55–56.

53. British descriptions of decorative gold coins were equally divided among accounts of Greece, Eastern Europe, Asia Minor, Egypt, and Palestine; more than half of the coins were attached to caps, with necklaces and braids rounding out the rest. The most popular coins were sequins, minted in Venice, Greece, or Syria; nearly all were worth seven shillings or less per coin. Based on a sample of 95 references in travel books and news articles.

54. George Gordon Byron, *Don Juan* (London: John Fairburn, 1820), 88; Benjamin Disraeli, *Tancred: or, The New Crusade* (London: Henry Colburn, 1847), 2: 232.

55. Charles Fellows, *A Journal Written during an Excursion in Asia Minor* (London: John Murray, 1839), 187–188.

56. James Dallaway, *Constantinople Ancient and Modern* (London: T. Bensley, 1797), 127.

57. Leigh Hunt, "Letters from Abroad: Genoa," *The Liberal* 1 (1822), 275; Charles Fellows, *An Account of Discoveries in Lycia* (London: John Murray, 1841), 189.

58. John George Francis, *Notes from a journal kept in Italy and Sicily* (London: Longman, Brown, Green, and Longmans, 1847), 180; "The Genoese," *Mirror of Literature* 14 (1829): 179.

59. *On the Principle of Compensation, as respecting the Condition of the Working Classes in Wales and England* (Cardiff: privately published, 1831), 7, 9.

60. Sydney Morgan, *Italy* (London: Henry Colburn, 1821), 1: 68; Samuel Laing, *Observations on the Social and Political State of the European People in 1848 and 1849* (London: Longman, Brown, Green and Longmans, 1850), 125.

61. Pardoe, *City of the Sultan*, 1: 38; Edmund Phipps, "A Week at Venice," *New Monthly Magazine* 60 (1840): 251.

62. *The Tyranny of Love* (London: C. Elliot and T. Kay, 1790), 1: 178–180.

63. "The Turkish Sabbath and the Late Sultan," *London Saturday Journal* 2 (1839): 385–386; Donald Quataert, "Clothing Laws, State, and Society in the Ottoman Empire, 1720–1829," *International Journal of Middle East Studies* 29 (1997): 403–425.

64. Geoffrey Nash, *From Empire to Orient: Travellers to the Middle East, 1830–1926* (London: I. B. Tauris, 2005), 113.

65. Henry Thoby Prinsep, *Origin of the Sikh Power in the Punjab and Political Life of Muha-Raja Runjeet Singh* (Calcutta: G.H. Huttmann, 1834), 167; *Times* February 14, 1839; Thomas Pennant, *The View of Hindoostan* (London: Henry Hughs, 1798), 2: 79; Robert Percival, *An Account of the Island of Ceylon* (London: C. and R. Baldwin, 1803), 406–407.

66. Thomas Maurice, *The Modern History of Hindostan* (London: W. Bulmer, 1803), 2: 165–166, 195–196, 390; Mountstuart Elphinstone, *The History of India* (London: John Murray, 1841), 2: 342–343, 434–435.

67. James Burnes, *Narrative of a Visit to the Court of Sinde at Hyderabad on the Indus* (Edinburgh: Bell and Bradfute, 1839), 35–36.

68. Digby Macworth, *Diary of a Tour through Southern India, Egypt, and Palestine, in the Years 1821 and 1822* (London: J. Hatchard and Son, 1823), 146.

69. John Hobart Caunter, *The Oriental Annual, or Scenes in India* (London: Edward Bull, 1834), 203–204; Nugent, *Journal*, 1: 308–309, 375–376. See Sujit Sivasundaram, "Trading Knowledge: The East India Company's Elephants in India and Britain," *Historical Journal* 48 (2005): 27–63.

70. "Notes of the Month on Affairs in General," *Monthly Magazine* 11 (1822): 86.

71. Thomas Campbell, *Frederick the Great, his Court and Times* (London: Henry Colburn, 1842), 1: 91; William Pitt Scargill, *Tales of My Time* (London: Colburn and Bentley, 1829), 3: 138–139.

72. John Crawfurd, *History of the Indian Archipelago* (Edinburgh: Constable, 1820), 1: 64.

73. George Francis White, *Views in India, chiefly in the Himalaya Mountains* (London: Fisher, Son, 1838), 82.

74. James Mill, *The History of British India* (London: Baldwin, Cradock and Joy, 1817), 1: 463.

75. "Turkish Improvements," *Chambers's Edinbugh Journal* 5 (1836): 308 (quoting the Prussian diplomat Friedrich Tietz); Grenville Temple, *Travels in Greece and Turkey* (London: Saunders and Otley, 1836), 2: 35–36.

76. T. Edward Bowdich, *Mission from Cape Coast Castle to Ashantee* (London: John Murray, 1819), 32, 36; Samuel Walker, *Missions in Western Africa* (London: Longmans, Brown, 1845), 27. On Bowdich's reception in Britain see Philip D. Curtin, *The Image of Africa: British Ideas and Action, 1780–1850* (Madison: University of Wisconsin Press, 1973): 201–226.

77. William Ellis (ed.), *History of Madagascar* (London: Fisher, 1838), 2: 417, 422, 425; "Coronation of the Queen Ranovalo Manjaka," *British Magazine* 1 (1830): 28. For context see Gwyn Campbell, *David Griffiths and the Missionary "History of Madagascar"* (Leiden: Brill, 2012), 205–211.

78. Henry Glassford, *A Narrative of the Late Military and Political Operations in the Birmese Empire* (Edinburgh: Constable, 1827), 68; "Regalia of Candy," *Asiatic Journal* 9 (1820): 522.

79. T. E. Ritchie, *Political and Military Memoirs of Europe* (Edinburgh: T. Maccleish, 1802), 2: 209; *Le Beau Monde* 1 (1809): 117; Joseph Nightingale, *The Beauties of England and Wales* (London: J. Harris, 1810), 10/2: 768. On the siege and its immediate aftermath see Maya Jasanoff, *Edge of Empire: Lives, Culture, and Conquest in the East, 1750–1850* (New York: Vintage, 2005), 149–196.

80. *Morning* Chronicle December 7, 1844; Morning *Post* May 5, 1832 and September 28, 1835.
81. Basil Jackson, *The Military Life of Field Marshal the Duke of Wellington, K.G. &c.* (London: Longman, Orme, Brown, Green, and Longmans, 1840), 1: 65–66; On Tipu see Kaushik Roy, *War, Culture and Society in Early Modern South Asia, 1740–1849* (New York: Routledge, 2011), 70–94.
82. Edmund Saul Dixon, *Ornamental and Domestic Poultry: Their History, and Management* (London: Gardeners' Chronicle, 1848), 13.

Chapter 8

1. Joseph Addison, *Remarks on Several Parts of Italy* (London: Jacob Tonson, 1705), 145–147.
2. John Moore, *A View of Society and Manners in Italy* (London: Strahan and Cadell, 1781), 1: 344–345, 348–349; Samuel Sharp, *Letters from Italy* (London: R. Cave, 1767), 42; Henry Swinburne, *The Courts of Europe at the Close of the Last Century* (London: Henry Colburn, 1841), 1: 310–311.
3. Napoleon Bonaparte, *A Selection from the Letters and Despatches* (Cambridge: Cambridge University Press, 2010), 140.
4. John Chetwode Eustace, *A Tour through Italy* (London: J. Mawman, 1813), 1: 165–166; J. E. Clarke, *Review of a Dissertation on the Dragon, Beast, and False Prophet of the Apocalypse,* quoted in "The Truth of God Defended," *Methodist Magazine* 37 (1814): 908.
5. "A Day at Loretto," *Fraser's Magazine* 7 (1833): 321; "The City of Loretto," *Saturday Magazine* 9 (1837): 3.
6. Much of this story echoes Linda Colley's observations on the importance of a Catholic "other" in the formation of Britishness during that time, while adding nuance to her suggestion that Catholicism became less effective at unifying Britons after the 1820s: Colley, *Britons: Forging the Nation* (New Haven: Yale University Press, 1992), chs. 1 and 8.
7. Addison, *Remarks,* 145.
8. On ex-voto offerings see Megan Holmes, "Ex-votos: Material, Memory, and Cult," in *The Idol in the Age of Art: Objects, Devotions and the Early Modern World,* ed. Michael Wayne Cole and Rebecca Zorach (Farnham: Ashgate, 2009), 159–181.
9. Henry Milman, *The History of the Jews* (London: John Murray, 1829), 3: 22, 58–59. For context see Simon Goldhill, *The Temple of Jerusalem* (Cambridge, MA: Harvard University Press, 2005), 1–18.
10. Exodus 3:22. 37:2–17; Joshua 6: 19; Judges 8: 20–26; 2 Samuel 8:7 and 12:30; 1 Chronicles 18:11 and 28:14–17. Plunderers included Egypt (1 Kings 14:26 and 2 Chronicles 36:2); Damascus (1 Kings 20:3–7), Assyria (2 Kings 18:16), Babylon (Daniel 5:2–3), Chaldea (2 Kings 25:15), and Samaria (2 Chronicles 25:24).
11. Matthew Henry, *An Exposition of All the Books of the Old and New Testaments ... with Practical Remarks and Observations* (orig. 1708; London: W. Baynes, 1804), 1: 235; William Thom, "The Revolt of the Ten Tribes" (1776), in *Works* (Glasgow: James Dymock, 1799), 81.
12. "On Antient Works of Art," *Director* 2 (1807): 134; Thomas Maurice, *Indian Antiquities: or, Dissertations, relative to ... Hindostan* (London: H. L. Galabin, 1800), 7: 491.
13. Andrew Dalzel, *Substance of Lectures on the Ancient Greeks, and on the Revival of Greek Learning in Europe* (Edinburgh: Constable, 1821), 1: 198–199; see Margaret M. Miles, *Art as Plunder: The Ancient Origins of Debate about Cultural Property* (Cambridge: Cambridge University Press, 2008), 255–256.
14. Adelaide O'Keeffe, *Zenobia, Queen of Palmyra* (London: Rivington, 1814), 2: 302–303; John Clark Marshman, *The History of India, from Remote Antiquity to the Accession of the Mogul Dynasty* (Serampore: Church Mission Press, 1836), 92; Thomas Maurice, *The Modern History of Hindostan* (London: Bulmer, 1803), 2: 25.
15. Charles Greenstreet Addison, "Sketches of Jerusalem," *Metropolitan Magazine* 26 (1839): 1–2; Adam Anderson, *An Historical and Chronological Deduction of the Origin of Commerce* (London: J. Walter, 1787), 1: 189; William Jacob, *An Historical Inquiry into the Production and Consumption of the Precious Metals* (London: John Murray, 1831), 1: 357.

16. Barbara Allan Simon, *The Ten Tribes of Israel Historically Identified with the Aborigines of the Western Hemisphere* (London: R. B. Seeley and W. Burnside, 1836), 98; James Silk Buckingham, *America, Historical, Statistic, and Descriptive* (London: Fisher, 1841), 1: 125.

17. R. Cole Heinowitz, *Spanish America and British Romanticism, 1777–1826: Rewriting Conquest* (Edinburgh; Edinburgh University Press, 2010), 115, 185–186, 216; Peter Cunningham, *A Handbook for London: Past and Present* (London: John Murray, 1849), 1: 287.

18. Lee Palmer Wandel, *Voracious Idols and Violent Hands: Iconoclasm in Reformation Zurich, Strasbourg, and Basel* (Cambridge: Cambridge University Press, 1994); Margaret Aston, *Broken Idols of the English Reformation* (Cambridge: Cambridge University Press, 2016); David McRoberts, "Material Destruction Caused by the Scottish Reformation," *Innes Review* 10 (1959): 126–172.

19. Samuel Maunder, *The Treasury of History* (London: Longman, Brown, Green, and Longmans, 1844), 276; G. Herbert Rodwell, *Old London Bridge* (London: Darling, 1848), 162.

20. Jane Taylor, "Prejudice," in *Essays in Rhyme, on Morals and Manners* (London: Taylor and Hessey, 1825), 20–21.

21. Maunder, *Treasury of History*, 295; Jacob, *Historical Inquiry*, 2: 54–55.

22. *Times* June 27, 1796; *Free Communing; or A Last Attempt to Cure the Lunatics, now Labouring under . . . the French Disease* (Edinburgh: J. Fairbairn, 1793), 13.

23. *Considerations on the Causes and Alarming Consequences of the Present War* (London: Jordan, 1794), 99. On millenarian responses, which persisted in subsequent histories of the French Revolution, see, e.g., "Answer to the Query," *Christian's Magazine* 3 (1792): 457 and Walter Henry, *A History of England . . . on Christian Principles* (London: Rivington, 1839), 7: 48.

24. "The Portuguese Observer," *Quarterly Review* 4 (1810), 13.

25. Gavin Daly, *The British Soldier in the Peninsular War: Encounters with Spain and Portugal, 1808–1814* (New York Palgrave Macmillan, 2013), 177–178; S. Samuel Trifilo, "Catholicism in Argentina as Viewed by Early Nineteenth-Century British Travelers," *The Americas* 19 (1963): 262–275.

26. Ebenezer Henderson, *Biblical Researches and Travels in Russia; including a Tour in the Crimea and the Passage of the Caucasus* (London: James Nisbet, 1826), 50.

27. Henry David Inglis, *Spain in 1830* (London: Whittaker, Treacher, 1831), 1: 385–386.

28. Donald Campbell, *A Journey Over Land to India* (London: Owen and Griffiths, 1796), 33.

29. Francis Collins, *Voyages to Portugal, Spain, Sicily, Malta, Asia-Minor, Egypt, &c.* (Philadelphia: Solomon Wiatt, 1809), 33; Charles Swan, *Journal of a Voyage up the Mediterranean* (London: Rivington, 1826), 6; "The City of Toledo," *Saturday Magazine* 25 (1844), 186; Thomas Raffles, *Letters during a Tour through Some Parts of France, Savoy, Switzerland, Germany, and the Netherlands* (Liverpool: Thomas Taylor, 1820), 254.

30. G. A. Young, "The Russo-Greek Church," *British and Foreign Review* 9 (1839), 377; William Jacob, *Travels in the South of Spain* (London: J. Johnson, 1811), 84, 86.

31. Philip Thicknesse, *A Year's Journey through France, and Part of Spain* (Dublin: J. Williams, 1777), 1: 222; Mary Boddington, *Slight Reminiscences of the Rhine, Switzerland, and a Corner of Italy* (London: Longman, Rees, Orme, Brown, Green, and Longman, 1834), 2: 140. On "going native" see Christopher Herbert, *Culture and Anomie: Ethnographic Imagination in the Nineteenth Century* (Chicago: University of Chicago Press, 1991), 150–203.

32. Thomas Henry White, *Fragments of Italy and the Rhineland* (London: William Pickering, 1841), 458; Michael Faraday to Benjamin Abbot, July 24, 1814, quoted in Frank A. J. L. James, *The Correspondence of Michael Faraday* (London: Institution of Electrical Engineers, 1991), 1: 77.

33. Frances Trollope, *A Visit to Italy* (London: Richard Bentley, 1842), 2: 75; "Storia d'Italia Narrata al Popolo Italiano," *Westminster Review* 53 (1850): 537. On "cultural dialogue" see Claudia Brosseder, "Cultural Dialogue and Its Premises in Colonial Peru: The Case of Worshipping Sacred Objects," *Journal of the Economic and Social History of the Orient* 55 (2012): 383–414.

34. Hester Lynch Piozzi, *Observations and Reflections made in the Course of a Journey through France, Italy, and Germany* (London: Strahan and Cadell, 1789), 85; Samuel D. Broughton, *Letters from Portugal, Spain, & France* (London: Longman, Hurst, Rees, Orme, and Brown, 1815), 174.

35. Britta Martens, "Vatican Ceremonies and Tourist Culture in Nineteenth-Century British Travelogues," in *Imagining Italy: Victorian Writers and Travellers*, ed. Catherine Waters et al (Newcastle: Cambridge Scholars, 2010), 22–23.

36. Seth William Stevenson, *A Tour in France, Savoy, Northern Italy . . . and the Netherlands* (London: Rivington, 1827), 1: 77; George Gardner, *Travels in the Interior of Brazil . . . between the Years 1836–1841* (London: Reeve, Benham and Reeve, 1849), 162; "A Voyage by Steam to Ceylon," *Church-Warder and Domestic Magazine* 1 (1847): 204–205; Michael Hobart Seymour, *A Pilgrimage to Rome: Containing some Account of the . . . General State of Religion in that City* (London: Seeleys, 1848), 353. On the emergence of a "majestic and bejeweled" Mary see Miri Rubin, *Mother of God: A History of the Virgin Mary* (New Have: Yale University Press, 2009), 306–310.

37. Seymour, *Pilgrimage to Rome*, 51.

38. Anna Eliza Bray, *The Mountains and Lakes of Switzerland: with Descriptive Sketches of Other Parts of the Continent* (London: Longman, Orme, Brown, Green, and Longmans, 1841), 3: 152, 110.

39. Louisa Stuart Costello, *A Tour to and from Venice, by the Vaudois and the Tyrol* (London: John Ollivier, 1846), 125.

40. William Bullock, *Six Months' Residence and Travels in Mexico* (London: John Murray, 1824), 82. On Bullock see Robert D. Aguirre, *Informal Empire: Mexico and Central America in Victorian Culture* (Minneapolis: University of Minnesota Press, 2005), 19–33.

41. James Murphy, *Travels in Portugal . . . in the Years 1789 and 1790* (London: Strahan and Cadell, 1795), 9.

42. "Bullock's *Six Months in Mexico*," *Eclectic Review* 22 (1824): 143–144.

43. James Abbott, *Narrative of a Journey from Heraut to Khiva, Moscow, and St. Petersburgh, during the Late Russian Invasion of Khiva* (London: William H. Allen, 1843), 2: 238–239.

44. William Wordsworth, *Complete Poetical Works* (Philadelphia: James Kay, 1837), 551. On Wordsworth as a champion of Protestant simplicity see Jo Carruthers, *England's Secular Scripture: Islamophobia and the Protestant Aesthetic* (London: Continuum, 2011), 58–62.

45. William Beattie, *The Castles and Abbeys of England* (London: George Virtue, 1842), 1: 109.

46. J. F. Merritt, "Puritans, Laudians, and the Phenomenon of Church-Building in Jacobean London," *Historical Journal* 41 (1998): 935–960; Maartin Delbeke and Anne-Françoise Morel, "Metaphors in Action: Early Modern Church Buildings as Spaces of Knowledge," *Architectural History* 53 (2010): 99–122.

47. Emma Rhatigan, "Preaching Venues: Architecture and Auditories," in *The Oxford Handbook of the Early Modern Sermon*, ed. Peter McCullough et al. (Oxford: Oxford University Press, 2011), 87–119.

48. *An Historical Account of the Antiquities in the Cathedral Church of St. Mary, Lincoln* (Lincoln: W. Wood, 1771), 40–41; Thomas Cromwell, *Excursions in the County of Kent* (London: Longman, Hurst, Rees, Orme, and Brown, 1822), 52.

49. James Peller Malcolm, *Londinium Redivivum, or an Ancient History and Modern Description of London* (London: John Nichols & Son, 1807), 4: 361; James Raine, *Saint Cuthbert: With an Account of the State in which His Remains Were Found upon the Opening of His Tomb in Durham Cathedral* (Durham: F. Humble, 1828), 130.

50. Peter Newcome, *The History of the Ancient and Royal Foundation, called the Abbey of St. Alban, in the County of Hertford* (London: J. Nichols, 1795), 49, 59, 76, 203, 241, 275.

51. Johnson Grant, *A Summary of the History of the English Church, and of the Sects Which Have Departed from Its Communion* (London: J. Hatchard, 1811), 1: 243.

52. E. C. Harington, "Papal Exactions in Britain consequent on Papal Dominion," *British Magazine* 23 (1843): 282; "Popish Relics," *Mirror* 19 (1832): 344. William Jacob, who had marveled at Seville's devotional gold in 1809, concluded in his later historical census of the precious metals that the Reformation merely "lessened what little disposition had existed of a profuse expenditure in decorating the churches" of northern Europe—noting that these had been "much less furnished with gold and silver utensils . . . than similar establishments in the peninsula": *Historical Inquiry*, 2: 66.

53. William Andrews, *Poetical Works* (Southampton: A. Cunningham, 1793), 60–61.

54. "Summary of Early Sculpture in England," *Arnold's Library of Fine Arts* 1 (1833): 385; "Report of the Commissioners on the Fine Arts," *British and Foreign Review* 15 (1843): 196.

55. Daniel Defoe. *A Tour thro' the Whole Island of Great Britain* (London: G. Strahan, 1724), 121–122, 127; *Times* June 6, 1787.

56. Malcolm, *Londinium Redivivum*, 3: 73–74.

57. Raine, *Saint Cuthbert*. 194, 202–213.

58. *History, Gazetteer, and Directory of Cumberland* (Beverley: Mannix and Whellan, 1847), 127; Fanny Burney, *Diary and Letters* (London: Henry Colburn, 1843), 5: 238 (diary entry from August 1791).

59. The quote is from *Times* June 30, 1786. All nine thefts were from Anglican churches. Although usually made of brass, the "eagle lectern" that was a fixture in most Anglican pulpits was occasionally gilded: see, e.g., William White, *History, Gazetteer, and Directory of Leicester* (Sheffield: William White, 1848), 548 (on Gopsal Hall); E. Wedlake Brayley, *A Topographical History of Surrey* (London: G. Willis, 1850), 5: 175 (on Cranleigh Church).

60. See, e.g., *Moral Reformer* 1 (1831): 216; *Temper: a Treatise on Its Use and Abuse* (London: R. B. Seeley., 1837), 32.

61. "Evangelical Gold-Eaters," *Penny Satirist* May 20, 1843; Cornelius Webbe, *Glances at Life in the City and Suburb* (London: Sherwood and Bowyer, 1845), 196. On beadles see M. Dodsworth, "'Civic' Police and the Condition of Liberty: The Rationality of Governance in Eighteenth-Century England," *Social History* 29 (2004): 212.

62. *Times* January 3, 1822.

63. *Times* April 8, 1818 and February 11, 1841.

64. Robert Huish, *Memoirs of Her Late Royal Highness Charlotte Augusta* (London: Thomas Kelly, 1818), 368–369; *Mirror* July 7, 1838 (on Victoria's coronation); *Times* February 11, 1841.

65. oldbaileyonline.org (trial of Francis Abbott and William Hill, January 11, 1786).

66. R. M. Beverley, *A Letter to His Grace the Archbishop of York on the Present Corrupt State of the Church of England* (Beverley: W. B. Johnson, 1831), 17.

67. *The Objects and Rules of the Northern Political Union: Passed at a Meeting Held in the Music Hall, Newcastle upon Tyne* (Newcastle: Mackenzie and Dent, 1831), 6 (John Carr); George Hows, *David's Sling at the State Church Goliath, and at Priestcraft in General* (London: Strange, 1849), 8.

68. Chris Brooks, "Introduction," in *The Victorian Church: Architecture and Society*, ed. Brooks and Andrew Saint (Manchester: Manchester University Press, 1995), 13.

69. Nicholas Wiseman, "Revelations of Spain, in 1845," *Dublin Review* 18 (1845): 422.

70. Hugh Roberts, *For the King's Pleasure: The Furnishing and Decoration of George IV's Apartments at Windsor Castle* (London: The Royal Collection, 2001), 36–37; Rosemary Hill, *God's Architect: Pugin and the Building of Romantic Britain* (New Haven: Yale University Press, 2007), 253; *History . . . of Cumberland*, 219.

71. A. Welby Pugin. *Contrasts* (London: privately published, 1836), 22; Pugin, "The Present State of Ecclesiastical Architecture in England," *Dublin Review* 12 (1842): 108.

72. John Cunningham, *The Velvet Cushion* (London: Cadell and Davies, 1814), 10, 16.

73. "Church Needlework, and Altar Hangings," *Ecclesiologist* 4 (1845): 97–103; John H. Sperling, "On Polychrome as Applied to Organ Pipes," *Ecclesiologist* 10 (1849): 375–378; "Oxford Architectural Society," *Ecclesiologist* 8 (1848): 47. See James F. White, *The Cambridge Movement: The Ecclesiologists and the Gothic Revival* (Cambridge: Cambridge University Press, 1962).

74. John Henry Newman, *Parochial Sermons* (London: Rivington, 1842), 6: 321, 334; 1 Chronicles 29:2. Newman would convert to Catholicism three years later, in 1845.

75. John Ruskin, *The Seven Lamps of Architecture* (London: Smith, Elder, 1849), 1: 13–14.

76. "Pugin's *Contrasts*," *British Critic* 25 (1839): 481; Marmion Wilard Savage, *The Falcon Family: Or Young Ireland* (London: Chapman and Hall, 1846), 269.

77. Nigel Yates, *Anglican Ritualism in Victorian Britain, 1830–1910* (Oxford: Oxford University Press, 1999), 59.

78. Numbers 31:50, as quoted in John Whitecross, *Anecdotes illustrative of a Select Passage in Each Chapter of the Old Testament* (Edinburgh: William Oliphant and Son, 1834), 74; "Proposals for a New and Ample Missionary Fund," *Literary Chronicle* 3 (1821): 331–332.

79. Brooks and Saint, *The Victorian Church*, 139–142, 156 (essays by Jeanne Sheehy and Chris Miele).
80. Wiseman, "Revelations of Spain," 421.

Chapter 9

1. *London Evening Post* August 7, 1773.
2. Alexander Dick, *Romanticism and the Gold Standard: Money, Literature, and Economic Debate in Britain 1790–1830* (Houndmills: Palgrave Macmillan, 2013), 162.
3. "Layard's Nineveh," *Fraser's Magazine* 39 (1849): 446; M. F. Tupper, "Cardwell and Akerman on Coins," *Quarterly Review* 72 (1843): 356–357.
4. Jeremy Bentham, *The Rationality of Reward* (London: John and H. L. Hunt, 1825), 85.
5. Joseph Addison, *Works* (London: Jacob Tonson, 1721), 1: 437.
6. Thomas Bankes, *A New and Authentic System of Universal Geography, Antient and Modern* (London: C. Cooke, 1788), 2: 837; John Ingamells, "John Ramsay's Italian Diary, 1782–84," *Volume of the Walpole Society* 65 (2003): 119; Rogers Ruding, *Annals of the Coinage of Britain and Its Dependencies* (London: Lackington, Hughes, Harding, Mavor, and Jones, 1819), 1: xix–xxvi. On medallic histories see Neil Guthrie, "Johnson's Touch-piece and the 'Charge of Fame': Personal and Public Aspects of the Medal in Eighteenth-century Britain," in *The Politics of Samuel Johnson*, ed. Jonathan Clark and Howard Erskine-Hill (Houndmills: Palgrave Macmillan, 2012), 98.
7. William Wyon, "Practice of Engraving and Multiplying Dies," *Mechanics' Magazine* 21 (1834): 189.
8. P. H. Sawyer, *The Wealth of Anglo-Saxon England* (Oxford: Oxford University Press, 2013); Roger Bland and Xavier Loriot, *Roman and Early Byzantine Gold Coins found in Britain and Ireland* (London: Royal Numismatic Society, 2010); Michael J. O'Kelly, *Early Ireland: An Introduction to Irish Prehistory* (Cambridge: Cambridge University Press, 1989), 173–188, 262–283.
9. Margarita Díaz-Andreu, *A World History of Nineteenth-Century Archaeology: Nationalism, Colonialism, and the Past* (Oxford: Oxford University Press, 2007); Shawn Malley, *From Archaeology to Spectacle in Victorian Britain: The Case of Assyria, 1845–1854* (Farnham: Ashgate, 2012).
10. Faraday to Thomas Joseph Pettigrew, May 4, 1835, in Frank A. J. L. James, *The Correspondence of Michael Faraday* (London: Institution of Electrical Engineers, 1991), 1: 259.
11. J. H. Burton, "Vestiges of the Ancient Inhabitants of Scotland," *Blackwood's Edinburgh Magazine* 69 (1851): 662.
12. Based on 177 accounts from British and Irish newspapers and local histories.
13. George Roberts, *The History of Lyme-Regis, Dorset, from the Earliest Periods to the Present Day* (Sherborne: Langdon and Harker, 1823), 122–125.
14. *Times* December 25, 1828.
15. G. Francis, *Dictionary of Trade, Commerce, and Navigation* (London: Brittain, 1844), entry Coroner.
16. "Discovery of Gold Coins at Southend near Lewisham," *Numismatic Journal* 1 (1837): 265; "Antiquarian Researches," *Gentleman's Magazine* 163 (1838): 303.
17. "Discovery of Ancient Coins," *Times* February 12, 1840; John Sykes, *Local Records: or, Historical Register of Remarkable Events* (Newcastle: John Sykes, 1824), 312; Ralph Ousley, "Account of Four Circular Plates of Gold Found in Ireland," *Transactions of the Royal Irish Academy* 6 (1797): 31–32.
18. Daniel Wilson, *The Archaeology and Prehistoric Annals of Scotland* (Edinburgh: Sutherland and Knox, 1851), 209; *Times* July 23, 1824.
19. Wilson, *Archaeology and Prehistoric Annals*, 318; Burton, "Vestiges of the Inhabitants of Scotland," 662.
20. "Archaeological Institute," *Athenaeum* May 11, 1850; "Museum at Copenhagen," *Chambers's Edinburgh Journal* 7 (1847): 75.
21. David Masson, *The British Museum, Historical and Descriptive* (Edinburgh: William and Robert Chambers, 1850), 411; Peter Cunningham, *A Handbook for London: Past and Present* (London: John Murray, 1849), 1: 132.

22. Jonathan Binns, *The Miseries and Beauties of Ireland* (London: Longman, Orme, Brown, 1837), 2: 264.

23. James H. Todd, "Irish Archaeology," *Athenaeum* October 26, 1850.

24. Edmund Spencer, *Travels in Circassia, Krim-tartary, &c... in 1836* (London: Henry Colburn, 1837), 2: 83; Thomas Smart Hughes, *Travels in Sicily, Greece, and Albania* (London: Henry Colburn and Richard Bentley, 1830), 1: 160–162; Anastasia Filippoupoliti, "Spatializing the Private Collection: John Fiott Lee and Hartwell House," in *Material Cultures, 1740–1920: The Meanings and Pleasures of Collecting*, ed. John Potvin and Alla Myzelev (London: Routledge, 2016), 53–70.

25. Henry Matthews, *The Diary of an Invalid* (London: John Murray, 1822), 1: 206; Edward Bulwer Lytton, *The Last Days of Pompeii* (Paris: Baudry's European Library, 1834), 5, 77, 139, 197.

26. Timothy J. Larsen, "Nineveh," in *Cities of God: The Bible and Archaeology in Nineteenth-Century Britain*, ed. David Gange and Michael Ledger-Lomas (Cambridge: Cambridge University Press, 2013), 124.

27. Charles MacFarlane, *Turkey and Its Destiny* (London: John Murray, 1850), 1: 331.

28. *Times* August 10, 1830; Caroline Amelia Halsted, *Richard III., as Duke of Gloucester and King of England* (London: Longman, Brown, Green, and Longmans, 1844), 2: 490–492.

29. William White, *History, Gazetteer, and Directory of the County of Essex* (Sheffield: Robert Leader, 1848), 507; Patrick Fitzgerald and J. J. M'Gregor, *The History, Topography, and Antiquities, of the County and City of Limerick* (Dublin: George M'Kern, 1826), 1: 117–118; John Bathurst Deane, *The Worship of the Serpent Traced throughout the World* (London: Rivington, 1833), 371. See Richard Hutton, *Blood and Mistletoe: The History of the Druids in Britain* (New Haven: Yale University Press, 2009), 1–49.

30. John O'Driscol, *The History of Ireland* (London: Longman, Rees, Orme, Brown, and Green, 1827), 1: 11; George O'Malley Irwin, *The Illustrated Hand-book to the County of Wicklow* (London: Newman & Co., 1844), 52–54.

31. Thomas Cromwell, *History... of the Ancient Town and Borough of Colchester* (London: Robert Jennings, 1825), 1: 15; Ruding, *Annals of the Coinage*, 2: 265; Dick, *Romanticism and the Gold Standard*, 165.

32. "A Gold Coin Found," *Weekly Entertainer* 53 (1813): 441; John Ayrton Paris, *Philosophy in Sport made Science in Earnest* (London: Longman, Rees, Orme, Brown, and Green, 1827), 97.

33. Alexander Pope, "Verses Occasioned by Mr. Addison's Treatise on Medals," in Addison, *Works*, 1: 433; Suvir Kaul, *Poems of Nation, Anthems of Empire: English Verse in the Long Eighteenth Century* (Charlottesville: University of Virginia Press, 2000), 101.

34. James Fitzjames Stephen (1862), quoted in Matthew Rubery, "Journalism," in *Cambridge Companion to Victorian Culture*, ed. Francis O'Gorman (Cambridge: Cambridge University Press, 2010), 177.

35. Wyon, "Practice of Engraving," 188; *Practical Economy; or, The Application of Modern Discoveries to the Purposes of Domestic Life* (London: Henry Colburn, 1822), 118.

36. Henry Wollaston, *British Official Medals for British Coronations and Jubilees* (Nottingham: Commemorative Collection Society, 1978), 10–19, 55; John Pinkerton, *An Essay on Medals* (London: James Dodlsey, 1784), 167.

37. Wollaston, *British Official Medals*, 12; Thomas Allen, *The History and Antiquities of London* (London: George Virtue, 1837), 5: 52.

38. Laurence Brown, *A Catalogue of British Historical Medals 1760–1960* (London: Seaby, 1980–87), 1: 70, 118.

39. Guthrie, "Johnson's Touch-piece," 90–95.

40. Brown, *Catalogue of British Historical Medals*, 1: 3–6; John Charnock, *Biographia Navalis* (London: R. Faulder, 1794), 1: 334.

41. J. E. Cookson, *The British Armed Nation, 1793–1815* (Oxford: Clarendon Press, 1997), 221; Lawrence L. Gordon, *British Battles and Metals* (Aldershot: Gale and Polden, 1962), 15–17, 49; Thomas Carter, *Medals of the British Army, and How They Were Won* (London: Groombridge and Sons, 1861), 6.

42. *Times* July 18, 1787; *London's Roll of Fame: being Complimentary Notes and Addresses from the City of London, on Presentation of the Honorary Freedom of that City* (London: Cassell, 1884);

Kenneth Snowman, *Eighteenth Century Gold Boxes of Europe* (Boston: Boston Book and Art Shop, 1966), 97.

43. Review of *London's Gratitude*, in *Monthly Review* 69 (1783): 244; *Monthly Miscellany* 4 (1776): 187 (Drapers); Bob Harris, "Patriotic Commerce and National Revival: The Free British Fishery Society and British Politics, c.1749–58," *English Historical Review* 114 (1999): 306–307 (Fishmongers); *Times* August 27, 1827 (Goldsmiths).

44. Hugo Arnot, *The History of Edinburgh* (Edinburgh: W. Creech, 1779), 231; *Edinburgh Weekly Magazine* 42 (1780), 119–120; *Times* October 7, 1791, May 9, 1794, August 31 and September 8, 1795, October 10, 1798, July 30, 1816, March 12, 1828, September 21, 1829. No women, in London or the provinces, received gold snuff boxes with the freedom of the city before 1850.

45. *London's Roll of Fame*, 20–21, 119; Paul Langford, "William Pitt and Public Opinion," *English Historical Review* 88 (1973): 54–80, quoting Horace Walpole at 54–55.

46. *A Register of the Premiums and Bounties given by the Society . . . for the Encouragement of Arts, Manufactures, and Commerce* (London: James Phillips, 1778): 11, 19.

47. RSA Archives PR/MC/103/10/327 (Richard Wynne to Charles Taylor, September 23, 1801); *Farmer's Magazine* 3 (1802): 508; n.s. 13 (1846), 271; 17 (1848), 104; John Knox, *A Tour through the Highlands of Scotland* (London: J. Walter, 1787), lxxxii; *Times* May 27, June 8 and 16, 1835, August 20 and September 15, 1841, and July 27, 1843; Francis Forbes, *The Modern Improvements in Agriculture* (London: T. Evans, 1784), 589; *Annals of Agriculture* 38 (1802), 467.

48. Thomas Galloway, "Recent History of Astronomical Science," *Edinburgh Review* 51 (1830): 105; *Times* February 20, 1837; *Journal of the Royal Geographical Society of London* 15 (1845), xxxv–xxxvi; Brown, *Catalogue of British Historical Medals*, 1: 311.

49. Adam Wall, *An Account of the Different Ceremonies observed in the Senate House of the University of Cambridge* (Cambridge: John Burges, 1798), 231, 258–261, 268–270; *Literary Panorama* 2 (1807), 1077; *Cambridge University Magazine* 2 (1842), 391; Holger Hoock, *The King's Artists: The Royal Academy of Arts and the Politics of British Culture 1760–1840* (Oxford: Clarendon Press, 2003), 57–62; Martin Archer Shee, *Address to the Students of the Royal Academy* (London: W. Clowes, 1832), 1.

50. *Times* July 12, 1787, October 1, 1839, May 6, 1841.

51. *New Sporting Magazine* 4 (1833): 288–297, 369–376; 6 (1834): 65–81; 8 (1835): 63–98; 10 (1836): 61–75; 12 (1837): 1–20; 14 (1838): 1–19; 16 (1839): 1–20.

52. *New Statistical Account of Scotland* (Edinburgh: William Blackwell and Sons, 1845), 9: 472; "Archery," *Sporting Magazine* 14 (1799), 229; John Kerr, *The History of Curling* (Edinburgh: David Douglas, 1890), 146; *Times* June 7, 1827 and August 9, 1833; *Lincoln, Rutland and Stamford Mercury* August 24, 1838; Eleanor M. McPeck, "George Isham Parkyns: Artist and Landscape Architect, 1749–1820," *Quarterly Journal of the Library of Congress* 30 (1973): 171–172.

53. Cookson, *British Armed Nation*, 221–222; Royal Mint Record Book, National Archives, MINT 1/22 (instructions for the coronation of George IV).

54. M. Yakub Bektas and Maurice Crosland, "The Copley Medal: The Establishment of a Reward System in the Royal Society, 1731–1839," *Notes and Records of the Royal Society of London* 46 (1992): 44–47; Joshua Dixon, *The Literary Life of William Brownrigg* (London: Longman and Rees, 1801), 23.

55. Thomas Dick, *On the Mental Illumination and Moral Improvement of Mankind* (Philadelphia: Key and Biddle, 1836), 374.

56. The Society was equally precise in the matter of gender: it generously awarded gold prizes to "ladies of various ages . . . for original drawings and paintings," and warmly welcomed women to its annual awards ceremony; but besides restricting recognition to these "polite arts," the Society usually awarded pallets in these categories rather than their usual circular medals: Frederick von Raumer, *England in 1835* (Philadelphia: Carey, Lee, and Blanchard, 1836), 257; *Transactions of the Society . . . for the Encouragement of Arts, passim*.

57. Thomas Mortimer, *A Concise Account of the Rise, Progress, and Present State of the Society for the Encouragement of Arts, Manufacture, and Commerce* (London: S. Hooper, 1763), 38; letter from Henry Baker, March 24, 1756, RSA Archives PR/GE/110/2/109; *Transactions*, vols.

3–17 (1785–1800), *passim*; Edward Presgrave to Samuel Moore, September 21, 1790, RSA Archives PR/MC/103/10/37.

58. Edward Thomason, *Memoirs during Half a Century* (London: Longman, Brown, Green, and Longmans, 1845), 1: 304–305, 384, 386–387.

59. James Mudie, *Historical and Critical Account of a Grand Series of National Medals* (London: Henry Colburn, 1820); Luke A. L. Reynolds, "Who Owned Waterloo? Wellington's Veterans and the Battle for Relevance" (City University of New York PhD dissertation, 2019).

60. Henry Matthews, *The Diary of an Invalid* (London: John Murray, 1824), 2: 50; Ruding, *Annals of the Coinage*, 4: 155.

61. Wollaston, *British Official Medals*, 76–82; "The Great Waterloo Medal," *Art Journal* 1 (1849): 334; G. P. Dyer and P. P. Gaspar, "Reform, the New Technology and Tower Hill, 1700–1966," in *A New History of the Royal Mint*, ed. C. E. Challis (Cambridge: Cambridge University Press, 1992), 478, 492–493.

62. Addison, *Works*, 1: 536.

63. "The Wiltshire Coursing Prize Picture," *New Sporting Magazine* 16 (1848): 221; *Times* September 13, 1828.

64. Dyer and Gaspar, "Reform," 489; National Archives, MINT 7/31 (letter to James William Morrison, April 28, 1826). See also the letter to the *Times*, December 1, 1817, referring to Pistrucci's rendering of George III on the new sovereign as "most vilely deformed."

65. Richard Thomson, *Chronicles of London Bridge* (London: Smith, Elder, 1827), 661–663; Charles Welch, *Medals Struck by the Corporation of London to Commemorate Important Municipal Events* (London: Corporation of London, 1894), xii, 1, 29.

66. Henry Baker, "Further Thoughts on the Medal," May 5, 1756, RSA Archives, AD/MA/100/10/4/404.

67. Exceptions included the £5 and £2 coins discussed in chapter 5; the Mint also sold some "specimen pieces" of new sovereigns in 1828, "struck *in medal fashion*, for the purpose of being placed . . . in the cabinets of persons who are collectors of coins": National Archives, MINT 7/112.

68. "Medal in Honour of the Late Sir John Sinclair," *Farmer's Magazine* 4 (1836): 352.

69. *Times* December 25, 1805, May 27, 1811, January 17, 1812.

70. "Fox Hounds and Fox Hunting," *Sportsman's Cabinet* 1 (1833): 227–228.

71. *Times* December 17, 1788, July 14, 1800, June 29, 1802, June 18, 1818, June 29, 1829; David Hughson, *London; being an Accurate History and Description of the British Metropolis* (London: J. Stratford, 1805), 1: 457, 596; *Edinburgh Annual Register* 4 (1811): 96, 178; *Wilson's Description of the New Royal Exchange* (London: Effingham Wilson, 1844), 86–87; National Archives, MINT 7/98.

72. *Athenaeum* 1 (1807), 528; Robert Chapman, *The Picture of Glasgow; or, Strangers' Guide* (Glasgow R. Chapman, 1812), 135, 146; Sykes, *Local Records*, 2: 44.

73. National Archives, MINT 16/15 (letter from Skelton to William Pole, July 11, 1821), and 1/22 (letter from James Morrison to Skelton, July 17, 1821); Robert Colton, *Pedestrian and Other Reminiscences at Home and Abroad* (London: Longman, Brown, Green, and Longmans, 1846), 157.

74. Helenus Scott, *The Adventures of a Rupee: Wherein Are Interspersed Various Anecdotes Asiatic and European* (London: J. Murray, 1782), 260, 263.

75. *A Catalogue of the Classic Contents of Strawberry Hill, collected by Horace Walpole* (London: George Robins, 1842), 95, 100, 102, 111–112.

76. Robert Aguirre, *Informal Empire: Mexico and Central America in Victorian Culture* (Minneapolis: University of Minnesota Press, 2005), 7–25.

77. "The Great Waterloo Medal," *Art Journal* 11 (1849): 333; *Bury and Norwich Post* December 22, 1819; G. Erving Scott, "Waterloo," *Classical Journal* 22 (1820): 195.

78. *Weekly Entertainer* 35 (1800): 410–411; *Times* May 2, 1801 and December 25, 1805; Robert Southey, *The Life of Lord Nelson* (Niagara: Henry Chapman, 1831), 71.

Chapter 10

1. Sophia Raffles, *Memoir of the Life and Public Services of Sir Thomas Stamford Raffles* (London: John Murray, 1830), 84–85, 255 (letters to Lord Minto and Lord Buckingham).

2. Two additional areas of interest appeared after 1790: the southern United States, which yielded more than 35,000 kg of gold between 1801 and 1850 but kept most of it in the country; and County Wicklow in Ireland, which yielded a surprising windfall of gold in the 1790s, then a series of disappointments afterward. On British interest in North American gold see Jeff Forret, "Slave Labor in North Carolina's Antebellum Gold Mines," *North Carolina Historical Review* 76 (1999): 139–142. On Wicklow see Timothy Alborn, "An Irish El Dorado: Recovering Gold in County Wicklow," *Journal of British Studies* 50 (2011): 359–380.

3. Byron, cited in R. Cole Heinowitz, *Spanish America and British Romanticism, 1777–1826: Rewriting Conquest* (Edinburgh: Edinburgh University Press, 2010), 172; Benjamin Disraeli, *Lawyers and Legislators: Or, Notes on the American Mining Companies* (London: John Murray, 1825), 68.

4. Henry English, *A General Guide to the Companies formed for Working Foreign Mines* (London: Boosey and Sons, 1825), 19–23, 35–36.

5. *State of Colombia* (London: Treuttel and Würtz, 1824), 83; W. B. Stevenson, *A Historical and Descriptive Narrative of Twenty Years' Residence in South America* (London: Hurst, Robinson, 1825), 3: 87–88; "Manifesto of the Prince Regent of Brazil to Friendly Governments and Nations," *Times* October 16, 1822.

6. Malcolm Deas, "Venezuela, Colombia and Ecuador: The First Half-century of Independence," in *Cambridge History of Latin America*, ed. Leslie Bethell (Cambridge: Cambridge University Press, 1984), 3: 510; Kendell W. Brown, *A History of Mining in Latin America from the Colonial Era to the Present* (Albuquerque: University of New Mexico Press, 2012), 91–122. Between 1820 and 1847, Colombia produced an annual average of 3289 kg of gold, more than Brazil (2548 kg), Mexico (1198 kg), Chile (1148 kg), and other South American countries (967 kg): Robert H. Ridgway, *Summarized Data of Gold Production* (Washington: USGPO, 1930), 32–36.

7. James Cook, *An Account of a Voyage Round the World* (London: Strahan and Cadell, 1773), 34; George Anson, *A Voyage Round the World*, ed. Richard Walton (Edinburgh: Alex. Chapman, 1796), 1: 68.

8. John Pinkerton, *Literary Correspondence* (London: Henry Colburn and Richard Bentley, 1830), 2: 171; "Mawe's *Travels in the Interior of Brazil*," *Monthly Review* 72 (1813): 338.

9. Herbert Heaton, "A Merchant Adventurer in Brazil 1808–1818," *Journal of Economic History* 6 (1946): 4–9, 18–21.

10. John Luccock, *Notes on Rio de Janeiro, and the Southern Parts of Brazil* (London: Samuel Leigh, 1820), 526; "Luccock's *Notes on Brazil*," *Eclectic Review* 16 (1821): 213; John Mawe, *Travels in the Interior of Brazil* (London: Longman, Hurst, Rees, Orme, and Brown, 1812), 77.

11. Mawe, *Travels*, 212; Alexander Caldcleugh, *Travels in South America* (London: John Murray, 1825), 2: 247–248; John Barrow, *A Voyage to Cochin-China, in the years 1792 and 1793* (London: Cadell and Davies, 1806), 106; Andrew Grant, *History of Brazil, containing a Geographical Account of that Country* (London: Henry Colburn, 1809), 165; Luccock, *Notes*, 492, 507.

12. Laird Bergad, *Slavery and the Demographic and Economic History of Minas Gerais, Brazil, 1720–1888* (Cambridge: Cambridge University Press, 1999), 34.

13. "Discovery of the Province of Minas Geraes . . . by a Mine Proprietor," *Monthly Magazine* 1 (1826): 401; Luccock, *Notes*, 503.

14. Mawe's *Travels*," *Eclectic Review* 8 (1812): 941; Luccock, *Notes*, 463–466; "Discovery," 397.

15. Mawe, *Travels*, 185–186, 241; Robert Southey, *History of Brazil, Part the Third* (London: Longman, Hurst, Rees, Orme, and Brown, 1819), 828.

16. Chris Evans, "Brazilian Gold, Cuban Copper and the Final Frontier of British Anti-Slavery," *Slavery and Abolition* 34 (2013): 121; Marshall C. Eakin, *British Enterprise in Brazil: The St. John d'el Rey Mining Company and the Morro Velho Gold Mine, 1830–1960* (Durham: Duke University Press, 1989), 23–29; *Times* August 26, 1837 and May 28, 1841.

17. Paul Ferrand, *L'Or à Minas Gerais, Brésil* (Ouro Preto, Estado do Minas Geraes, 1894), 1: 110; Eakin, *British Enterprise*, 40.

18. English, *General Guide*, 11–12; *Twelfth Report of the Directors* (London: Imperial British Mining Association, 1832), 41, 85; George Gardner, *Travels in the Interior of Brazil* (London: Reeve, Benham and Reeve, 1849), 379–380; *Times* February 3, 1828.

19. Robert Walsh, *Notices of Brazil in 1828 and 1829* (London: Frederick Westley and A. H. Davis, 1830), 2: 114.

20. See chapter 1.

21. Evans, "Brazilian Gold," 121–126; Eakin, *British Enterprise*, 34; Joseph Kelly, "The Problem of Anti-Slavery in the Age of Capital: Britain and Transatlantic Slavery, c.1833–1888" (University of Liverpool PhD dissertation, 2018), 203–254; "Imperial Brazilian Mining Company," *Anti-Slavery Reporter,* June 2, 1841; *Times,* May 5, 1841.

22. "The Slaves of the St. John del Rey Mines," *Anti-Slavery Reporter* 4 (1849), 189; Evans, "Brazilian Gold," 119.

23. Leslie Bethell, *The Abolition of the Brazilian Slave Trade: Britain, Brazil, and the Slave Trade Question, 1807–1869* (Cambridge: Cambridge University Press, 1970), 62–87, 242–266.

24. Charles Cochrane, *Journal of a Residence and Travels in Colombia* (London: Henry Colburn, 1825), 3: 329; Richard Vowell, *Campaigns and Cruises, in Venezuela and New Grenada* (London: Longman, 1831), 209–210.

25. Charles Thomson, *The Ordinances of the Mines of New Spain* (London: John Booth, 1825), 27; Stevenson, *Twenty Years' Residence in South America,* 2: 352. For context see John Silver, "The Myth of El Dorado," *History Workshop* 34 (1992): 4.

26. Francis Bond Head, *Reports relating to the Failure of the La Plata Mining Association* (London: John Murray, 1827), 9; John Miers, *Travels in Chile and La Plata* (London: Bladwin, Cradock and Joy, 1826), 1: 402; James Franklin, *The Present State of Hayti* (London: John Murray, 1828), 294.

27. H. G. Ward, *Mexico in 1827* (London: Henry Colburn, 1828), 2: 17–18, 595, 604–608; Andrew Ure, *A Dictionary of Arts, Manufactures, and Mines* (London: Longman, Orme, Brown, Green, and Longmans, 1839), 606–607; Deas, "Venezuela, Colombia and Ecuador," 510.

28. David Rock, "Porteño Liberals and Imperialist Emissaries in the Rio de la Plata: Rivadavia and the British," in *Connections after Colonialism: Europe and Latin America in the 1820s,* ed. Matthew Brown and Gabriel Paquette (Tuscaloosa: University of Alabama Press, 2013), 214–219; "Andrews' Travels in South America," *Monthly Review* 6 (1827): 234; *The Present State of Colombia* (London: John Murray, 1827), 321.

29. Alexander von Humboldt, *An Essay on the Fluctuations in the Supplies of Gold* (London: Simpkin, Marshall, 1839), 19; *Parliamentary Papers* 1847–1848 [904]; J. D. Magee, "The World's Production of Gold and Silver from 1593 to 1905," *Journal of Political Economy* 18 (1910): 54.

30. A. Bruce Lincoln, *The Conquest of a Continent: Siberia and the Russians* (New York: Random House, 1994), 185–188; Augustus Granville, *St. Petersburgh: A Journal of Travels to and from that Capital* (London: Henry Colburn, 1828), 2: 150–151; James Edward Alexander, *Travels to the Seat of War in the East, through Russia and the Crimea, in 1829* (London: Henry Colburn and Richard Bentley, 1830), 109.

31. Charles Herbert Cottrell, *Recollections of Siberia, in the Years 1840 and 1841* (London: John W. Parker, 1842), 225.

32. Thomas Atkinson, *Oriental and Western Siberia* (London: Hurst and Blackett, 1858), 1: 129–134; John Cochrane, *Narrative of a Pedestrian Journey Through Russia and Siberian Tartary* (London: Charles Knight, 1824), 2: 204–205.

33. Robert A. Stafford, *Scientist of Empire: Sir Roderick Murchison, Scientific Exploration, and Victorian Imperialism* (Cambridge: Cambridge University Press, 2002), 11–14; John L. Morton, *King of Siluria: How Roderick Murchison Changed the Face of Geology* (Horsham: Broken Spectre, 2004), 107; James Secord, "King of Siluria: Roderick Murchison and the Imperial Theme in Nineteenth-Century British Geology," *Victorian Studies* 25 (1982): 425–429.

34. Lincoln, *Conquest of a Continent,* 187; George Simpson, *Narrative of a Journey Round the World, during the Years 1841 and 1842* (London: Henry Colburn, 1847), 2: 400.

35. Cochrane, *Narrative,* 1: 127; Thomas Esper, "The Incomes of Russian Serf Ironworkers in the Nineteenth Century," *Past and Present* 93 (1981): 141–146.

36. Stafford, *Scientist of Empire,* 13; Roderick Murchison, *The Geology of Russia in Europe and the Ural Mountains* (London: John Murray, 1846), 1: 337.

37. Cochrane, *Narrative,* 1: 127–128; John Macgregor, *Commercial Statistics* (London: Whittaker, 1847), 2: 755; Alexander, *Travels to the Seat of War in the East,* 1: 109–112.

38. Forty-three percent of the gold extracted from the Ural Mountains between 1830 and 1846 came from government mines, compared to only 12 percent of Siberian gold between 1830 and 1842: *Examiner* August 18, 1849.

39. "Russian Gold," *Economist* August 3, 1844; "Gold From Russia," *Examiner* July 27, 184; Leitch Ritchie, *The British World in the East* (London: W.H. Allen, 1846), 2: 16–17.

40. Bank of England Archives C61/4, 9A 47/1; Rudiger Dornbusch and Jacob A. Frenkel, "The Gold Standard and the Bank of England in the Crisis of 1847," in *A Retrospective on the Classical Gold Standard, 1821–1931,* ed. Michael D. Bordo and Anna J. Schwartz (Chicago: University of Chicago Press, 1984), 248–249; *Dundee Courier* May 25, 1847; Benjamin Davidson to Rotshchilds, October 2 and December 2, 1847, Rothschild mss XI/38/81B/122-123.

41. *Standard* October 13, 1836; Charles Frederick Henningsen, *Revelations of Russia: or The Emperor Nicholas and his Empire, in 1844* (London: Henry Colburn, 1844), 2: 159; *The Era* June 28, 1840; "The War Betwixt Turkey and Russia," *Reynolds's Newspaper* March 5, 1854.

42. *The American Mines: Shewing their Importance, in a National Point of View* (London: Effingham Wilson, 1834), 13–14.

43. Robert Bremner, *Excursions in the Interior of Russia* (London: Henry Colburn, 1840), 1: 316.

44. "The Anti-Gold Law League," *John Bull* November 20, 1847; "Prospects of Hungary and Italy," *The Plain Speaker* August 4, 1849.

45. James Stanier Clarke, *The Progress of Maritime Discovery: From the Earliest Period to the Close of the Eighteenth Century* (London: Cadell and Davies, 1803), lxxxi; Timothy Alborn, "King Solomon's Gold: Ophir in an Age of Empire," *Journal of Victorian Culture* 20 (2015): 491–508.

46. Ridgway, *Summarized Data,* 6; Philip D. Curtin, "Africa and the Wider Monetary World, 1250–1850," in *Precious Metals in the Later Medieval and Early Modern Worlds,* ed. John F. Richards (Durham: Carolina Academic Press, 1983), 246–252.

47. Michael Adas, *Machines as the Measure of Men: Science, Technology, and Ideologies of Western Dominance* (Ithaca: Cornell University Press, 1989), 112–113; Philip Curtin, "The Lure of Bambuk Gold," *Journal of African History* 14 (1973): 623–631.

48. George Waddington, "Cailliaud's *Travels to Meroé,*" *Foreign Quarterly Review* 2 (1828): 470; Hassan Ahmed Ibrahim, "The Egyptian Empire, 1805–1885," in *Modern Egypt, from 1527 to the End of the Twentieth Century,* ed. M. W. Daly (Cambridge: Cambridge University Press, 1998), 206–207.

49. Debbie Lee, *Slavery and the Romantic Imagination* (Philadelphia: University of Pennsylvania Press, 2004), 24–25; James Bruce, *Travels to Discover the Source of the Nile* (Edinburgh: G.G.J. and J. Robinson, 1790), 1: 458–459; 4: 327.

50. "Metals—Their Compounds and Uses," *Bradshaw's Journal* 3 (1842): 133; Sarah Lee, *Stories of Strange Lands; and Fragments from the Notes of a Traveller* (London: Edward Moxon, 1835), 66; William Hutton, *A Voyage to Africa... in the Year 1820* (London: Longman, Hurst, Rees, Orme, and Brown, 1821), 334–335.

51. John Howison, *European Colonies in the Various Parts of the World* (London: Richard Bentley, 1834), 2: 126, 131–132.

52. Ty M. Reese, "'Eating' Luxury: Fante Middlemen, British Goods, and Changing Dependencies on the Gold Coast, 1750–1821," *William and Mary Quarterly* 66 (2009): 870; Jennifer Mori, *William Pitt and the French Revolution 1785–1795* (Edinburgh: Keele University Press, 1997), 34–35; Robert Isaac and Samuel Wilberforce, *The Life of William Wilberforce* (London: John Murray, 1838), 1: 162–163; *Proceedings of the Association for Promoting the Discovery of the Interior Parts of Africa* (London: C. Macrae, 1790), 206; *Eighteenth Report of the Directors of the African Institution* (London: Ellerton and Henderson, 1824), 40, 199–200.

53. English, *General Guide,* 39–40.

54. *Times* February 13, 1819; James M'Queen, "British Tropical Colonies," *Blackwood's Edinburgh Magazine* 34 (1833): 623–624.

55. See, e.g., John Adams, *Remarks on the Country extending from Cape Palmas to the River Congo* (London: G. and W.B. Whittaker, 1823), 236–237; Howison, *European Colonies,* 1: 60, 124–125. For context see Reese, "'Eating' Luxury," 867–868.

56. William Waterston, *A Cyclopaedia of Commerce* (Edinburgh: Oliver and Boyd, 1843), 118; Ridgway, *Summarized Data,* 6, 16, 50–59; Reese, "'Eating' Luxury," 870.

57. R. Montgomery Martin, *The British Colonial Library* (London: Whittaker, 1837), 8: 249.

58. Frederick Burr, "Remarks upon the Auriferous Deposits of India, considered with especial Reference to their Economical Value," *Madras Journal of Literature and Science* 12 (1840): 30–31, 36.

59. Proby Cautley, "Notes on the Gold Washings of the Gúmtí River," *Journal of the Asiatic Society* 4 (1835): 279; John Warren, "Observations on the Golden Ore Found in the Eastern Provinces of Mysore in the Year 1802," *Journal of the Asiatic Society* 3 (1834): 5–7.

60. James Baillie Fraser, *Journal of a Tour through Part of the Snowy Range of the Himala Mountains* (London: Rodwell and Martin, 1820), 191–192; T. J. Newbold, "Mineral Resources of Southern India: Gold Tracts," *Journal of the Royal Asiatic Society* 7 (1843): 203; T. H. Baber, "Geology of Malabar," *Asiatic Journal* n.s. 3 (1830): 311; F.T. Grant, "Mode of Extracting the Gold Dust from the Sand of the Ningthee River," *Journal of the Asiatic Society* 1 (1832): 148.

61. Newbold, "Mineral Resources," 208; Cautley, "Notes," 280; Warren, "Observations," 1, 6.

62. Burr, "Remarks," 31; Newbold, "Mineral Resources," 203; J. Abbott, "Account of the Process Employed for Obtaining Gold from the Sand of the River Beyass," *Journal of the Asiatic Society of Bengal* 16 (1847): 268.

63. *Assam: Sketch of Its History, Soil, and Productions* (London: Smith, Elder, 1839), 30; J. R. Ouseley, "Note on the Process of Washing for the Gold Dust and Diamonds at Heera Khoond," *Journal of the Asiatic Society* 8 (1839): 1057–1058.

64. Alborn, "King Solomon's Gold," 497–499; Samuel Jennings, *My Visit to the Goldfields in the South-east Wynaad* (London: Chapman and Hall, 1881).

65. William Vincent, *The Commerce and Navigation of the Ancients in the Indian Ocean* (London: Cadell and Davies, 1807), 2: 607–610.

66. William Milburn, *Oriental Commerce* (London: Black, Parry, 1813), 311; T. J. Newbold, *Political and Statistical Account of the British Settlements in the Straits of Malacca* (London: John Murray, 1839), 1: 18, 431; John Crawfurd, *History of the Indian Archipelago* (Edinburgh: Constable, 1820), 3: 482–486.

67. William Jacob, *An Historical Inquiry into the Production and Consumption of the Precious Metals* (London: John Murray, 1831), 2: 332; Milburn, *Oriental Commerce*, 311.

68. Crawfurd, *History*, 3: 472; William Marsden, *The History of Sumatra* (London: Thomas Payne and Son, 1783), 135; John Crawfurd, *Journal of an Embassy . . . to the Courts of Siam and Cochin China* (London: Henry Colburn, 1828), 36; Horace S. R. St. John, *The Indian Archipelago, Its History and Present State* (London: Longman, Brown, Green, and Longmans, 1853), 1: 76.

69. Crawfurd, *History*, 3: 473; Ritchie, *British World in the East*, 2: 125; John Macdonald, "On the Gold of Limong," *Asiatic Researches* 1 (1799): 336.

70. Rodney Mundy, *Narrative of Events in Borneo and Celebes, down to the Occupation of Labuan* (London: John Murray, 1848), 2: 50–51; Ooi Keat Gin, *Of Free Trade and Native Interest: The Brookes and the Economic Development of Sarawak, 1841–1941* (Kuala Lumpur: Oxford University Press, 1997), 122–123; Craig A. Lockard, "The 1857 Chinese Rebellion in Sarawak: A Reappraisal," *Journal of Southeast Asia Studies* 9 (1978): 85–98.

71. Maria Graham, *Journal of . . . a Voyage from Chile to Brazil in 1823* (London: Longman, Hurst, Rees, Orme, Brown, and Green, 1824), 32–33.

72. Roderick Murchison, "A Few Observations on the Ural Mountains, to Accompany a New Map of a Southern Portion of that Chain," *Journal of the Royal Geographical Society of London* 13 (1843): 270; Morton, *King of Siluria*, 158.

73. Morton, *King of Siluria*, 158–160.

Conclusion

1. "A Voice from the West," *British Friend* 8 (1850): 44–45; John Capper, *The Emigrants' Guide to Australia* (London: Whittaker, 1852), 77.

2. Robert H. Ridgway, *Summarized Data of Gold Production* (Washington: USGPO, 1930), 10, 28, 59–60; R. H. Patterson, "Gold and Social Politics," *Blackwood's Edinburgh Magazine* 94 (1863): 507.

3. Patrick Brantlinger, *Rule of Darkness: British Literature and Imperialism, 1830–1914* (Ithaca: Cornell University Press, 1988), 112–124.

4. Albert L. Hurtado, *John Sutter: A Life on the North American Frontier* (Norman: University of Oklahoma Press, 2006), 106, 222–224 and *passim*; Douglas Fetherling, *The Gold Crusades: A Social History of the Gold Rushes, 1849–1929* (Toronto: University of Toronto Press, 1997), 12–13.
5. Ridgway, *Summarized Data of Gold Production*, 14.
6. Fetherling, *Gold Crusades*, 21–25; Carey McWilliams, *California: The Great Exception* (Berkeley: University of California Press, 1998), 66; Oxford Dictionary of National Biography online, entry Edward Hargraves; Malcolm J. Rohrbough, *Days of Gold: The California Gold Rush and the American Nation* (Berkeley: University of California Press, 1997), 155–184.
7. *Presidential Documents*, ed. J. F. Watts and Fred L. Israel (New York: Routledge, 2000), 108; McWilliams, *California*, 49.
8. *Morning Chronicle* September 7, 1848; *Daily News* October 3, 1848.
9. Rothschild Archives XI/38/81/2/26, 15, 32 (Davidson to Rothschild, September 29 and May 29, 1848; Davidson to Charles Scharfenberg, November 29, 1848); Giles Constable, "The Rothschilds and the Gold Rush: Benjamin Davidson and Heinrich Schliemann in California, 1851–52," *Transactions of the American Philosophical Society* 105:4 (2015): 5–6.
10. Rothschild Archives XI/38/82A/6 (Davidson to Rothschild, January 31, 1850), VII/6/18-19; Constable, "The Rothschilds and the Gold Rush," 28; Stanley Chapman, *The Rise of Merchant Banking* (London: Unwin Hyman, 1984), 22; Miguel A. López-Morrell, *The House of Rothschild in Spain, 1812–1941* (Farnham: Ashgate, 2013), 96–97.
11. Timothy Green, *Precious Heritage: Three Hundred Years of Mocatta and Goldsmid* (London: Rosendale Press, 1984), 27; William D. Rubinstein (ed.), *The Palgrave Dictionary of Anglo-Jewish History* (Basingstoke: Palgrave, 2011), 680.
12. Bank of England Archives C61/5, 9A 181/1, and C129/11 (Liverpool Branch Letter Book, entries from June 27 and December 11, 1851).
13. Fetherling, *Gold Crusades*, 43–48; John William Knott, "Imperial Settlement," in *The Australian People*, ed. James Jupp (Cambridge: Cambridge University Press, 2004), 35–38.
14. Ridgway, *Summarized Data of Gold Production*, 14–15, 28, 59; Bank of England Archives 9A 181/1.
15. National Archives, MINT 9/32.
16. G. P. Dyer and P. P. Gaspar, "Reform, the New Technology and Tower Hill, 1700–1966," in *A New History of the Royal Mint*, ed. C. E. Challis (Cambridge: Cambridge University Press, 1992), 502; John Clapham, *The Bank of England: A History* (Cambridge: Cambridge University Press, 1966), 2: 180.
17. "A Proclamation for declaring Gold Coins made at the Branch Mint at Sydney . . . a Legal Tender within the United Kingdom," copy in Bank of England Archives, 3A47/1; Robert Torrens, *Political Economy and Representative Government in Australia* (London: James Ridgway, 1855), 28–32.
18. *Dramatic Register* (London: Thomas Hailes Lacy, 1853), 79; "The Two Lands of Gold," Online Archive of California (http://oac.cdlib.org); Richard D. Altick, *The Shows of London* (Cambridge, MA: Belknap Press, 1978), 489; "Panorama of an Australian Voyage and of the Gold Diggings," *Morning Chronicle* August 11, 1852; "To Australia for a Shilling," *Punch* October 2, 1852.
19. Robert Ellis, *Official Descriptive and Illustrated Catalogue [of the Great Exhibition]* (London: W. Clowes and Sons, 1851), 2: 1431, 1449; Robert Stafford, "Preventing the 'Curse of California': Advice for English Emigrants to the Australian Goldfields," *Historical Records of Australian Science* 7 (1988): 215–230.
20. "The Gold Seekers of California," *Illustrated London News* February 10, 1849; "Arrival of Californian Gold and Mexican Dollars at the Bank of England," Ibid., September 22, 1849; "The Australian Gold District," Ibid. October 25, 1851; David Tatham, *Winslow Homer and the Pictorial Press* (Syracuse: Syracuse University Press, 2003), 19–29.
21. Rothschild Archives XI/38/82A/11 (Davidson to Rothschild, January 31, 1850); Constable, "The Rothschilds and the Gold Rush," 21.
22. "New South Wales," *Wesleyan Missionary Notices* 10 (1852): 186 (letter from Samuel Wilkinson, Bathurst).

23. "Mrs. Chisholm and Emigration," *Rambler* 11 (1853): 165; "Historical and Geographical Sketches of North America," *Preston Guardian* September 27, 1856.

24. Maria Abdy, "There Is Gold in California," *Metropolitan Magazine* 54 (1849): 347.

25. "Ship-Passage in Central America to the Pacific," *Eclectic Review* 27 (1850): 712; "A Run for Gold," *Bristol Mercury* January 6, 1849.

26. "The New Nation," *Dublin University Magazine* 37 (1851): 101; George Croly, "Johnston's Physical Geography," *Blackwood's Edinburgh Magazine* 65 (1849): 416.

27. R. H. Patterson, "The Celestials at Home and Abroad," *Blackwoods Edinburgh Magazine* 72 (1852): 98.

28. "A Digger's Wedding," *Household Words* 7 (1853): 512. See also David Goodman, *Gold Seeking: Victoria and California in the 1850s* (St. Leonards: Allen & Unwin, 1994), 149–178 and 236.

29. W. K. Tweedie, *Man and His Money: Its Use and Abuse* (London: James Nisbet, 1855), 77.

30. Charles Reade, *Gold! A Drama in Five Acts* (London: John Dicks Press, 1853), 4; "Metropolitan Theatres," *Theatrical Journal* (February 1853), 4.

31. "Moral Effects of the Gold Discoveries," *Lady's Newspaper* October 30, 1852.

32. Keith D. Lilley, "'One Immense Gold Field!': British Imaginings of the Australian Gold Rushes, 1851–59," *Landscape Research* 27 (2002): 70–75; *Leeds Mercury* November 1, 1851.

33. "Mrs. Chisholm and Emigration," 166; "Australia and Colonization," *Christian Spectator* September 15, 1852; William Butters, "State and Prospects of Methodism at the Victoria Gold-Fields," *Wesleyan Missionary Notices* 12 (1854): 67.

34. Jeremiah Dodsworth, *The Better Land; or, The Christian Emigrant's Guide to Heaven* (London: T. Holliday, 1853), 83.

35. Fetherling, *Gold Crusades*, 50–64; Angela Woollacott, *Settler Society in the Australian Colonies: Self-Government and Imperial Culture* (Oxford: Oxford University Press, 2015), 98–122.

36. Joseph Beete Jukes, "Australia and Its Gold Diggings," *Dublin University Magazine* 39 (1852): 617.

37. *A Visit to Australia and Its Gold Regions* (London: Society for Promoting Christian Knowledge, 1853), 200–201.

38. "The Progress of Victoria (From the *Times*)," *Freeman's Journal* September 16, 1856; "Morals of the 'Diggings,'" *Punch* November 20, 1852.

39. "Gold in Australia," *Times* January 20, 1852; Patterson, "Gold and Social Politics," 516–520.

40. "Startling Effect of the Gold 'Diggins,'" *Punch* July 24, 1852; "The Golden Age," *Punch* May 1, 1852.

41. Goodman, *Gold Seeking*, 34–35, 235; "Chamber of Commerce," *Caledonian Mercury* January 22, 1852 (speech of J. F. Macfarlan).

42. "Change for a Sovereign," *Household Words* 5 (1852): 279.

43. J. R. McCulloch, *Treatises and Essays on Subjects Connected with Economical Policy* (Edinburgh: Adam and Charles Black, 1853), 47; Frank Whitson Fetter, *The Development of British Monetary Orthodoxy, 1797–1875* (Cambridge, MA: Harvard University Press, 1965), 242–246.

44. Robert A. Stafford, *Scientist of Empire: Sir Roderick Murchison, Scientific Exploration and Victorian Imperialism* (Cambridge: Cambridge University Press, 1989), 38.

45. William Miller, "Estimate . . . of the total amount of the Gold Currency in the United Kingdom," Bank of England Archives M 5/592.

46. Niall Ferguson, *The Cash Nexus: Money and Power in the Modern World, 1700–2000* (New York: Basic Books, 2001), 147, 328–330; Ridgway, *Summarized Data of Gold Production*, 14, 58.

47. H. R. Grenfell, "What Is a Pound?" *Nineteenth Century* 9 (1881): 942; Rowena Olegario, *The Engine of Enterprise: Credit in America* (Cambridge: Harvard University Press, 2016), 80–87; Barry Eichengreen, *Globalizing Capital: A History of the International Monetary System* (Princeton: Princeton University Press, 1996), 17–19.

48. Benjamin Mountford and Stephen Tuffnell, eds., *A Global History of Gold Rushes* (Berkeley: University of California Press, 2013), 143, 209–228.

49. Fetherling, *Gold Crusades*, 94–148.

50. Ted Wilson, *Battles for the Standard: Bimetallism and the Spread of the Gold Standard in the Nineteenth Century* (Aldershot: Ashgate, 2000), 65–89; Mike Davis, *Late Victorian Holocausts: El Niño Famines and the Making of the Third World* (New York: Verso, 2002), 303–305; E. H. H. Green, "Rentiers versus Producers? The Political Economy of the Bimetallic Controversy c. 1880–1898," *English Historical Review* 103 (1988): 606–607.
51. Martin Daunton, *State and Market in Victorian Britain: War, Welfare and Capitalism* (Woodbridge: Boydell Press, 2008), 226–244; Wilson, *Battles for the Standard*, 90–137.
52. D. T. Coulton, "California versus Free Trade," *Quarterly Review* 90 (1852): 499.
53. "Gold—Its Past—Its Present—Its Future," *New Quarterly Review* 2 (1853), 149.
54. "The Dethronement of Gold," *London Journal* 12 (1851): 412; W. B. Adams, "Human Progress," *Westminster Review* 52 (1849): 38; Charles Whitehead, "El Dorado," *Bentley's Miscellany* 25 (1849): 191.
55. Thomas Gaspey, "My Grandson's Life and Times, to be Written by Himself in 1925," *Spirit of the Public Journals* (London: Sherwood, Gilbert and Piper, 1826), 29.
56. "Gold and Emigration," *Fraser's Magazine* 46 (1852): 132; Oxford Dictionary of National Biography online, entry for George Elkington; William Bates, *A Pictorial Guide to Birmingham* (Birmingham: Josiah Allen, 1849), 172; Harriet Martineau, "The Magic Troughs at Birmingham," *Household Words* 4 (1851): 114.
57. "Glorious Effects of Californian Gold," *Satirist* March 10, 1849; Richard and Susan Wales, *Souvenirs from the Diamond Jubilee of Queen Victoria* (Milton Keynes: AuthorHouse UK, 2012), 10, 22, 28, 30, 38, 52, 72.
58. Barbara J. Morris, *Victorian Embroidery: An Authoritative Guide* (New York: Thomas Nelson, 1962), 89–94; "Aesthetics of the Thanksgiving," *Saturday Review*, March 2, 1872.
59. "National Prosperity and Individual Panic," *Chambers's Edinburgh Journal* August 7, 1852.
60. Linda Jones, "Subversive Jewellery: Challenges to Conservative Power from the Victorian Goldfields," *reCollections* 7 (2012): 6–8.
61. Michel Chevalier, *Remarks on the Production of the Precious Metals, and on the Depreciation of Gold* (London: Smith, Elder, 1853), 45–48; Patterson, "Gold and Social Politics," 505.
62. Patterson, "Gold and Social Politics," 499–500.
63. Ferguson, *The Cash Nexus*, 325.
64. For a recent example see Mountford and Tuffnell, eds., *A Global History of Gold Rushes*, 42–136.
65. Marcello De Cecco, *Money and Empire: The International Gold Standard, 1890–1914* (Oxford: B. Blackwell, 1974).
66. David Cannadine, "The Context, Performance, and Meaning of Ritual: The British Monarchy and the 'Invention of Tradition,' c. 1820–1977," in *The Invention of Tradition*, ed. Eric Hobsbawm and Terence Ranger (Cambridge: Cambridge University Press, 1992), 128; W. J. Jackman, *The Illustrious Life and Reign of King Edward VII* (Guelph: World Publishing, 1910), 41, 53, 69, 78.
67. Eichengreen, *Globalizing Capital*, 15–44; Karl Polanyi, *The Great Transformation: The Political and Economic Origins of Our Time* (Boston: Beacon Press, 1957), 195.
68. Karl Marx, *Capital* (London: Lawrence and Wishart, 1959), 3: 337.

SELECTED BIBLIOGRAPHY

Adas, Michael. *Machines as the Measure of Men: Science, Technology, and Ideologies of Western Dominance.* Ithaca: Cornell University Press, 1989.

Aguirre, Robert. *Informal Empire: Mexico and Central America in Victorian Culture.* Minneapolis: University of Minnesota Press, 2005.

Alborn, Timothy. *Conceiving Companies: Joint-Stock Politics in Victorian England.* London: Routledge, 1998.

Alborn, Timothy. "Coin and Country: Visions of Civilisation in the British Recoinage Debate, 1867–1894." *Journal of Victorian Culture* 3 (1998): 252–281.

Alborn, Timothy. "An Irish El Dorado: Recovering Gold in County Wicklow." *Journal of British Studies* 50 (2011): 359–380.

Alborn, Timothy. "Money's Worth: Morality, Class, Politics." In *The Victorian World,* ed. Martin Hewitt (London: Routledge, 2012), 209–224.

Alborn, Timothy. "King Solomon's Gold: Ophir in an Age of Empire." *Journal of Victorian Culture* 20 (2015): 491–508.

Alborn, Timothy. "The Greatest Metaphor Ever Mixed: Gold in the British Bible, 1750–1850." *Journal of the History of Ideas* 78 (2017): 427–447.

Aravamudan, Srinivas. *Enlightenment Orientalism: Resisting the Rise of the Novel.* Chicago: University of Chicago Press, 2012.

Aston, Margaret. *Broken Idols of the English Reformation.* Cambridge: Cambridge University Press, 2016.

Attman, Artur. *Dutch Enterprise in the World Bullion Trade, 1550–1800.* Göteborg: Vitterhets-Samhället, 1983.

Attman, Artur. *American Bullion in the European World Trade, 1600–1800.* Göteborg: Kungl. Vetenskaps- och Vitterhets Samhallet, 1986.

Bakewell, Peter. "Mining in Colonial Spanish America." In *Colonial Latin America,* ed. Leslie Bethell (Cambridge: Cambridge University Press, 1984), 105–149.

"The Bank of England Note: A Short History." *Bank of England Quarterly Bulletin* 9 (1969): 209–222.

Beer, Anna. "Textual Politics: The Execution of Sir Walter Ralegh." *Modern Philology* 94 (1996): 19–38.

Bektas, M. Yakub and Maurice Crosland. "The Copley Medal: The Establishment of a Reward System in the Royal Society, 1731–1839." *Notes and Records of the Royal Society of London* 46 (1992): 43–76.

Bergad, Laird. *Slavery and the Demographic and Economic History of Minas Gerais, Brazil, 1720–1888.* Cambridge: Cambridge University Press, 1999.

Bernstein, Peter L. *The Power of Gold: The History of an Obsession.* Chichester: John Wiley and Sons, 2005.

Bethell, Leslie. *The Abolition of the Brazilian Slave Trade: Britain, Brazil, and the Slave Trade Question, 1807–1869*. Cambridge: Cambridge University Press, 1970.

Bethell, Leslie, ed. *Colonial Brazil*. Cambridge: Cambridge University Press, 1987.

Blair, Claude, ed. *The Crown Jewels: The History of the Coronation Regalia in the Jewel House of the Tower of London*. London: The Stationery Office, 1998.

Bonar, J. "Ricardo's Ingot Scheme." *Economic Journal* 33 (1923): 281–304.

Booker, John. *Travellers' Money*. Stroud: Alan Sutton, 1994.

Bor, Joep. "Mamia, Ammani and Other *Boyadères*: Europe's Portrayal of India's Temple Dancers." In *Music and Orientalism in the British Empire, 1780s–1940s: Portrayal of the East*, ed. Martin Clayton and Bennett Zon (Aldershot: Ashgate, 2007), 39–70.

Bordo, Michael J. *The Gold Standard and Related Regimes*. Cambridge: Cambridge University Press, 1999.

Bordo, Michael J. and Eugene N. White. "A Tale of Two Currencies: British and French Finance During the Napoleonic Wars." *Journal of Economic History* 51 (1991): 303–316.

Boxer, C. R. *The Golden Age of Brazil, 1695–1750*. Berkeley: University of California Press, 1964.

Boxer, C. R. "Brazilian Gold and British Traders in the First Half of the Eighteenth Century." *Hispanic American Historical Review* 49 (1969): 454–472.

Brantlinger, Patrick. *Rule of Darkness: British Literature and Imperialism, 1830–1914*. Ithaca: Cornell University Press, 1988.

Brantlinger, Patrick. *Fictions of State: Culture and Credit in Britain, 1694–1994*. Ithaca: Cornell University Press, 1996.

Brewer, David. *The Greek War of Independence: The Struggle for Freedom from Ottoman Oppression and the Birth of the Modern Greek Nation*. Woodstock: Overlook Press, 2001.

Brewer, John. *The Sinews of Power: War, Money, and the English State, 1688–1783*. Cambridge: Harvard University Press, 1990.

Brooks, Chris and Andrew Saint, ed. *The Victorian Church: Architecture and Society*. Manchester: Manchester University Press, 1995.

Brown, Kendell W. *A History of Mining in Latin America from the Colonial Era to the Present*. Albuquerque: University of New Mexico Press, 2012.

Brown, Laurence. *A Catalogue of British Historical Medals 1760–1960*. London: Seaby, 1980–1987.

Brown, Wallace Cable. "The Near East in English Drama, 1775–1825." *Journal of English and Germanic Philosophy* 46 (1947): 63–69.

Browning, Logan Delano. "Reading Dickens's Misers." University of North Carolina PhD dissertation, 1999.

Bury, Shirley. *Jewellery 1789–1910: The International Era*. Woodbridge: Antique Collectors' Club, 1991.

Cain, Peter J. and A. G. Hopkins. *British Imperialism: Innovation and Expansion 1688–1914*. London: Longman, 1993.

Cannadine, David. *Aspects of Aristocracy: Grandeur and Decline in Modern Britain*. London: Penguin, 1994.

Cannadine, David. *The Decline and Fall of the British Aristocracy*. New York: Vintage, 1999.

Cannadine, David. *Ornamentalism: How the British Saw Their Empire*. Oxford: Oxford University Press, 2001.

Carman, W. Y. *British Military Uniforms from Contemporary Pictures*. New York: Arco, 1957.

Chapman, Stanley. *The Rise of Merchant Banking*. London: Unwin Hyman, 1984.

Chard, Chloe, *Pleasure and Guilt on the Grand Tour: Travel Writing and Imaginative Geography, 1600–1830*. Manchester: Manchester University Press, 1999.

Checkland, S. G. "John Koster, Anti-Bullionist." *Manchester School* 20 (1952): 174–202.

Claeys, Gregory. *Machinery, Money and the Millenium: From Moral Economy to Socialism, 1815–1860*. Princeton: Princeton University Press, 1987.

Clancy, Kevin. "The Recoinage and Exchange of 1816–17." University of Leeds PhD dissertation, University of Leeds, 1999.

Clapham, John. *The Bank of England: A History*. Cambridge: Cambridge University Press, 1966.

Colley, Linda. *Britons: Forging the* Nation. London: Pimlico, 2003.

Constable, Giles. "The Rothschilds and the Gold Rush: Benjamin Davidson and Heinrich Schliemann in California, 1851–52." *Transactions of the American Philosophical Society* 105:4 (2015): 1–130.

Cookson, J. E. *The British Armed Nation, 1793–1815*. Oxford: Clarendon Press, 1997.

Costa, Leonor Freire, Mariel Manuela Rocha, and Tanya Araújo. "Social Capital and Economic Performance: Trust and Distrust in Eighteenth-Century Gold Shipments from Brazil." *European Review of Economic History* 15 (2011): 1–27.

Crawforth, Michael A. *Weighing Coins: English Folding Gold Balances of the 18th and 19th Centuries*. London: Cape Horn Trading Co., 1979.

Crouzet, François. *L'Economie Britannique et le Blocus Continentale (1806–1813)*. Paris: Presses Universitaires de France, 1958.

Cunnington, Phillis and Catherine Lucas. *Occupational Costume in England from the Eleventh Century to 1914*. London: Adam and Charles Black, 1967.

Curtin, Philip D. *The Image of Africa: British Ideas and Action, 1780–1850*. Madison: University of Wisconsin Press, 1973.

Curtin, Philip D. "The Lure of Bambuk Gold." *Journal of African History* 14 (1973): 623–631.

Dalrymple, William. *Return of a King: The Battle for Afghanistan, 1839–42*. New York: Alfred A. Knopf, 2013.

Daly, Gavin. "Napoleon and the 'City of Smugglers', 1810–1814." *Historical Journal* 50 (2007): 333–352.

Daly, Gavin. *The British Soldier in the Peninsular War: Encounters with Spain and Portugal, 1808–1814*. New York: Palgrave Macmillan, 2013.

Daunton, Martin. *State and Market in Victorian Britain: War, Welfare and Capitalism*. Woodbridge: Boydell Press, 2008.

Davies, Glyn. *History of Money*. Cardiff: University of Wales Press, 2002.

Davis, Mike. *Late Victorian Holocausts: El Niño Famines and the Making of the Third World*. New York: Verso, 2002.

Deas, Malcolm. "Venezuela, Colombia and Ecuador: The First Half-century of Independence." In *Cambridge History of Latin America*, ed. Leslie Bethell (Cambridge: Cambridge University Press, 1984), 507–538.

De Cecco, Marcello. *Money and Empire: The International Gold Standard, 1890–1914*. Oxford: B. Blackwell, 1974.

Delbeke, Maartin and Anne-Françoise Morel. "Metaphors in Action: Early Modern Church Buildings as Spaces of Knowledge." *Architectural History* 53 (2010): 99–122.

De Marly, Diana. *Costume on the Stage, 1600–1940*. London: B. T. Batsford, 1982.

Desan, Christine. *Making Money: Coin, Currency, and the Coming of Capitalism*. New York: Oxford University Press, 2015.

Dick, Alexander. *Romanticism and the Gold Standard: Money, Literature, and Economic Debate in Britain 1790–1830*. Houndmills: Palgrave Macmillan, 2013.

Dickson, P. G. M. *The Financial Revolution in England: A Study in the Development of Public Credit, 1688–1756*. London: Macmillan, 1967.

Dobson, Michael and Nicola J. Watson. *England's Elizabeth: An Afterlife in Fame and Fantasy*. Oxford: Oxford University Press, 2002.

Dodsworth, M. "'Civic' Police and the Condition of Liberty: The Rationality of Governance in Eighteenth-Century England." *Social History* 29 (2004): 199–216.

Dornbusch, Rudiger and Jacob A. Frenkel. "The Gold Standard and the Bank of England in the Crisis of 1847." In *A Retrospective on the Classical Gold Standard, 1821–1931*, ed. Michael D. Bordo and Anna J. Schwartz (Chicago: University of Chicago Press, 1984), 233–264.

Dutton, H. I. and J. E. King. "An Economic Exile: Edward Stillingfleet Cayley, 1802–1862." *History of Political Economy* 17 (1985): 203–218.

Dyer, G. P. and P. P. Gaspar. "Reform, the New Technology and Tower Hill, 1700–1966." In *A New History of the Royal Mint*, ed. C. E. Challis (Cambridge: Cambridge University Press, 1992), 398–606.

Eacott, Jonathan. *Selling Empire: India in the Making of Britain and America, 1600–1830*. Chapel Hill: University of North Carolina Press, 2016.

Eakin, Marshall C. *British Enterprise in Brazil: The St. John d'el Rey Mining Company and the Morro Velho Gold Mine, 1830–1960*. Durham: Duke University Press, 1989.

Eichengreen, Barry J. *Globalizing Capital: A History of the International Monetary System*. Princeton: Princeton University Press, 2008.

Einaudi, Luca. *Money and Politics: European Monetary Unification and the International Gold Standard (1865–1873)*. Oxford: Oxford University Press, 2001.

Eldon, William. *England's Subsidy Policy towards the Continent during the Seven Years' War*. Philadelphia, University of Pennsylvania Press, 1938.

Elliott, J. H. "Self-Perception and Decline in Early Seventeenth-Century Spain." *Past and Present* 74 (1977): 41–61.

Esper, Thomas. "The Incomes of Russian Serf Ironworkers in the Nineteenth Century." *Past and Present* 93 (1981): 137–159.

Evans, Chris. "Brazilian Gold, Cuban Copper and the Final Frontier of British Anti-Slavery." *Slavery and Abolition* 34 (2013): 118–134.

Ferguson, Niall. *The House of Rothschild: Money's Prophets 1798–1848*. New York: Viking Penguin, 1998.

Ferguson, Niall. *The Cash Nexus: Money and Power in the Modern World, 1700–2000*. New York: Basic Books, 2001.

Festa, Lynn. *Sentimental Figures of Empire in Eighteenth-Century Britain and France*. Baltimore: The Johns Hopkins University Press, 2006.

Fetherling, Douglas. *The Gold Crusades: A Social History of the Gold Rushes, 1849–1929*. Toronto: University of Toronto Press, 1997.

Fetter, Frank Whitson. *The Development of British Monetary Orthodoxy, 1797–1875*. Cambridge, MA: Harvard University Press, 1965.

Finucane, Adrian. *The Temptations of Trade: Britain, Spain, and the Struggle for Empire*. Philadelphia: University of Pennsylvania Press, 2016.

Fisher, H. E. S. *The Portugal Trade: A Study of Anglo-Portuguese Commerce, 1700–1770*. London: Methuen, 1971.

Fitzmaurice, R. M. *British Banks and Banking: A Pictorial History*. Truro: D. Bradford Barton, 1975.

Flandreau, Marc. *The Glitter of Gold: France, Bimetallism, and the Emergence of the International Gold Standard, 1848–1873*. Oxford: Oxford University Press, 2004.

Forbes, J. S. *Hallmark: A History of the London Assay Office*. London: Unicorn Press, 1999.

Forret, Jeff. "Slave Labor in North Carolina's Antebellum Gold Mines." *North Carolina Historical Review* 76 (1999): 135–162.

Franklin, Michael J. *Romantic Representations of British India*. London: Routledge, 2006.

Freedgood, Elaine. *The Ideas in Things: Fugitive Meaning in the Victorian Novel*. Chicago: University of Chicago Press, 2010.

Gambles, Anna. *Protection and Politics: Conservative Economic Discourse 1815–1852*. London: Royal Historical Society, 1999.

Gaskill, Malcolm. *Crime and Mentalities in Early Modern England*. Cambridge: Cambridge University Press, 2000.

Geczy, Adam. *Fashion and Orientalism: Dress, Textiles and Culture from the 17th to the 21st Century*. London: Bloomsbury Academic, 2013.

Geggus, David Patrick, *Slavery, War, and Revolution: The British Occupation of Saint Domingue, 1793–1798*. Oxford: Clarendon Press, 1982.

Gin, Ooi Keat. *Of Free Trade and Native Interest: The Brookes and the Economic Development of Sarawak, 1841–1941*. Kuala Lumpur: Oxford University Press, 1997.

Godfrey, Esther. *The January–May Marriage in Nineteenth-Century British Literature*. Basingstoke: Palgrave Macmillan, 2009.

Goldhill, Simon. *The Temple of Jerusalem*. Cambridge, MA: Harvard University Press, 2005.

Goodman, David. *Gold Seeking: Victoria and California in the 1850s*. St Leonards: Allen & Unwin, 1994.

Gordon, Lawrence L. *British Battles and Metals*. Aldershot: Gale and Polden, 1962.

Graeber, David. *Debt: The First 5,000 Years*. Brooklyn: Melville House, 2011.

Green, E. H. H. "Rentiers versus Producers? The Political Economy of the Bimetallic Controversy c. 1880–1898," *English Historical Review* 103 (1988): 588–612.

Greig, Hannah. *The Beau Monde: Fashionable Society in Georgian London*. Oxford: Oxford University Press, 2013.

Guthrie, Neil. "Johnson's Touch-piece and the 'Charge of Fame': Personal and Public Aspects of the Medal in Eighteenth-century Britain." In *The Politics of Samuel Johnson,* ed. Jonathan Clark and Howard Erskine-Hill (Houndmills: Palgrave Macmillan, 2012), 90–111.

Haberly, David T. "Colonial Brazilian Literature." In *Brazilian Literature*, ed. Roberto Gonzalez Echevarria and Enrique-Pupo (Cambridge: Cambridge University Press, 1996), 47–68.

Hampson, Norman. *The Perfidy of Albion: French Perceptions of England during the French Revolution*. Houndmills: Palgrave Macmillan, 1998.

Harling, Philip. *The Waning of Old Corruption: The Politics of Economical Reform in Britain, 1779–1846*. Oxford: Clarendon Press, 1996.

Hartmann, William K. *Searching for Golden Empires: Epic Cultural Collisions in Sixteenth-Century America*. Tucson: University of Arizona Press, 2014.

Hartop, Christopher. *Royal Goldsmiths: The Art of Rundell and Bridge, 1797–1843*. Cambridge: John Adamson, 2005.

Heal, Ambrose. *The London Goldsmiths, 1200–1800*. Cambridge: The University Press, 1935.

Heaton, Herbert. "A Merchant Adventurer in Brazil 1808–1818." *Journal of Economic History* 6 (1946): 1–23.

Heinowitz, R. Cole. *Spanish America and British Romanticism, 1777-1826: Rewriting Conquest*. Edinburgh: Edinburgh University Press, 2010.

Herbert, Christopher. *Culture and Anomie: Ethnographic Imagination in the Nineteenth* Century. Chicago: University of Chicago Press, 1991.

Herbert, Christopher. "Filthy Lucre: Victorian Ideas of Money." *Victorian Studies* 44 (2002): 185–213.

Hill, Rosemary. *God's Architect: Pugin and the Building of Romantic Britain*. New Haven: Yale University Press, 2007.

Hilton, Boyd. *Corn, Cash, Commerce: The Economic Policies of the Tory Governments 1815–1830*. Oxford: Oxford University Press, 1977.

Hilton, Boyd. *The Age of Atonement: The Influence of Evangelicalism on Social and Economic Thought, 1795–1865*. Oxford: Oxford University Press, 1988.

Hobsbawm, Eric and Terence Ranger, eds. *The Invention of Tradition*. Cambridge: Cambridge University Press, 1992.

Hodgkins, Christopher. "Stooping to Conquer: Heathen Idolatry and Protestant Humility in the Imperial Legend of Sir Francis Drake." *Studies in Philology* 94 (1997): 428–464.

Holmes, Megan. "Ex-votos: Material, Memory, and Cult." In *The Idol in the Age of Art: Objects, Devotions and the Early Modern World,* ed. Michael Wayne Cole and Rebecca Zorach (Farnham: Ashgate, 2009), 159–181.

Holton, Woody. *Unruly Americans and the Origins of the Constitution*. New York: Hill and Wang, 2007.

Hont, Istvan. *Jealousy of Trade: International Competition and the Nation-State in Historical Perspective*. Cambridge, MA: Harvard University Press, 2005.

Hoock, Holger. *The King's Artists: The Royal Academy of Arts and the Politics of British Culture 1760–1840*. Oxford: Clarendon Press, 2003.

Hoock, Holger. *Empires of the Imagination: Politics, War, and Arts in the British World, 1750–1850*. London: Profile Books, 2010.

Howell, Martha C. *Commerce Before Capitalism in Europe, 1300–1600*. Cambridge: Cambridge University Press, 2010.

Hunt, Alan. *Governance of the Consuming Passions: A History of Sumptuary Law.* New York: St. Martin's Press, 1996.

Hurtado, Albert L. *John Sutter: A Life on the North American Frontier.* Norman: University of Oklahoma Press, 2006.

Ibrahim, Hassan Ahmed. "The Egyptian Empire, 1805–1885." In *Modern Egypt, from 1527 to the End of the Twentieth Century,* ed. M. W. Daly (Cambridge: Cambridge University Press, 1998), 198–216.

Ingrao, Charles W. *The Hessian Military State: Ideas, Institutions, and Reform under Frederick II, 1760–1785.* Cambridge: Cambridge University Press, 1994.

Jasanoff, Maya. *Edge of Empire: Lives, Culture, and Conquest in the East, 1750–1850.* New York: Vintage, 2005.

Jastram, Roy W. *The Golden Constant: The English and American Experience 1560–2007.* Cheltenham: Edward Elgar, 2009.

Jones, Linda. "Subversive Jewellery: Challenges to Conservative Power from the Victorian Goldfields." *reCollections* 7 (2012): 1–13.

Jungnickel, Christa and Russell McCormmach. *Cavendish.* Philadelphia: American Philosophical Society, 1996.

Jusdanis, Gregory. *Political Nations.* Princeton: Princeton University Press, 2001.

Kaplan, Herbert H. *Nathan Mayer Rothschild and the Creation of a Dynasty. The Critical Years, 1806–1816.* Stanford: Stanford University Press, 2006.

Kaul, Suvir. *Poems of Nation, Anthems of Empire: English Verse in the Long Eighteenth Century.* Charlottesville: University of Virginia Press, 2000.

Kelly, Joseph. "The Problem of Anti-Slavery in the Age of Capital: Britain and Transatlantic Slavery, c.1833–1888." University of Liverpool PhD Dissertation, 2018.

Knafo, Samuel. *The Making of Modern Finance: Liberal Governance and the Gold Standard.* London: Routledge, 2013.

Laidler, David. "The Bullionist Controversy." In *Money,* ed. John Eatwell, Murray Milgate, and Peter Newman. New York: W.W. Norton, 1989.

Lamb, Jonathan. *The Things Things Say.* Princeton: Princeton University Press, 2011.

Lane, Kris. "Gone Platinum: Contraband and Chemistry in Eighteenth-Century Colombia." *Colonial Latin American Review* 20 (2011): 61–79.

Langford, Paul. "William Pitt and Public Opinion." *English Historical Review* 88 (1973): 54–80.

Langford, Paul. *Englishness Identified: Manners and Character 1650–1850.* Oxford: Oxford University Press, 2002.

Larsen, Timothy J. "Nineveh." In *Cities of God: The Bible and Archaeology in Nineteenth-Century Britain,* ed. David Gange and Michael Ledger-Lomas (Cambridge: Cambridge University Press, 2013), 111–135.

Leask, Nigel. *Curiosity and the Aesthetics of Travel Writing 1770–1840.* Oxford: Oxford University Press, 2002.

Lee, Debbie. *Slavery and the Romantic Imagination.* Philadelphia: University of Pennsylvania Press, 2004.

Lepler, Jessica M. *The Many Panics of 1837: People, Politics, and the Creation of a Transatlantic Financial Crisis.* Cambridge: Cambridge University Press, 2013.

Lethbridge, Lucy. *Servants: A Downstairs History of Britain from the Nineteenth Century to the Modern Times.* New York: W.W. Norton, 2013.

Li, Sumaio. "Fashionable People, Fashionable Society: Fashion, Gender and Print Culture in England, 1821–1861." University of Michigan PhD dissertation, 2008.

Lilley, Keith D. "'One Immense Gold Field!': British Imaginings of the Australian Gold Rushes, 1851-59." *Landscape Research* 27 (2002): 67–82.

Lincoln, A. Bruce. *The Conquest of a Continent: Siberia and the Russians.* New York: Random House, 1994.

Linton, Marisa. *Choosing Terror: Virtue, Friendship, and Authenticity in the French Revolution.* Oxford: Oxford University Press, 2013.

Lockard, Craig A. "The 1857 Chinese Rebellion in Sarawak: A Reappraisal." *Journal of Southeast Asia Studies* 9 (1978): 85–98.

López-Morrell, Miguel A. *The House of Rothschild in Spain, 1812–1941*. Farnham: Ashgate, 2013.

Lydon, J. G. "Fish and Flour for Gold: Southern Europe and the Colonial American Balance of Payments." *Business History Review* 39 (1965): 171–183.

Mackrell, Alice. *An Illustrated History of Fashion: 500 Years of Fashion Illustration*. New York: Costume& Fashion Press, 1997.

Macleod, Dianne Sachko. "Cross-Cultural Dressing: Class, Gender and Modernist Sexual Identity." In *Orientalism Transposed: The Impact of the Colonies on British Culture*, ed. Julie F. Codell and Dianne S. Macleod (Aldershot: Ashgate, 1998), 63–86.

Magee, J. D. "The World's Production of Gold and Silver from 1593 to 1905." *Journal of Political Economy* 18 (1910): 50–58.

Malley, Shawn. *From Archaeology to Spectacle in Victorian Britain: The Case of Assyria, 1845–1854*. Farnham: Ashgate, 2012.

Maltby, William S. *The Black Legend in England: The Development of Anti-Spanish Sentiment, 1558–1660*. Durham: Duke University Press, 1971.

Mandler, Peter. *The Fall and Rise of the Stately Home*. New Haven: Yale University Press, 1997.

Marcílio, Maria Luiza. "The Population of Colonial Brazil." In *Colonial Latin America*, ed. Leslie Bethell (Cambridge: Cambridge University Press, 1984), 37–64.

Marcuzzo, Maria Cristina and Annalisa Rosselli. *Ricardo and the Gold Standard: The Foundations of the International Monetary Order*. London: Macmillan, 1991.

Marino, Elisabetta. "Three British Women Travelers in Egypt: Sophia Lane Poole, Lucie Duff Gordon, and Emmeline Lott." In *The Legacy of the Grand Tour: New Essays on Travel, Literature, and Culture,* ed. Lisa Colletta (Lanham, MD: Farleigh Dickinson University Press, 2015), 51–70.

Martens, Britta. "Vatican Ceremonies and Tourist Culture in Nineteenth-Century British Travelogues." In *Imagining Italy: Victorian Writers and Travellers,* ed. Catherine Waters et al. (Newcastle: Cambridge Scholars, 2010), 14–31.

Mathias, Peter. *The First Industrial Nation: An Economic History of Britain, 1700–1914*. London: Methuen, 1969.

Mathias, Peter. *The Transformation of England: Essays in the Economics and Social History of England in the Eighteenth Century*. Abingdon: Routledge, 2006.

Maxwell, Alexander. *Patriots Against Fashion: Clothing and Nationalism in Europe's Age of Revolutions*. Houndmills: Palgrave Macmillan, 2014.

McDermott, James. *Martin Frobisher: Elizabethan Privateer*. New Haven: Yale University Press, 2001.

McFarlane, Anthony. *Colombia Before Independence: Economy, Society, and Politics under Bourbon Rule*. Cambridge: Cambridge University Press, 1993.

McGowen, Randall. "Managing the Gallows: The Bank of England and the Death Penalty, 1797–1821." *Law and History Review* 25 (2007): 241–282.

McKay, Ruth. *"Lazy, Improvident People": Myth and Reality in the Writing of Spanish History*. Ithaca: Cornell University Press, 2006.

McPherson, Heather. "Caricature, Cultural Politics, and the Stage: The Case of *Pizarro*." *Huntington Library Quarterly* 70 (2007): 607–631.

McRoberts, David. "Material Destruction Caused by the Scottish Reformation." *Innes Review* 10 (1959): 126–172.

Merritt, J. F. "Puritans, Laudians, and the Phenomenon of Church-Building in Jacobean London." *Historical Journal* 41 (1998): 935–960.

Michie, Elsie. *The Vulgar Question of Money: Heiresses, Materialism, and the Novel of Manners from Jane Austen to Henry James*. Cambridge: Harvard University Press, 2011.

Miles, Margaret M. *Art as Plunder: The Ancient Origins of Debate about Cultural Property*. Cambridge: Cambridge University Press, 2008.

Morton, John L. *King of Siluria: How Roderick Murchison Changed the Face of Geology*. Horsham: Broken Spectre, 2004.

Mountford, Benjamin and Stephen Tuffnell, eds. *A Global History of Gold Rushes.* Berkeley: University of California Press, 2018.

Muldrew, Craig. "'Hard Food for Midas': Cash and Its Social Value in Early Modern England." *Past and Present* 170 (2001): 78–120.

Munich, Adrienne. *Queen Victoria's Secrets.* New York: Columbia University Press, 1996.

Munting, Roger. *An Economic and Social History of Gambling in Britain and the USA.* Manchester: Manchester University Press, 1996.

Myerly, Scott Hughes. *British Military Spectacle from the Napoleonic Wars through the Crimea.* Cambridge: Harvard University Press, 1996.

Nash, Geoffrey. *From Empire to Orient: Travellers to the Middle East, 1830–1926.* London: I. B. Tauris, 2005.

Neal, Larry. *The Rise of Financial Capitalism: International Capital Markets in the Age of Reason.* Cambridge: Cambridge University Press, 1993.

Nechtman, Tillman W. *Nabobs: Empire and Identity in Eighteenth Century Britain.* Cambridge: Cambridge University Press, 2010.

Newman, Gerald. *The Rise of English Nationalism: A Cultural History 1740–1830.* New York: St. Martin's Press, 1997.

Nunokawa, Jeff. "The Miser's Two Bodies: 'Silas Marner' and the Sexual Possibilities of the Commodity." *Victorian Studies* 36 (1993): 273–292.

Ormrod, David. *The Rise of Commercial Empires: England and the Netherlands in the Age of Mercantilism, 1650–1770.* Cambridge: Cambridge University Press, 2003.

Paquette, Gabriel B. *Imperial Portugal in the Age of Atlantic Revolutions: The Luso-Brazilian World, c. 1770–1850.* Cambridge: Cambridge University Press, 2013.

Parthasarathi, Prasannan. *The Transition to A Colonial Economy: Weavers, Merchants and Kings in South India, 1720–1800.* Cambridge: Cambridge University Press, 2001.

Pinto, Virgflio Noya. *O Ouro Brasileiro e o Comércio Anglo-portugues.* Sao Paulo: Companhia Editora Nacional, 1979.

Polanyi, Karl. *The Great Transformation: The Political and Economic Origins of Our Time.* Boston: Beacon Press, 1957.

Poley, Jared. *The Devil's Riches: A Modern History of Greed.* New York: Berghahn Books, 2016.

Poovey, Mary. *Genres of the Credit Economy: Mediating Value in Eighteenth- and Nineteenth-Century Britain.* Chicago: University of Chicago Press, 2008.

Quataert, Donald. "Clothing Laws, State, and Society in the Ottoman Empire, 1720–1829." *International Journal of Middle East Studies* 29 (1997): 403–425.

Rajan, Supritha. *A Tale of Two Capitalisms: Sacred Economics in Nineteenth-Century Britain.* Ann Arbor: University of Michigan Press, 2015.

Rapport, Michael. *Nationality and Citizenship in Revolutionary France: The Treatment of Foreigners 1789–1799.* Oxford: Clarendon Press, 2000.

Redish, Angela. "The Evolution of the Gold Standard in England." *Journal of Economic History* 50 (1990): 789–805.

Redish, Angela. *Bimetallism: An Economic and Historical Analysis.* Cambridge: Cambridge University Press, 2000.

Reese, Ty M. "'Eating' Luxury: Fante Middlemen, British Goods, and Changing Dependencies on the Gold Coast, 1750–1821." *William and Mary Quarterly* 66 (2009): 851–872.

Reynolds, Luke A. L. "Who Owned Waterloo? Wellington's Veterans and the Battle for Relevance." City University of New York Ph.D. dissertation, 2019.

Rhatigan, Emma. "Preaching Venues: Architecture and Auditories." In *The Oxford Handbook of the Early Modern Sermon,* ed. Peter McCullough et al. Oxford: Oxford University Press, 2011.

Richards, Eric. "Darién and the Psychology of Scottish Adventurism in the 1690s." In *Imperial Expectations and Realities: El Dorados, Utopias, and Dystopias,* ed. Andrekos Varnava (Manchester: Manchester University Press, 2015), 26–46.

Ridgway, Robert H. *Summarized Data of Gold Production.* Washington: US Government Printing Office, 1930.

Roberts, Hugh. *For the King's Pleasure: The Furnishing and Decoration of George IV's Apartments at Windsor Castle*. London: The Royal Collection, 2001.

Rock, David. "Porteño Liberals and Imperialist Emissaries in the Rio de la Plata: Rivadavia and the British." In *Connections after Colonialism: Europe and Latin America in the 1820s*, ed. Matthew Brown and Gabriel Paquette (Tuscaloosa: University of Alabama Press, 2013), 207–222.

Rowlandson, Matthew. *Real Money and Romanticism*. Cambridge: Cambridge University Press, 2010.

Roy, Kaushik. *War, Culture and Society in Early Modern South Asia, 1740–1849*. New York: Routledge, 2011.

Roy, Rama Dev. "Some Aspects of the Economic Drain from India During the British Rule." *Social Scientist* 15 (1987): 39–47.

Rubin, Miri. *Mother of God: A History of the Virgin Mary*. New Have: Yale University Press, 2009.

Russell-Wood, A.J. R. *The Black Man in Slavery and Freedom in Colonial Brazil*. New York: St. Martin's Press, 1982.

Sargent, Thomas J. and François R. Velde. *The Big Problem of Small Change*. Princeton: Princeton University Press, 2001.

Schaffer, Talia. *Novel Craft: Victorian Domestic Handicraft and Nineteenth-Century Fiction*. New York: Oxford University Press, 2011.

Schumpeter, Joseph. *History of Economic Analysis*. Oxford: Oxford University Press, 1954.

Secord, James. "King of Siluria: Roderick Murchison and the Imperial Theme in Nineteenth-Century British Geology." *Victorian Studies* 25 (1982): 413–442.

Selgin, George. "Steam, Hot Air, and Small Change: Matthew Boulton and the Reform of Britain's Coinage." *Economic History Review* 56 (2003): 478–509.

Sharp, William F. "The Profitability of Slavery in the Colombian Chocó, 1680–1810." *Hispanic American Historical Review* 55 (1975): 468–495.

Sherwig, John M. *Guineas and Gunpowder: British Foreign Aid in the Wars with France 1793-1815*. Cambridge: Harvard University Press, 1969.

Shin, Hiroki. "Paper Money, The Nation, and The Suspension of Cash Payments in 1797." *Historical Journal* 58 (2015): 415–442.

Sideri, S. *Trade and Power: Informal Colonialism in Anglo-Portuguese Relations*. Rotterdam: University of Rotterdam Press, 1970.

Silver, John. "The Myth of El Dorado." *History Workshop* 34 (1992): 1–15.

Sivasundaram, Sujit. "Trading Knowledge: The East India Company's Elephants in India and Britain." *Historical Journal* 48 (2005): 27–63.

Smith, Anthony. *Explorers of the Amazon*. Chicago: University of Chicago Press, 1990.

Smolenski, John. "Violence in the Atlantic World." In *The Atlantic World*, ed. D'Maris Coffman, Adrian Leonard, and William O'Reilly. London: Routledge, 2015.

Snowman, Kenneth. *Eighteenth Century Gold Boxes of Europe*. Boston: Boston Book and Art Shop, 1966.

Spang, Rebecca. *Stuff and Money in the Time of the French Revolution*. Cambridge: Harvard University Press, 2015.

Spencer-Smith. Jenny. *Portraits for a King: the British Military Painting of A.J.-Dubois Drahonet*. London: National Army Museum, 1990.

Stafford, Robert A. "Preventing the 'Curse of California': Advice for English Emigrants to the Australian Goldfields." *Historical Records of Australian Science* 7 (1988): 215–230.

Stafford, Robert A. *Scientist of Empire: Sir Roderick Murchison, Scientific Exploration, and Victorian Imperialism*. Cambridge: Cambridge University Press, 2002.

Styles, John. "'Our Traitorous Money Makers': The Yorkshire Coiners and the Law, 1760-83." In *An Ungovernable People: The English and Their Law in the Seventeenth and Eighteenth Centuries*, ed. John Brewer and John Styles (New Brunswick: Rutgers University Press, 1980), 172–249.

Sutherland, Lucy. *A London Merchant 1695–1774*. Oxford: Oxford University Press, 1933.

Taws, Richard. *The Politics of the Provisional: Art and Ephemera in Revolutionary France*. University Park: Pennsylvania State University Press, 2013.

TePaske, John Jay. "New World Gold Production in Hemispheric and Global Perspective 1492–1810." In *Monetary History in Global Perspective, 1500–1808,* ed. C.E. Núñez et al. (Seville: Universidad de Seville, 1998), 21–34.

Thompson, James. *Models of Value: Eighteenth-Century Political Economy and the Novel.* Durham: Duke University Press, 1996.

Thompson, Noel W. *The People's Science: The Popular Political Economy of Exploitation and Crisis 1816–34.* Cambridge: Cambridge University Press, 1984.

Trentmann, Frank. *Free Trade Nation: Commerce, Consumption, and Civil Society in Modern Britain.* Oxford: Oxford University Press, 2009.

Trifilo, S. Samuel. "Catholicism in Argentina as Viewed by Early Nineteenth-Century British Travelers." *The Americas* 19 (1963): 262–275.

Trudell, Scott A. "Occasion." In *Early Modern Theatricality,* ed. Henry S. Turner. Oxford: Oxford University Press, 2013.

Valenze, Deborah. *The Social Life of Money in the English Past.* Cambridge: Cambridge University Press, 2006.

Vamplew, Wray. "The Protection of English Cereal Producers: The Corn Laws Reassessed." *Economic History Review* 33 (1980), 382–395.

Vickery, Amanda. *Behind Closed Doors: At Home in Georgian England.* New Haven: Yale University Press, 2009.

Vilar, Pierre. *A History of Gold and Money 1450 to 1920.* London: Verso, 1976.

Wallace, Willard. *Sir Walter Raleigh.* Princeton: Princeton University Press, 1959.

Walton, Charles. "The Fall from Eden: The Free-Trade Origins of the French Revolution." In *The French Revolution in Global Perspective,* ed. Suzanne Desan, Lynn Hunt, and William Max Nelson (Ithaca: Cornell University Press, 2013), 44–56.

Wandel, Lee Palmer. *Voracious Idols and Violent Hands: Iconoclasm in Reformation Zurich, Strasbourg, and Basel.* Cambridge: Cambridge University Press, 1994.

Ward, S. G. P. *Wellington's Headquarters: A Study of the Administrative Problems in the Peninsula 1809–1814.* Oxford: Oxford University Press, 1957.

West, William N. "Gold on Credit: Martin Frobisher's and Walter Ralegh's Economies of Evidence." *Criticism* 39 (1997): 315–336.

White, James F. *The Cambridge Movement: The Ecclesiologists and the Gothic Revival.* Cambridge: Cambridge University Press, 1962.

Wilson, Ted. *Battles for the Standard: Bimetallism and the Spread of the Gold Standard in the Nineteenth Century.* Aldershot: Ashgate, 2000.

Wollaston, Henry. *British Official Medals for British Coronations and Jubilees.* Nottingham: Commemorative Collection Society, 1978.

Woollacott, Angela. *Settler Society in the Australian Colonies: Self-Government and Imperial Culture.* Oxford: Oxford University Press, 2015.

Yates, Nigel. *Anglican Ritualism in Victorian Britain, 1830–1910.* Oxford: Oxford University Press, 1999.

INDEX

For the benefit of digital users, indexed terms that span two pages (e.g., 52–53) may, on occasion, appear on only one of those pages.

Note: figures are indicated by *f* following the page number